THE RED DECADE

By EUGENE LYONS

The Life and Death of Sacco and Vanzetti

Moscow Carrousel

Six Soviet Plays (*ed.*)

We Cover the World (*ed.*)

Assignment in Utopia

Stalin, Czar of All the Russias

Herbert Hoover

David Sarnoff

Workers' Paradise Lost

THE RED DECADE

The Classic Work on Communism
in America During the Thirties

Eugene Lyons

Simon Publications
2001

8-13-19

Library of Congress Control Number: 72139886

ISBN: 1-931541-07-8

Printed by Lightning Source Inc. La Vergne, TN

Published by Simon Publications, P.O. Box 321, Safety
Harbor, FL 34695

TABLE OF CONTENTS

CHAPTER   PAGE

     Author's Preface to the New Edition   i
     Introduction: In Defense of Red-Baiting . . .   9
   I   The Five Ages of the Communist International .   20
  II A Party Is Born   29
 III Boring from Within   37
  IV The Moscow Solar System   47
   V The American Party Is Purged   53
  VI A Milquetoast Takes Command   63
 VII The Red Decade Dawns   70
VIII Fascism Has the Right of Way   82
  IX The Cult of Russia-Worship   92
   X The Liberals Invent a Utopia   102
  XI Apologists Do Their Stuff   114
 XII The Red Cultural Renaissance   128
XIII More Planets Are Launched   141
 XIV Moscow Adopts the Trojan Horse   158
  XV Communism Becomes Americanism   170
 XVI The Incredible Revolution Spreads   183
XVII American League for Soviet War Mongering . .   195
XVIII Stalin's Children's Hour in the U.S.A.   204
 XIX Stalin Muscles in on American Labor   219
  XX Russian Purges and American Liberals   235
 XXI Hooray for Murder!   246
XXII "Friends of the G.P.U."   257
XXIII Cocktails for Spanish Democracy   268
XXIV Revolution Comes to Hollywood and Broadway .   284
XXV America's Own Popular Front Government . .   298
XXVI The Typewriter Front   311
XXVII Intellectual Red Terror   324
XXVIII The Last Loony Scene   342
XXIX The Melancholy Retreat of the Liberals . . .   355
XXX New Fronts for Old   365
XXXI And They Called It "Peace"   382
XXXII The Menace Today   393

AUTHOR'S PREFACE
TO THE NEW EDITION

THE term "Red Decade" to characterize American political and intellectual life in the 1930's has entered the national language. Not all who use it are aware that it derives from the title of a book published in the fall of 1941 that has been out of print since the initial year or two, and hard to obtain even through second-hand book channels.

The appearance of a new unabridged edition nearly thirty years after its original publication is naturally agreeable to the author—who is a bit astonished to be still around to witness the event. My private gratification aside, however, I believe readers today, especially in the generations without personal recollection of this extraordinary period, will find the account fascinating simply as a piece of nearly forgotten history. Moreover, I believe that they will recognize its pertinence to the explosions of radicalism in the present time.

There have been a great many books about the Depression, the New Deal and other aspects of the crowded Thirties. Necessarily they touch upon the rebellious, utopia-oriented moods and movements of that disturbed time. But the press, then massively "colonized" by communists and fellow-travelers, had tactical reasons for playing down the communist role in public affairs, and historians thereafter tamely followed their lead. Some of them do allude, briefly and superficially, to the communist upsurge in the United States under Soviet management; but *The Red Decade*, as far as I can ascertain, is the only full record of that phenomenon.

Never before—or since—had all areas of American society been so deeply penetrated by a foreign nation and a foreign ideology. Never before had the country's thinking, official policies, education, arts and moral attitudes been so profoundly affected by the agents, sympa-

i

thizers and unwitting puppets of a distant dictatorship. America lived through what I called "a grotesque and incredible revolution," largely run by "a swarming, disciplined, obedient and fanatically self-righteous army of Muscovite agents."

Literally millions of Americans, some knowingly and most innocently, allowed themselves to be manipulated by a small group under tight control from Kremlin headquarters. They chanted in unison slogans devised in Moscow; abandoned them for diametrically opposite slogans on signal from Moscow; lustily crusaded for prescribed causes through organizations formed for the purpose by communists or infiltrated and captured by communists. Professing themselves "liberals," they meekly followed totalitarian leadership into the most illiberal movements.

Apart from its social and political significance, the spectacle had dimensions of irony and absurdity, hilarious for the string-pullers. Hollywood celebrities around their swimming pools posturing as proletarian wage slaves. Flocks of professors and scientists guaranteeing, sight unseen, the fairness of Moscow blood-purge trials. Young Republicans and Young Democrats making united fronts with Young Communists in the name of "peace" and "freedom." Cabinet members and New Deal stalwarts addressing or "greeting" communist-run conferences. Trade unions calling strikes in American defense industries at Stalin's instigation for his temporary ally Hitler. Men of wealth paying the bills for efforts to hasten their own "liquidation as a class." Student rebels, guests of the First Lady, booing the President on the White House grounds. Books and authors judged or ignored in top-shelf publications strictly by Party-line standards. Lifelong pacifists lending themselves to drives for "defense of the Soviet Union." Government-financed theatre and art projects agitating for the overthrow of the government.

Random samples, these, out of the bookful in your hands. Myriad Americans were corralled into hundreds of local and nationwide Trojan-horse committees, leagues, mobilizations, councils, all controlled and maneuvered by their communist staffs. In retrospect, probably the most befuddled and gulled were the writers, academics, actors, etc., who rushed to the defense of the blood purges in Russia in the late 1930's. The full measure of their fatuity did not become apparent until 1956, when Nikita Khrushchev turned on his deceased master. Most of those executed, he confessed in his "secret speech," were innocent victims of Stalin's paranoia, and the murder of Kirov, which touched off the holocaust, had been arranged by Stalin himself.

The American apologists for the great blood-letting were thus left holding the bag, humiliated by the belated proof of their idiocy as long-distance experts on Soviet jurisprudence. On a later occasion, in 1961, Khrushchev, returning to the attack on Stalin, said that some day a monument would be erected in the Kremlin to the communist victims of the purges. That seemed a good idea and I proposed to the foremost of the American apologists that he initiate a fund-raising campaign for the monument, to atone for his egregious error. For some reason the proposal only made him volubly angry.

Reviewing the book in the New York Times, Max Eastman said that the Red Decade "combines the charms of the South Sea Bubble and the insane pathos of the Children's Crusade," and complained that in recounting it I "erred slightly . . . on the side of moderation." He was the only one who charged me with sins of moderation; in the perspective of time I should admit to some immoderate verbal exuberance.

On the political Left, in the intervening years, some objections have been raised—notably in a magazine article by Granville Hicks—that the decade was not as Red as Lyons painted it; that the name I imposed on the time-period was excessive. These strictures, however, belabored a straw man. I did not imply that those years were *all* Red, any more than the Nineties were all "gay" or the Twenties all "flaming."

My intention was to describe and document the magnitude of the communist influence, its amazing successes and the methods used to achieve them. "It is easy, of course, to exaggerate the strength of the phenomenon," I cautioned in the Introduction, but added: "It is even easier to brush aside the whole thing as a negligible and rather amusing aberration. The fact is that the complex United Front tinctured every department of American life while it lasted and has left its color indelibly on the mind and moral attitudes of the country."

That summation has stood the test of time. Since the book was written, its accuracy has been overwhelmingly corroborated by post-war Congressional investigations and by defectors from the communist and crypto-communist enterprises. Even Earl Browder, the sagging Kansas bookkeeper who was Stalin's chief impresario of the political extravaganza, writing after his expulsion from the Communist Party, credited it with the initiative or complete control of activities and organizations in which communist primacy, when alleged, was vociferously denounced as "red-baiting."

Re-reading the book after twenty-nine years, I find nothing that calls for change. If anything, in the light of information available later, it could be charged with under- rather than over-statement. The Red penetration and pollution of the New Deal government, for instance, was more pervasive and mischievous than we could know at the time. Infiltration of the churches, as later revealed by Dr. J. B. Matthews and others, was more extensive than the book conveyed.

And one vital phase of the Red Decade was hardly covered at all —namely, the massive Soviet espionage conducted by American citizens. I was quite aware of the existence of spy networks and there are allusions to them throughout the volume. Most of the operations subsequently uncovered had been planted before the war. By its nature, however, espionage did not lend itself to the kind of examination and documentation I was able to bring to other aspects of the story. A full picture of the affliction did not emerge until after the war, through years-long hearings in Congress and the revelations of repentant agents like Elizabeth Bentley and Whittaker Chambers.

The Red Decade, of course, did not end with the advent of the 1940's; history does not conform so neatly to the calendar. Communist organization and influence would not again attain the leverage they exerted in that bizarre decade, but they were in large measure carried over and have persisted, in varying degrees, to this day.

The Communist Party, U.S.A. and most of its appendages (some under refurbished names) survived the body-blow of the Moscow-Berlin pact in August, 1939. Overnight they turned militantly "pacifist" and neutralist on the Axis side—worldwide and especially American support against the Allies was for Hitler a valuable part of his bargain with Stalin. The years of shrill anti-Nazi and anti-fascist fervor quite forgotten, the comrades now assumed a substantial role in the debate between advocates of isolationism and interventionism, covering the liberal and Left flanks of public opinion not so accessible to the America First Committee. Their strong position in the labor movement enabled them to sabotage defense production and slow up arms shipments to Britain.

The next dramatic somersault came in June, 1941, when the Germans invaded Soviet Russia. The main slogan for twenty-two months had been, "The Yanks are not coming!" Now it was slightly amended to read, "The Yanks are not coming too late!" With Pearl Harbor and American entry into the war, both official and popular opinion in the United States generously forgot and forgave their zigzagging past and American communists were accepted at face value as patriotic allies. Not only were they again in good odor but they were so respectable that anyone who dared mention their endemic duplicity and subservience to Moscow, or doubted that Stalin would be a trustworthy partner for a peaceable world, risked denunciation as a traitor.

The effulgence of Red respectability faded fast at the war's end and the unfoldment of Moscow's designs to gobble up as much of Europe and Asia as it could. Browder, hapless symbol of four years of native patriotism, was ousted and his Party once more became rabidly revolutionary and anti-American. Again fake-pacifist, the communist apparatus was well to the front in the successful neo-isolationist campaign to "bring the boys home" and dismantle American military power. Stalin's aggressive hostility, particularly after the Soviet seizure of Czechoslovakia, turned public opinion sharply against communism, domestic and foreign. The Cold War—the old contest since 1917 now under a new title—intensified. That, plus the exposure of false-front operations in the preceding decade, narrowed the scope for new Innocent Clubs and transmission belts.

Yet even in these lean years, amazingly, the communists directly and indirectly played a lead role in shaping disastrous American policies in China. Well entrenched in the prestigious Institute of Pacific Relations, which had its claws deep in the flesh of government, and still strategically deployed in the press, universities and book publishing, the communists and their minions succeeded in persuading Americans that the Chinese communists were merely "agrarian reformers." The resulting misdirection of Washington diplomacy helped put Mao Tse-tung in power: an epoch-making calamity for which we paid and are still paying in Asia, from Korea to Vietnam and Cambodia.

What needs underlining is that the Kremlin's fifth column in the United States, even after its decline in numbers and strength by Red Decade standards, helped bring about the two most fateful setbacks for the world of freedom: the eviscerating of American military stamina in the critical post-war years, thereby giving unimpeded right of way to Soviet expansionism, and the surrender of China to communism.

A new lease of public tolerance came to the American communists and their camp-followers with the death of Stalin. Khrushchev revived Stalin's trick-slogan of "peaceful coexistence." Eager faith in supposed "mellowing" trends inside Soviet Russia and its empire was industriously nurtured in the West. Americans, fatigued and bored by the protracted conflict, now had the excuses they craved for relaxing into complacency. Those who maintained that the Cold War and the Red menace were still grim realities seemed disturbers of peaceful slumber —doctors blamed for unpleasant diagnoses.

And so in time "anti-communist" became a more disparaging epithet than "communist." Forgetting how well anti-Nazism and anti-fascism served as rallying cries for counteraction, it was now argued, even by some conservatives, that anti-communism was a "negative" approach, and anti-anti-communism, though doubly negative, prevailed.

For the Party and its teeming entourage this was a major semantic triumph. Their success in turning anti-communism into a dirty word (chiefly the handiwork of liberals) should rate with the loss of Eastern Europe and China among the great defeats for freedom since the World War. In the United States it cancelled out the thrust of anti-communist sentiment and organization which had acquired great vigor in the late Forties and early Fifties. It conferred upon communists a large measure of the immunity in public opinion which they still enjoy and exploit.

To bring the thumbnail sketch of Red history down to the present, known and self-identified communists today, just as in the Red Decade, are acceptable and openly active in non-communist and even professedly anti-communist student, youth, Negro, consumer, women's liberation, anti-pollution and other current movements. Their opponents, if too vocal and ardent, are dismissed as reactionaries "stuck in the swamps of primitive anti-communism."

Such is the atmosphere that again opens to communists of all denominations glowing opportunities in critical areas of national life and policy. Anyone who follows their press can attest that they are excited by the prospects and gearing to make the most of them. That, in turn, makes an understanding of the Thirties indispensable, if only for the light it sheds on communist techniques and allegiances. The Red Decade seems to me relevant, to use the code word of contemporary radicalism, to our present condition.

The Communist Party is no longer the potent apparatus it was in the Red Decade, when it claimed 100,000 members at the peak and did have about 75,000. Now it claims 13,000 and presumably does have some 8,000—approximately its size in the early 1930's. Its periphery, those concentric circles of non-dues-paying communists, witting fellow-travelers and collaborators in varying stages of innocence, which thirty-odd years ago could be safely estimated in many millions, has shrunk sharply. But Gus Hall, the American *Gauleiter* at this writing, has boasted that for every real communist there are ten "state of mind communists." Now as always, Party pressures radiate outward from the hard core of zealots to affect the minds of some millions, especially among the young and in the so-called Liberal Establishment.

From the beginning it has been Leninist dogma that numbers are less important than disciplined organization. When we regard communism in America—as we decidedly should—as extensions of power centers abroad, branch offices of established regimes, the numerical decline ceases to be decisive. With Chinese and Cuban forces added to the Soviet apparatus, the world communist enterprise is vastly larger and more powerful than at any time in the past. Its American agencies are therefore correspondingly more dangerous to our institutions and domestic peace.

More important than numbers, in appraising the movement today, is the fact that it is no longer subject to manipulation by a single High Command. There are communists loyal to the Soviets, others to Peking and Havana, and an assortment of Marxist-Leninists without specific foreign alliances. Moreover, other varieties of radicalism such as anarchism, nihilism, Blanquism (not new, as the more ignorant adherents proclaim, but throwbacks to nineteenth-century philosophies) are in ferment. These are surrounded and inter-penetrated by newly fashionable "life styles" of the hippies, yippies, crazies, essentially devoid of political purpose or commitment, all soaked through with drug addiction, sex pathologies, mystic cults, sheer destructive urges.

The radical milieu of the Sixties and Seventies is thus strikingly unlike what it was in the years covered by this book. What was then a near-monolithic movement is now unstable, fragmented, kaleido-scopic pluralism.

Ironically, the role played by pervasive *poverty* in the Depression years has nowadays been taken over to a large extent by pervasive affluence—its guilt-ridden beneficiaries acting in the name of the poor. As John W. Aldridge put it in his stimulating recent book, *In the Country of the Young*, "the underprivileged once again occupy the center of our attention" and "their interests dominate our view of American society far more completely than they did even in the Thirties." That perhaps is what J. Edgar Hoover meant when he wrote (New York *Daily News*, May 24, 1970): "Not since the De-pression has the Communist Party found more fertile fields of agita-tion," and went on to say that the Party sees ready weapons for its war on America in "New Leftism, Black Power and civil disobedi-ence."

The function of the communists today is defined by the very con-fusions of the radical scene: it is to penetrate and exploit the shifting mass, prodding it closer and closer to Old Left positions. Whether of the Muscovite persuasion, or the Peking-oriented Progressive Labor Party and its splinters, or Trotskyist formations like the Socialist Workers Party and its affiliated Young Socialist Alliance, only the older communists have historic training in revolutionary strategy and the anchorage of fixed beliefs. They alone can offer programs, ideol-ogy, roadmaps to bogus utopias to the herds of protesters, dissenters, compulsive vandals and other rebels without a rational cause.

It is hardly surprising, therefore, that the New Left consistently tends to move closer to the Old Left. "During 1969," the F.B.I. Di-rector recently testified before a Congressional committee, "leading proponents of the New Left movement in the U.S. more clearly estab-lished themselves as Marxist-Leninist revolutionaries dedicated to the destruction of our society and the principles of free government. . . . Hard core communist elements are intensifying their efforts in the New Left movement."

The present-day Party-line for the West, in both the Kremlin and Maoist camps, prescribes cooperation with any radical aggregation (except with each other), even unto formerly outlawed anarchist tendencies. For one thing, these represent opportunity for recruit-ment: subversion of a few leaders or potential leaders usually suffices to give disciplined communists a stranglehold on an organization.

More important, all the groupings merit communist support because they serve the fundamental objective, which is *to weaken the United States* as the main obstacle to communist ambitions. Anything that erodes the nation's traditional values, rips into its social fabric, emasculates natural patriotism, is obviously grist for the communist mills.

This applies in particular to activities calculated to cut down American military vitality, from attacks on ROTC and the draft to violence against defense research projects and plants making weapons. There is a pattern in the concentration of radical leaders on selected universities of second or even lesser rank. What such institutions have in common is the fact that they harbor scientific undertakings related to national security.

For several years before the tragic events of 1970, for instance, Kent State University of Ohio was favored by the energetic attention of outsiders. The reason, I suggest, is that it has been engaged in apparently vital research projects for the Institute of Defense Analysis, a civilian enterprise funded by the government. Relatively unimportant schools without such military significance may develop protest measles locally, but they rarely rate the intervention of top-echelon national leaders.

The main and most successful communist activity in the Red Decade was the fabrication of endless Innocent Clubs, false-fronts, transmission belts. The technique has not been jettisoned but it no longer holds top priority.

Only a handful of the fronts created in the Thirties have survived: the National Lawyers Guild, the American Committee for Protection of Foreign Born, the National Council of American-Soviet Friendship, Veterans of the Abraham Lincoln Brigade, for example. Others, while not direct progeny, have similar assignments. Thus a Citizens Committee for Constitutional Liberties carries on in the area once occupied by the International Labor Defense; the current National Emergency Civil Liberties Committee is remarkably like the defunct National Emergency Conference for Civil Liberties of the 1930's. Although communists have taken a licking in organized labor, they still dominate several unions and exert influence in a few others.

On a far more restricted scale than in the past, new fronts are being set up, each with its facade of innocents. New organizations are constantly being announced, on and off campus; it is not always clear, however, which of them are of communist inspiration. In some cases communist participation is overt. This is true of the S.D.S. (Students for a Democratic Society), which includes warring anarchist and Maoist sections. Communists were identifiable in the National Mobilization Committee to End the War in Vietnam, which staged the big demonstrations in 1969, and in the steering committee of its successor group, the so-called New Mobe, which includes people, as reported by Hoover, "who are or have been affiliated with old-line communist groups" and "are coordinating their activities with international communist elements." The Young Communist League on the campuses of the Thirties has had a series of reincarnations, from the W.E.B. Dubois Clubs to the recently announced Young (Communist) Workers Liberation League.

But for the most part the communist involvement, if any, in an array of new outfits is carefully concealed. Newspaper advertisements by Veterans for Peace were financed by at least one prominent fellow-traveler, but that does not necessarily prove communist origins. The Freedom and Peace Party launched in New York, a Medical Committee for Human Rights, a G.I. Civil Alliance for Peace, the rash of "G.I. Coffeehouses" planted near military installations to lure and "politicalize" soldiers—to what extent are communists connected with such enterprises? One coffeehouse organizer said publicly that it represented a coalition "ranging from orthodox Communist Party to New Left types."

In any case, the false-front technique of the 1930's has not been abandoned. More to the point, the nature of communism—its utter immoralism; its genius for conspiracy, deceit and double-talk; its subservience to foreign masters and dedication to foreign purposes—has remained unchanged. The contempt for truth, the skills in manipulating the discontented and guilt-ridden and unwary idealists, have remained unchanged. Adapted to the new situation, the strategy and morality on view in The Red Decade, almost as in laboratory demonstrations, are being applied here and now.

The experience of that time has left scars on intellectual life and moral attitudes. The brain damage and ethical trauma have been passed along to the succeeding generations. It was a period when, for large segments of the intellectual community, thinking and value judgments became "relativist," blurring the frontiers between good and evil, truth and falsehood. Expediency, justified in the name of self-righteous ends, blotted out for them what Russell Kirk calls "the permanent things." The scythe of time having done its work, only a few of those whose minds were shaped by the "incredible revolution" are still teaching in our schools, writing in avant-garde periodicals, preaching from our pulpits. But thousands of others in the following decades who were conditioned mentally and morally by such men and women of the Thirties today hold influential posts in education, journalism, government, the arts and professions. In this sense, at least, the Red Decade has been carried over into our time. It was then that the breed of totalitarian liberals swept the nation, occupying academia, the press, book publishing; and it has been with us ever since in the Liberal Establishment.

The book, I suggest, is uniquely pertinent to the so-called youth rebellion. I am constantly astonished, in talking to young people, that the generation without direct memory of the Red Decade assumes that youth dissent, including "anti-war" crusades, is something new in America. A reading of this book should, at any rate, apprise them that a vast and raucous youth movement under communist management was shaking the country long before they were born.

In sheer dimensions, though without the extremes of violence and vandalism and pornography of the present period, that youth agitation was much larger than its manifestations today. Today's youth will learn, for instance, that an American Youth Congress was able to assemble young people, as individuals and through other organizations, literally by the millions to implement secret Kremlin directives; that campus strikes, "peace mobilizations," revolutionary rhetoric against the power structures are not recent inventions; that then, as now, confused or cynical grown-ups and political demagogues proved their piety as liberals by flattering and cheering on the young militants.

Perspective is needed even more urgently for the larger picture. The Cold War does not date from the end of the Second World War, as is so widely assumed. Only the label is new—the struggle it connotes has been under way ever since the Bolsheviks hijacked the Russian Revolution and made the country a staging ground for world revolution. And wishful thinking to the contrary notwithstanding, that epochal confrontation between communism and freedom has not been resolved. It takes new forms, throws up new slogans and diversions on both sides, but the Cold War remains the overarching reality of the world we live in.

For more than fifty years the ambitions and pretensions of communism have kept the world in a state of turmoil, violence and uncertainty. The obsessive drive for One Communist World has sowed chaos on all continents, inspired declared and undeclared wars, imposed back-breaking burdens of armaments on our country. From the Middle East to Southeast Asia, in Latin America and in the riotous streets of the United States, the struggle continues unabated. It is primarily for control of the world communist movement that Red Russia and Red China are contending. Why would they seek dominance over fifth columns in eighty-odd countries if the Cold War were ended?

The fact is that not one responsible spokesman for any communist power center has renounced or retreated from the goal of global dominion. Not one of them has conceded even the possibility of an enduring compromise or détente. All the consoling talk of the convergence of the two systems of life, of "bridges" of cooperation, has come from our side, not theirs. It is only in our world that such formulas as "peaceful coexistence" are taken seriously.

Those whose job it is to monitor Soviet propaganda know that there has been not even a marginal diminution of anti Western and particularly anti-American invective. During the Lenin Centennial in 1970, as in the celebration of the fiftieth anniversary of Bolshevik power in 1967, Soviet oratorical and editorial emphasis was on the supreme communist mission to "liberate" humanity from its capitalist chains.

On April 14, 1969, a congress of the Chinese Communist Party explicitly pledged its support of "the 'justice struggle' of the proletariat, youths and students in the United States." Cuba, entrenched in the inviolable sanctuary we awarded to communism as part of the price for removing Moscow's nuclear missiles, inflames hostility to the United States throughout the Western Hemisphere. Attorney General John Mitchell, whose sources of information are surely adequate, told the American people on May 12, 1970 (on the CBS program, "Sixty Minutes"), that not only ideology but funds for extremists in our country are flowing in from foreign countries; he didn't name them but that was hardly necessary.

To evade or minimize the continuing challenge of communism calls for exceptional powers of self-deception. I dare to hope that the re-publication of this book, nearly thirty years after it was written, will help some Americans meet the challenge more intelligently and effectively.

In open societies like ours the turnover in the ranks of communists, their camp-followers and their dupes has always been large and rapid. The great majority of those whose names figure in this account of communist-led enterprises in the 1930's, especially in the non-Party periphery to its most gullible reaches, long ago abandoned the movement. Many, of course, have died. The survivors will understand, I trust, that history cannot be erased or amended, and that the record of those years does not necessarily reflect on their subsequent and present views and associations.

Disillusioned communists and fellow-travelers have often become the most knowledgeable and effective opponents of communism. A courageous few of the men and women mentioned in *The Red Decade* belong in that category, while others continue at the same old stands of subversion. The rest, perhaps embarrassed by the realization that they served as stooges, have faded into political anonymity. In any case, the new edition of the book is presented purely as history.

—Eugene Lyons

November, 1970

THE RED DECADE

IN DEFENSE OF RED-BAITING

1

O N THE day when this book was ready for the press, Nazi Germany invaded Russia. The attack, as Vice-Premier Viacheslav Molotov charged, was wholly unprovoked. Stalin had appeased Hitler and supported Hitler's cause with unflagging and demonstrative energy. For twenty-two months the Communist International and its endless open and clandestine extensions had preached defeatism to the French, immediate negotiated peace to the British, anti-Yankee sentiments to the Latin Americans, rigid isolationism to the people of the United States. The communist "line" for America had been indistinguishable from the Nazi line: non-intervention in European affairs, promotion of strikes in defense industries, class and group hatreds and the rest.

That line was hastily and clumsily reversed within a few hours after the blitzkrieg was unloosed against Stalin's country. Yesterday's "imperialist" and "plutocratic" war was magically transmuted into a people's war for freedom and justice. Conscription, national armaments, aid to Britain were mysteriously sanctified in a flash for all American Stalinists, whether acknowledged or disguised.

Through an act of Hitler's, the despised "pluto-democracies" were instantly converted into crusaders against evil in the eyes of all good comrades. Two notoriously Stalinoid organizations, the American Youth Congress and the National Maritime Union, happened to be holding conventions soon after the Nazi ingrates double-crossed their Soviet associates; both had been conspicuously active in fighting any sort of aid to Britain; both now came out for unstinted and undelayed American help to the British. The national organization especially created to promote the strictest isolationism and non-intervention, the American Peace Mobilization, called off its "peace vigil" at the White House and announced its support of aid to Britain. The whole communist "peace front"—until the night of June 22 so loud and busy

9

and crowded—was soon silent and deserted, except for the faint wailing of honest pacifists trampled in the ignominious retreat of the comrades from fake-isolationism.

By the time this volume is in print, it is certainly not impossible that this somersault of late June may have turned into a double somersault. I can give no assurances that the democratic crusade against Hitlerite aggression will not have turned once more into an imperialist crime. The only way to keep up with the permutations of communist policy is on a loose-leaf basis.

The crux of the matter, however, is not in the character of communist propaganda at any given moment, but in the fact that such propaganda, always and unswervingly, is determined by the Kremlin's needs and the Kremlin's instructions. It has not the remotest relation to American affairs. Whether the "line," in its zigzag course paralleling Stalin's whims or desperations, coincides with American national interests or contradicts them is sheer accident. Stalin's Fifth Column in America, as in all other nations, has only one set of "principles": blind obedience to the will of Moscow. It has only one "ideal": allegiance to a foreign dictator.

The reversal of June 22 came as a dramatic demonstration of the truth of the main thesis of this volume. An allegedly American political movement had made two major turns in its "policies" in less than two years—both based exclusively on the altered position of a foreign nation. Each of the turns took in a full 180 degrees, completing a circle which encloses the most sinister case of political cynicism and subservience to a foreign overlord in American history.

The circumstance that Soviet interests for any period happen to run close to American interests must not obscure the underlying danger represented by the presence of a swarming, disciplined, obedient and fanatically self-righteous army of Muscovite agents in our midst. It is a gun pointed at the heart and mind of America—not to be complacently mistaken for a toy pistol merely because it is not, at a given moment, being fired.

2

A great many books and a multitude of articles have been published in recent years exposing the native and foreign purveyors of fascism and Nazism in America. But we have yet to hear their authors denounced as brown-baiters, black-baiters or silver-baiters. The charges are assayed on the basis of their truth or falsity. They are not arbitrarily dismissed with a hackneyed epithet. There is as yet among us, it happens, no taboo against examining and if necessary condemning the operation of Mussolini, Hitler and their direct or indirect agents.

Books and articles attacking native and foreign purveyors of Stalin's special brand of totalitarianism, however, are condemned automatically by a portion of the American public as "red-baiting." Their authors are branded without further ado as "red-baiters." Their charges and their reasoning are not measured by the ordinary yardsticks of veracity or good sense, but swept aside angrily without measuring.

The American public, especially in its Left and so-called liberal reaches, is the victim of an irrational and indefensible taboo against criticizing the Great Experiment in Stalin's Russia or its extensions and machinations in our own country. There is no use reasoning or arguing against this fact. We can merely note the phobia, in a scientific spirit, and observe its fantastic effects. And we can merely warn the great mass of Americans which has escaped the phobia that the taboo is no innocent and accidental gadget. It is a neatly contrived device for heading off free and uninhibited discussion of such little things as man-made famines, horrifying blood purges, forced labor on a gigantic scale—if they happen to occur in Russia. It is no less useful in preventing or discrediting in advance all exposures of Stalinist activities directed against the institutions or even against the life of non-Soviet nations.

The self-righteous outcries about red-baiting with which this book, for instance, will be greeted in certain predictable quarters will have little or nothing to do with the specific contents of the volume. They will be simply a conditioned reflex on the part of those in the grip of the taboo—and they include, unluckily, a good many literary critics, book reviewers and political commentators. These people cannot be blamed. They shriek "red-baiter!" at the first contact with sharp criticism of communists as automatically as they cry "ouch!" at the first contact with a hot stove.

There are some exceedingly curious ingredients in the taboo. The most curious of all is that it is primarily, often exclusively, attack on a particular brand of red ideology or practice which causes a blackout of logic in the victim, namely the brand approved by Moscow at any given moment. Attacks on anarchism, syndicalism, single tax, social credit or any other non-Stalinist radical movement leave these folk cold and collected. Only criticism aimed directly at communism and its preachers touches off their specialized indignations.

Nay, not even communism as such. One may expose Trotsky's variety or de Leon's, or Jacques Doriot's version of communism without being ostracized from decent "liberal" and "intellectual" society. It is specifically attack against Stalin's blessed and subsidized communism—and particularly the demonstration that it isn't communism at all but an approximation of the fascist ideologies—which throws the afflicted liberals into a panic of violent, know-nothing resistance.

Because the Communist Party and its great array of subsidiaries have had the resources and the prestige of a big nation behind them, they have succeeded in imposing that prohibition on American liberals and even a good many conservatives. They have succeeded so well, in fact, that thousands who do not hesitate to speak their minds vigorously about other social philosophies or political regimes stop short, panic-stricken, when it comes to speaking their mind on communism and its ways. It takes money and power and psychological leverage to condition great numbers of people in this fashion. Among the radicals, only Stalin's subjects and employees have possessed these things in ample measure.

When the New York *PM*, a few days after General Walter Krivitsky's death, attacked the dead man in vulgar and vicious style, did it occur to anyone to charge it with red-baiting? Did the liberal magazines raise the red-baiting clamor when liberals and radicals were pounced upon in an Open Letter in August, 1939? Of course not. But let the same daily insult a live or dead stooge of Stalin, let some Open Letter "smear" Browder or Marcantonio or the communist leader of an outlaw strike—and instantly the fumes of red-baiting charges will fill the air and becloud the issue. When the government took sadly belated steps looking toward the deportation of one Harry Bridges, an Australian communist, the cry of red-baiting echoed through the pseudo-liberal press. No such outcry met the deportation proceedings against Jan Valtin, anti-communist radical. Indeed, the aforementioned *PM* ran an editorial protesting the Bridges affair in the same week when it virtually demanded the deportation of Valtin.

Incidentally, there is a portion of the press in America which is devoted almost exclusively to vilifying "reds." Its pages run over with bilious invective against social-democrats, anarchists, syndicalists, communists of other than Muscovite persuasion and, in open season, also against the liberals. I refer, of course, to the Stalinist press here. Every issue of the *Daily Worker*, for instance, is hectic with insults in words and cartoons directed against those "reds" whom Moscow disapproves. It occurs to no one, notwithstanding, to call the *Daily Worker* a red-baiting rag. Yet the social-democratic *New Leader* or Norman Thomas' *Socialist Call*, when they unmask Stalinist agents, are instantly accused of red-baiting.

3

The communist achievement in obtaining a monopoly of protection under the taboo has been one of the Kremlin's most effective forces in undermining American life and thought. The dread of being labeled a red-baiter has kept droves of disillusioned communists and their fellow-travelers from announcing and explaining their change of heart and mind. The epithet has been a mark of Cain to outlaw critics of the Russian terror or the Stalinist infiltration of American life. Whenever the communists are under fire, it has served to divert attention from the subject matter to futile discussion of personal motives, the critic's private life and other deliberate tricks of befuddlement.

When someone belabors the Nazis or the Silver Shirts, the Town-sendites or the Technocrats, it is not assumed or implied that he has been "bought" by some nation or bank or publisher, even though that may be the case. Let the same person attack Russia or its creatures abroad, and instantly it is assumed by the muddled and inhibited among the liberals that he has "sold out" to somebody or other. In the old days Hitler, Mussolini and the Mikado were regarded as natural purchasers; after the Kremlin had made friends with these three, the market was presumably cornered by Hearst. Which may explain why he was selling his art treasures—he couldn't have everything. After the Nazi invasion of Russia, Hearst presumably again faced competition in that market.

Certain of my colleagues, having lived in Nazi Germany and learned to recognize Hitler's methods, have written books exposing the Nazi regime and its intrigues on American soil. As far as I am aware they have not been reprimanded for not saving the Southern share-croppers instead. No book reviewer or liberal commentator has sneered at them, "Why must you carry on about concentration camps and political murder in Germany? What about Sacco and Vanzetti and Negro lynchings?" It is assumed, sensibly, that they happen to know more about Germany.

But this gracious leeway is denied to writers hostile to Stalinist Russia and its foreign conspiratorial empire. When they mention millons of corpses in a Ukrainian famine, they are told off neatly with a scathing reference to the Okies in California. Should they allude to the Soviet purges, they are hit over the head with Mooney and Billings. Until the Soviet-Nazi Pact made the procedure a bit awkward, their indictment of terror in Soviet Russia was instantly canceled out by reference to Nazi terror in Germany.

That, obviously, is just another aspect of the same taboo against testing the rosy illusions about communism à la Stalin. It constrains me to give public notice herewith—as I did in *Assignment in Utopia*—that the horrors of Bolshevism do not, in my view, justify horrors elsewhere, including those apparent under capitalism; that the Soviet invasion of American life does not for a moment justify the Nazi invasion or the totalitarian abominations preached by our native fascists and social nihilists. This book, believe it or not, devotes itself exclusively to the story of the Stalinist attack on our institutions and on our mental integrity for the simple reason that it is a book on that subject.

The so-called liberals are actually paralyzed by the hobgoblin of red-baiting. If ever they are tempted to question Stalin's paradise, they no doubt have nightmares in which they see themselves surrounded by animate megaphones all hooting, "Red-baiter! Red herring!" The story is told that Austrian Nazis, before the Anschluss, had a standard device for keeping the police at bay when engaged in beating up adversaries. As soon as the police approached, the Nazis began to sing the national anthem. Automatically the policemen snapped to attention and stood rooted to the spot—long enough for the ringleaders to escape. In the same way, the cry of red-baiting halts liberals in their tracks when they are tempted to go after communism.

There can be no clear thinking, no clear examination of the issues raised by the Kremlin's intrusion in American life until the red-baiter taboo has been exorcised. A beginning, at least, can be made if those who expose communist skulduggery walk up boldly to the terrible hobgoblin and, taking their courage in their hands, say "Boo!" right in its face. After that, I can assure them, they will be able to wear the red-baiter tag with a flourish of pride, and their sleep will be as sweet as a healthy infant's.

Here, by way of beginning, I propose to say "Boo!" If an attempt to tell the truth about Russia-at-home and Russia-abroad is red-baiting, then I proclaim myself a red-baiter. I trust that this book, indeed, may merit top ranking as a better-than-average exemplar of honest and effective red-baiting as thus defined.

What is more, I challenge all intellectually honest liberals to break through their inhibitions by saying "Boo!" They will not find it easy at first, of course, and may have to practice it before their mirrors with doors closed and blinds drawn. But after a while they will discover that neither thunder nor lightning will descend on their heads, but only a spatter of harmless sparks unloosed from Thirteenth Street, off Union Square in New York. In the end they will be cured, and will be able to examine the mythology of Stalinism as calmly as the folklore of capitalism or the mythology of Hitlerism.

I invite them, in fact, to test their psychological courage on the pages which follow. If they can read them through without one apoplectic fit or one frenzied yelp of "Red-baiter!" they may consider themselves emancipated at long last.

4

This book does not pretend to be an academic and comprehensive history of communism in America; that remains to be done by someone of more scholarly temper. It is frankly journalistic and polemic; a needed exposure in a moment of national and world-wide crisis. It is intended as an informal account of Bolshevism in our country—the strange Bolshevism that reached a bizarre climax in the amazingly successful People's or Popular Front phase of Muscovite activity outside its Russian homeland.

In the decade before Stalin and Hitler made the infamous bargain that touched off the Second World War—our Red Decade—the United States lived through a grotesque and incredible revolution. The fact that it was neither communist nor revolutionary, in the normal sense of these words, is not an incidental paradox. It is a clue to the essential nature of the event—its Machiavellism. The distinguishing mark of the Red Decade was hypocrisy, manifest in false-front societies, secret inner-caucus controls, duplicate and triplicate names, high-minded lying and deceptions. Its methods are implicit in key words and phrases which it contributed to our political vocabulary: words like fellow-traveler, party line, Innocents' Club, transmission belts, front organizations, social fascists.

We are not dealing with candid revolutionists who have the courage of their convictions, men and women whose moral stature we can respect. We are dealing, for the most part, with people who could not even understand the "inspired frenzy" of honest rebels from Spartacus down to Tom Paine and John Brown, Eugene V. Debs and Emma Goldman. During the Red Decade we are confronted, in the main, with a horde of part-time pseudo-rebels who have neither courage nor convictions, but only a muddy emotionalism and a mental fog which made them an easy prey for the arbiters of a political racket.

At the core of the incredible revolution was a small group of leaders, some known to the public, others obscure but no less powerful, still others—the official resident agents of the Moscow hierarchy—secret but most powerful of all. Around them was the solid ring of Communist Party members, the mass of them acknowledging their allegiance but an effective minority concealing their membership under fake names and even protesting with outraged vehemence when accused of being members. Beyond them were deployed the more diffuse and vastly more numerous fellow-travelers, consciously working within the movement, though obeying a moral rather than an organizational discipline. And farther out were concentric ring after ring of wholly or partly innocent camp-trailers.

Clearly we can have more human esteem for the open party members, accepting the yoke and facing the music, than for the fellow-travelers and "sympathizers" who played the game without risking any of their own chips.

All of it was more of a conspiracy than a political movement, more a hoax than a social upsurge. The innocence of so many victims, and their eagerness to be taken in, does not detract from the chicanery but makes it more mischievous. And because the whole thing was conspiratorial and vague at its edges, any attempt to measure its magnitude or effects statistically must fail. The burlesque revolution whispered or shouted, as occasion required, now disclaiming any influence, now boasting of direct control of the minds of millions. The same officials who wailed about red-baiting exaggerations when credited with fomenting certain events or dominating certain organizations, insisted on such credit in reports to the higher-ups in Moscow.

Our own American Popular Front, though never officially in power as it was in France and for a brief period in Spain, penetrated, in various degrees, the labor movement, education, the churches, college and non-college youth movements, the theatre, movies, the arts, publishing in all its branches; it bored deep into the Federal government and in many communities also into local government; it obtained a stranglehold on great sectors of national and local relief setups and made-work projects through domination of the Workers Alliance, capture of key jobs and other stratagems. At its highest point—roughly about 1938—the incredible revolution of the Red Decade had mobilized the conscious or the starry-eyed, innocent collaboration of thousands of influential American educators, social workers, clergymen, New Deal officials, youth leaders, Negro and other racial spokesmen, Social Registerites, novelists, Hollywood stars, script writers and directors, trade-union chiefs, men and women of abnormal wealth. Its echoes could be heard, muted or strident, in the most unexpected places, including the supposed citadels of conservatism and respectability.

It is easy, of course, to exaggerate the strength of this phenomenon. But it is even easier to brush the whole thing aside as a negligible and rather amusing aberration. The fact is that the complex communist United Front tinctured every department of American life while it lasted and has left its color indelibly on the mind and moral attitudes of the country. Our labor movement, politics, art, culture and vocabulary still carry its imprint. Even those who are most repentant and shamefaced in the present sour aftermath still carry the scars of the planned hypocrisy on their minds and souls. Something devious clings to their thinking on the affected subjects. In organized labor, where it operates chiefly as the Left Wing of the C.I.O. and at this writing still enjoys the patronage of John L. Lewis, it is even more deeply entrenched than it was before the Moscow-Berlin partnership was announced, and, until the German invasion of Russia, was consciously sabotaging the national defense effort under trade-union banners. A generation of college youth has been poisoned by communist amoralism and has carried the disease into manifold post-collegiate activities.

In exposing the past and current machinations of the Kremlin junta and its multitudes of innocents and stooges, I am decidedly not beating a dead horse. The animal is very much alive and gets its oats regularly from the central international fodder stocks. Because the stakes are particularly important at this time, the Kremlin unquestionably is investing more cash and effort than ever before in the game. American Bolshevism, now—in 1941—in its twenty-first year, has reached its majority. It has learned a lot from its successive experiences and political incarnations, period after period, and by this time feels as much at home in the open or underground, among maritime workers or bishops, as the pampered favorite of government officials or as their special target of attack. There is no corner of American life where it does not have its outright agents or complacent and dependable "sympathizers." And behind it—to guide and to chide, to urge and to purge—is the Communist International, the greatest world-wide agitational, propaganda, espionage and sabotage organization ever built in the whole history of human society. The arts of propaganda, as practiced by the Comintern, are effectively supplemented by direct action ranging from slander to murder.

That organization is in our midst, for the most part as a secret underground movement in its immediate phase, but functioning above ground in a new array of Innocents' Clubs and a new set of transmission belts. In the measure that it operates through camouflaged stooge-organizations under disarming names behind respectable show-window committees, it is even more reprehensible and more dangerous. *Stalinism in America today represents the most serious single sabotage-potential.* It is widely diffused, effectively disguised, firmly entrenched in government and other influential spheres. Beguilingly "packaged" in pseudo-idealistic wrappings, it finds takers among well-meaning Americans who would never succumb to the unsubtle Hitlerite salesmanship.

I am aware that much of this indictment, even after I have set it down in considerable detail, will sound farfetched to the uninitiated. But the reader should recall that the story of social disintegration and totalitarian skulduggery in important sectors of life in France would have sounded farfetched had anyone told it before the collapse of that country made those things only too obvious and too credible. The complacency of the average American has operated to facilitate the work of the communists as of other foreign agents. The success or failure of the current Muscovite line for America—a line revised constantly by absentee masters—will depend on the temper of America, on its moral stamina. It will depend also on its comprehension of the Kremlin's techniques. This volume, I hope, may contribute a little to that comprehension.

5

I wish to acknowledge gratefully the invaluable help of S. L. Solon, who did the spadework for this volume in gathering and organizing basic data and documents. I wish to express my thanks, also, to those who have generously helped with suggestions, corrections and information, especially to Victor Riesel, Benjamin Stolberg, Ben Mandel, Hugo Pollock, Nelson Frank, Sam Baron, William G. Ryan and Suzanne La Follette. In the writing of the initial historical chapters, I found Benjamin Gitlow's fine autobiography, *I Confess*, particularly valuable as a source book and herewith acknowledge my indebtedness to it.

Many of those whose names appear in the following pages in connection with activities of the Communist Party and its subsidiaries have since broken with Stalinism. Some of them, indeed, have become fervent opponents of the Stalinist penetration. Since this is a history, told as far as convenient chronologically, it has not been possible or always desirable to expunge names from the historical record. I can only proffer apologies in advance for any incidental embarrassment the record may cause to such people.

Fortunately, most of them have the intellectual integrity not to conceal their Stalinist "past." With few exceptions, as I have tried to underline in these pages, they were victims of their own idealistic urges and of a conjuncture of social pressures. The Depression, the moral disintegration of the intelligentsia and the middle classes as the economic debacle developed, these were more potent in shaping the Red Decade than any of the masterminds on New York's Union Square. Those who were sucked into the vortex of that bizarre "revolution" were not always to blame. I have tried to understand the social phenomenon, rather than to lambaste its dupes, and it is possible that I have not always succeeded in this feat of fairness.

CHAPTER I

THE FIVE AGES OF THE COMMUNIST INTERNATIONAL

1

T HE essential fact about the Third or Communist International, more commonly known as the Comintern, is its stubborn and greedy nationalism. This fact is the passkey to an understanding of any of its foreign branches, such as the Communist Party of the United States. A remarkable number of Americans, Britishers, Chinese and Patagonians, it is true, have relished the delusion that they are "internationalists" because they serve Soviet Russia instead of their own country. That is a proof of their gullibility; certainly it is no mitigation of the self-centered Russian spirit of the International. Actually the Comintern is international in about the same sense that the American Express Company is international; that is, it has branches in many foreign countries. Its policies and purges and leadership have been from the start determined wholly by the internal and foreign interests of the Soviet state. The dizzy factional wars, the hairpin turns in program and strategy, the rise and fall of leaders within any given branch office have been simply reflections of Soviet events, Soviet needs, Soviet blunders, Soviet hopes—reflections distorted by distance.

From the outset the Russian leaders made it clear that the Comintern was their show, and comrades from other lands simply extras. Non-Russian communists who wouldn't play on those terms joined some other show; the world is littered with small heretical companies playing for the most part to empty houses. Though outwardly a Comintern affiliate like the other national affiliates, only the Communist Party of Russia has explicit authority to review and revise Comintern decisions. This makes the Comintern simply an instrument of Russia's ruling party, which is to say, of the clique or the dictator in control of that organization. The American, British or

20

Patagonian communists have a simple choice between obeying orders from the Russian party—transmitted through Communist International channels for appearances' sake—and getting out.

The prestige of the Russians as leaders of the only successful communist revolution gave them from the start an overwhelming moral authority. Their control of the purse strings clinched it. At no time in the history of the Comintern did the dues-paying membership of all other Communist Parties of the world put together equal the membership of the Russian party. The pretense of national equality in the bosom of the International has therefore been too thin to fool anyone but the most naïve among the faithful. I happened to be present in 1921 at the Leghorn Congress of the Socialist Party of Italy, where the Italian Communist Party was born. A bearded and bustling Russian was in constant attendance as official mid-wife, determined to split the socialist movement rather than compromise on a comma of the new International's catechism. It was that split in the powerful socialist forces which, more than any other single factor, opened the path to power for the fascists under Benito Mussolini.

In later years, while residing in Moscow as press correspondent, I watched the leaders of foreign communist movements come and go. Big fish in their native radical puddles, here they were small fry, treated with insulting contempt if politically in disgrace, and no less insultingly patronized if in good standing. They connived and licked muddy Russian boots for the favor of their Soviet bosses. I visited some of them at the Lux Hotel where they were usually quartered, and they seemed to me so many pensioners and poor relations of the Kremlin crowd. Stalin manipulated the Browders and Doriots, the Pollitts and Thaelmanns, as wilfully as he did any of his Russian puppets.

In all the history of this supposedly international organization there is not a single major case of successful defiance of the Russian leaders by any non-Russian Communist Party. There has never been a time when Russian and Comintern leadership did not coincide; the removal of any communist, big or small, from political influence in Russia has automatically canceled out his influence in the world-wide body. What is more, this Russian domination of the International became more undisguised, cruder, more unreasonable in direct proportion to the Soviet Union's growing strength.

By this time the Kremlin is so contemptuous of its foreign creatures that it stands Comintern policies on their head without the courtesy of an advance tip-off to foreign branch managers. Witness the humiliating position of Earl Browder, head of the American Communist Party, when the Soviet-Nazi Pact of August, 1939, caught him unawares.

The Comintern was founded in the Kremlin, in March, 1919, by thirty-five delegates and fifteen guests. All but one of them were Russians, hand-picked representatives of non-existent Communist Parties in the fragments of the former Russian Empire, returned Russian emigrés self-designated to represent the lands of their recent exile. The manifesto that announced the launching was signed by Lenin, Trotsky and Zinoviev, all Russians; by Christian Rakovsky, a completely Russianized Bulgarian, and Fritz Platten, a Swiss.

No Bolshevik at that moment believed it possible for the new regime to pull through without successful Bolshevik revolutions in one or more industrialized West European countries. The absurdity of a communist island surviving in a capitalist ocean was one of the fundamental dogmas of the Bolshevik faith at the time. Lenin and his associates thought of all internal measures as strategy for saving Russia "until such time as the revolution takes place in other countries." Moreover, Soviet Russia was invaded and beleaguered by foreign armies and choked economically by a blockade. Pro-Soviet internationalist sentiment in non-Soviet countries was desperately needed to foment the hoped-for revolutions and to help break those strangling attacks.

Under these circumstances a militant internationalism was not merely good communist doctrine. It was good Soviet policy. In trumpeting the world revolution, all stops were pulled out. Russia was not so much a nation as the nucleus of an inter-nation, destined to embrace the whole earth. This was the *First Period* of the Comintern—shrilly revolutionary, conspiratorial and glorying in outlawry, appealing in all countries to genuine social rebels and to bold romantics.

With the end of the Russian civil wars, the collapse of intervention and the reluctant postponement of world revolutionary hopes, Russian interests demanded that the Comintern trumpets be muted. The country had to adjust itself to the realities of its unexpected survival. Diplomatic relations had to be cemented somehow with capitalist countries. Trade channels had to be blasted through the debris of the fevered war years. Inside Russia the military communism of the first years gave way to the New Economic Policy—NEP—which was, in effect, a compromise between state and private economy. A great political opportunist, Joseph Stalin, more interested in power than in revolution, forged ahead to dictatorial leadership under the compromise slogan of "socialism in one country."

Analogous tactics of compromise were inevitable outside Russia. The fiction of a separation between the Soviet government and the Communist Party which runs it was evolved to make possible political traffic with other governments. The larger fiction of a separation between the Communist International and the Russian Communist Party which decides its every word and accent was fostered and embellished with painstaking camouflage. This was the *Second Period* in the career of the Comintern and hence of its every extension abroad, roughly from 1921 to 1928. Wherever possible the Communist Parties retreated from plotting to mild propaganda within the laws of their respective countries. In many countries, among them the United States, the parties climbed out of romantic subcellars to the prosaic sidewalks of legality.

The key words of this period were "united front" and "boring from within." The whole technique of snaring and exploiting sympathetic liberals and progressives abroad was evolved, though its magnificent perfection was to come much later. Typical episodes of this period were efforts to collaborate with other organizations or to capture them outright: such as the Anglo-Russian Committee in England, the fake and sterile communist farmer-labor organizations and the blundering flirtation with the La Follette progressive movement in America, and Soviet Russian co-operation with the Kuomintang revolution under General Chiang Kai-shek.

All these episodes were black failures. But we are not concerned here with the wisdom or stupidity of the policies. We want to underline the fact that such policies were conditioned almost exclusively by the situation inside Russia, not by conditions in the countries where the "party line" of the period was applied. The Soviet regime needed to consolidate its position at home. Those who had grabbed Lenin's and Trotsky's leadership needed a lull in world revolutionary propaganda abroad—time for the rising bureaucracy to entrench itself—even as they needed to placate the *kulaks* or richer peasants and the "Nepmen" or new middle class at home.

2

The year 1928, which marked the start of the first Five Year Plan in Russia, also marked the start of the *Third Period* in Comintern history. It is no coincidence. Once more the turn of affairs in Russia dictated a violent swing in the conduct of its foreign satellites.

Having wrested all power from the so-called Lefts, from the Trotsky opposition, and imprisoned or exiled their leaders, Joseph Stalin proceeded to out-Left them all. NEP was wiped out, private farming was slated for forcible socialization, a brutally speeded-up industrialization was begun. Though the Soviet State was more committed than ever to "socialism in one country," it required ultra-revolutionary slogans to fire the zeal of its own population. It needed the same slogans, also, to overcome lingering Trotskyist influence among supporters abroad and to stoke the furnaces of revolutionary enthusiasm, chilled nearly everywhere by the Second Period failures.

The Leftward stampede of communists the world over had little if any relation to events outside Russia. In a good many countries, indeed, among them the United States, the leaders were overwhelmingly Right and spoke for a majority of their local parties. But the majorities were summarily kicked out by Moscow and the minorities recognized as the official branches of the Comintern. Arbitrarily Stalin and his clique had decided that a new "revolutionary upsurge" was upon the world, and individual communists in Germany or South Africa, in China or America had to behave accordingly or be booted out of the comradely fold.

But there was something suspiciously perverted about the resuscitated revolutionary zeal. Its sharp edge was directed, curiously, less against out-and-out capitalists than against socialists, conservative trade unionists, liberals and progressives. These were now classified as "social fascists," and so much of the ammunition was assigned for their special annihilation that precious little remained for the out-and-out fascists. Under the new system of labeling, Mussolini and the National Socialist leader who was making such strides in Germany, Adolf Hitler, were merely fascists, whereas Leon Blum, George Lansbury, Norman Thomas and the German social-democrats, were social fascists.

To deal with these reprobates, Moscow devised one of the slickest hypocrisies on record. It decreed a new sort of united front—the united front *from below*. No longer were the faithful to co-operate in the slightest way with the social fascists at the head of labor and radical movements. Instead they must go over the heads of the leaders and unite with all those whom they could *detach* from such organizations. The Comintern, in other words, aimed at the unity achieved by the cat that swallows a canary, or the leech that unites with another creature's blood.

The consequences of this lopsided Leftism were to prove disastrous. In place of the promised "revolutionary upsurge," the world, under the impact of economic depression, experienced a fascist upsurge. But the theory of social fascism precluded any chance of united action against the new scourge. Moscow's verbal Leftism, binding on every member party, in practice meant civil war in the ranks of labor and liberalism—and a clear road ahead for fascism. Stalin accomplished the feat of attitudinizing as Leftest of the Left while actually helping clear the ground for fascism. There is no reason for believing that this was his deliberate purpose, despite his subsequent united front from above with Hitler. But it was the practical result of his tactics. Stalin needed revolutionary pyrotechnics at home and abroad to provide a smoke screen to cover terrorism, famine and despair inside Russia. He decidedly had no use for actual Bolshevik or socialist revolutions, which might have diverted energies from the building of "socialism in one country."

The social fascism slogan—amounting to war on the democratic governments and institutions in tacit co-ordination with other anti-democratic movements—did the trick. More starkly and tragically than ever before, the foreign branches of the Comintern followed the line of the Soviet Union's national purposes at a fearful cost to their own countries. Germany was merely the most tragic victim. Other nations, too, paid for Russia's blunder. What made the blunder possible was the subjection of a supposed international movement to the commands of a profoundly nationalistic political coterie.

Even after Hitler had come to power and triumphant Nazis were cramming their morgues and concentration camps with German communists, the Kremlin did not at once abandon its Third Period policies. First there were assiduous efforts on Stalin's part to win over the new Germany. One year after Hitler's accession, Stalin was still explaining to a Moscow conference for Hitler's benefit:

Of course, we are far from being enthusiastic about the fascist regime in Germany. But fascism is not the issue here, if only for the reason that fascism, for example in Italy, did not prevent the U. S. S. R. from establishing very good relations with that country.

Only when Hitler rejected the "very good relations," preferring to set himself up temporarily as Europe's policeman against Bolshevism, did Moscow veer gloomily to its "democratic" anti-fascist line of recent memory. The epoch of People's Fronts, Popular Fronts, collective security and elaborate pseudo-democratic mummery, the *Fourth Period*, was thus virtually forced upon the Communist International by the German Führer.

The period unfolded slowly. The reconciliation with capitalist democracies, however cynically undertaken, went too much against the grain of Bolshevik habits. It contrasted too crudely with the ever more rigid totalitarianism within Russia. But the fear that Europe might use Hitler as its fist to smash Soviet Russia, coupled with obstreperous Japanese militarism on the other side, left no pleasanter alternative. Moscow began its flirtations with Poland, the Little Entente in Central Europe, and with France—until then considered the spearhead of anti-Soviet plotting. It subscribed to the Kellogg Pact. It began to construct a system of non-aggression pacts with its neighbors. It negotiated a pact that was almost an alliance with France. And it entered the League of Nations—until then, in Lenin's phrase, "the League of Robber Nations."

The Fourth Period, during which a whitewashed Bolshevism was to attain unprecedented political influence in the democracies of the world, was officially launched at the Seventh Congress of the Comintern in the summer of 1935. The world revolution was not merely postponed, it was explained away as a "comic misunderstanding," as Stalin described it a few years later. Some surface embellishments were undertaken in Russia itself, including a bizarre document called the Stalin Constitution. The surface decorations, of course, did not interfere with an even bloodier terror and a more thorough erasure of human, let alone democratic, rights.

Russia's urgent national interests, its hope for allies against the German-Japanese threat, were at the bottom of the revised policies. The sections of the Communist International revamped their programs, from the cellar up, in a panic of fervent obedience. Again their about-face had no reference, necessarily, to conditions within their respective countries. The fascist danger had been no less rife during the preceding period. But miraculously the social fascists were sanctified in communist eyes, and wooed with the same ardor that they had until then been walloped. In every country the communists suddenly announced themselves as the real friends of democracy, the guardians of every tradition of freedom and civil liberty. A decade of agitation for revolution was coyly disclaimed. Respectability became the communist guiding star in everything from national politics to neckties. Communist radicalism was so thoroughly watered down to meet a Russian emergency that every conceivable "cause," from patriotism to poetry, could swim in it at ease.

And the nations which had been untouched by communist vitriol now succumbed rather ludicrously to communist honey. Statesmen, novelists, bridge-hounds, ministers, social workers, army heads flocked to the refurbished standards of the cooing comrades. France soon had its People's Front, headed by ex-social fascist Blum. In Spain the suppression of a fascist-nationalist uprising was taken over bodily by native and imported communists under beguiling communist slogans—thus dooming the Loyalist cause.

In the United States, too, the new Comintern policy produced a curious revolution—a pervasive communist infiltration of American life. It penetrated more deeply than the general public ever realized. Frequently it was so beautifully masked that some of its most overworked dray horses have not yet realized who held the reins. Many of those who considered themselves leaders—in government posts, in the world of art and culture, in education and in youth movements—are still smarting from the humiliating discovery that they were despised stooges of communist masterminds. The realization that those masterminds were none too brilliant salted the wounds of humiliation.

The story of that incredible revolution is the primary task of this book. But an understanding of the phenomenon is impossible without some knowledge of the world-wide machinery operated from Moscow, and of the general history of Bolshevism in America.

The Fourth Period came to an abrupt end in August, 1939, with the Soviet-Nazi Pact. Its sudden death, like its slow birth, had nothing to do with conditions in America or any other non-Soviet country. On the contrary, the world was never riper for a real democratic united front than at the moment when that front was kicked over by a Russian boot. The whole fantastic tale makes sense only in relation to the national interests of Russia. The history of Bolshevism in America makes sense only as a shifting shadow thrown on the screen of American life by a far-off dictatorship.

The *Fifth Period*, after the pact, unfolded smoothly enough for twenty-two months—until it was smashed on June 22, 1941, by the treachery of the Berlin partner. While it lasted, the Comintern swung back to world revolutionary pretensions and slogans, utilized primarily in the service of the very forces it had presumably been fighting against in the preceding period.

Chapter II

A PARTY IS BORN

1

THE notion that radicalism is somehow "alien" to America is deeply rooted here. The American Credo has it that "reds" are foreigners. This is a strange idea in a country settled by religious nonconformists, born as a nation in a long and violent revolution, and kept together through a bitter civil war. In truth the United States has a rich radical tradition, beginning with those newfangled democratic ideas of Paine, Franklin, Jefferson and others. The tradition includes the bumptious agrarian radicalism of the frontier that put Andrew Jackson into the President's chair. It includes the Abolitionists and slave-running and John Brown, Brook Farm and Single Tax and Technocracy. The first great association of American trade unions, the Knights of Labor, was militant in temper, embracing skilled and unskilled workers of all races and colors. Our native syndicalist movement, the I. W. W. (Industrial Workers of the World), which appealed chiefly to lumberjacks, fruit pickers and migratory laborers generally, was as picturesquely American as its leader, the bulky one-eyed Bill Haywood. The I. W. W. songs have the authentic idiom and accent of the American spirit and the lusty I. W. W. "free-speech fights" were as American as the Boston Tea Party.

Naturally, industries manned overwhelmingly by immigrant labor, such as mining, textiles and the needle trades, involved a lot of foreigners in their strikes. But the most violent chapters in the story of American trade unionism were written by native workmen under native leaders—the eight-hour day strikes of 1886, the celebrated Pullman strike of 1894, the several steel strikes, the General Strike in Seattle after the World War, and so on.

If anything, the American soil has been especially congenial for unorthodox ideas, from social Utopianism to sheer crackpotism. There are more queer messiahs and Utopian reformers in any corner of Los Angeles than in all of London or Moscow. Philosophies and programs

29

of action originating in Europe became in time thoroughly American. Social ideas, like the waves of immigration, fertilized the American world. By the time the United States took the plunge into the World War in 1917, a dozen radical organizations were clamoring for the chance to remake the country.

The more influential among them stemmed from the teachings of Karl Marx—half economic science, half mystic religion of progress. This is not the place for a discussion of the theories nor of the cleavages between the many competing interpreters. The various brands of socialism were no more un-American because Karl Marx was a German Jew than the various denominations of Christianity are un-American because Jesus Christ was a Palestinian Jew.

The radicalization of the laboring people, it happens, took place much sooner in Europe than in America. This was not because of any special ingredient in the American mind that made it immune to radical preachments. It was because free land, a frontier civilization, the rapid expansion of American economy provided a pleasanter escape from the working-class levels—an escape, that is, to better-off levels—than any theory of revolution. Having already been touched by radicalism, many European immigrants brought with them, along with their gifts of labor and their passion for liberty and learning, various socialist ideas. But those ideas took root and flourished only to the extent that the soil of American conditions permitted.

This, however, does not invalidate the claim that the American Communist Party, in particular, is alien. Far from being typical in this regard, it is a notorious exception among the Left and labor movements in our country.

Not even Stalin and his manifold agencies of espionage and pressure can make an American organization an absolute replica of the Russian original. Imitation has certain physical and psychological limits. A great deal of the communist ballyhoo and bombast in America in recent years, for instance, took peculiarly American forms. Much of its magnetism for middle-class Americans derived from our national love for safe conspiracy—from the weakness for passwords, pig Latin and secret handclasps on which fraternities and fraternal orders batten. But American communism is as nearly a true replica of the Muscovite original as possible under such unlike conditions.

The zigzag course of Russian Bolshevism has some inner logic. It can be explained by reference to Russian events or Russian struggles for power. There is no such logic in the zigzag course of American Bolshevism. It has merely trotted along parallel to the Russian line, with almost mechanical exactitude. Normally that line led the comrades clear outside American realities. It forced them to act on Soviet premises that did not exist here. Again and again it split their organization on issues that in America were wholly artificial and often meaningless to the uninitiated. Now and then, as in the fantastic fellow-traveler era, the line did cut deeply into American life, and that gave the movement a temporary semblance of reality. But as soon as it suited Moscow's purpose, the zigzag would swerve once more, taking the comrades for another ride to futility.

Thus, there has always been an aura of make-believe around American communism; something shrill, exaggerated, remote from everyday bread-and-butter existence. The mechanical alignment with the viewpoints and arbitrary orders of a nation thousands of miles away—a nation as different as possible from America in mentality, background and historical experience—drove the American party from melodrama to comedy, from legality to outlaw status and back again. An ostensibly American movement geared to the needs, the whims, the policies of an Asiatic dictatorship in a far-off backward country—how could it help becoming absurdly unrealistic?

2

The Communist Party began as an offshoot of the Socialist Party, but of a Socialist Party suddenly diluted by the inflow of Slavs and other foreigners in American immigrant centers. During the war the socialist membership had declined sharply, because of a deep split on the war question. New recruits came almost entirely from immigrant layers of the population. The astonishing change that had taken place in the Socialist Party by 1919—the year when its growing Left Wing broke away to form communist organizations—was summed up as follows by Morris Hillquit, an outstanding socialist leader:

Its dues-paying membership jumped to 108,000 and practically the entire increase was furnished by recent arrivals from Russia and its border states. The membership in the foreign-language federations rose to 57,000 or 53 per cent of the total, and the bulk of it was represented by Russian, Ukrainian, South Slavic, Finnish, Lithuanian and

Lettish organizations. It was the Soviet revolution that had primarily stimulated the interest of the workers of these countries in the Socialist movement at home and in the foreign centers of their emigration, and these new recruits were Bolshevik to the core.

It was out of these immigrant groups, principally, that the first communist fragments were formed. They tended to push American intellectuals to the fore as American façade: men like the gifted and impetuous Harvard-trained John Reed; or Jay Lovestone and Bertram Wolfe, recently out of college; or more seasoned socialists and labor men who had been fighting the older leaders even before America's entry into the war, like Charles E. Ruthenberg, William Z. Foster, Benjamin Gitlow, James Cannon. But the voting strength and the political manipulation came from the foreign-language "federations" within the party.

Along with ardor for the new Russia and its exciting slogans, there was an impatience with the stodgy reformism of the old-timers in the Socialist Party. Younger men were coming into the movement. Some of them had swallowed Marxism in one gulp, and were under psychological pressure to regurgitate it in action, almost any kind of action. They were determined to capture the organization or wreck it, although Reed, Gitlow and the tiny native American contingent generally still hoped to capture the party without a split.

There were faction conferences, caucuses, tendencies within each faction, and, above all, a spirited contest for places of leadership in the revolution a-borning. Until then socialism had been an abstraction. Its plums of leadership had been pretty tough and dry. But now, Bolshevism regnant in a great if distant country seemed to offer juicy rewards. There was revolutionary passion in the communist ranks— but there were also nostrils aquiver to the sweet scent of power.

The Communist International had declared the job of its adherents the world over to be the bringing about of "the immediate universal dictatorship of the proletariat in view of the present dissolution of the capitalist regime of the whole world." This was to be done by "the seizure of governmental power, the disarmament of the bourgeoisie, the general arming of the proletariat, and the suppression of private property." And that, believe it or not, was the assignment which the Left Wing Socialists solemnly accepted for post-war America. School-boys playing cops and robbers are far closer to reality.

On February 16, 1919, the Left Wingers met in an East Side hall in New York. They adopted a magniloquent "Manifesto and Program" which urged, in all seriousness, that the American workers immediately do what the Russian workers had done. In relation to the America of the moment this sounds lunatic. It was. And the lunacy that marked the inception of American Bolshevism was to remain a constant in a career wherein nearly everything else was variable.

The new leaders of the newest revolutionary enterprise were for the most part congenital romantics, immigrants ignorant of American life, and young intellectuals ignorant of any kind of life. The cooler and more experienced heads among them were turned by the general contagion of enthusiasm. The Socialist Party elders, being in control of the organization machinery, acted to expel the hotheads. When the New York State Executive kicked out its Bolsheviks, one of them shouted: "You are Right Wing enemies of the Revolution! Go ahead with your dirty work! Expel us from the party! We will soon meet you in bloody battles on the barricades!" The split spread through the country. The final act of the purge was set for the national convention of the party in Chicago on September 1.

The foreign-language groups summoned a counter-convention for the same day and the same city, to be held in the Russian federation headquarters, which they romantically named Smolny after the Petrograd headquarters from which Lenin and Trotsky had directed their putsch. Some of the Americans, among them Ruthenberg, went to Smolny. The others, among them Reed and Gitlow, tried to storm the convention of the parent body at Machinists Hall, only to be ejected with the help of Chicago police. The ejected group thereupon met in rump session a floor below. Their bid to the Smolny crowd to join forces was spurned—it was a contest for the glory of being the founding fathers.

The Bolshevism that emerged from these gatherings was born triplets. Smolny-on-the-Chicago launched a Communist Party. The Machinists Hall group launched a Communist Labor Party. And soon the Michigan section broke away from the Smolny to form its own Proletarian Party. Among them all they counted at the start perhaps 25,000 supporters, all that remained of the 60,000 they had torn away from the Socialist Party. The members dwindled rapidly under the pressure of a terrific red scare, out of all proportion to the threat.

Attorney General A. Mitchell Palmer, the American Legion, a

section of the press and certain superpatriotic alarmists shared the Moscow delusion that the revolution was around the corner. They therefore unloosed a nightmare of official and extra-legal persecutions. It was a case of post-war jitters of which the country was subsequently thoroughly ashamed. There was an orgy of raids, smashed offices, mass deportations that decimated the infant communist movement, but left those who remained even more passionately consecrated to their private melodrama.

A few months after the threefold birth, the three parties could claim no more than 10,000 members for their little job of "immediate universal dictatorship" and "the seizure of governmental power." In driving them more or less underground, Mr. Palmer and the American Legion completed the illusion of impending revolution by forcing the American communists into an outlaw political life resembling that of Russian communists under the Czars.

3

Underground the several parties in time got together, though the intense personal feuds and the rough elbowing for power grew even more bitter. In fighting one another desperately, the groups had a titillating illusion of fighting a desperate revolution.

By 1921 a Workers Party had been formed as the aboveground legal instrument of the undercover organization. The membership of the two was identical, except that the legal party drew in a handful of sympathizers unwilling to risk the hazards of the illegal one. These were, in a way, the first fellow-travelers—the foundation stones of the towering edifice of fraud in later years. The illegal Communist Party was affiliated with the Communist International. Its legal duplicate presumably was independent—for the record. This piece of tactical chicanery set the style for greater things to come. Among the conditions for affiliation with the International was concurrence with the tenet: "The class struggle in almost every country of Europe and America is entering the phase of civil war." The tiny American Communist Party was thus an imaginary army engaged in an imaginary war and proud of its imaginary victories.

Spokesmen of all the factions shuttled frantically between the U.S.A. and Moscow to plead their cases. The Kremlin, for its part, sent over "Comintern Reps" or representatives to help bring order out of the mess. Naturally, they only added to the tangle of intrigue. The initial lot of plenipotentiaries arrived with authority to straighten out the party quarrels. A secret convention for the purpose was summoned to Bridgeman, a village in Michigan, in August, 1922. Stupidly or in an excess of rebel daring, Michigan was selected though it had a sharp-toothed Criminal Syndicalism law on its books. The batches of mysterious city folk, many of them foreigners and outlandishly bearded, were as inconspicuous as a circus parade. Besides, the organization was honeycombed with government agents. But the amateur plotters enjoyed the comedy while it lasted.

Sessions were held in the woods, by torchlight, though the conspiratorial voices carried for hundreds of yards. William Z. Foster and Earl Browder, relatively recent recruits, made their maiden speeches. Foster had been in turn a Bryan Democrat, a socialist, an I. W. W. and a rabid syndicalist before the World War, but had sold Liberty Bonds and turned into a conservative A. F. of L. organizer under Samuel Gompers after 1917. Now he was a burning communist, though a secret one. In the Bridgeman woods he talked of coming glory—a communist-led labor movement, presumably with himself at its head. Earl Russell Browder, a native of Kansas, was a political hanger-on of Foster's. He had also been in the I. W. W., but during the war he had served a prison term as conscientious objector.

The Bridgeman gathering patched up a peace that was merely the prelude to bigger and better factional tussles. Then the inevitable government raid came. The detectives caught only a few of the participants, but they obtained a full list of delegates, complete with addresses and biographical data. The Bridgeman case, as a result of which several comrades served prison terms, was one of the earlier communist *causes célèbres*.

The years of the birth of American communism were tense with social struggles. There was a wave of strikes in 1919-20 involving more than four million workers. On the political side, labor leaders and others formed a Conference for Progressive Political Action which was the start of the La Follette progressive movement of four years later.

But the communists were out of all this. They fitted nowhere into the pattern of reality. Theirs was a tiny supercharged world isolated from America, though they hurled bombastic manifestoes into the void, and scattered leaflets calling for instant insurrection. This underground epoch in America corresponded to the First Period of the Comintern, the period of intransigeant trumpeting for the immediate overthrow of capitalism. Whatever meaning the intransigeance had in Hungary or Bavaria, in Finland or Italy, it was gibberish in the United States. The melodrama of those first years, earnest enough for its actors, seems comedy of a low order in historical retrospect. But nearly all the future leaders were trying their political wings and their polemic swings, learning to please the Kremlin overlords, and taking one another's measure.

On the whole it was an inept lot of would-be revolutionary prima donnas. I do not know enough about the peculiar qualities of bookkeepers to explain why two of them, Ruthenberg and after him Browder, should have been tagged by fate for supreme command in the following years. Of the two, Ruthenberg was by far the bigger and more competent man. In the lot were also Robert Minor, a first-rate cartoonist who preferred to be a fourth-rate Left politician, and who had jumped all the way from anarchism to its communist opposite; the big gruff labor leader, Jim Larkin, who returned to his native Ireland soon after serving a prison term in New York; Gitlow, Katterfeld, Wagenknecht, Bittelman, Ludwig Lore, scores of others. Some of them were able enough, but not one was a truly great, magnetic leader.

They had not succeeded—nor really tried—to establish living contact with the larger American public. From 80 to 90 per cent of their nine or ten thousand followers were in Russian, Ukrainian, Jewish, German, Finnish and other foreign-language branches. Less than a thousand were in English-speaking branches and their English was nothing to boast about. In an inner-circle discussion over a matter of policy at that time Robert Minor declared: "The interests of Russia must always be our first consideration." This was a sentiment fully shared by the new rulers of Russia. It was a sentiment that explains much which is otherwise inexplicable in the strange life and hates of the American Communist Party.

Chapter III

BORING FROM WITHIN

1

THE *sub rosa* Communist Party was dissolved early in 1923. The aboveground Workers Party took over all its functions, among them its secret membership in the International. It was a secret advertised on every page of the party press and confided daily to Western Union.

The fact is that the Kremlin has never troubled to conceal its control. Its decisions and "directives" on "the American question"—slavishly obeyed by the comrades on this side of the ocean—have been published and broadcast. American leaders have been demoted, expelled, or lifted to glory by overseas decree. They have raced to Moscow with their quarrels and theological problems, hung around anxiously for audiences with the mighty, and swallowed the Kremlin's bitterest verdicts. Ex-leaders, in the aftermath of their purging, have put the minutiae of the Russian domination copiously on record. The volumes of sworn testimony gathered by official investigations on the subject of the American party's subservience to the Comintern therefore demonstrate that the hardest thing to prove is the obvious.

The legalization of the party, as noted at the outset, was a conditioned reflex to the falling revolutionary temperature in Russia. Until then the Comintern had regarded labor agitation useful only as a preliminary to insurrection. Strikes were dress rehearsals for revolution or they were a waste of time. Now, however, the Comintern instructed its scattered legions to join these unions and purify them by their presence. A resolution bade them "learn how to influence unions without attempting to keep them in leading strings." Of course, they need not be too squeamish about the methods used to win the confidence of their fellow-workers. Lenin explained that in his *Left-Wing Communism*:

It is necessary to be able . . . to agree to any and every sacrifice, and

37

even—if need be—to resort to all sorts of devices, manoeuvres, and illegal methods, to evasion and subterfuge, in order to penetrate into the trade unions, to remain in them, and to carry on communist work in them at all costs.

By 1924 this angelic reasonableness spiced with evasion and subterfuge had gone to the point where the International warned that "Leninism on the field of the trade-union movement is the struggle against splitting in any form." A similar softening of temper was carried into all other fields. In the political arena, for example, no comrade in the first years would have deigned to associate with the unbaptized of other parties. The new dispensation of the Second Period ended this "isolation from the masses." It no longer frowned on joint action with respectably "progressive" organizations among the unsaved.

On a planetary scale, the International launched a *Profintern* or Red Trade Union International, willing and anxious to enroll all unions everywhere on its lists. The Profintern's work was fairly fruitful. It absorbed many trade-union federations in the Balkans, Latin America and the Far East, though it made no headway in Germany, England or the United States. Its paid agents and unpaid enthusiasts wormed their way into hundreds of big and little unions in all countries, planting everywhere the seeds of Profintern ideology, current version. There was the *Krestintern* or Red Peasant International, which remained notoriously ineffective. (Among the American "peasantry" it had an extremely faint echo in the Farmers Union.)

Then there was a lengthening array of special world-wide bodies for special purposes—friendship with Russia, defense of class-war prisoners, anti-imperialist propaganda, tutelage of the youth, etc.—where infidels might have the privilege of serving the cause without baptism in the communist church. The slogans of the period stressed the united front, contact with the masses, unity of labor and, of course— the one principle that never changed—defense of the Soviet fatherland.

The primary method worked out for implementing these slogans was to become celebrated, accursed and feared under the phrase "boring from within." It meant entering an organization and reforming or capturing it from inside, instead of torpedoing it from outside as in the past. Communists the world over were obligated to join everything from trade unions to their nation's defense forces and begin to bore.

Secretly or openly, depending on local conditions, communists in non-communist bodies must constitute themselves "fractions" or "nuclei" or "cells" to carry out the orders of their party chiefs. Where possible they must bore upward into posts of leadership, and in any event they must use their disciplined strength to make life burdensome for "reactionary" leaders and to awaken the complacent membership to a sense of their wrongs. Acting as organized units, under the guidance of experienced party people outside, the fractions and nuclei could make themselves felt way beyond their numerical strength. They could guide the rank and file along the paths of radical righteousness.

The American party, what there was of it, revised its character in line with these new policies. In the First Period it had failed to start Soviets in factories. In the Second it would fail to capture the American Federation of Labor. The Kremlinesque blueprints for boring from within the citadels of American capitalism were decidedly too ambitious for a party whose membership, during the next ten years, hovered around twelve or fifteen thousand, all but a thousand or two living in immigrant pockets of America. A few thousand communists whispering mysteriously underground had made a sizable conspiracy—enough to frighten the Department of Justice and extralegal alarmists. The same people in the light of day made a pitifully small movement, forgotten even by professional anti-red head-hunters except for rhetorical purposes.

Yet the party made a noise out of proportion to its size. The energy of its leaders and the fanatic zeal of the members made up for the paucity of numbers. After all they were backed by a gigantic foreign nation, subsidized from Moscow when necessary, and in a position to exploit that vague, amorphous "sympathy" for the Bolshevik "experiment" which had touched a sector of the American people.

The activities of the Workers Party from about 1923 to 1928 were not in themselves important. They left few permanent traces on the social physiognomy of the nation. The Trade Union Educational League, the abortive Farmer-Labor political undertakings, the first of the united front organizations in other directions, the fratricidal contests for leadership made no real impress on American life and thought. But those activities are extremely important for our narrative. They amounted to a prelude to the Red Decade. The operating techniques which later wrought curious miracles in our midst were developed during this period.

2

In boring from within the American labor movement, communists used the Trade Union Educational League (TUEL) as their drill. It had been started back in 1915 by William Z. Foster in his ultra-syndicalist days, but had become very rusty from disuse. In 1921 Foster was induced to lead a hand-picked labor delegation, including Earl Browder and Ella Reeves Bloor, to the first congress of the Profintern. He returned with a Communist Party card in his pocket, as leader of the boring brigades in the labor domain. Publicly and to the honestly progressive labor men whom he drew into his work, Foster for many years vehemently denied that he was a communist. He threw up his hands in holy horror at the suggestion, then hurried to meetings of the Communist Central Executive Committee, of which he was a member. There was no doubt that he had the makings of a communist leader.

The TUEL was the first, and in the 'twenties the most successful, communist decoy organization. Foster was secretary-treasurer of the League and editor of its paper, the *Labor Herald*, of which his rather meek and slow-witted hanger-on, Browder, became managing editor. Ostensibly "independent," the first national conference of the League—in Chicago, August, 1922—saw not only Foster and Browder in the forefront but a bevy of other well-known communists. A Profintern overseer, under the party name of Scott, was on hand to direct the gathering. The fact that a good many non-communist labor leaders worked with the TUEL in its initial years merely shows how easy it was to fool them. Nevertheless, organized labor in later years proved itself on the whole less open to united front blandishments than journalists, teachers, shopkeepers and Social Registerites.

The inside boring was startlingly successful in the needle trades unions centered in New York. The leadership in those unions had always been more or less socialistic and a vociferous Left Wing had enjoyed large followings. Sidney Hillman, the head of the Amalgamated Clothing Workers of America, was able to evade communist domination of the Amalgamated though some of its locals were badly scarred by the intrusion. The other great needle organization, the International Ladies Garment Workers Union, however, came to know the disease in all its virulence. By 1925 the communist faction was in complete command of some of the largest locals, and the union was being run from communist headquarters. It took the more conservative leaders a few years, fighting fire with fire, before the communists were ousted. The Fur Workers International Union, captured bodily at that time, has remained in the communist grip to this day, with the communist leader Ben Gold in command.

Foster and his lieutenants succeeded in lining up progressive labor leaders like John Fitzpatrick and Edward Nockles of the Chicago Federation of Labor, John Brophy and Alexander Howat of the United Mine Workers. But the communist control of the TUEL became too obvious. More and more, the genuine progressives fell away and the TUEL became almost all-communist, pure but futile. To mask the boring from within more effectively, special decoy organizations had to be built in various industries: a Railroad Workers Amalgamation Committee, a Progressive Miners Committee, equivalent propaganda groups in the textile, shoe-manufacturing and food industries. Being an additional length or two removed from the Muscovite wire-pullers, their connection was a bit more difficult to prove. The sheer mechanics of such outfits are worth looking at, since they were to become standard.

At the head of the group invariably stood a non-communist carefully selected by the party, though he did not necessarily know this. Frequently he might be someone genuinely interested in the alleged objectives of the group. But the secretary, who handled records, correspondence and money, was invariably a party member under absolute discipline—interested only in maintaining the party's grip on the whole business. The executive board was usually loaded with party people or "sympathizers" willingly taking party guidance. Thus there was always a respectable façade, and behind it the machinery of communist control. Since the group was normally dependent on direct or indirect subsidies, there was small enough chance of insubordination.

The most notable boring-from-within chapter was written in the United Mine Workers of America. The TUEL and its decoy Progressive Miners Committee placed themselves not merely behind but all around and on top of the opposition movement which was trying to displace John L. Lewis. The finances for the drive, as Gitlow and

others subsequently revealed in convincing detail, came directly from
the Profintern in Moscow, upon authorization of the Comintern.
The Kremlin was always especially solicitous about the basic industries—mining, transportation, communications, metallurgy, the things
most essential to the life and military strength of nations—and ready to
invest generously in their domination.

The coal miners' situation developed into a bitter struggle of many
years' duration. In the course of it Lewis was elaborated into an ogre-
like creature by his communist-led opposition. He had long stood out
for his ruthless ways, even among labor leaders. Now propaganda
rubbed in the stains. In the communist press he was a labor faker,
strikebreaker, capitalist toady, murderer—the whole colorful vocabulary of radical vituperation was emptied on his leonine head. Until
the very hour when he formed the C.I.O. and took the Moscow men
into his camp, he remained in communist eyes a very Beelzebub of
reaction.

The Lewis machine in the end vanquished the insurgents. TUEL
work in most other fields came to nothing. The attempt to co-ordinate
the Leftist labor unions with a political movement, as we shall see,
ended in burlesque. Foster's dream of boring his way to the top of
the A.F.of L., or building a new labor empire out of the pieces,
petered out as a nightmare of futility. The borers were expelled wholesale from the established unions, leaving the communists in control of
only a few corners of the clothing trades and some scattered and ineffectual independent unions in other industries. Even the most dramatic strike action under all-communist leadership, a textile strike in
Passaic, New Jersey, boiled down to exactly nothing.

The first major campaign of applied Machiavellism under Moscow direction failed. But the American generals learned a lot about
strategy in the process.

3

Moscow's first grand venture into American politics cries for
another Gilbert and Sullivan team to do it justice. The trouble, of
course, was that the Kremlin, then and always, tried to fit a standardized policy on all countries. The British Labor Party was heading for
power. If the British communists could share in that power, they
would be useful in Moscow's foreign affairs. In other countries, like-

wise, a Muscovite nucleus, if not outright control, in political life
would be valuable. Hence the orders went forth to rally all possible
socialist, labor, liberal, farmer and progressive elements for political
action under hidden communist aegis.

The American comrades complied with alacrity. The third-party
idea was very much in the air, and Senator Robert M. La Follette was
known to be toying with the temptation. The unsavory Harding
Administration, heading for the Teapot Dome scandal, had stirred a
yen for righteousness. A Conference for Progressive Political Action
had been launched by the Railroad Brotherhoods, the Machinists
Union, Hillman's Amalgamated and other independent labor groups.
The communists, and especially Foster as generalissimo of the TUEL,
saw the organization of a strong labor party as a magic short cut to
influence. Here was within-boring to thrill the most sluggish comrades!

A convention to found a national farmer-labor party was called
for July 3, 1923, in Chicago. Naturally the summons was not issued
frankly by the Workers Party, but by Farmer-Labor groups in the
Northwest under communist prodding. The comrades can work hard,
if nothing else. They mobilized more than five hundred "delegates"
for the convention, all but a handful of them representing out-and-out
communist stooge-organizations, paper constituencies with fine-
sounding names, or just themselves. They acted like outraged innocents when the press accused them of being communists—and
regularly took part in the party caucuses. In describing the gathering,
Robert Morss Lovett wrote that the uninvited guests "came into the
house and carried off the ice-cream." (The experience, alas, did not
save Mr. Lovett in the balmy fellow-traveler years to come from energetic participation in some two dozen stooge-organizations.)

Genuine labor delegates who thought they were using the communists realized soon enough that it was the other way around. They
argued that the gathering should postpone the actual formation of a
party until other and stronger third-party elements, particularly the
Conference for Progressive Political Action and the Minnesota
Farmer-Labor Party, could be brought into line for a concerted move.
What such men failed to understand until too late was that the communists didn't want a labor party—but a communist party decked out
in labor-party labels.

The convention jammed through a resolution solemnly bringing to birth a Federated Farmer-Labor Party. The handful of uncontrolled delegates, including the only real labor representatives, fled the convention. The minor Machiavellis had captured themselves. They had bored diligently, only to find they had broken into their own empty safe. All the same, it was a famous victory. A new "epoch in American history," General Foster called it, and promised the faithful that the Federated Farmer-Labor Party, bought with a Kremlin appropriation and a mess of lies, "will break the chains with which the Gompers bureaucracy keeps the workers of this country bound to the political chariots of their industrial masters." Privately, however, the plotters were embarrassed and chagrined no end.

But that was only the first act. Bigger and better buffoonery was in the script. The La Follette movement was gaining ground. The Conference for Progressive Action had issued a call for a nominating convention to be held in Cleveland on July 4, 1924. Obviously the only hope for horning in on the third-party excitement was to ride the La Follette tide. The communist scheme, therefore, was to take the Minnesota Farmer-Labor Party in tow, stage a convention earlier than the one scheduled for Cleveland, and thus steal the lead in nominating La Follette. The Minnesota Farmer-Laborites proved easy marks for the impressive communist strategy. How could they doubt the sincerity of the comrades, who were outdoing everybody else in their support of La Follette? One Clarence Hathaway, representing the Machinists Union of St. Paul in the Farmer-Labor Party, was particularly active—only the communist leaders knew that this Hathaway (later the editor of the New York *Daily Worker*) was secretly and passionately a Workers Party member.

Thus a nominating convention, ostensibly under joint auspices of the Minnesota Farmer-Labor Party and Foster's private Federated Farmer-Labor Party, was summoned to St. Paul for June 17. The party press and communists on non-party labor papers lambasted the coming Cleveland convention and held up the St. Paul gathering as the only real thing. La Follette was industriously "sold" to the American "masses"—meaning all the ten or twenty thousand who heeded the voice of Moscow.

But within the party there was an anti-La Follette minority, eager to plow under the current leadership and usurp its places. It had access to the Kremlin's ear, and before long Moscow took a hand. Foster and others rushed to Moscow. The upshot of these hegiras was tragic or comic, depending on the point of view. Moscow, for reasons of its own, decided against support for La Follette under any circumstances! A convention elaborately rigged to nominate La Follette had been prepared by every device of double-dealing and camouflage. And now—twenty-two days before the great event—the bosses "over there" ordered that it be turned into an anti-La Follette occasion. The thought of disobeying the Muscovite dictates never crossed the minds of the American leaders. God forbid!

Six hundred delegates, perhaps 90 per cent of them communists or communist stooges, gathered in St. Paul on June 17 to nominate the Wisconsin Senator. The Minnesota Farmer-Laborites, imagining themselves in control, had no misgivings. But by the time the convention was opened, the about-turn order had been passed down the line of astonished but obedient delegates. The first mention of La Follette did not bring the expected and solemnly promised storm of cheers but a tornado of catcalls and jeers. Were the Minnesota innocents surprised!

La Follette himself, smarter than the Minnesota statesmen, had repudiated the St. Paul gathering on the eve of its meeting, indicating that he was playing with the Cleveland group. The St. Paul convention, now passionately in reverse for reasons beyond its understanding, adopted the title of National Farmer-Labor Party. It dragged a couple of hapless delegates from their obscurity and nominated them to the highest offices in the land: Duncan McDonald of Illinois, a former miners' official, for President, and William Bouck, a farmer from the State of Washington, for Vice-President. Once more the miniature Machiavellis and the masterminds in the Kremlin had captured a corpse, with a duo of Presidential candidates to tote it triumphantly through the land. Meanwhile the Cleveland convention nominated La Follette, scores of independent groups, including the Socialist Party, jumped on the band wagon, and the great plotters were out of it all.

The farce was too hilarious to last. New decrees came through from Russia. The ludicrous McDonald-Bouck campaign was called off a few weeks after its start. In a sudden spurt of revolutionary spirit, intended to save face, a Workers Party conference in Chicago on July 10 washed its hands of counter-revolutionary farmer-labor puttering and nominated its very own candidates: William Z. Foster for President, Benjamin Gitlow for Vice-President. The comedy ended in anticlimax.

For the first time in American history the communists had their own candidate for President. The Vice-Presidential candidate many years later testified under oath that Moscow had sent through $50,000 for his own and Foster's campaign. The spirited campaign was directed mainly against La Follette and his socialist supporters. It was hoped to divert some socialist votes and impress the bosses seven thousand miles away with the vigor of their American agents. Then the votes were counted. The Workers Party total was 33,361. The communists who had been able to pack conventions and pull the wool over well-meaning labor men in Chicago and Farmer-Labor politicians in St. Paul were helpless when it came to snaring the ordinary American. Their talents, it was clear, were for behind-the-scenes conniving rather than open agitation. This simple truth would be demonstrated again and again in the future course of American Bolshevism. It was, in the final analysis, a foreign agency pulling off jobs for its employers, and not in the remotest sense an American social movement.

The useless thrashing of political waters, however, was duly reported to the Fifth Congress of the Communist International in Moscow by a Comrade Kolarov as a colossal achievement: "In the United States the small farmers have founded a Farmer-Labor Party which is becoming ever more radical, drawing closer to the communists and becoming permeated with the idea of the creation of a workers' and peasants' government in the United States." The American job holders in the International evidently were lying to the bosses to magnify the importance of their job and their own accomplishments. The bosses in turn were translating the lies into general principles to keep the whole world-communist movement pepped up and hopping happily to the snap of Soviet fingers.

CHAPTER IV

THE MOSCOW SOLAR SYSTEM

1

THE phase of the Second Period policies of the Moscow International which concerns us most closely, because it was fated to carve deep scars on American life many years later, was its initial success in building false-front organizations: groups for carrying out communist plans under seemingly "neutral" auspices. "Sympathizing mass organizations for special purposes" was the formal description of the idea offered by a Comintern resolution in 1926. The resolution went on to explain the obvious: that while self-governing and independent in appearance, these bodies must be "in reality under communist leadership."

A more candid statement of the case was given by Karl Radek in 1922. Discussing the need for simulating friendship with the British socialists, he had this to say about the method of the United Front: "It is easier and pleasanter to smash things, but if we have not the power to do so, and if this method is necessary, we must make use of it . . . in the firm trust that this method will do harm to Social Democracy, not to us . . . and in the conviction that *we shall crush them in our embrace.* . . ." Certainly a cute statement of applied amoralism!

And Otto Kuusinen—the same Kuusinen who figured briefly as head of Stalin's puppet government for Finland fourteen years later—summed up the idea graphically in 1926: "We must create a whole solar system of organizations and smaller committees around the Communist Party, so to speak, smaller organizations working actually under the influence of our party (not under mechanical leadership)." The cryptic parenthesis was crystal clear to the comrades. He meant that the *seeming* leadership need not be communist, but only the actual behind-the-throne direction.

Another piece of incidental candor for insiders may be credited to a German comrade once high in the Muscovite hierarchy, Willi

47

Muenzenberg.* Willi was one of the earliest and most prolific builders of communist structures behind "liberal" false fronts. His handiwork was known familiarly to his comrades as "Muenzenberg shows." They included relief organizations, publishing houses, defense outfits, fake "cultural" enterprises. Well, Willi was talking once about his favorite "show," the W.I.R. or Workers International Relief, and other such undertakings, and his remarks are on record in the published minutes.

"The W.I.R.," he said, "can take steps which political parties cannot take. . . . Now we must get hold of other groups under other names." Then he grew whimsical about his own distaste for the business of roping a lot of nitwits into camouflaged organizations. "Personally," he said, "these do not interest me very much, and it is not really interesting to form these Innocents' Clubs." One can imagine him sighing as he faced the necessity, continuing, "We must penetrate every conceivable milieu, get hold of artists and professors, make use of cinemas and theatres, and spread abroad the doctrine that Russia is prepared to sacrifice everything to keep the world at peace. We must join these clubs ourselves. . . ."

Thus the ironical designation Innocents' Clubs for these fake organizations comes out of the mouth of one of its chief leaders. And it is a telltale description. It betrays the real attitude of the communists toward those whom they inveigle into their schemes. Contempt—pitiless and jeering contempt. For enemies they harbor deadly hatred, but for their fellow-travelers and supine tools—only contempt. The "artists and professors," the leaders of "cinemas and theatres," the clergymen and novelists, Cabinet members and rich men's sons, who in due time would populate Willi's Innocents' Clubs, have from the beginning been despised and insulted behind their backs. They have been looked upon as puppets unworthy even of the playful affection a ventriloquist accords to his wooden dummy.

Comrade Kuusinen's "solar system" is indeed a curious universe, and we astronomers have no easy time of it trying to study its ways. Every planet and satellite in the system is purposely colored to escape detection and shrieks denials when detected. There has never been another world-wide complex of prevarication on such a scale. The illusion that the International is "international" is the fundamental lie.

---

* Muenzenberg was found murdered in France late in 1940, apparently the victim of G.P.U. killers. He had broken with Stalin and was regarded as dangerous by the Kremlin because he had been privy to so many Stalinist crimes.

The continuous revision of policies and principles, while retaining the old socialist, communist and Marxist labels, is an essential part of the deception. The development of Innocents' Clubs is the fraud that concerns us most in this narrative. Each of them represents a multiple lie. Not only is it an organization posing as something other than it really is, but its own adherents, in many cases, are unaware of its real aims and its real control.

2

The Friends of Soviet Russia, renamed Friends of the Soviet Union when the country changed its name, was one of the first and remained one of the longest-lived of the Innocents' Clubs* The frankness of its title is in itself a proof of early origin. As the Comintern became more proficient in the arts of hoaxing the public, the enclosures in which the gullible and unwary were corralled were less honestly named. Indeed, a variation of the Friends in our own country which came into being later called itself the Russian-American Institute, though it was manipulated by the comrades as dexterously as the earliest model.

In the initial years the Friends were more candidly communist than in the later stages, when Corliss Lamont was put at their head. Those in charge at that time did not deny that they were party members working under party orders. Their first big undertaking was to collect money for the relief of distress brought about by the great Russian famine of 1921. Those who worked on it little dreamed that a bigger undertaking of the Friends, more than a decade later, would be to conceal the second and greater Soviet famine, the one hand-made by the Stalin regime in 1932-33.

Another false-front group of an early vintage is the International Labor Defense, "section of the International Red Aid," to quote its own constitution. The more formal name of that international is MOPR, those being the Russian initials for International Class War Prisoners Aid Society. As late as 1939, Congressman Vito Marcantonio of New York, then head of the American section of MOPR, would deny that it was a communist front. But Gregory Zinoviev, as President of the Comintern, did not share Marcantonio's shyness in

---

* Dissolved by fiat from above soon after the Soviet-Nazi Pact.

the matter. "The Executive Committee of the Comintern," he said in 1925, "regards the International Red Aid as one of its branches, and indeed as one of the most important of them."

The international president of the Red Aid, until her death, was the famous German communist veteran, Klara Zetkin, and the international secretary, until he resigned from the party, was Muenzenberg. The first head of the American section was James P. Cannon, among the key leaders of the party until his expulsion in 1928. Not until the lush years of the fellow-traveler masquerade did the party deem it necessary to put a Republican Congressman between the American "masses" and the truth.

The American section of MOPR was born officially in June, 1925. The birth was ordered by Moscow, supervised by a MOPR emissary and the accouchement was paid for by a Moscow appropriation. "All the details for the convention to organize the International Labor Defense were worked out by the Central Executive Committee of the Party," Gitlow later revealed. "Out of the conference emerged a strictly communist organization. Of course, the fact that it was affiliated with the Soviet MOPR was not then made public." The I.L.D. propaganda was raucously communist, its publications undisguised in their Muscovite orientation. One of the unkind tricks of "red-baiters," in fact, was to suggest out loud that the I.L.D., being so deeply devoted to radical political prisoners, do something to help the imprisoned socialists, anarchists, Tolstoyans and even communists in the Soviet Union.

The Anti-Imperialist League, too, must be mentioned among the hardiest United Front fabrications. It dates back to 1925, with the redoubtable Willi among its founders and officials. Since it dealt with the uncertain stuff of Soviet foreign policy, it was destined to go through more names, liquidations and reincarnations than any other single Innocents' Club. Its greatest blossoming in America, and all other countries, would wait for the 'thirties, under such titles as League Against War and Fascism, League for Peace and Democracy, and finally the American Peace Mobilization.

These and a batch of other planets set spinning during the Second Period may be considered experimental. Some exploded, others survived, many altered their shapes and orbits. But the Moscow divinities saw their work and found it good—so good that the Never-Never universe for innocents would ultimately become crowded with heavenly bodies of all sizes, contours and colors. In its best days the solar system would become more important and command more of the communist energies than the Communist Parties themselves. Moscow had stumbled on a magnificent technique of befuddlement.

The principal assignment for all the innocents and not-so-innocents, whatever their particular corrals might be called, was to "defend the Soviet Union." The euphemism covered a wide range of effort to suppress unpleasant truths about life under the Soviet dictatorship. Most of the "fronts" put out magazines. Many of their members had the public ear, as speakers or writers. It was thus possible not only to spread fairy tales about the Bolshevik paradise, but to tear down the character of anyone who reported doubts of its paradisiacal wonders. Dozens of comrades who had gone to the shrine to worship returned to exhibit the broken pieces of their pretty illusions. Several of the men and women deported to the land of their dreams by the American authorities in the Mitchell Palmer era—among them Emma Goldman and Alexander Berkman—fled Russia to report it as a nightmare. These "renegades" were the special butt of calumny. The mere fact that they objected to torture of their nonconformist comrades in Russia was prima facie evidence that they had sold their souls to the capitalist devil.

No communist questioned the doctrine that the interests of Russia came before every other moral or national claim. Hence they really were aware of no violation of conscience in doing the dirtiest jobs if ordered by the party. On the contrary, the more distasteful the chore, the greater the credit. They broke up socialist and labor meetings as a matter of course. Boring from within under instructions took Moscow's men in America into factories, into the army, everywhere to ferret out information for transmission to headquarters. They manned mud guns and swung blackjacks and concocted lies for the greater glory of the Soviet Union. As Gitlow phrased it subsequently:

We were volunteer members of a militarized civil service, pledged to carry out the decisions of our supreme rulers resident at Moscow anywhere in the world but particularly in the land we were colonizing for communism, the United States.

And in this he hit on the perfect formulation. The American communists in effect became colonial agents of Moscow. The fact that many of them were native Americans strengthens the resemblance—many of Britain's civil servants in India or Italy's in Libya are likewise natives. The test is in the basic allegiance, not in race or nationality.

The open or underground Communist Parties, the proliferating solar system of "fronts," the individual "sympathizers" or purchased propagandists add up to a new sort of world empire. Its domain is not geographical. It is in the loyalties and enthusiasms and self-interests of millions in all countries directly or indirectly in the service of the Soviet regime.

CHAPTER V

THE AMERICAN PARTY IS PURGED

1

IN FOLLOWING the course of Bolshevism in America, one cannot fail to be impressed and astonished by the consistent mediocrity of its leaders. It has great villainies to its credit, but no great villains. Something cramped and pettifogging lies like a gray dust over its entire high command. I can think of only one exception: John Reed, whom death removed from the communist scene very early, before he had a chance to leave it voluntarily as he was about to do when he died. The rest—Ruthenberg, Foster, Lovestone, Minor, Olgin, Cannon, Trachtenberg, Engdahl, Bittelman, Bedacht, Stachel, Hathaway, Krumbein, Browder, Ford—included capable men, even personable and amusing men. A few were better than average as politicians and connivers. A few were touched by the flame of idealism, at least at the outset of their careers. But among them is not one great orator or inspiring leader, one forceful demagogue or eloquent writer. This is not necessarily derogatory, since I am measuring them with the yardstick of genuine greatness.

The American Socialist Party had its Eugene V. Debs, a magnetic leader and a great speaker; its Morris Hillquit, the brilliant lawyer whose mind was admired even by his dearest enemies. The Socialist Labor Party had a great theoretician, Daniel de Leon. The I.W.W.'s had Big Bill Haywood, a rough-hewn leader of classic mold. The anarchists had Emma Goldman. The moderate labor movement had Samuel Gompers, an organizer on the grand scale. But the communist movement in its upper reaches has been almost uniformly drab, uninspired and boring. At various stages in its history it attracted brilliant writers and speakers. Especially in the heyday of its "democratic" incarnation it would draw lavishly upon the talents of gifted Americans in many fields. But these remained in the hazy periphery. The authority always rested with men and women without color or lift, let alone attributes of greatness.

53

The reasons for this poverty of human material are not far to seek, once we understand that servility is the first test of communist leadership. An original mind and a robust spirit could not conceivably survive under conditions where every thought is predigested seven thousand miles away and shipped to the United States in neat capsules. The mental quality needed for survival is a chameleon-like ability to take on the color of a far-off dictator's thoughts and wishes. After all, the virtues that make an excellent butler do not make a revolutionary leader. An American communist chief who has wriggled through twenty years of purges along the zigzag of an alien party line might qualify as a contortionist but scarcely as a hero.

The communist leaders have risen to power, and held on to it, not by achievement at home, but by success in mollifying Moscow. The itch for power has in consequence afflicted little men who in other political movements would have been content to remain ward heelers. Among those at all capable of rising above the inert mass of naïvely faithful rank-and-filers, there were few so meek that they did not for a time reach for the higher rungs of the communist ladder. It meant being kicked in the teeth and kicking others in the teeth, running to the Kremlin fathers with complaints and denunciations.

Factionalism was the endemic disease of the American, as of every other, Communist Party in the period of which we are speaking— the period that ended with the enthronement of Browder. I use the past tense because after 1929, with the final ascendancy of Stalin as the unquestioned dictator of world communism, the internal struggles were mostly driven below the surface. They continued to boil and sputter in the depths, of course, but a "monolithic" unanimity—the unanimity and peace of death—was maintained on the surface.

The disease was devastating while it lasted. Contending groups within an organization may be an aspect of democratic give-and-take. Among the communists, however, factionalism was a function of the dictatorial setup, and particularly of foreign domination. The competition was not primarily for mass support or majorities. It was simply for the support of the Comintern overlords. Under the banners of "unity," "discipline," and "loyalty to the Comintern," internecine warfare went on for the mastery of the American party and its "neutral" extensions—warfare, that is, for the favor and patronage of Moscow. From the beginning, intrigue, rotten diplomacy and mutual knifing were routine procedures in the higher brackets of American Bolshevism. These refinements absorbed more time, energy and emotional substance in a week than the job of making the revolution did in a year.

The internal warfare, moreover, was if anything more unreal than the alleged revolution. If the factional quarrels had any intrinsic connection with American problems, there might have been some sense to them. But they were invariably American battles fought to the death on issues which did not exist in America. Right or wrong, Trotsky and Stalin, then Stalin and Bukharin, went at each other with all the weapons of comradely homicide over realities. The Ruthenbergs, Fosters, Cannons and Lovestones used the same weapons over chimeras and windmills. These Kansas and City College politicos fought for hegemony over the coming American revolution on the issue of liquidation of Russian *kulaks* and similar pressing American problems. Whether they won or lost depended entirely on whether they guessed right about those far-off and, for them as Americans, utterly fictitious values.

Their noisy wars were especially pathetic when taken together with the small and ineffectual role the party enjoyed in American life after a decade of fulmination. Foster's vote as Presidential candidate was 33,076 in 1924, and 48,288 four years later. Actually this was a considerable loss, as the 1928 figure represents candidacy in thirty-three states, against only thirteen states in the previous election. In 1924-25 the party claimed 17,000 dues-paying members. In 1926 the paid-up rolls fell to 8,698; in 1927 they stood at 9,642. The party membership, moreover, was extremely unstable, probably undergoing a nearly total turnover in three or four years.

It must be granted that party adhesion is not the only test of influence. Already the organization exercised control over a "periphery," composed in part of people herded in Innocents' Clubs and in part of unattached and vaguely "sympathetic" individuals, many times larger than the core of enrolled believers. These lay members, below the pitch of faith or courage for accepting discipline and obligations, were more important than the group actually in orders, because they were drawn from more influential sections of the American people. But when all credits are added, the party still remained an insignificant sect among American political faiths. When the factions appealed to their standing with the "American workers" or their status as "vanguard of the revolutionary forces," they were indulging in their game of make-believe.

Yet the struggle for jobs and honors proceeded in deadly earnest. It involved for the participants frequent and hurried journeys to Moscow. When Comrade A took off for the Kremlin, Comrade B of necessity did likewise—A could obviously not be allowed to monopolize the Infallible Ear. On occasion the Russian leaders drafted American comrades for "important work" in China or Patagonia or in Moscow itself, to get them conveniently out of the way of the current favorite. The bickerings also involved the constant presence of "Reps" from Russia invested with the omniscience of the masters. Sometimes entire Comintern commissions arrived, every member under a false name. Again and again the whole future of American communism hung on whether this faction or that cornered Moscow's latest ambassador first and kept him properly mellowed for its own side.

2

The scope of this account does not allow for detailed stories of even the more important factional campaigns. Reluctantly I pass over the glorious ganging up on Ludwig Lore in the fifth and sixth years of the party's labors. The echoes of that crusade against Loreism (not even Lore knew what the word meant) have long ago died down. The campaigns in which General Foster stole the army and equipment from General Ruthenberg and the manner in which Ruthenberg retrieved the losses in time for a state funeral and a hero's grave on Red Square—these, too, tempt me. But the price of historical writing is self-denial. I must limit myself to bare outlines of the great battles which wound up the Second Period and introduced the Third in the life of the Communist Party of the United States. All the battles, I need hardly add, were won by Stalin.

The first of these was related to the Stalin-Trotsky contest in Russia. This must not be taken to mean that one American faction supported Trotsky and the other supported Stalin. Nothing so straightforward could be expected. All factions supported the winner, but some were quicker or luckier than others in realizing who the winner would be, and louder in making their discovery manifest.

American leaders naturally followed the Stalin-Trotsky tussle with great avidity. But they followed it cagily, fearing a move that might place them irrevocably on the wrong side. As late as 1927, when Trotsky's fate was sealed, the American comrades had not yet caught up with the facts and were publishing routine but heretical compliments to Lenin's closest associate. Foster's control of the TUEL and the importance of that "front" organization in the farmer-labor farce had for a time given him supreme leadership. But the failure of those enterprises put the party back into the hands of Ruthenberg, whose major-domo was Jay Lovestone.

Foster intrigued relentlessly for the crown, seconded by Cannon and others. That is, of course, oversimplifying the picture. Nearly every chieftain had a foot or a few toes in both camps, ready to desert his colleagues for a price. Only fear restrained him, or the fact that said colleagues moved first. The comrades rifled one another's private files and stole brief cases from suspected factional traitors. They used non-party gangsters at professional rates against obdurate fellow-idealists and maintained factional legations in Moscow.

The sudden death of Ruthenberg on March 2, 1927, raised intrigues to a fever level. American Bolshevism saw a minor version of the scramble for power which had marked the death of Lenin in Russia. Caucuses met before, during and immediately after the funeral and memorial mass meetings for "the American Lenin." (Now that he was dead even Foster conceded that insulting title to him—insulting to Lenin, that is.) In the end all the deals and cross-deals were thrown into the wastebasket. Stalin made it clear he would choose Ruthenberg's successor himself.

The result was that practically the whole American party leadership packed its bags, equipped itself somehow with passports, and headed for Moscow. The passionate pilgrims included Lovestone, Foster, Gitlow, Cannon, Weinstone, not to mention lesser lights and the resident American representatives in the Soviet capital, such as Robert Minor and Bill Kruse. This panicky exodus to Moscow provides more impressive proof of Moscow's complete domination— for the formalists who want the obvious proved—than any documents cited by legislative investigators.

The Lovestone group, partly because it arrived on the scene a bit sooner and got the drift of things faster, stole a march on their enemies by demanding the expulsion of Trotsky from the International. This fawning alignment with Stalin gave them the decisive edge in the elaborate haggling that kept them all in Moscow for many weeks. Lovestone and Gitlow returned home as official heirs to Ruthenberg's place. They also brought permission to move the party headquarters from Chicago to New York, where their faction had better maneuvering capacity. If I am vague about the concrete differences of opinion which separated the factions, it is because everyone else was no less vague. Opinions were little more than expedients for hitting an opponent on the head and snatching his political capital.

Foster and Cannon had agreed to abide by the Kremlin decision, but few expected that they would. They continued to plot more industriously than ever, being pushed closer and closer to the dangerous Trotskyist camp by the exigencies of the struggle. Naturally the new bosses made the attack on Trotskyism their foremost concern. The American workers whom they were theoretically piloting to Utopia might know nothing about Trotskyism and care less. But Moscow was watching, and the surest way to eliminate rivals was to tar them with the "Left deviation" or Trotskyist brush. Foster was shrewd enough to edge away. Cannon, less agile, was maneuvered into taking an "Oppositionist" position that made his elimination inevitable.

His expulsion, along with Max Shachtman and some fifty others in 1928, was the first major purge of the American ranks. The official or Stalinist party remained the party. From this time forward, indeed, Stalinism became a more accurate description of the American Bolshevik movement. In using "communist" and "communism" to identify it I am merely avoiding complications. The words had been taken over by the winners along with the apparatus and funds of the party, and were no longer descriptive of the aims or behavior of the official party. These conformed strictly to Stalin's shifting ideas and methods, no matter how far they moved from the original conceptions.

The party members accepted the Moscow decrees blindly. They joined in the howls of hatred against the Cannon faction, just for the emotional exercise. The American Trotskyists began their career of martyrdom in the outer darkness of excommunication as the Communist League of America (Opposition). Not for six or seven years did they acknowledge the expulsion as final, regarding themselves as the Left Wing of the party destined to return to the fold and assume control. When finally they set out as a new party, a section of Leon Trotsky's Fourth International, it spoke in thunderous accents for perhaps five to seven hundred members.

3

The second great purge merely paralleled Stalin's furious revenge on those who had helped him crush Trotsky and Zinoviev. He invariably punished his confederates, thus wiping out their claims on him. In the summer of 1928, Nikolai Bukharin, second only to Lenin among Bolshevik theoreticians, presided over a Congress of the Communist International. Moscow buzzed with reports that Stalin was preparing to lynch Bukharin after the Congress. (I was there at the time reporting these matters.) The Caucasian chief ridiculed these rumors with every show of sincerity. Lovestone and others in the American delegation were foolhardy enough to believe him. While cleverer delegates from various nations shunned Bukharin, these Americans maintained cordial relations with him. They were thus committing political suicide.

Soon after the Congress, Bukharin was tagged as leader of a new "Right Deviation," which included Premier Rykov; the former trade-union head, Mikhail Tomsky; and a great many others. A sizzling campaign of Bukharin-baiting was ordered, and mayhem on his character became compulsory for all sections of Stalin's political empire. The American section complied with its customary enthusiasm for refined knavery, adopting a vigorous resolution impaling Bukharin and his friends on pointed adjectives.

It was wasted perfidy. The new leadership, only recently installed by Stalin himself, was slated for sacrifice. Having ousted the Cannonites and launched the anti-Trotsky campaign, Lovestone, Gitlow et al had served their purpose and must be discarded. If they were not now partisans of Bukharin, they easily might be later. Despite their piteous protestations of loyalty to the Kremlin boss, the leaders of American Bolshevism were in their turn tagged as Right Deviators and slimy tools of the suddenly sinister Bukharin. Ordinary Americans in those critical months went about their work and play quite unaware that the nation was menaced by the Bukharinist infection. But such was the case. Had Stalin failed to act with his usual speed and vigor, our country by this time might have been devastated by the horrors of Right Deviationism.

A National Convention of the American party was scheduled for February, 1929. To impress Moscow with the size of their popular following, the Lovestone-Gitlow group lined up delegates and foiled

Foster's every attempt to do likewise. The convention met at Irving Plaza Hall in New York, with 90 per cent of its delegates vociferously behind the administration. It might have been 100 per cent, except that a tenth part was assigned to Foster for tactical reasons. It was a victory, they felt, that even Stalin could not ignore.

When Lovestone, Gitlow and a large staff once more departed for Russia, they knew they were at a disadvantage. They only had the whole American party behind them, whereas their factional foes had the whole of Stalin behind them. In Moscow, a Comintern commission was set up to study the eternal "American question." Viacheslav Molotov, Stalin's dull but hard-working man Friday, was put at its head. The hearings were a long-drawn farce, with everyone perfectly aware what the verdict must be. The overseas criminals argued that they could not be held guilty of traffic with Bukharin at a time when Stalin himself was publicly doing likewise. They exhibited their anti-Bukharin resolution.

It did them no good. The commission ordered what amounted to a Russian receivership of the American party, and the removal of Lovestone and his friends from the leadership. A verdict was composed by the Molotov court which in effect charged the American leaders with treachery, stupidity, rotten diplomacy, unprincipled opportunism and much more. Then the culprits were instructed, in the name of Comintern discipline, to accept the verdict. When eight of the ten Americans on trial refused to do so, the Russians were flabbergasted. They had quite forgotten the taste of defiance.

Stalin lost his temper. He raged at such insubordination and "stubbornness." How dared they, he shouted, "refuse to subordinate their will to the will of the higher collective." "True courage," said he, "consists in being strong enough to master and overcome one's self and subordinate one's will to the will of the collective, the will of the higher party body."

Translated into less euphemistic language, it means that Stalin was demanding that eight Americans confess to vague crimes they did not commit and sign their names to a judgment that called them fools and scoundrels. Neither Stalin nor Molotov, nor some of the Americans considered that this was an excessive demand. "The party"—which is to say, Stalin—had the right to demand a sacrifice of reputation in the interests of "unity." In later years, when Bukharin and dozens of other leading Bolsheviks confessed to impossible crimes and called themselves insulting names, the world was bewildered. Those familiar with the curious communist ethics of self-immolation for "the party" could understand what had happened.

The American majority was canceled out. The rebels were thrown out of the party in disgrace. Even before they returned to America the campaign to discredit them was raging in the communist press and it overflowed into the capitalist press. The rank-and-file membership accepted the new Muscovite orders as enthusiastically as ever and now joined in the howls of hatred against Lovestone, Gitlow and the rest. Later it became known that Stalin had transmitted the necessary orders and cash for outlawing the American party and starting a new one if the rebels should manage to retain the party machinery with rank-and-file backing. But it was unnecessary. The party was completely and jubilantly obedient to his whip.

The whole to-do had been far removed from the simple party membership, on trumped-up issues beyond their understanding. The explanations in their press were not especially enlightening, unless they could figure out statements such as this, announcing a new department aiming—

To make the *Daily Worker* and our other party press reflect not only the general political struggle of the party and of the American working class, but also to involve the *Daily Worker* in the inner struggles of the party for the correct party line, against all deviations from our present struggle against the right wing group of Lovestone and against all negations from the correct communist position that may occur in any section of the party. . . .

The new purgees organized as the Communist Party, U.S.A., (Majority Group), and in time came to be known simply as the Lovestoneites. Like the Trotskyites, they continued for years to knock on the doors of the official party, begging for admission. For years the membership of the new communist "splinter" remained under 350, though it included several labor leaders with a personal grip on union locals totaling thousands. In January, 1941, Lovestone formally announced the dissolution of his "splinter" party.

Foster's victory, however, was short-lived. Having used him as a club against the Right Deviators, Stalin paid him off in insults. He had neither forgotten nor forgiven Foster's brief flirtation with the Trotskyist faction. The Moscow Führer was good and sick of the "American problem" and "insubordination." He needed someone more pliable, someone with a real talent for carrying out orders, an agility for squirming from one party line to another, and made in Stalin's own moral image. Casting around for such a paragon of negative virtues, he picked on Earl Russell Browder. At last he had his dream leader for the U.S.A.

Chapter VI

A MILQUETOAST TAKES COMMAND

1

A *Daily Worker* cartoon once portrayed Earl Russell Browder as skipper at the helm of the S. S. *Working Class*, presumably steering the stout craft for the harbor of communism. The artist used his crayon boldly, adding heft and a virile storm coat to the figure. But all his efforts to make the man look masterful ended by making him look fatuous and plainly embarrassed.

The nervous little man who—until his incarceration in March, 1941—headed the Communist Party of the United States simply doesn't lend himself to heroic roles. There is a seedy, unkempt tone about him that has nothing to do with clothes; it is an emanation from the inside. The droop of his ragged mustache is not rebellious but just tired. That sandy cowlick is neither show-off nor defiant but rather apologetic. There is a sag to his shoulders and a distinct slouch to his walk and a furtive unease in his pale blue eyes.

Journalists who have described their impressions of Browder invariably express their astonishment over his washed-out personality. Hubert Kelley, writing in the *American Magazine*, referred to "a wistful, somewhat beaten look" about the American Stalin, and summed him up as "one of the mildest, most harmless-looking men I know. He resembles a cartoonist's idea of Mr. John K. Public, or the Taxpayer, more than he does a funny-paper Bolshevik." A writer in *Current History* declared, "Mr. Browder is a sweet-natured almost wistful person, looking more like a lyric poet than the leader of a revolutionary faction." And the perspicacious John McCarten wrote in the *New Yorker*:

Browder is a haggard little man with grizzling hair and a stubbly mustache who looks as though he's just eaten something that didn't agree with him. His pinched gray face is creased with troubled lines. His restless, red-lidded eyes are set in worried pouches. There is a trace of distress in his quick, uneasy smile.

63

Browder is neither the idealized Great Leader of the communist propaganda nor the idealized Great Villain of the anti-communist imagination. The contrast between the faded reality and these dramatic fictions usually upsets those who do not understand the nature of communist leadership in the Stalin epoch. Thus Hubert Kelley posed his confusion: "Nobody back home can account for his rise. Some said he had a routine mind like an adding machine. I have often heard persons who know him wonder how he got the job and kept it." Mr. Kelley then proceeded to explain the mystery as wrongly as possible. He assumed that the small-bore Kansas Milquetoast "made good" despite his mediocrity, whereas in truth he rose—or rather, was hoisted bodily—to the top because of his mediocrity.

Browder was elected to the Führership of the U.S.A. by one vote—Stalin's vote. In party circles he was known as "the book-keeper." His designation early in 1930 to succeed and supersede Foster, for whom he had been from the beginning a pathetic sort of understudy, amazed the comrades no end. The subsequent years, however, confirmed the wisdom of Stalin's selection. They underlined Stalin's greatest political asset: his uncanny knowledge of men and his gift for exploiting their weaknesses. In Browder, Stalin had found the perfect resident sales manager for one of the lesser of his foreign branches—too meek and ineffectual ever to set up in business on his own.

In Russia itself the long years of political bickering were brought to an end with the outlawing of the Left or Trotskyist Opposition and the squelching of the Right or Bukharinist heresies. A police regime of absolute uniformity was passed off as "unity." Stalin now had a "monolithic" party and a "monolithic" nation. Inevitably he made the totalitarian rule unanimous by enforcing a "monolithic" Comintern as well. In all countries, the obdurate or temperamental or overly ambitious communist chieftains were expelled or reduced to the ranks. Some of them were lured to Moscow and actually stuck away in Soviet "isolators" and concentration camps. In their place Stalin put smaller, more "disciplined" men—men who owed their careers neither to talents nor achievements at home but exclusively to the Kremlin's favor. The elevation of Browder was merely the American phase of the general policy.

In his small-town Kansas youth, Browder had been a conscientious hack by day, doing dull jobs for small wages and giving his employers their money's worth. In his spare time he was an earnest rebel against injustice. He tootled a flute, tried his hand at verse that wasn't poetry, and dreamed vaguely of a better world. In his maturity as communist leader he was still a conscientious hack, giving the far-off boss his money's worth, and getting a thrill from the gaudy fittings of the loads he pulled. He strained to sell the new "line" of communist goods each time that headquarters changed patterns and prices with as much unimaginative seriousness as he sold the old lines.

Under this humdrum existence he is still, perhaps, a rebel. Maybe he daydreams of facing Stalin one day and shouting into his face, "From now on, quit shoving me around!" But the hack in him is far stronger than the revolutionary. So he held on to his titillating and humiliating job. Little wonder he carries a harassed expression and a sad, furtive look in his pale eyes.

2

In the years when the party line called for red-white-and-blue Americanism and an American eagle topped the crossed hammer and sickle, the communists made a lot of political capital out of Earl Browder's impeccably American background. He comes of Colonial and pioneer stock. His forebears fought in the Revolutionary and Civil Wars. Grandfather Browder rode the circuit in Illinois as a Methodist parson. Papa Browder prepared for the ministry but succumbed to a strain of skepticism that diverted him to schoolteaching in Kansas and a life of penury. The comrades even professed to see a certain political symbolism in the fact that Wichita—where their leader, the second of ten Browder offspring, was born in 1891—is "somewhere near the exact geographical center of the United States."

Earl's youth was hard and grubby. There is no doubt of that phase of the Horatio Alger story proudly told by his disciples. It was in the Alger mood that one of them, Moissaye Olgin, told the American leader's tale to the party faithful. His account of Browder's life, the most complete available in the official literature, has about it the flavor of a highly moral success story. It abounds in injunctions like "Behold the growth of the man!" and moral comments like "The satisfaction of work well done was Browder's only reward."

Comrade Alger-Olgin, with an immigrant's envy for the deep-rooted native, begins his biography of The Leader with panegyric excitement about his authentically American ancestry. "Our candidate is blood and bone of America," he quotes the ecstatic tribute of the ex-anarchist Robert Minor. Then he goes on to tell of young Browder's poverty-ridden but high-minded childhood. Papa Browder's skepticism had taken him to Unitarianism, thence to Populism and finally into the bosom of the Socialist Party. Earl thus grew up in a mildly radical home, in a tradition of unorthodox thought salted with the tears of continuous poverty. The boy peddled the *Appeal to Reason* not only for the pennies but for his soul, and while yet in his 'teens joined the Socialist Party in Kansas City, Missouri, where his family now was living.

There he sided always with the more impatient dissenters, and soon joined a tiny group with a big name: The Syndicalist League of North America, led by another young American, William Z. Foster. He helped Foster get out a paper and did a lot of other chores with missionary zeal. Grubbing wearily at his figures ten hours a day, helping to provide bread for an invalided father and a crowded houseful of children, Earl was impatient with the reformism of the socialists. He was all for militancy and direct action, though these things never took him beyond words. It was all really in line with his devotion to the flute and his inept forays in the fields of poesy.

Then America entered the World War. Browder, now twenty-six, married, but still a nobody in both his workaday book-keeping world and his revolutionary dreamworld, found a focus for his resentments. Together with his brothers he refused to register for the military draft and spent the next year in the Platte County, Missouri, jail. We have his own assurances that he was treated exceedingly well and given ample opportunity to catch up on revolutionary reading. Then he was transferred to the Federal penitentiary at Leavenworth as a conscientious objector. Again he has no complaint to make about his treatment. For a while he worked in the book-keeping department of the prison, and then in the musical division, and spent most of his time tootling in the prison band.

"Prison has ever been a proving ground for revolutionaries," the pious *New Masses* explained in one of its lives-of-the-saints pieces on The Leader. Unfortunately for the picture, Browder's trials and tribulations as a martyr to pacifism were exceedingly on the mild side. They impelled him to nothing more startlingly revolutionary than the composition, while in the county jail, of an extremely dull pamphlet on

A System of Accounts for a Small Cooperative. Clearly the future Lenin of America was not breaking new philosophical ground.

When he emerged from Leavenworth in November, 1920, rested and in better health than ever before, the Communist Party had already been launched. He made several dismal and short-lived attempts to earn a living. Then he stopped trying and attached himself permanently to the communist pay roll. It is casting no slur on his sincerity to state that his economic problem was settled for the first time and for keeps—human motivations are too complex for harsh judgment. Foster, with whom he had maintained respectful relations despite that gentleman's lapse into war patriotism and Gompers respectability, was being primed for a communist role. Browder went along.

Browder was with Foster in the trumped-up American "labor delegation" to the first congress of the Profintern (Red International of Trade Unions) in Moscow in 1921. In fact, he went on a fake passport bearing the name of Nicholas Dozenberg, a minor communist functionary who in later years became a Soviet spy of some stature. Though he had belonged briefly to a book-keepers union, Browder knew approximately nothing about labor organization, red or otherwise. Such was Moscow's poverty of labor contacts in America, however, that Browder to his own amazement found himself elected to the Executive Committee, no less, of the Red International. He had done nothing, of course, to merit this distinction except to agree discreetly with all that was said. It was a negative technique guaranteed to put him ahead of the parade ultimately.

Foster, as we have seen, hid his communist membership for a number of years. His man Browder, whom he gave the job of editing the TUEL paper, was not important enough to need such concealment. Thereafter his career was little more than a twisted shadow of Foster's. Being a poor writer and a monotonous speaker—an embodiment of the tedious and the commonplace in his works as in his person—he aroused neither violent antagonisms nor anything resembling affection. Foster ran—for President, for party leadership, for glory—and Browder also ran. He kept accounts for his factional chief as he had kept them for a Wichita drug house.

In 1927, however, Browder was separated from his chief and set adrift. Having gone to Moscow for another congress, he was told off for a routine assignment way off in China.

3

He was made part of an "international labor delegation" from the Profintern to the workers of China, then engaged in their nationalist war headed by Chiang Kai-shek and his Soviet advisers. Browder was most inconspicuous in a group that included the British labor leader Tom Mann and the French communist leader Jacques Doriot. Of Doriot's participation neither Browder nor his party biographers say very much, since he later became the leader of a French fascist movement.

This delegation was the last Muscovite contribution to the communist tragedy in China. Even while Browder and the others were exhorting Chinese meetings to follow Comrade Chiang Kai-shek, the latter turned on his Moscow friends, who fled for their lives, while General Chiang proceeded to slaughter thousands of Chinese communists. In the midst of the debacle and in the hope of salvaging a few shreds of influence, the communists staged at Hankow a conference of what they called the Pan-Pacific Trade Union Secretariat. Browder, who was not needed for serious work elsewhere, was picked on to remain as secretary of this organization, with headquarters at Shanghai. The Chinese episode in his life has been inflated by party propaganda. But in truth he merely edited an insignificant underground party paper and acted as Moscow's fiscal agent in local espionage and propaganda pay-offs.

His record as Shanghai paymaster was the reverse of brilliant. Indeed, Browder was brought up on charges of incompetence and criminal neglect when he and his staff showed up in Moscow after a police raid on the Shanghai headquarters. Browder's political head was saved by Stalin himself. The shrewd Georgian had been watching his blundering American creature. Browder's very awkwardness and mediocrity appealed to him. Here was a man whom he could use without fear of insubordination, a man who would owe his glory solely to Stalin.

It was precisely on that basis that the Soviet dictator selected his other human tools. From his early pre-revolutionary days Stalin had carried over a deadly hatred of intellectuals. Men of genius or passion or even great talent stirred him to a slow and murderous fury. This hatred was deepened in the early Soviet years, when he found himself insultingly neglected, though he was among the top leaders. His whole life, in a sense, has been a long vengeance against brilliance.

In the Comintern, too, he was crushing the intellectuals, the clever ones, and putting hand-picked servants wearing his own drab livery in their place. Browder had been fashioned by the gods for Stalin's service. Long before the American communist even suspected it, the Caucasian schemer had no doubt earmarked him for future greatness.

When Browder got back to America after nearly two years of Chinese muddling, the Lovestone-Foster feud was under way, and he threw himself loyally into the service of his own faction. At the famous convention where Lovestone polled 90 per cent of the votes for leadership, Browder was hooted down when he attempted to defend Foster. But he was with the minority favored by Moscow. The convention, as we know, was nullified by Stalin. A mixed secretariat was set up to rule the American branch of the Soviet ideological export business. Though Foster was temporarily the nominal head, he was given no power. Then he was put out of the way with a face-saving title and Browder was designated as the Secretary-General, a post corresponding to the one held by Stalin in the Russian party.

Stalin has had no reason to regret his choice. The job fitted Browder to perfection—it gave him the semblance of leadership without any of the burdens of initiative. He needed only to carry out orders, transmitted from headquarters or conveyed to him by Moscow's "Reps" on the scene. Gitlow and others who should know, assert that the real power rested with Jack Stachel, a crafty fellow with an instinct for the wishes of the distant bosses and a taste for behind-the-scenes control. Earl Russell Browder, a 100 per cent American, too uncertain of himself to risk anything but the shadow of power, made a satisfactory figurehead.

Milquetoast and Mr. Chips and the cartoonist's Average Man have their virtues and their places. The fact that a little man embodying the worst features of all three—on the whole a pathetic little man—stood for so many years at the head of organized American Bolshevism is a measure of the degradation of the movement. It is a measure, in particular, of its subservience to something bigger outside. Browder's figure, in fact, seemed more shrunken and ludicrously inadequate as the movement which he ostensibly commanded grew to amazing size and influence in the Red Decade, after Stalin, lifting him between thumb and finger, had placed him on the giddy pinnacle.

Chapter VII

THE RED DECADE DAWNS

1

THE bulk of the American people did not suspect, in the years 1929-35, how close they were to their day of social reckoning—in the communist literature. They rode complacently on the crest of a world-wide "revolutionary upsurge," officially identified and proclaimed as such by the highest authorities in the Soviet Union. The identification was promptly and heatedly confirmed by Comintern underlings in every sub-nation, including those in the United States. The few who whispered that America was not quite ready for the ultimate upheaval were instantly adjudged guilty of the heresy of "American exceptionalism." It goes without saying that they got what was coming to them—expulsion from the ranks of true believers.

If some future historian were to piece together a portrait of America at this time solely from Stalinist documents, it would certainly wear a strange face. Its chief features would be: 1) American capitalism, decrepit and staggering. 2) The socialists, the A.F.of L., President Hoover and after him President Roosevelt, and the Wall Street boys working desperately to keep old capitalism from collapsing. 3) The Communist Party, alone, too proud to associate with lesser breeds, pushing to hasten the fall and preparing to establish the Dictatorship of the Proletariat in a Soviet America. The behavior of the communists here, like their words, jibed with the assumption of Bolshevik conquest around the corner. Everything was Revolutionary with a great rumbling R.

"I think the moment is not far off when a revolutionary crisis will develop in America," Joseph Stalin said on May 6, 1929. The future tense was swiftly discarded. All subsequent tracts said that the crisis was developed. America, of course, was not alone in this impending cataclysm. A cycle of uprisings, the final revolutionary explosion, was promised by Moscow for the whole globe. Stalin's extraordinary Third Period, committed to the immediate and inevitable doom of capitalist civilization, was under way—at any rate in the Muscovite proclamations.

With a revolution so close at hand, there was plainly no time for compromises and half-measures. The more moderate radicals and laborites everywhere, because they doubted or delayed "the moment," were more dangerous and despicable even than capitalists and fascists. They were *social* fascists. The term was especially coined for them and carried overtones of rascality beyond the ken of straight fascists. The monolithic communists must storm the citadels of the old order over the dead bodies of these social fascists—and no detours allowed, even where a road less cluttered with corpses might be open. The Comintern, Profintern and other assorted Internationals met in red-hot plenums and composed sizzling funeral orations for capitalism and its social fascist lackeys. They also launched long and unreadable "theses" which, when deciphered by initiates, turned out to be commands to the workers and peasants to arise and rule. All national sections of the Internationals repeated the command, likewise in a theological lingo remote from the speech of Iowa and Bolivian peasants. The order echoed down the line through manifold open and secret communist affiliates, from labor circles to sewing circles.

The social crisis discovered by American communists was not only part of the larger crisis discovered by Moscow, but clothed in the identical words. It was another of those miracles of coincidence familiar on that level of political hallucination. The thesis of the Communist Party of the United States (as it was by this time known) greeted the "revolutionary upsurge of the working masses of the U. S.," manifest in "increasing militancy of the workers" and "mass interest in revolutionary unionism." Angrily the thesis made it clear that only William Green, Norman Thomas, John L. Lewis and the other social fascists held up the consummation of that lovely surge.

The command to revolt was therefore aimed in the first place against the labor leaders and non-communist radicals and their organizations. As I explained earlier, this world-wide agitation was in effect a ruthless war on independent labor and Left movements everywhere. It suited the propaganda needs of the Soviet regime, giving Stalin the semblance of world revolution without the embarrassment of actual upheavals. On the one hand, it diverted attention from the growing horrors of forcible industrialization, liquidation of the *kulaks*, mass executions and man-made famine inside Russia. On the other, it provided a backdrop of trouble in the capitalist lands for the most cynical lying about "marvels of achievement" under the Five Year Plans.

The economic Depression gave the Soviet newspapers ample material to prove that the capitalist world was in violent dissolution. Imagination did the rest. A Moscow paper published pictures of some ordinary excavations on Broadway with captions about apocryphal "bombings" and "riots." Orders went out for "the capture of the streets" by "the masses." Whereupon demonstrations were staged in Union Square, New York, and several other cities—and the brethren reported to headquarters that the streets had been captured.

At one time they were ordered to "Bolshevize" their party. Thereupon "cells" and "nuclei" in factories, "street nuclei" in neighborhoods, and an array of other formations came into being, and the humblest holder of a red card felt himself a soldier fighting in many armies on many fronts at once. The membership being small and the number of factory workers among them even smaller, the Bolshevization was largely rhetorical—but rhetorical victories sufficed in a purely verbal revolution. Partly the comrades went drunk on ultra-Left phrases, partly they prevaricated to impress the bosses in Moscow.

Certainly the workers and "peasants" of the U.S.A. had better cause for revolt than ever before. The Depression left millions of them without work or food or hope, bewildered and without leadership. But no party taking its slogans and blueprints of action readymade from another country could hope to make contact with America's common humanity. The opportunity for radical action may have been at hand. But the Stalinists, acting mechanically on "directives" not even vaguely related to American realities, devoted themselves and their subsidies from the International treasury to making trouble on the Left. They promulgated the "united front from below," the frank aim of which was to sow distrust of their leaders in all working-class organizations.

For ten years Foster's Trade Union Educational League had sought to "capture" the American Federation of Labor and all other unions by boring from within. Now the slow process was discarded. Foster's dwindling and inept army was renamed Trade Union Unity League (the word "unity" is always a tip-off on communist plans for splitting) and set itself up as a complete substitute for the A.F.of L. Communist factions in all individual unions seceded to form dual unions, or remained only for the purpose of smashing unions from within.

In every other field of activity these tactics of mock revolutionism became obligatory. No one in his senses really believed that *Der Tag* was dawning. But the Comintern said it was: hence a painted dawn in lurid colors on smudged canvas was improvised and treated as the real thing.

2

The workers and "peasants" of America didn't spurn the command to revolt—they never heard it. They were too numbed by the shock of lay-offs, foreclosures, the evaporation of small life's savings to do more than pray with Herbert Hoover for the return of prosperity.

The middle classes and even a portion of the moneyed minority, however, did try revolt. Their sudden misgivings and fears drove them into more-or-less fascist movements at one extreme, into more-or-less communist movements at the other extreme. Having lost their sense of security and self-reliance, they grabbed in panic at the nearest formulas of reassurance or revenge. Planning and collective enterprise, as preached shrilly by both fascists and communists, seemed wonder-working gadgets to steady a reeling economic world. At both extremes it became the fashion to sneer at democracy as "doddering," "hypocrisy" and "sham."

Thus it happened in the years that followed the market crash that the Communist Party of the United States became the magnetic center for a large and fast-growing mass of near-communists, sympathizers, fellow-travelers, spare-time insurgents, frightened liberals and masochistic capitalists. It was the dawn of a Red Decade. Many a bankrupt broker hesitated between jumping out of his skyscraper window and jumping out of his class. Intellectuals, so-called, hesitated between joining the Catholic Church and joining the Communist Party—they yearned for a faith and surcease from thinking. (A few compromised ultimately by joining both Moscow and Rome.)

Professors and financiers and clergymen argued earnestly when, precisely, the revolution would break out. If the very poor didn't believe in the promised upheaval, a good many of the very rich did. They bought themselves farms or Caribbean islands against the dire moment. Others associated themselves with the revolution by way of psychological insurance; not in the front trenches, of course, but somewhere far back in the intellectual and emotional commissary departments. A good many, I happen to know, did both, hurrahing for the revolution and buying an island to escape it.

The comic futility of the bogus communism which became increasingly fashionable as the Red Decade developed may be measured by reference to its core, the Communist Party. At the peak of its "revolutionary upsurge" in 1930, it claimed only some 8,000 members. Two years later, though the magazines and penthouses and thousands of cocktail parties had rocked with bold revolutionary discussion—of communism, proletarian culture, dialectic materialism—the membership reached only 12,000.

It was, moreover, a most volatile adherence. The trade journal for party functionaries, the *Party Organizer*, complained in 1932 that member turnover or "fluctuation" is "as high as 75 per cent. Many of these are old members. In the last registration we found that only 3,000 members had been in the party as much as two years." This "vanguard of the revolution," as it called itself in routine modesty, thus had no more than 3,000 members of more than twenty-four months' standing, in a party that had existed for thirteen years and that could mobilize fifty thousand cocktail revolutionists any evening for any of its projects. By 1934 it had enrolled about 47,000 new members, but only 12,000 of them had stuck, making a total of about 24,000.

A small, unstable, neophyte party it was, no matter how the resident agents might alibi to Moscow.

But around it was that solar system of "mass organizations," a mushrooming universe of interlocking causes, unions, committees, leagues, centers, etc. Around these, in turn, were agitated clouds of Depression Bolsheviks, and beyond them thinnish vapors of tentative sympathizers, admirers of the Soviet "experiment," innocent trailers of fashionable phobias, mobs of intellectuals without intelligence, half-literate proletarian *litterateurs*, and unassorted proletarian social climbers.

The phony foundations were being laid for a phony revolution still to come. Both in magnitude and in variety, of course, the pseudo-communism at the start of the Red Decade was just a preliminary sketch of the incredible revolution still in the womb of time.

In February, 1931, the *Party Organizer* boasted that it had, *in the New York District* alone, "100 different mass organizations." Some of these were national, others local; every other district had its own regional groupings. While many of these dissolved, in the following years even more were formed, so that the aggregate for the nation unquestionably ran into hundreds. Here is a partial list of the communist-led societies and activities of the moment in the New York area toward the end of the Third Period, omitting the out-and-out trade-union organizations which we shall consider separately:

Communist Party, Young Communist League, International Labor Defense, International Workers Order, Friends of the Soviet Union, Workers International Relief, Workers Ex-Servicemen's League, League against War and Fascism, National Student League, City Council of Associated Workers Clubs, United Council of Working Class Women, John Reed Clubs, League of Struggle for Negro Rights, National Committee to Aid Victims of German Fascism, Labor Sports Union, Anti-Imperialist League, Labor Research Association, National Committee for the Defense of Political Prisoners, Chinese Anti-Imperialist Alliance, Icor, World Tourists, Workers School, Workers Bookshops, International Publishers, Workers Library Publishers, Pen and Hammer, Artef, Workers Music League, Film and Photo League.

Though incomplete, the list conveys some sense of the expanding enterprise, especially remarkable considering the tiny core of actual party members. The magazine Common Sense, familiar with the facts of life on the Left, said in 1934: "It may be hazarded that the periphery of (communist) mass organizations and sympathizers amount to some 500,000." Each of the organizations, institutions, newspapers involved a batch of paid secretaries, editors, directors, organizers. The volunteer and decorative officialdom was drawn from the agitated periphery. But the paid jobs were reserved for party stalwarts. Of some 3,000 members in the New York District in 1934, at least 1,000 were paid functionaries, and doubtless a lot of the others were hoping to be.

Party affiliation had, in fact, become a trade as well as a sacred trust. Since a large part of the wages was syphoned off into party coffers, this officialdom was a financial asset, besides saving deserving comrades from the pangs of unemployment. More significant was the political advantage; the paid staff, doing the day-to-day work, could control the organizations and channel their work into the mainstream of current Muscovite purposes.

3

In the United States and in every other country the Third Period rested on an inflated fraud—on that upsurge that turned out to be a still life. Such surging as transpired—in Germany, Austria, China, portions of the Balkans, Japan—was decidedly downward, into the sloughs of fascism.

The one thing that might have halted the steady fall of the level of human freedom was honest joint action by all democratic and anti-fascist elements. This was explicitly forbidden by the Stalinist cate-chism, on pain of instant excommunication. The stigmata of a Right Deviationist, indeed, were his tendency to treat social fascists as possible allies. The Kremlin's orders were unmistakable: to split, destroy and undermine every group unwilling to yield unconditionally to com-munist leadership. It amounted to cold-blooded sacrifice of the trade unions and democratic institutions of many lands to the self-interest of Russia, or what it stupidly assumed to be its self-interest.

In America the consequences of this criminal attitude were of relatively small importance. In countries where the communists were a great political force, as in Germany, the results were utterly disastrous. Yet in America, too, the Third Period policies left their mark. Verbal violence, denunciation of democracy, pretense of imminent seizure of power—all of this fitted into the deepening mood of desperation. Thousands of liberals and frustrated conservatives who could not ac-cept fascism in its black, brown or silver wrappings, accepted it with a self-satisfied glow of "emancipation" in red packages. For them and for thousands of others Stalinism became a school for totalitarian think-ing and feeling.

Professors and journalists, coupon-clippers and Junior Leaguers who lacked the moral boldness to abandon liberal democratic ideas by moving Right, did so by moving Left. The formulas of the communist milieu enabled them to edge away from democracy with a clearer conscience, even with a delusion of courage. It was a more respectable outlet for their cynicism, their economic frustrations, their nihilistic angers. The communist role—obviously in Germany, less obviously in America—was to condition middle-class liberals and traditionalists to totalitarian thinking. It cured them of their hang-overs of prejudice against dictatorship, mass slaughter, and the crushing of the human spirit.

Those of us who tried to watch and understand the phenomenon can have little doubt of the general pattern. We shall not be surprised to see yesterday's pseudo-communists emerge, when the occasion offers itself as the theorists and apologists of tomorrow's fascism. (In some measure it was already happening, as fervent "anti-fascists" of the Red Decade carried on the Stalin-Hitler propaganda of appeasement and capitulation to the Nazi "New Order" during the life of the Moscow-Berlin Axis.) In Germany I saw how Depression Bolsheviks among the intelligentsia stepped lightly over the line to become Nazis. Knowing that they were already primed for it, Hitler's party made it easier for an ex-communist to enter its ranks than for other people. Returning to the United States from Germany, I saw the same process of conditioning of future Nazis by the Communist Party in full blast.

The breed which I christened "totalitarian liberals" was really born at this time and nurtured on ultra-revolutionary pap imported from Moscow. That upbringing enabled them to swallow the precept that a noble end justifies the most terrifyingly ignoble means. It enabled them to shout "Hallelujah, it's wonderful!" for mass murder in Stalinland. Ultimately it made it possible for them to insist that a Hitler victory "served England right," since the Second World War was just a dogfight of competing imperialisms.

4

While it lasted, the imaginary revolution gave its promoters a great emotional kick, which is what many of them chiefly craved. Not only were the streets captured, but the Negroes were "liberated." Among America's twelve million colored citizens the party managed to find a handful willing—through moronic enthusiasm or inflamed ambition—to serve as its tools. The completely cynical fashion in which the communists exploited the fears and hopes of Negroes for Moscow's purposes makes one of the ugliest chapters in the unpretty story of American Bolshevism. At communist instigation courageous members of the Negro race went to futile injury and death to make "copy" and "causes" for the communist press here and abroad.

How little the Moscow masterminds understand American Negroes may be judged from this curious episode: The Comintern decided to produce in Moscow a great propagandist film for the Negro population of the United States. It selected a German scenario writer and director for the task. His recommendation for the job was that he had spent some time in Africa *filming jungle aborigines.* This obviously equipped him to write and film an epic of Negro life in Mississippi, Georgia and Harlem. Unfortunately for fanciers of grotesquerie, the project was dropped on the urging of certain white Americans doing business with Russia.

Communist policy for Negroes at this time was as extreme as policy in all other matters. Only the demand for "Negro self-determination in the Black Belt" and the establishment of a separate "Negro nation" in the South suited the lunatic temper of the moment. What was good enough for Czechs, Armenians and Hindus was good enough for American Negroes. The Comintern gave instructions and left no margin for local variations. Non-communist Negro organizations which refused to follow such insanity were maligned as fascists or worse, social fascists. Harry Haywood reported to a party conference:

In all this work it is necessary to bring forth more energetically our full program for Negro liberation, equal rights, right of self-determination, confiscation of land. We carry through the widest popularization of the achievements of the Soviet Union in the solution of the national question.

These parrot phrases had been drummed into heads like Haywood's in Moscow schools. In the Soviet capital I met dozens of America's Negroes training to lead their promised Black Belt Soviet Republics—just to write the name is to bring the fraud into stark relief. A few of these students—like James W. Ford, perennial candidate for Vice-President on the communist ticket—were shrewd careerists. The rest were simple-minded, befuddled and tragic victims of political exploitation.

Early in its career the American party had created a Negro Department. This was later transformed into the American Negro Labor Congress. In 1930, at a convention in St. Louis, the name was changed to League for Struggle for Negro Rights, in line with the more revolutionary character of the new shipment of Kremlin orders. The communist control was not hidden; the national council of the League included Foster, Browder, Hathaway, Gil Green. A young Negro poet, Langston Hughes, having thrown himself passionately into the communist movement, served as president of the League. Like many

gifted, emotional artists of all races—stronger in heart than in
mind—Langston Hughes accepted the shadow of communist phrases
for the substance of reality.

The League never really touched the Negro masses, attracting
largely careerists and black bohemians. It remained a sectarian enterprise, until it was transformed into the National Negro Congress in
the years of the Popular Front.

One of the principal revolutionary activities of the Communist
Party was to break up socialist meetings and demonstrations. The
blood that flowed in the major physical battles of the curious revolution was therefore the blood of comrades.

This grand strategy of overthrowing capitalism by egging socialists
reached an ugly climax at Madison Square Garden in February, 1934.
Socialists and liberal trade unions called a mass meeting to protest
against the shooting down of Social Democrats and the bombardment
of their workers' apartment houses by the Dolfuss government in
Vienna. There was widespread public sympathy for the victims.
Mayor LaGuardia was among the scheduled speakers. Clearly the
communists could not let such a "counter-revolutionary" demonstration for Austrian social fascists get away with it. They came in force
to disrupt the gathering and to prevent the "fascist LaGuardia" from
addressing it. What is more, they succeeded—turning the meeting
into a riot and shambles. It was the high point of the "revolutionary
upsurge."

And yet, slugging a socialist, physically or verbally, is emotionally
satisfying to those with a yen for slugging. The communist literature
of those years is a veritable slug-fest of fevered rhetoric. It calls shrilly
for "a revolutionary way out of the crisis." Said an introductory note
to the manifesto of the Eighth Convention of the Communist Party
of the U.S.A.:

The idea of the storming of capitalism is maturing in the minds
of the masses . . . rallying them around its [the party's] program for the
overthrow of capitalism and for the establishment of the dictatorship
of the proletariat—for a Soviet Government. . . . The bitter truth is
rapidly being learned that Roosevelt and his New Deal represent the
Wall Street bankers—finance capital—just the same as Hoover before
him, but carrying out even fiercer attacks against the living standards

of the masses of the people. . . . A struggle which must shatter the entire bourgeois system, including its government, a struggle which increases the forces of the revolution, consciously leading them to the overthrow of capitalism and the establishment of a Soviet government. . . . The violent winning of the power, demanding sacrifice, demanding victims, is what the communists must help the workers to realize in their experience of everyday struggle.

One of the most dastardly heresies then raising its horned head was the idea of a labor or a farmer-labor party. Forgetting its own ludicrous experiments along those lines, the Communist Party and all its side-line enthusiasts denounced the notion in classic periods of invective. Even John Strachey, the peripatetic salesman of the changing party line, wrote an article in an American journal under the title "Against an American Third Party." His peroration is fairly typical of the smug ultra-Leftism of the well-fed, whether in Strachey's country or the U.S.A.:

Is it not possible for the American masses to leap over a whole historical phase, the phase of that nauseating thing, social-democratic reformism, and to pass direct from the domination of capitalist ideas to the clear-sighted revolutionary struggle for communism?

The import of his article was that this gymnastic historical leap was quite possible. Why, therefore, have any truck with democratic-minded reformists, with labor parties, with makeshifts? Such was the distemper of the fabulous Third Period. Its propaganda bristled with mouth-filling and soul-stirring talk of "ideological subjugation," "opportunist deviations," "chauvinistic demagogy," "true Bolshevik intolerance," "Leninist firmness," "renegade theatricalism," "social fascist betrayal." The comrades wore caps and leather jackets and unshaven faces. The girls in the movement disdained lipstick and cut their hair short and lived demonstratively with Negroes.

The liberal periphery was hectic with amorphous excitement— which I shall analyze in some detail later. For the moment suffice that writers and painters, Social Register gals and a few bankers had discovered the proletariat and greeted it tumultuously in the persons of John Strachey, Corliss Lamont, Granville Hicks, Theodore Dreiser, Henri Barbusse and other sons of toil. Only the masses (except for twenty thousand or so drawn into Unemployment Councils) were unaware of the revolution.

The revolution, to put it tersely, did not exist, but had a glorious career notwithstanding. Stalin needed the fiction as a smoke screen for his "Iron Age" of liquidations and executions; the American comrades and near-comrades obliged.

Chapter VIII

FASCISM HAS THE RIGHT OF WAY

1

WHAT of the American workers in the era of upsurge? The "peasants" may be counted out. They refused to recognize their lowly status and continued almost unanimously to suffer in ideological darkness. But some tens of thousands of workers at various times did submit themselves to Stalinist leadership, with consistently dire results.

The TUEL, as we saw, had become the TU Unity League, determined, as its new program phrased it, "to sharpen, deepen and unite the scattered economic struggles of workers into a general political struggle aiming at the abolition of capitalism and the establishment of a workers and farmers government." Nothing less, of course. In unions where the moderate leaders had long tried to ferret out and expel the communists, the latter now did them the favor of withdrawing and setting up their own red unions, affiliated with the TUUL, which in turn was openly and proudly an affiliate of the Profintern. In unorganized industries the communists tried to lead strikes, handicapping the effort from the start by setting up fantastic "revolutionary" aims. The most prominent of these attempts, such as the textile strike in Gastonia, North Carolina, petered out in bloodshed and abortive propaganda for social revolution.

That it was a policy of deliberate union-busting is not a deduction on my part. It was the loud boast of Stalinists, high and low, at this juncture in their history. "The task of the TUUL," a Comrade Mingulen wrote, "is to mobilize the masses, win them to its side, embrace them organizationally within its fold and destroy the American Federation of Labor, the most reliable support of American capitalism." And Comrade Lozovsky, head of the Profintern, stated it no less frankly, in a pronunciamento in 1932:

That we want to break up the reformist unions, that we want to

82

weaken them, that we want to disrupt their discipline, that we want to wrest the workers from them, that we want to break up and destroy the trade union apparatus—of that there cannot be the slightest doubt.

The enormity of the social crime implied by such a destructive policy was not too evident in America. Here it merely resulted in isolating the communists and turning them into a sect fashionable with portions of every group in the country except the workers and farmers. But it was amply evident in nations like Germany, where another and more dynamic anti-union movement was pushing forward tumultuously. That movement triumphed, Hitler ruled a new Reich, and communist blood ran in rivers. Yet the Moscow geniuses did not call a halt to their suicidal rampage. Not until two years later—after Hitler had rejected every self-abasing offer of friendship by Moscow—was the communist "line" of the Third Period reluctantly abandoned.

Until then it was the duty of every Comintern stooge to explain Hitler's ascendancy and the advance of fascism generally as indirectly a victory for the communist revolution! At this distance it sounds incredible, but the record is clear enough. "After them, our turn!" was the official Kremlin consolation. As late as April, 1934, the Presidium of the Comintern solemnly declared that the Nazi dictatorship,

by destroying all the democratic illusions of the masses and liberating them from the influence of Social Democracy, accelerates the rate of Germany's development towards proletarian revolution.

And poor Browder parroted such nonsense to the inane applause of the totalitarian liberals. Addressing a party conference in January, 1934, about a year after Hitler's accession to power, he ridiculed those of small faith who think that "the victory of Hitler inaugurates a protracted period of fascist reaction and a long-time defeat of the revolution." Browder actually hailed fascism jubilantly as a forerunner of his own brand of dictatorship. Fascism, he explained,

destroys the moral base for capitalist rule, discrediting bourgeois law in the eyes of the masses; it hastens the exposure of all demogogic supporters of capitalism, especially its main support among the work-

ers—the socialist and trade union leaders. It hastens the revolutioniza-
tion of the workers, destroys their democratic illusions and thereby
prepares the masses for the revolutionary struggle for power.

Let no one claim, therefore, that communists opposed Nazism
and fascism on "democratic" grounds. On the contrary, the communists vociferously cheered the Hitlerite destruction of "democratic
illusions" and the fascist crushing of social fascist radical and labor
organizations. Whatever they may have objected to in fascism, it was
surely not its totalitarian character or its stamping out of democratic
institutions. The inner moral identity between communism and
fascism, far more real than any of the outer differences, explains why
Stalinists, despite their numerical strength, were helpless to keep Hitler
from power. In their hearts they were unwilling to do so. Was not
Hitler clearing the ground for their own revolution? It helps explain
why, after the years of the great "democratic" hoax, the communists
in the end formed the inevitable united front with Hitler—and adhered
to it faithfully for nearly two years, until Hitler smashed it.

The droves of American liberals and middle-class muddleheads
generally who supported Bolshevism in its Third Period—the period
which gave the right of way to fascism—must share the guilt for the rise
of Hitlerism. I am not pretending to indict them as individuals, but
"objectively," as Marxists say, and as a class. They were victims of the
Depression and of their emotional and mental panic. Theirs was a
mass aberration, a sort of unconditioned reflex to the hurts and un-
certainties of a world shaken by economic earthquake. Which may
exonerate them as individuals, but removes not a jot of their responsibility for helping along the nightmare of bloodletting in Russia, in
Germany and now in the whole world.

2

Let us look at the union-splitting program of dualism midway in its
career, about the end of 1930. There was a dual Stalinist organization in
the clothing industry, the Needle Workers Industrial Union, claiming
6,000 members out of a possible half million. There was the National
Textile Workers Union under TUUL control; except for a few highly
publicized martyrs in strike riots, it had nothing to show for years of
investments and noise. Instead of helping the anti-Lewis opposition
· in the miners' union, as in the past, the Stalinists now set up their own

National Mine Workers Union with a few hundred dues-paying members. Similarly the Amalgamated Food Workers and Independent Shoe Workers Union counted their membership in three figures, and negligible dual unions were set up in the furniture, steel and a few other industries.

The new policy merely resulted, as J. B. S. Hardman put it in an analysis at that time, in pitting "the Communist Party versus the labor movement." In several directions, however, they made beginnings destined to bring rich results for Moscow and first-rate headaches for America.

The Profintern was especially eager to obtain a foothold on the waterfronts and in world shipping. The strategic importance of possessing devoted allies among the shore and ship crews in the event of war is self-evident. Moscow made no bones on this subject. Communist organizations had long wooed the sailors of the world. Openly where possible and under disguise elsewhere, Red clubs for sailors had become a standard feature in the harbors of many nations. Along with hospitality and entertainment, the visiting seamen were dosed with fairy tales about Stalin's "socialism" and their opportunity to seize power from the capitalists. Jan Valtin, a German sailor who during these years was working for the Comintern as its secret agent in maritime undertakings, has told part of that story in lurid detail in his remarkable confession, *Out of the Night.*

The campaign to capture the American waterfronts had been going on for years. It was now intensified and greased with larger appropriations than ever in the past. The work was administered by Roy B. Hudson, George Mink, Tom Ray and other trusted comrades, some of them, like Mink, directly connected with Soviet espionage. A Marine Workers Industrial Union was set up, as the American section of the Profintern's International of Seamen and Harborworkers. The new setup gained some minor following, because of the sluggishness of the existing conservative union even more than because of its own energy. In time it would flourish as the Maritime Workers Union, the organization headed by Joseph Curran.

In 1934 the shipping tie-up on the West Coast took place, with Harry Bridges, an Australian communist, in the limelight for the first time. Moscow's undisguised purpose of obtaining a strangle hold on the transportation and communications of all countries was being put into effect in America too.

A fruitful beginning was also made in extending communist influence among the unemployed of the nation. There were so many millions of them, their confusion and despondency were so deep, that the most inept fishermen could make a good haul. The Communist Party needed only to place itself in the forefront with rousing slogans to rally some following among the out-of-work. Specifically this following was channeled into Unemployment Councils, which multiplied until they counted over 20,000 adherents—loosely organized, often out of sympathy with their communist spokesmen, yet a sufficient force for demonstration, hunger marches and sheer nuisance activities.

At any stage in its career, the shifting membership of the Communist Party has included idealistic men and women with honest faith in the current slogans. Their very honesty has been a guarantee that sooner or later they would renounce the party. In the Depression years, such men and women were stirred into a fury of action by the great misery that engulfed the country. It is to these earnest rank-and-file communists, rather than to the job holders above them, that the relative success of the work among unemployed must be credited. They put themselves in the front lines of desperate groups demanding relief. They organized rent strikes and led protests against evictions. They bore the brunt of police violence and sometimes popular anger evoked by their noisemaking.

The top-shelf party bureaucrats were taken unawares and rather scared by the unexpected response to their initial efforts. Only gradually they thawed out and soon instructions were issued for the formation of Councils—the word is a literal translation of "Soviets"—wherever possible. Local and sporadic Councils were then merged in a national organization.

But after a fine start the Councils began to lose strength. Droves of the unemployed were scared off by the Third Period slogans foisted on them: "Down with Yankee imperialism! Defend the Soviet Union! For a Soviet America!" At the same time a rival organization began to make great strides. It was the Workers Alliance, sponsored by the Socialist Party and liberal elements, and headed by a young, vigorous and capable socialist, David Lasser. The communists realized that their salvation lay in a merger. They were convinced, and rightly so, that once an amalgamation was achieved, they would control it. Besides, the Third Period was drawing to a close—symptoms of Moscow's abandonment of the "revolutionary upsurge" were multiplying.

So the comrades promised to be good, to refrain from boring from within and to show for once that a real United Front was possible. The Alliance yielded. Ostensibly it absorbed the Councils; actually the communists took over the Alliance, which became just another Moscow front. Herbert Benjamin, one of the most obsequious of Browder's lieutenants, became secretary-treasurer and hence the strategic master of the organization. Lasser needed only a pilgrimage to Moscow to abandon the Socialist Party and to become a useful instrument for the communists, until the very end of the Red Decade, when he broke away from them.

The labor aspect of American Bolshevism in the years under discussion can therefore be summarized roughly as follows: Union-busting activities that netted Moscow nothing; a good start in control of American harbors and shipping for the Kremlin; and the capture of the organization of unemployed destined to become a power in the New Deal system in the immediate future.

3

The paper revolution of 1929-35 did not spare President Roosevelt and his New Deal. In the later love affair between the communists and some of the New Dealers the early hatreds were so thoroughly buried that it takes an effort of the memory to disinter them. The merciless communist attacks on Hoover were transferred in their entirety to his successor. In fact, in the measure that Roosevelt was closer to labor, he opened himself to the more deadly vituperation reserved for the social fascists. The endorsement of his program by socialists and by trade-union leaders made him doubly vulnerable, as at once a tool of Wall Street and a tool of social fascism.

The formal Communist Party manifesto, published as late as February, 1935, in the *Communist International*, was captioned: AGAINST THE "NEW DEAL" OF HUNGER, FASCISM AND WAR! This, little more than a year before Comrade Browder and his party stepped to the front of the stage and announced their sudden affection for the New Deal! The manifesto was no more than a summation of two years' unsparing communist denunciation of the Roosevelt administration. It painted the President as the architect of the coming American fascism, put into the White House to delude the masses with false promises while forging chains for the workers. Here are some random excerpts, merely to suggest the flavor of the thing:

Under Roosevelt and the New Deal policies, the public treasury
has been turned into a trough where the big capitalists eat their fill. . . .
The NRA and the industrial codes have served further to enrich capitalists. . . . The labor provisions of the NRA, which were hailed by the
A. F. of L. and socialist leaders as a new charter of labor, have turned
out in reality to be new chains for labor. . . . The policies of the government in Washington have one purpose, to make the workers and
farmers and middle classes pay the costs of the crisis, to preserve the
profits of the big capitalists at all costs, to establish fascism and to
wage imperialist war abroad.

No Economic Royalist of any year's vintage could have done the
job more lustily. Every one of the dozens of party publications in all
languages ran over with foul language aimed at the New Deal and its
leader. A typical *Daily Worker* article on the New Deal (November
11, 1933) is captioned "Roosevelt and Mussolini—Blood Brothers."
The *New Masses*, cultural fortress of the cause, rarely let an issue go to
press without its quota of anti-Roosevelt bile. It lauded the communists, in a quotation before me, for their sagacity in underlining the
resemblance "between the Roosevelt Administration and the pre-
fascist Bruening government which, with the aid of Social Democratic
leaders, smoothed the way for Hitler."

Stalinist cartoonists had a field day of it caricaturing Roosevelt as
the American Hitler and the lackey of Big Business. His compromising
tactics were contrasted with the beauties of the Five Year Plans in
Russia. The side-line cheering squads of Depression Bolsheviks yelled
themselves hoarse in approval—the vocal exercise helped them forget
their troubles. Few political love affairs on record had a less propitious
prelude.

4

"Defense of the Soviet Union" is the least common denominator
of all Comintern periods and policies. In the final analysis every other
slogan and activity is an aspect of this fundamental purpose. The
Third International was founded, as we have seen, as a bulwark of the
young Soviet State. In its every subsequent transformation it remained
true to that essential purpose. The least important or most important

communist undertaking anywhere can be traced back to its source in Moscow's anxiety to safeguard the physical existence of the Bolshevik power.

Over and above all other assignments, member parties therefore had the clear-cut task, in the Third Period, of undermining the military strength of their particular nations. The assumption was that every capitalist nation was a potential enemy of Russia, hence must be kept at the lowest possible level of military preparedness. The fear of foreign assaults had haunted the mind of the Kremlin from the earliest hours of the Bolshevik Revolution. That fear reached fever pitch in the Five Year Plan epoch. In part, no doubt, the outside danger was played up as an alibi for the horrifying burdens and sacrifices loaded on the backs of the Russian people. In part, however, it was a genuine apprehension that some countries might seek to escape the economic impasse by the gamble of war—and what more convenient target than Soviet Russia?

Moscow's orders were therefore simple and straightforward. On this most crucial problem it could not risk ideological circumlocutions. Those orders were: Prevent expansion of armed forces! Block military and naval appropriations! Penetrate the war industries to hamper their productivity! Stir up disloyalty among soldiers and sailors! Seize control of trade unions in any way connected with defense problems, and especially unions of longshoremen, seamen, telegraph operators, munitions workers! These injunctions were accepted by the American Communist Party and transmitted to its members and sympathizers. They were translated into action—as far as a tiny party could do so—with the help of the non-communists who flocked innocently to "anti-war" mass organizations.

Instructions of this nature from a foreign nation had never before in American history been carried out on such a scale and with so little concealment. Certainly there was little concealment when Herbert Benjamin—later the dominant figure in the Workers Alliance—wrote in the Daily Worker on January 18, 1930:

Our struggle against imperialist war for the defense of the Soviet Union and in support of the revolutionary struggles of the colonial masses can become really effective and assume revolutionary form only if we take these struggles into the factories and especially those factories where war materials are produced; onto the waterfronts from

which the war materials are shipped and upon the ships on which they
are conveyed.

Or when the American party published and distributed such decisions
by the Comintern as this, adopted in December, 1933:

In fighting against war, the communists must prepare even now for
the transformation of the imperialist war into civil war, concentrate
their forces in each country at the vital parts of the war machine of
imperialism.

A Moscow resolution, adopted in 1935 just before the change of
"line" on the subject, instructed Communist Parties of all capitalist
countries to "fight against military expenditures [war budgets] . . .
against militarization measures taken by capitalist governments. . . ."
A few months later the same parties would be howling for bigger armaments! Treason can scarcely be more self-righteously candid than this,
from an article in The Communist by an American party leader in
September, 1933:

The center where these central tasks outlined above are to be
carried out must be the factories, particularly the war industries. . . .
Only if our anti-war campaign is developed in the factories, munition
plants, docks and ships can our struggle against war be effective. . . .
Only in this way can the Soviet Union be defended from American
imperialist intervention. . . . The next strategic places for the anti-
war activities of the Party and the Young Communist League must be
within the armed forces, as well as within the various semi-military
reforestation and concentration camps of adult unemployed and
homeless youth.

Writing at this time, in Can These Things Be!, George Seldes gave
pages to exposing such an "out and out call to treason" on the part
of the Russians. (This was before Seldes, growing more communistic
as Russia grew less so, changed from a good reporter into a poor
politician.) He declared that Moscow was "planning mutiny, rebellion, civil war in the armies of her potential enemies," including the
U.S.A. "Propaganda seems better than high explosives" to the comrades, he showed. Then he proved from documents that Moscow, far
from opposing military service, expects every young comrade to sign

up for the purpose of "carrying on a revolutionary propaganda" and "learning the use of army weapons which he can turn against the bourgeoisie."

The citations could be continued to fill a volume. Few party documents and agitational publications on any subject failed to drag in "defense of the Soviet Union" and its concomitant penetration of the Army, the Navy, the munitions factories, the national transportation arteries. The American communists were under unequivocal orders to betray their country in the event that it should be useful to Russia, and were trying to obey.

Of course, there is a tremendous distance between willingness and accomplishment. It is more likely that the serious Soviet spy and sabotage work was done, like such work by other nations, by the professionals in their military and G.P.U. intelligence services. Individual members of the American party were often drawn into the professional Russian military services—in which case they normally severed all open connections with the party. The American movement was a vast reservoir of potential spies, if nothing else.

But the record on the party's intentions is crystal clear. Its ready response to the voice of the Kremlin on matters like national defense and infiltration of munitions plants dramatizes the allegiance of the party to a foreign nation. I am not here arguing their moral or constitutional right to such allegiance; all of them regarded Russia as their *real* fatherland, even if their ancestors had come over in the *Mayflower* and they had breathed their first lungful in Kansas or Texas. I am establishing the fact itself. And I am establishing it primarily because it is significant in relation to the extraordinary communist pretense of American patriotism and loyalty to the United States in the following Comintern period.

The only phase of the Kremlin's military program for America which was successful beyond cavil was in roping well-meaning liberals, pacifists, literary fellow-travelers and their like into the "anti-war" planets of the expanding solar system.

CHAPTER IX

THE CULT OF RUSSIA-WORSHIP

1

WHAT was happening inside the Soviet Union is a part of this American story. That country was the jealous and headstrong overseer of American Bolshevism, snapping the whip, punishing the stragglers, rewarding the diligent. But it would be false to present the picture as a simple case of physical and fiscal domination. Normal men do not transfer their loyalties blindly from their own to a foreign land for bread alone; not even for the bread of political power. When the American communists and their fellow-travelers acclaimed Russia as their "spiritual fatherland" they were truly exhibiting a deeper relationship—on the plane of emotional fixations.

Needing a faith into which they could sink themselves luxuriantly— an earthly faith of the here and now—they had found it in far-off Russia. Its very distance was an advantage. It is no accident that the countries closest to Russia geographically, such as Finland, the Baltic republics, Poland, Rumania, were least infected with Bolshevism. They could hear the cries of the anguished across the frontier. To the eager seekers for consoling enthusiasm far removed from the scene, the Kremlin's propaganda presented a systematized delusion. It was materialist in form, with its Five Year Plans, industrialization, statistics; yet it was spiritual in mood, presenting objects of adoration and devils for hating.

Those who accepted the gift endowed it with the lush colors of their own yearnings. They attacked as a vandal anyone who cast doubts on their glowing symbols of hope and salvation in our own time. The longer and the more earnestly they committed themselves to that foreign allegiance, in fact, the more compelling was their inner need to make the foreign object flawless. Russia had to be, for them, potentially if not actually perfect. Anything less would have admitted the possibility that they were dupes and traitors.

Those who accused such people of lying about Russia were vulgarizing the affair. The communists were lying in the first place to themselves. When they ganged up on anyone who tried to bring them a bit of the truth, they were merely protecting their spiritual retreat from infidel assaults. Certainly there were bevies of charlatans among them, especially in the inner circles of their leadership; faithless men and women flocked to the Muscovite jam pots for the sweet jobs, the social and intellectual prestige, the sheer nervous exhilaration of it all. But in the larger sense the phenomenon of Russia-worship had in it more of religious ecstasy than political chicanery. The Russia they worshipped was in their own minds. The circumstance that there was a real country of the same name was an annoyance that they could not allow to spoil the fun.

I do not believe I am exaggerating the element of self-delusion in the process. I lived in Russia, close to its grim realities, precisely in years when the strange Russia-worship overcame so many Americans. At the height of the tourist invasion, in the early 'thirties, as many as 85 per cent of the foreign hordes were from the United States. I watched literally thousands of my countrymen prostrate themselves at the shrines of their new inspiration.

Their minds surely were not involved in the business, even with those who had first-rate minds. I heard them exclaim in hushed wonder over marvels that existed only in their quivering imaginations. I saw them stiffen in desperate resistance at the first contact with doubt. I watched them move like somnambulists among the food queues and horrors of a throttled and policed population, clapping their hands in glee over the lovely "sacrifices."

But I will not say that these visitors were dishonest. For the most part the fault was in their vision, not in their conscience. The professional American Russia-boosters who sometimes conducted special tours, and with careful formulas of befuddlement explained away the evidences of terror and pervasive poverty, were often purposeful liars. But not the bleating flocks of schoolteachers, clergymen, writers, dentists, shopkeepers, etc. whom they shepherded.

The resident correspondents (including those who posed in the "liberal" journals as angels in Stalin's paradise) had a scathing contempt for the adoring pilgrims. Soviet officials despised their gullibility and cackling self-importance. We could scarcely blame the tourist guides who, in the privacy of friendship, wondered whether all Americans were blind and stupid. Yet looking back at it all, I admit we may have been too harsh in judging these innocents. They were more deserving of pity than of ridicule, for only men tortured by a terrible thirst could have lapped up putrid ditchwater with such relish.

A number of American physicians looked at hospitals which, in their own country, would have been condemned as a menace—hospitals without cleanliness, order or elementary competence—and went home to sing hymns of praise to Soviet medicine. It was enough for them that the mess was labeled "socialized medicine." They never bothered to see the confusion underneath. One honest Russian physician, if he had dared talk and the visitors had dared to listen, could have set them right.

The almost inescapable fact about Soviet life was the fearful pressure on people's nerves, because of overcrowding, the eternal threat of arrest, the murderous "tempo" of industrialization, the endless worry over food and other essentials. But American psychiatrists wrote solemn volumes based on the staggering lie that nervous disorders had "disappeared" in nerve-shocked Russia.

Prison reformers went through a few "model" prisons and boys' camps. Then they composed books and reports that somehow overlooked the millions of political and criminal prisoners in concentration camps, isolators, harsh areas of punitive exile. They lacked the mental perseverance to take note of the intimate pictures of Soviet prison life from the inside by the Tchernavins, Solonevich, George Kitchin, Ciliga, Victor Serge, Julia de Beausobre and others; there happens to have been a sizable documented literature on the subject. Nor did it occur to them to bring back, along with their hand-tooled statistics, the medieval Soviet laws that impose capital punishment for theft of a few bushels of grain, that make innocent relatives guilty for alleged crimes by their sons and brothers, that impose death sentences on twelve-year-olds.

Honest educators like Professor John Dewey and Dr. George S. Counts, hundreds of them from all countries, flocked to study the new Russian education and wrote high-pitched volumes on its beauties. Many of them are by now ready to admit, shamefacedly, that they had recorded their imported elations rather than the physical facts. They had been taken in by their own eagerness, accepting plans and paper curricula and fine phrases for the reality. They did not take the time to look at the ordinary schools, to watch the ordinary backward teacher, or to ask themselves about the value of an education that distorts the truth and makes thinking a crime.

An American couple who had devoted years to the "simple life" and to inveighing against the modern machine age, somehow found themselves glorifying Soviet industrialization. Lifelong pacifists gushed happily over the Red Army and the military training of women and little children. Once I watched a well-fed female exulting over the marvels of a linotype machine in action in the pressrooms of the Moscow *Izvestia*. I asked her where she was from and she confessed to Brooklyn. Whereupon I led her to the rear of the machine and showed her the inscription, "Mergenthaler, Brooklyn." Young women "studied Russia" for delirious months with the aid of robust male Bolsheviks and returned to America ultimately to extol the "freedom" of Soviet society. And always there were the mobs of tourists, grimly determined not to be cheated out of their state of grace by mere facts.

The few who were shocked by what they saw usually rationalized it all on the homeward trip. I remember when the Rev. Dr. Harry F. Ward of Union Theological Seminary sat in my Moscow office. He had come to investigate "new motivations" in the "socialist" land. He complained, sadly not bitterly, that he found the age-old spurs of greed and grab were still rampant here. Unfortunately he had arrived at a time when those motives had been restored to respectability. I tried to console the reverend tourist. It was not necessary—in due time he wrote a passionate volume in praise of the new motivations in Soviet society. He had discovered them after all, I suppose, somewhere on the homeward route.*

Naturally, there were a few who were disillusioned or came without illusions in the first place. A few of them tried to tell America about what they had seen and felt. But their voices were drowned out by the chorus of hallelujah-shouters. They were howled down ferociously in the press and among their friends and dismissed as "petty bourgeois" or red-baiters or plain stupid. How could they, how dared they, set their puny impressions against history-on-the-march, against the authority of the professional whoopers-up for Stalin?

2

Here is a little story. I heard it years later, from the chief actors. It seems to me to sum up the whole delusion symbolized by Russia.

He is a New York painter. As a reaction against economic misery

---

* *In Place of Profit, Social Incentives in the Soviet Union*, by Harry F. Ward, 1933.

all around him he had drifted into the Stalinist way of thought and had been comforted. Came the great day when he could make the pilgrimage, which he undertook in a state of self-hypnosis in the company of his mother. The woman, Russian-born and less complicated psychologically than her son, looked at Stalin's empire with sober eyes and did not like it. Her son argued with her throughout the journey and refused to be influenced by the piled-up horror around them. Back in New York, the painter delighted his communist friends with the warmth of his reports on Russia.

There was only one flaw in his own happiness, and it grew into a sort of guilty secret. During the long weeks in Russia he had carried sketchbooks and his gifted pencil had recorded the life around him: groups huddled on railway stations, hungry bodies, faces drained of all interest in life, ragged beggars, prostitutes, food lines. He had filled his books with graphic notes on the living reality. And to his dismay these did not at any point check with his honest verbal reports. His mind and his art had made entirely different records of the experience. The drawings reflected his mother's observations rather than the happiness and enthusiasm about which he was talking to his circle.

In confusion he hid those sketchbooks, showing them only to trusted friends. Then, years after the journey, he read certain books about Russia. He pondered what he read. And gradually it became clear to him that his artist's pencil had told the truth, despite himself,— the truth that his mother had seen at once—even while his mind lied to protect its comforting faith. He brought out the sketchbooks and transferred some of these notes to canvas and engraving blocks. He was no longer ashamed of their truth, which made him whole at last.

3

I cannot hope in a few pages here to summarize the terrifying reality of Russia under Stalin in the years immediately after he established his monopoly of power. I could do little more than suggest it in the 650 pages of Assignment in Utopia.

The hundred and seventy million Soviet people were herded and driven and starved by armies of secret agents, by threats, by promises. Literally millions died in their tracks. Under the sober-sounding slogan of "liquidation of the kulaks as a class," at least a million peasant families were torn up by the roots, stripped of all their goods and cast into the tropic or Arctic wildernesses. New and subtle crimes against the omnipotent state were invented as an excuse for mobilizing forced labor battalions to clear harbors, cut canals, lay rails and dig minerals where ordinary labor could not be lured. Concentration camps larger than any in the whole history of mankind—larger than the slave labor contingents at the disposal of the Pharoahs—multiplied through the land. Entire sections of the population—pre-revolutionary intellectuals or former Nepmen or farmers owning more than one cow—were systematically persecuted even unto death.

The last sparks of mental independence were stamped out among scientists, academicians and creative writers. The very memory of unorthodox speech or thought was expunged by terror. G.P.U. executions without trial took thousands of victims. We were all aware that a score or a hundred were being slaughtered without the formality of a press report for every one noted in the papers. Amazing "show trials" were staged in which engineers or professors or former socialists "confessed" elaborately to impossible crimes. Undernourished workers were driven to exertions beyond their physical strength. They lived in verminous barracks while blueprints of splendor-to-come filled the propaganda at home and abroad.

In the winter of 1932-33 a famine greater than any in Russia's history devastated the humanity of the Ukraine, North Caucasus and Central Asia. What made it unspeakably sadistic was that it was not an act of God but an act of man, a planned famine, allowed to take its gruesome course against the protests of some of Stalin's own associates. We all saw it coming. We all knew that the government could head it off by spending a few million dollars for Canadian or South American grain. But these little men in the Kremlin, turned into mad gods, decided to "punish" a population of forty or fifty million for their sullen passive resistance against the state's seizure of their land, tools and livestock. Then they proceeded to conceal the tragedy from the world to prevent even sympathy from reaching the stricken population.

How many millions died? Maurice Hindus, while still among the leading apologists for Soviet horrors, "admitted" three million corpses. Soviet officials and journalists in private conversation put it at seven millions—mentioning the figure, sometimes, even a little boastfully. But whether three millions or five or seven makes little difference. There is a point at which catastrophe can no longer be measured mathematically. The horror is beyond the figure, even beyond the wagons that went daily through Ukrainian cities collecting the night's corpses, beyond the blown-up bellies of children and the instances of cannibalism confided to me by Soviet newspapermen. It was rather in the deliberateness with which the crime was perpetrated and hidden from the outside world. The cynicism of absolute power can be more dreadful than wholesale murder.

Because the Kremlin needed gold and precious stones to pay for foreign machines, the G.P.U. built up a special *valuta* department. Its job was to torture Soviet citizens into "contributing" such possessions to the state. Thousands of suspects were sweated for weeks, tortured by men with a sinister genius for inflicting pain, driven to physical collapse and mental collapse until they gave up their legal possessions. And those who had something to give up were fortunate. Worse was the fate of the suspects who had nothing but could not convince their official tormentors of it. The torture of their children before their eyes could not produce dollar bills or diamond rings where they did not exist. The *valuta* episode, which lasted for several years, has never been openly admitted and had no sanction in law—*a government was deliberately engaged in robbing its own citizens.*

A system of internal passports was instituted. It turned every city and agrarian district of the nation into a "pale," where the population was tied to the place. Not since ancient Egyptian days has an entire country been thus "organized." Meanwhile the everyday living conditions were going from bad to worse. Every last article of food and clothing was rationed as in time of a great siege. The industrial undertakings yanked millions from the soil into urban centers where there were no housing accommodations for them. The mere task of keeping body and soul together soaked up all people's thoughts and energies and feelings, turned them into prowling, scavenging animals in a barren land. A great wretchedness spread and festered.

And all for what? For an industrialization that Japan had achieved even more rapidly without slaughtering millions; that Czarist Russia had got well started in its day; that other backward countries were introducing without mass killings for a "noble cause." The industrialization produced a vast machine structure which was lopsided, worked with fantastic inefficiency, and needed to be "purged" continuously by execution squads. Four or five men, living on a level which an American or a German on the dole would have considered impossible, did the work that a single laborer did elsewhere. Transportation was in a continuous state of semi-collapse. Tractors rusted in the fields for lack of spare parts or through misuse. The output of entire industries was frequently, according to the Soviet press itself, chiefly brak or spoiled goods.

And all for what? A "socialized" agriculture forced down the gullets of the peasantry, killing millions of them in the process. When it was finally accomplished the "socialized" farmers were merely serfs on government estates, every last item of their existence prescribed from headquarters, their machines belonging to the state landlord, without the right to leave the land. The term "collective farm" sounds to the Western ear like a brand of co-operative farming. Actually it is no more than a euphemism for a modernized, mechanized brand of serfdom.

And all for what? A "socialism" without a trace of the freedom, the proletarian control or the physical rewards foreseen by the prophets of the Marxian creed. The G.P.U. station attached to every important factory or mine was the symbol of the enslavement that dared call itself socialism. The trade unions, even as under fascism, had become extensions of the all-powerful state and hence "company unions" in the worst sense of the term. Entire families worked for wages that barely covered their semi-starvation rations, fearful of uttering a word or making a gesture that would put them on the blacklist of the only employer, the state.

And all for what? A "racial equality" that gave all races parity under conditions of terror and enslavement. Armenians, Kazaks, Volga Germans, Jews, Ukrainians could use their own language—provided that they said and read only what Moscow permitted. They could develop their own national cultures—provided those were twisted to conform strictly to the precepts prescribed by Moscow. They might have their own schools—provided they taught that Stalin was god and his enemies monsters to be murdered at sight. They had equality, except that the Kremlin could shoot the heads of their governments, their favorite national writers, even the leaders of their local Communist Parties whenever it so desired; except that they lived under a terror controlled at the center. In the final analysis their racial autonomy boiled down to the right to worship Stalin and denounce their racial heritage in their own tongues.

Such were the "achievements" upon which rested the cult of Russia-worship that gained sway in America in the Third Period and became epidemic in the following period. Such was the background of the Red Decade.

4

In 1931 I came to America for a vacation from my Moscow post. The Depression had begun during my absence, so that the curious cult of Russia-worship which was one of its strangest consequences was new to me. I had seen some of the cultists in the preceding years in the Soviet Union, but the great trek of tourists did not come until later.

The cult was dramatized for me by a banquet to which I was invited at Town Hall in New York. It was designed as a get-together of Americans who had been to Mecca and therefore enjoyed a special prestige among the worshipers. I shall plagiarize myself by excerpting the scene from *Assignment in Utopia*:

The exhibit styled itself a "We-Have-Been-to-the-U.S.R.R. Dinner" and contained first-rate specimens of practically every variety of eulogist of the Russian myth, from the simple third-category tourist through the high-powered salesman with a fat Soviet contract in view. The pep-it-up booster spirit that moves mountains and sells real estate prevailed, and indiscriminate enthusiasm for everything Soviet gushed and popped and crackled.

"Down with us!" would have been the appropriate slogan for the dinner, since a large majority of the guests, had they been Russians, would have been crushed long ago in one or another purge: liberal intellectuals with kind hearts and fuzzy minds, exactly the breed which was just then being liquidated wholesale in their "spiritual fatherland." A few of those at the speakers' table, indeed, would have been liquidated on their looks alone, they were such clear-cut bourgeois types.

Several score ladies and gentlemen who had made the pilgrimage fortified themselves with a large dinner, and proceeded to pile up superlatives. Could it be the same Russia which I left a few weeks earlier that they were exclaiming over in such childish delight? Did this gray-haired little lady from some college really approve the bloody works of Comrades Menzhinsky and Yagoda of the G.P.U.? Did this cheerful Rotarian defender of civil liberties actually believe that Russia was the "freest country in the world" and the home of "real democracy"? And the baldheaded little clergyman with spectacles on the tip of his nose, why was he of all people so thrilled with the Five Year Plan for the Liquidation of God? The Soviet officials present must have blushed for the monumental simplicity of these Americans. The hardships and sacrifices which they mentioned in passing seemed, in their speeches, merely to add a fillip of excitement to the thrilling Russian game.

These enthusiasts, of course, were typical of their kind. Thousands like them were attending dinners under the aegis of the Friends of Soviet Russia. Their names decorated a growing crop of false-front societies, and they were practicing the pig Latin of communist obfuscation. By the time I returned to America for good, in 1934, their breed was legion. The myth of a "socialist Russia" was firmly established.

Where had all these enthusiasts been in the thirteen years of the Bolshevik Revolution before 1930? Certainly there was a larger element of honest idealism, a smaller admixture of horror, in those years. No less certainly the Soviet regime had more need of their enthusiasm in its earlier stages. These Americans became pseudo-communists at precisely the juncture when Russia became less communistic in its thinking, more brutally totalitarian in its life. They were drawn to the Great Experiment by its magnitude and seeming strength. Under the guise of a nobly selfless dedication they were, in fact, identifying themselves with Power.

They were going through an ecstatic semi-religious experience. But not one of them gave up his stocks and bonds, his capitalist job, his lucrative pulpit, his last yacht. Few of them went so far as to join the party and accept the bonds of discipline. They preferred to be voluntary totalitarians. It was a faith which, being in large part a political racket, cynically and often contemptuously permitted them the thrill of "belonging" without the inconvenience of living up to its precepts. They could make their sacrifices comfortably by overeating at banquets and overdrinking at cocktail parties for the cause. They starved too—but vicariously, in the persons of Russian workers and peasants.

CHAPTER X

THE LIBERALS INVENT A UTOPIA

1

W HY should the Russians have all the fun of remaking a world?" This is the concluding sentence in A New Deal, a book by Stuart Chase published late in 1932. The rhetorical question was not irony but genuine envy. It about sums up the monumental self-delusions of the period when American liberals fashioned a wonderland of the imagination and called it, amazingly enough, Soviet Russia. I single out Mr. Chase only because of his unhappy choice of words. Never before, I suppose, had a reputable economist mistaken heaped-up horror and multiple catastrophes for "fun." He was simply reflecting the compelling assumptions of the group he moved in; personally Mr. Chase escaped the mass hypnosis of the Soviet myth somewhat sooner than most of them.

At the time those remarkable words were written, the Russians were having fun in a rather curious fashion. For instance, tens of thousands of them were dying of hunger every day in the Ukraine, North Caucasus and Central Asia. About a quarter of a million more were digging a canal in the Arctic region under indescribably brutal conditions, thousands of them dropping dead as the work progressed. The Soviet state was then engaged in liquidating pre-revolutionary intellectuals—men and women in general like Mr. Chase and the editors of the New York liberal weeklies—as well as engineers, professors, specialists. Day and night in sub-zero weather millions of Russians stood in queues in the desperate hope of buying a little food or kerosene or a few yards of cotton goods.

Were the Russians having fun! Victor Serge, French novelist and once a leader of the French Communist Party, saw the funmaking at close range. He described it in terms that are only now beginning to make sense to the liberals of that period: "The industrialization is directed like a march through conquered territory. . . . The collectivization is like installing an army in a conquered land, according to the *worst rigours of war.*" Before these processes had run their course, Russia had paid for them with more lives than it lost in the World War! Some of these Russians were having fun in the "steam rooms" and on the "conveyors" of the G.P.U. torture divisions. Thousands of others tried to cross the frontiers into Rumania, Poland, Finland, despite the death penalty for attempted escape from the fun-making.

The fact is that American liberals were hopelessly dazzled by the idea of "planning." They would not and could not see the planlessness under the Soviet blueprinted pretensions. It would take them years to recognize that the "plan" was one of the most costly pieces of national blundering in all history, whether reckoned in human or in economic terms. Ultimately nearly all the men responsible for the planning and for carrying it out were executed by the Soviet government, accused of having bungled and butchered the whole business.

The American liberal aberration had its house organ, the *New Republic*, which led all the rest in avid and undiscriminating acceptance of the myth of Stalin's Utopia. The *Nation* contended for the honors but never could master quite so much brilliant misinformation on the subject. The dullish and platitudinous stuff of its Louis Fischers, Maxwell Stewarts and Freda Kirchweys was not quite a match for the *New Republic's* Bruce Blivens, George Soules, Malcolm Cowleys and outside talent. Both journals in these years ran over with superlatives on the Russian theme—even the letter columns hummed with hymns.

The less liberal press, even unto Tory newspapers, did not escape the contagion. They might argue against Soviet "planning," but they often lacked the courage to deny its "achievements." The facts about the plan in action, even after we toned them down for foreign consumption, seemed too harsh to be credited. I suspect that hard-boiled capitalist editors, let down by their own system, were eager deep inside to believe that someone somewhere had the answer. I remember sending a few sketches of Moscow life—satirical bits about "love in the red" which even a Soviet journal could have published—to a reputable conservative magazine in America. They were returned to me with an acid note from an editor; he did not care to go in "for red-baiting."

Nearly every college professor, poet, social worker, engineer or schoolboy who returned from Russia brought the stereotyped formulas and statistical patterns to swell the shiny mountain of self-deception.

The more articulate wrote books. Almost as many books on the "Soviet experiment" were published in 1931 as in the preceding thirteen years. The least articulate sounded off in interviews or verbal reports to their own circles. When the clippings and newly-minted volumes reached us in Moscow, we could only wonder whether these good people had visited the same Russia in which we were living.

We read stray copies of the liberal weeklies as though they were comic supplements to the somber Soviet reality. Besides earnest reports by professional writers, there were the outpourings of those who shared their knowledge by a kind of intuition. They knew in their bones that the millennium was dawning over Siberia. There, for instance, was a simple reader of the *New Republic* (February 11, 1931,) achieving publication by reporting about a plain housewife, his own sister, and her miraculous instinct for the truth:

To my great surprise, for she reads comparatively little and in no sense is a student of world economic conditions, she manifested a knowledge of Russia approximating my own. Furthermore, she assured me that others in her circle were observing Russia closely. . . . They are aware of the significance of Russia and all it portends.

The editors of the journal, manifesting a knowledge approximating their reader's, took a peculiar personal pride in the tidings of glory from over there. They published charts contrasting key economic indexes in America and in Russia, never questioning the doctored Soviet figures, never discounting for quality factors or for cost in life and substance, never alluding to the march of death and terror through the land. At the end of 1930, when the Five Year Plan was bogged down and kicking wildly in the morass, the *New Republic* (December 12, 1930,) hailed its "success" and poked fun at the discomfiture of capitalist observers. "The progress of the Five Year Plan," it boasted, "is causing the American newspapers to react wildly, in fact an atmosphere of panic seems to prevail."

When the discomfited press dared criticize the epidemic of executions—at that time chiefly of people like the editors of the *New Republic*—that magazine exploded in anger:

Well, in America we executed people for murder and for holding unorthodox political opinions, in Russia they execute people for abusing positions of high responsibility. Are official rifle squads of the Cheka any more depressing to the morale of the workers than the hired Cossacks of the American mill towns? Are they any worse than the New York police?

Thus lightly and cheerfully these liberals continued to dismiss every enormity of the growing terror which in the end would kill the Plan and the Revolution which they worshiped. Against official terror as a principle of government and on a millionfold scale unmatched in history, they cited rough New York cops or a few miscarriages of justice in California and Massachusetts; against concentration camps holding literally millions of peasants and workers and intellectuals, they cited the company police of textile towns. No rationalization was too farfetched if it helped salvage their faith.

In the March 8, 1933, number, the same journal presented an extraordinary article under the title "Is Human Nature Changing in Russia?" The author, a social worker named Eduard C. Lindeman, had just sojourned in Utopia. The date is significant—it was the hardest and bloodiest moment in Soviet Russia's existence up to that time, a moment of wholesale starvation, intensified terror, inner tensions in the ranks of the ruling party itself which would have frightful consequences in the gigantic blood purges of a few years later. It was a period, I can attest, when even the most optimistic friends of Stalin who knew the facts whispered in private about the sharpening dangers. The professional press agents of the regime among foreign writers, indeed, had to admit the horrors of the crisis, if only to explain them away. But this American tourist somehow missed it all. Had he set out to compose a satire to kid his fellow-liberals, he could have done no better than in this lightheartedly earnest article.

Lindeman reported that "in the first place, there is stability in contemporary Russia and there is solidarity." It must have shocked the G.P.U. under the pathologically bloodthirsty Henry Yagoda, then engaged on his most ambitious mass production of corpses, to learn from the American weekly that "revolutionary vigilance tends to relax in all spheres because there is no longer any real danger of counter-revolutionary movements from within." Of course, "the primary hungers are not satisfied," but the Russians, being a peculiar breed of animal, enjoy that: "There are other goals which have thus far served to release energies and to promote faith."

The investigator also reported that "prostitution, homosexuality and suicide" were "disappearing." Homosexuality was so rampant in Moscow and Leningrad at the time that the government soon thereafter exiled hundreds of the afflicted men and women, among them certain high officials, from those cities. The preceding year, in connection with the domestic passport edict, there had been a terrifying wave of suicides in the larger cities; I knew personally of several families which had killed themselves en masse. Little girls below the age of puberty were offering themselves for a little bread on the streets of Kiev and other cities in the famine area at the very moment Lindeman was making his report.

On and on his report went, making one "deduction" from non-existing but gratifying facts after another. "Is it possible for human nature to change with sufficient rapidity and depth to attain those revolutionary goals which constitute the essence of the communist program?" he asked, and answered with a resounding YES. The Russians, he proved to the satisfaction of American liberals, "are teaching the world . . . the latent capacity of human nature to adapt itself to changing circumstances." They were indeed—adapting themselves to life by decree, chronic undernourishment, mass executions. But that, of course, is not what he referred to. He actually detected a revision of human character exactly in the period when the Kremlin leaders, to meet the clamoring insistence of the old character, were restoring piecework, bonuses and a thousand other devices, along with increased police pressure.

The temper of such imaginative "studies" of Russia on the spot may be judged from one episode elaborated by Lindeman. He saw a crowd of Muscovites assisting an officer in disentangling a traffic snarl resulting from an accident. Such gregariousness and helpfulness has always been common in Russia. But the American tourist eagerly read a socialist moral into it. He "meditated" on the "event," and decided that "Here, then was an illustration of voluntary collectivism. No, it was more than that; it was a demonstration of unity between the citizen and his government." This meditated proof, of course, outweighed for him the involuntary collectivism and the tragic disunity between state and citizens at that very moment being demonstrated in the South Russian famine.

I use that article only as typical of its kind, rather than exceptional. The liberals had invented a Utopia and were finding it good.

2

A young man who has since become a fervent opponent of Stalinism began a review of a batch of books about Russia in 1931 with roughly this remark: "Can it really be that there are still honest and intelligent people who doubt the wonderful achievements of the new Russia?" In that spirit, every outcropping of heresy was swiftly detected and exposed. William Henry Chamberlin ventured to warn that "it is perhaps too soon" to assume that Russia had finally solved the problem of employment. Instantly a gentleman in Toledo, Ohio, apprised Mr. Chamberlin in Moscow, via the *New Republic* of course, that soon "in the Soviet economic system there will be no unemployment, but there will be leisure for all."

No group of the population was without its own discoverer of the Never-Never land. Josephine Herbst stumbled on it in the midst of a literary inquisition that was muzzling gifted Soviet writers and driving Soviet critics to untimely deaths and making suicides epidemic among men and women in cultural pursuits. "The excitement about writing is good," she exulted (*New Republic*, April 29, 1931). "Make no mistake about it, something is up in the Soviet Union. And the proof that they are keeping their heads seems to be as much in their attitude toward literature and writers outside the Soviet Union as in anything else." Scores of those to whom she referred would lose their heads and their lives in the years to come, at the hands of the firing squads.

Professor Counts of Columbia produced a eulogy of his largely subjective Russia and the foremost living American philosopher, John Dewey, hailed the mirage, adding, of Russia: "In some respects, it is already a searching spiritual challenge as it is an economic challenge to coordinate and plan." The spiritual challenge, presumably, was in the current arrests and liquidations of philosophers, historians and professors accused of "rotten liberalism" in their thinking. Professor Dewey also chided William C. White for writing a book in which some of the Russians, alas, were not having much fun. He reminded Mr. White that "the universal habit of grumbling is especially chronic among Russians." Professor Dewey did not add—because he did not learn it until much later—that the universal habit of *not* grumbling, of fatalistic submission to suffering and tyranny, of extraordinary meekness, is even more chronic among Russians.

Bruce Bliven, of the *New Republic* staff, reassured prospective pilgrims "who feel a little squeamish about coming to a country where so many persons are underfed, lest they take sustenance from the mouths of the hungry." Their American dollars, he consoled them, would help the Five Year Plan.

An American city-planning expert, Edgar Chambless, wrote blithely, in the February 10, 1932, issue, "One reads of expert city planners traveling over Siberia in a special train, leaving the ground plans of new communities behind them as they go." The grotesqueness of this fantasy can be felt only by those who have seen any of the drab, lopsided, overcrowded, insanitary and quickly verminous new industrial towns. But the liberal faithful had what they wanted—a sort of R.F.D. tossing bright new cities from train doors in passing. If only the long-distance enthusiast could have known the heartbreaking experiences of imported housing specialists like Dr. Ernst May, the famous builder of the Frankfurt project! After several years of frustration and futility in the Soviet bureaucratic mess, Dr. May fled the country—bound for the heart of Africa, he told me, to forget the Russian disaster.

Dozens of well-meaning Americans, on the basis of hearsay or a supervised tour, were ready to attest in print that reports about forced labor in Russia were lies. They were cruelly let down by the Kremlin itself and by Stalin's most servile press agents, in later years, when it became the fashion not only to admit mass use of prisoners but to boast of it. The most cynical apologists found mealy-mouthed formulas to avoid the term "forced labor"—one of them, as we shall see, would call the forced employment of "myriads" of Russians under police overseers an "educational" enterprise—but not one of them dared deny the facts. The government soon would claim credit for gigantic prison jobs like the White Sea Canal, railroads in Siberia, harbors in the Arctic, irrigation projects in Central Asia, involving in the aggregate millions of G.P.U. slaves. It even published, at one time, a long list of such projects under exclusive G.P.U. control; American engineers familiar with Soviet labor productivity estimated for me that those projects alone called for at least three million prisoners.

It is in the light of this record that we must read the "denials" of forced labor by Americans who spoke honestly, cocksure in their ignorance. Even General William N. Haskell declared, on returning from a Soviet tour in 1930, "I was led to the conclusion that the Russian worker as a rule is more willing and enthusiastic than the American." The choice of the word "led" to the conclusion was decidedly apt. To fill the cup brimful the General added another heaping spoonful: the Soviet worker's "voice is the controlling factor in industry and politics," he asserted.

Sherwood Eddy informed his liberal audiences that "there is a healthy trade-union democracy among the workers" and that "there is very little convict labor in Russia." (N. Y. *American*, November 16, 1930.) The Soviet trade-union system is about as democratic as Hitler's and Mussolini's. Congressman Henry T. Rainey of Illinois required only a brief taste of Utopia to proclaim: "I particularly investigated the question of forced labor in Russia and there isn't any there. Labor is freer in Russia than in any other country in the world." (*U. S. Daily*, October 26, 1931.)

At the time of the Congressman's visit there was a fantastic turnover of labor in Russian plants. Droves of workers quit their jobs in the hope of a little more bread somewhere else. Soon the government would stop the tragic migration by a "passportization" plan that in effect tied workers to their machines. But Mr. Rainey reported back that "the workers of Russia have more money than ever before, and they are spending it liberally in traveling, literally by the tens of thousands." He had swallowed whole the standard explanation of the tragedy handed out to gullible foreigners. Another American did as well as the legislator. He returned from a business trip to Russia convinced, on the basis of this labor turnover, that "the average Russian seems inherently to crave a change." That, no doubt, is why generation after generation of average Russians remained in the same village. It did not occur to these Americans that the migrant workers craved a meal.

Especially noteworthy among the liberals was their vicarious valor in making sacrifices for their Utopia. "What if a million die?" they said sanctimoniously. What were a few million Russian deaths, a generation or two of misery, against the miracle of "Backward old Russia, suddenly springing on the civilized world the most advanced Utopian ideas and actually trying them out!" The quotation is from the writings of a Russian countess, transplanted to America, after her first view of the Soviet State. For some reason she did not linger to submit to the try-out procedures, though tens of thousands of aristocrats cowering in corners or rotting in prisons would gladly have taken her place in America among the benighted émigrés.

Ah, the magnificent courage of the Americans who took Russian sacrifices so nonchalantly in their stride! A Mr. Simpson, in the *New Republic* of December 16, 1931, dismissed such trifles with the greatest of ease. "The violence which has marked the agrarian revolution," he wrote, "seems . . . an inevitable accompaniment of so profound and far-reaching, etc. . . . A new order of social relations cannot, it seems, be made with sweetness and light." Pour out another ocean of Russian blood, comrades, the Simpsons are with you to the last Ivanovich!

Lincoln Steffens recorded for *New Republic* customers that it was "heart- and head-breaking to see the job begun and carried on over there by a dictator and a small minority using force," but he did not permit that circumstance to chill his fervor. Despite everything he "rejoiced" with the rest "that the deed was done and a path blazed for us." As he told Moscow friends, according to his own story: "What do I care for setbacks on the American continent now that you and I— we have won the great battle of Russia in Asia." Even if everything at home in benighted America fails, he exclaimed, "Then you and I and the world, if it pleases, can always lie down and say: 'Oh well, anyhow, there's Russia.'" And there certainly *was* Russia, even if the Steffenses and Lindemans could not see it through their tears of jubilation.

Boris Pilnyak, a Soviet writer visiting America, pulled his hosts' legs by "pitying" America publicly for its lack of Soviet blessings. The literal liberals were thrilled. American capitalists, the *New Republic* gushed, "will find it odd to be pitied by a Russian," but "the experience is good for them." Pilnyak had recently been put through a Soviet wringer for having written too truthfully about Russian life and was desperately proving his loyalty by kidding American audiences. The liberals did not know, of course, that the one person for whom Pilnyak cared most in the world, his father, had been taken into custody as soon as the novelist left the country—a hostage for the speedy return of his son and his good behavior while among the Americans.

Even the attempts to report Russia objectively were vitiated by the standardized assumptions. Thus Dr. Elisha M. Friedman, in one of the more restrained books on Russia, took it for granted throughout that the Soviet rulers, in visiting horror on their subjects, were motivated by lofty patriotism rather than party power-politics. He brushed away the libel that the Soviet State had anything to hide, attesting:

"Every request I made was granted."* I ventured to guess at the time the book appeared that he had not requested to visit the concentration camps, or to witness a lusty G.P.U. torture session when some old woman suspected of concealing five American dollars in the rafters was being "educated."

Many of those who acknowledged the dictatorial violence explained it away in a manner most unflattering to the inmates of Utopia. The Russians, they said in effect, are not quite human and can only be managed with whips, bayonets and execution squads. As engineer Walter A. Rukeyser put it in a book,† "Without an iron-bound dictatorship, Russia could not survive, for it is the only thing the Russian people know and understand." The same theory runs all through the curious political dissertations of Walter Duranty. Here is a sample from his book, *I Write as I Please:*

Most foreigners who go to Russia or try to analyze it fail to understand that Russia is Asiatic. . . . Stalin deserved his victory . . . because his policies were most fitted to the Russian character and folkways in that they established Asiatic absolutism.

3

In the early years of the Russian experiment, American eulogists were relatively few. Their books showed a romantic, almost lyrical acceptance of the revolution. The facts, no matter how harsh, were usually admitted and assimilated as part of the agony of birth. Such was the spirit of the writings of John Reed, Louise Bryant, Albert Rhys Williams, Lincoln Steffens and others. But in the years now under discussion the attitude in most pro-Soviet writings is quite different. Theirs is for the most part a literature of apologetics, ranging from panicky rationalization and self-deception to deliberate concealment.

The early literary eulogists wrote as inspired prophets of an embattled revolution; their latter-day successors—Fischer, Duranty, Hindus, Anna Louise Strong, the Webbs, Jerome Davis, Sherwood Eddy, John Strachey, Ella Winter, Harry Ward, etc.—wrote like the press agents of a going, if rather unpleasant, business. The emphasis of the new recruits is no longer on the coming freedom and equality.

---

* *Russia in Transition,* by Elisha M. Friedman, 1932.
† *Working for the Soviets,* by Walter A. Rukeyser.

It is upon factories, percentages, machinery, tractors. Few of them reveal any awareness that socialism ever meant more than the government ownership of all life and its rigid organization under a police regime.

Much of the earlier mystic element, however, survived and found voice in the more literary evangels. I shall never forget my shock, in reading Waldo Frank's exuberance on the Soviet theme, when I reached the passage in which he records that in Leningrad he could not eat—because he must sing. . . . This at a time when native Leningraders could not eat for less lyrical reasons. Another of the literary fraternity betrayed his fond preconceptions in the very title of his book, *Travels in Two Democracies*. Edmund Wilson has learned a lot more about Stalin's "democracy" since the book was written. But it's in the record and cannot be ignored. Arriving in Leningrad, Mr. Wilson was distressed by its "dingy and mute and monotonous hordes." But soon he came upon a bronze statue of Lenin in a theatre lobby:

A statue of Lenin, one of the most effective in Leningrad, the right arm and hand outstretched and in the eyes a look both piercing and genial, at once as if he were giving back to labor what it had made and inviting it to share for the first time in its heritage of human culture, and as if he were opening out to humanity as a whole a future of which for the first time they were to recognize themselves the masters, with the power to create without fear whatever they have minds to imagine.

Mr. Wilson has defended this passage against my interpretation; but I submit again that it is the most eloquent eyeful ever taken down stenographically. No dead bronze orbs have ever before lectured an onlooker at such length and in such elaborate detail. I submit we are correct in guessing that their message was a direct crib from the observer's mind.

It is essential to recognize such efforts by visiting believers to salvage their imported faith. They help explain many of the fervent reports from Mecca. Always the believer found some symbol to mirror his own thoughts. Less subtle visitors than Mr. Wilson seized upon grosser symbols: a day nursery, a row of houses, a model prison, a street scene in which citizens help a policeman untangle the traffic. I have seen the beauty of a Caucasian landscape, the equalitarian shabbiness of a city crowd, the traditional singing of Russian soldiers while marching, hailed excitedly as final proofs of the rightness of Marx and the wisdom of Stalin.

Thus, in a crescendo of enthusiasm, the American liberals molded their myth. I do not want to imply that they were consciously dishonest. The process was too intricate for any such pat moral judgments. For the most part they sought, like cornered animals, to escape from the wreckage of their complacent past, now that prosperity was in ruins. Russia offered a convenient gateway to hope.

No such justification, however, can be advanced for the group of writers, professional Russian specialists, who were most influential in discovering Utopia for the liberals. Though they knew some if not all of the reality, they were content to rest their case on official documents, statistics, promises. Ignazio Silone has coined the phrase "juridical cretinism" to describe a mental condition in which the afflicted prefer documents, laws and figures to the living truth all around them. The phrase applies to the believing readers of such books and articles even more than to the writers.

We may exempt from the definition out-and-out communists who, as they sometimes admitted, "sacrificed the truth for the cause." In the famine year of 1932, for example, Joseph Freeman, then a leader of the communist literati, published *The Soviet Worker,* an idyllic picture of life in Russia based wholly on official claims. Its descriptions of the happy frolicsome Russians sounded to us in the heart of Utopia like a deliberate joke intended to taunt and bait the sufferers. The whole thing rested on the assumption that every last statistic issued by Moscow was a scientifically checked fact, and on the even more egregious assumption that every Soviet ruble was worth 50 American cents, though its purchasing power (when there was anything to purchase) was between two and three cents. Long after Mr. Freeman himself would have repudiated such a literary atrocity, his book was making converts among young people in American schools.

But there were those others, denying truthfully that they were communists, yet for psychological or other reasons of their own, acting in effect as mouthpieces for the Kremlin.

Chapter XI

APOLOGISTS DO THEIR STUFF

1

THOUSANDS if not tens of thousands of Americans "found" Russia through the ministrations of Maurice Hindus. The Russia they found was populated by earthy and terribly talkative peasants (mostly from Mr. Hindus' native White Russian village) and rather theatrical proletarians—all engaged continually and self-consciously in being uprooted, socialized, awakened, and generally revised by force for the great future that awaited them beyond their present sorrows. It was a Dostoievsky country with a few dashes of Edgar Guest and Horatio Alger, and on the whole the customers came to like the place. It had such a vast soul and was so sad and so hopeful.

Mr. Hindus wears a poetic coiffure, a permanently pained expression and a preoccupied air. He plainly suffers. The suffering is on every page of his writing, where he swings from earthy sentimentality to sad but ecstatic visions of nirvana-to-come. Other apologists for Stalinism may have enjoyed their job, but Mr. Hindus, I was always convinced, wept inwardly for the victims of his historical necessities. He could "take it," and make his readers "take it," only by concentrating on the paradise beyond the immediate purgatory. In writing a book which, for all its labored alibis for the Stalin clique, reveals a lot of incidental butchery, Mr. Hindus was constrained to exclaim: "And yet like the tide of the ocean in the midst of wind and storm the Revolution continues to roll on and on."

A disingenuous platitude? It might sound like that to strangers. But we who knew the author doubted not that it was the cry of an aching heart—a consolation for others and above all for himself. We had watched him wring his hands, as it were, over the things he had seen on the last trip to his native village. We could understand, therefore, how greatly he must have suffered in adjusting those things for his liberal American following. Their stomachs, he knew, were too weak for the unadulterated facts, and he would be the last man to force indigestion upon them.

114

Mr. Hindus' success as a writer and lecturer depended on his subject more than on his talents, though the latter are considerable. It was primarily as a Soviet specialist that he lived and prospered, so that exclusion from Russia might be a personal disaster for him. But those considerations, I am certain, were not conscious factors in curbing his pen. It was rather that he suffered so much for the murdered revolutionary dream that he had to tell himself over and over again, "Despite everything, it's still alive. It must be alive. It's rolling on and on. . . ." I once saw a movie on the analogous theme: a mother who pretended that her dead son was still alive, and set the table for him every evening. Mr. Hindus after his every Soviet journey set the table for the departed communism.

He wrote *The Great Offensive* at the very end of the famine of 1932-33. It abounds with reportorial equivocation. Yet I stand ready to testify that it is but another proof of his kind heart. After the glowing pictures of Utopia a-borning in previous books and lectures, he simply could not let his audience down by giving them the horror straight. So he diluted it, scattered it, avoided unlovely words. About two years later he would give a stronger dose, actually referring to "at least three million" famine corpses. Ultimately he would pour out the whole bitter medicine without restraint. But not now, not now— this was 1933 and his book had to spare readers unnecessary pain.

So he skirted around the famine with a coy earnestness and with every evidence of embarrassment, like an old-fashioned mamma hiding the facts of life from little Betty. Those who knew the facts would understand he was talking about the famine, but the others would retain their pristine innocence. "If since the beginning of 1929 the food situation has been steadily growing worse," he wrote, "with the winter and spring of 1932 and 1933 bringing distress and privation to the North Caucasus, to parts of the Ukraine and to Kazakstan, the fault is not of Russia but of the Russians . . ."

Thus he gave the dates and the geographical position of the stricken area, but with a nice consideration for the feelings of his readers he avoided the use of the nasty word famine. "Distress" and "privation" served as substitutes. He kept returning guiltily to the scene of his suffering, but by sheer will power prevented himself from mentioning you-know-what. Just a few hints of horror, thrice removed. He wrote of "the wounds" that "mismanagement and mistreatment from above and below have inflicted on the collectives, especially in the Ukraine and in the North Caucasus." He chided the Bolshevik chiefs for their heartless policies. He may even have sounded to himself, as his typewriter rattled under his peasant fingers, like the voice of the afflicted *moujiks* crying for justice as the Revolution rolled on and on. But nary a candid word about the famine.

The pity of it is that his large audience, being a literal lot, got none of the hints. For years they continued to cite Mr. Hindus' book as proof that there had been no great famine. "Distress" and "privation," "mistakes" and "mismanagement," but assuredly no such major catastrophe as the one Chamberlin and Lyons and others—all obviously subsidized by Hearst and the Mikado—were talking about. (As late as 1936 the *Daily Worker* editorially sneered at "the famine invented by Hearst and Lyons.") Little wonder that the long-suffering Mr. Hindus was shaken to his depths by a book like *Assignment in Utopia*. Why, he probably asked himself, must such cruelty be visited on innocent-minded Americans while the Revolution was still rolling on and on? In his disgust with the vandal he groped wildly for a bludgeon-epithet with which to floor the inconsiderate author and finally settled on "Dr. Goebbels." It was in a letter to—yes, you guessed it, dear reader—the *New Republic*.*

2

Louis Fischer, the *Nation's* eyes and ears in Utopia, did not go in for any of Mr. Hindus' bouts of public pain. His revolution rolled on less sentimentally, with fewer inhibitions, and strictly in the partyline ditches. If occasionally he implied that there were stains on Soviet perfection, it only served to fortify his standing as a neutral commentator. Once he suggested cautiously in an article that Joseph Stalin could be wrong. For months thereafter he boasted of that feat of daring, while waiting for the lightning to strike. One of the hilarities that enlivened our Muscovite existence was *Izvestia's* habit of quoting Mr. Fischer's *Nation* pieces as the views of a "bourgeois American economist." By some miracle of coincidence those views fitted exactly into *Izvestia's* views.

Mr. Fischer was the least squeamish of the Kremlin's foreign favorites. Though he started his career as political *litterateur* as a

---

* After the Hitler-Stalin pact Hindus, like droves of others, finally became openly critical of the Soviet dictatorship.

Zionist, he could record the Soviet liquidation of Zionists with the same calmness that he reported liquidations of Left or Right Deviationists, straying professors, rotten liberals and other unideological dogs. He relished most in life, even more than physical comfort, the sense of being close to the boys on top. He fairly glowed with the knowledge that Soviet officialdom accepted him as one of its very own. In private conversation, as in his writing, he liked to mention casually that he had just been consulted by Chicherin or Litvinov or Radek. There was always the suggestion in his manner that even The Mightiest of All was aware of his, Fischer's, existence.

Once he was betrayed briefly by sentiment. That was when he associated too closely with followers of Leon Trotsky. On my way into Russia in January, 1928, the Berlin correspondent of the Moscow *Izvestia* warned me in a friendly spirit to avoid Mr. Fischer because he was suspected of maintaining contacts with the infidels. But when the Trotskyists were clearly licked, Mr. Fischer quickly retrieved his place within the aroma of power. He outdid all other foreigners in Moscow thereafter in his attacks on Beelzebub and his fallen angels. It was no fault of his own, surely, that his two-volume history of Soviet foreign affairs was never published in Russian translation. Even Chicherin had rebuked him in connection with this book, saying that he "writes like a Stalinist." But evidently there were still crumbs of heresy on its table of contents.

The famine, being the most sinister skeleton in Stalin's closet, may serve as a test of any man's writing. How did Mr. Fischer handle it? Neither during the famine nor for years after did he take his readers completely into confidence on the subject, leaving them self-righteously indignant against those who mentioned the "invention." His book *Soviet Journey* was published in 1935, three years after the event. It actually refers twice to "the 1932 famine." Time had passed, nearly everybody in Moscow was mentioning the skeleton out loud by then, and Mr. Fischer could be no less bold. But you will search the book in vain for a straightforward, specific and detailed description of the catastrophe, for an estimate of deaths and damage, for any other precise information that might reasonably be expected from an authoritative writer. Having casually admitted a major event which he had somehow overlooked when it was taking place, he now skipped any elaboration of the facts, limiting himself instead to this extraordinary apology for its perpetrators:

The peasants accordingly sabotaged—and had nothing to eat. It was a terrible lesson at a terrific cost. History can be cruel. . . . The peasants wanted to destroy collectivization. The government wanted to retain collectivization. The peasants used the best means at their disposal. The government used the best means at its disposal. The government won.

Can anything be simpler and neater? Some forty million Russians, after being "successfully" and "voluntarily" collectivized in issue after issue of the *Nation*, turn out to have been engaged in a war against the government instead! They seem to have used the weapons of passive resistance and non-co-operation which the *Nation* and its kind found so noble when used by peasants in India. And there is nobility in the spectacle of millions of simple people preferring the risk of death to submission to what they consider injustice.

I shall not pause to argue the illogic of the cozy interpretation of a popular national revulsion against systematic cruelty in terms of a street-corner brawl. I mean only to point out that here was an admission of the famine, a recognition that it was man-made, which yet left the controversy hazy. It failed to say with an open mouth, "Yes, Hearst is right—there was a man-made famine and it did take millions of lives." Perhaps it would then have been less easy to add, as he did in the book with a straight face: "Slowly the peasants are beginning to see the advantages of collective effort."

On a later occasion Mr. Fischer collaborated with his magazine in a piece of journalism, again with reference to the famine, that deserves recording. The Hearst press had published a series of articles and photographs purporting to be about the Russian famine. The stuff was so patently doctored that someone must have put it over on an overanxious editor. For instance, the famine was placed in 1934 instead of 1932-33. Mr. Fischer quite legitimately exposed the series in a *Nation* article (March 13, 1935). However, he merely conveyed the impression that there had been no famine at all!

Nowhere did the article disclose that, though the Hearst series was false, the famine was not a Hearst invention; that though it had not occurred in 1934, it had occurred a year earlier. Mr. Fischer declared that he was himself in the Ukraine in 1934 and saw no famine, and that another newspaper man who visited the region, likewise in 1934, saw no famine. He did not add that had those journeys been made in the winter of 1932-33 they would have seen plenty of famine. The dispute as to whether there had been a famine at all was still noisily under way in liberal quarters. That kind of refutation, I submit, was considerably worse than the publication by the Hearst press. It was what lawyers call a "negative pregnant," and under any name unfair to the readers.

Incidentally, this is a convenient spot to state that, for all their exaggerations, the Hearst newspapers were nearly the only ones at that time which told the facts about Russia. Their excesses in one direction were mild compared with the excesses of the *Daily Worker*, the *New Masses* and the liberal weeklies in the other direction. Many of those who finally wrote their Russian memories or impressions for the Hearst dailies had first tried desperately but without success to obtain publication in other newspapers and magazines. Everywhere they had been turned away with platitudes about not wishing to "attack Russia." It did not occur to those editors that an installment of truth as a counterweight to the liberal raptures might be a defense of Russia and its people.

One more sample of Mr. Fischer's methods must suffice. Only those aware of the staggering brutality of the concentration camps, the millionfold liquidations of peasants, the forced labor under G.P.U. aegis, can appreciate this to the full. He wrote happily of that whole ugly process as a "cure through labor" and added:

The G.P.U., in fact, has administered this "cure" to untold myriads in all parts of the country. The G.P.U. is not only an intelligence service and militia. It is a vast industrial organization and a big educational institution.

Hallelujah! More "untold myriads" having fun in all parts of the country with the benevolent help of G.P.U. sadists. I suggest that in any future editions of the books of the Tchernavins and Solonevich, this citation from Mr. Fischer should be used as frontispiece. Euphemism has rarely been carried to such an unsavory extreme. For a deeper appreciation of this description of the G.P.U. under Yagoda we must place it side by side with Fischer's words on the same subject six years later, after he, too, had renounced the Soviet Utopia with reservations-just-in-case. In an autobiography he would tell how, driven by a torturing "passion for truth," he had dug deep beneath the Soviet surface and made profound analyses. After seventeen years of these Herculean labors he came up, grim and grimy, with the vast discovery that Soviet Russia is a dictatorship and Stalin a tyrant! But incidentally he revealed that when he praised Yagoda's academy he was only pulling the liberals' legs. As a matter of fact, he wrote in 1941, he had always hated the G.P.U. and its works and all Russians had hated them likewise. Also: "During the years he had tortured Russia as head of the G.P.U., Yagoda executed, exiled and arrested millions of men, women and children."

Why he kept that little secret so long, concealing it under the label of "educational institution," we shall not know until his next book appears. Mr. Fischer's self-restraint in such matters is truly magnificent. By 1936, he now writes, he had finally given up Stalinism as a bad job. He was "tormented" by what was happening. It was "making him sick." Did he rush to the typewriter to share his sufferings with the Nation and Town Hall audiences which doted on his words? Not at all. Like other martyrs in other ages, he took a vow of silence which he did not break—except to praise the works of Stalin in Spain and to attack those who doubted the validity of the blood purges in Russia—for more than three years! Thus for three years longer his votaries were spared the pangs of doubt and disillusionment. Rarely has literary self-denial been carried that far.

3

Anna Louise Strong arrived at my office in Moscow one afternoon in a state of agitation. What had I done to her poor father? Well, I had merely talked to him, frankly but with considerable restraint, about subjects on which he asked for information. Being a sensitive and frail person, it had apparently been too much for the man's constitution, and he had taken to bed. Miss Strong therefore wanted a favor and a promise, to which I agreed gladly and rather contritely. I would not tell her father any more disturbing truths while he remained in Moscow. . . .

Miss Strong, like her father, is sensitive on these matters. She is not one-tenth part as cocksure and ruthless about the sad Soviet business as she seems to be in books and on the platform. Under her social worker's zeal burns a Puritan conscience. Again and again the impact of Soviet life has been hard on her nerves. I recall days when she sat

in my office, on returning from a trip outside Moscow, in a condition
of spiritual near-collapse. The mountainous confusions, sorrows, and
brutalities were too much for her. Her Junoesque person quivered with
honest emotion.

But always her sense of duty triumphed over these sensibilities.
The poor blundering revolution needed her mothering and understanding. Bravely she strode to a typewriter and indited another paean of
joy for "the achievements" of Stalin. Her whole emotional life was
invested in this Russia. She could not go back on it. At all costs she
must rationalize the facts themselves and rationalize the need for
withholding these facts from those with too little understanding in her
native America.

In *This Soviet World* she came dangerously near to confessing that
she was concealing things from the readers:

I tell not the "whole truth," for truth is never "whole"; there are
always at least two truths, the truth that is dying and the truth that is
coming into existence.

In a pious concern for the unborn truths, she helped the dying ones
to their appointed graves. In handling the same famine, for instance,
she avoided even the inept denials and evasions of other apologists. A
hint so remote that only a perspicacious insider could know what she
meant was quite sufficient for her purposes. Indeed, in *This Soviet
World*, much of it given over to the peasant problem, the famine was
reduced to a mere footnote, in tiny type, in the course of a discussion
of censorship:

The most striking recent example was the suppression of information during the difficult year of 1932, a suppression which turned
several American journalists permanently against the Soviets. The
Soviets believed with some reason that detailed knowledge of their
difficulties would provoke the threatened Japanese invasion.

And not another word about the famine in the entire volume! In
the quoted footnote Miss Strong's implication is that the suppression
of the facts *rather than the facts themselves* turned the journalists. I
am one of the journalists involved and had discussed the matter with
her repeatedly. She therefore knew full well that it was the horror of

the millions of corpses in a human slaughterhouse that went against my grain, not the fact that we were confined to Moscow for the duration of the great killing. A further implication is that while she, these journalists, and a hundred million Soviet citizens knew all about the famine, the simple-minded and trusting Japanese embassy people, correspondents and spies were being fooled! And to cap it all, Miss Strong, having hinted at a story, fails to tell what precisely dangerous information was suppressed, and why she was continuing to ignore it in her book now that the Japanese Ambassador had found it out.

<h2 style="text-align:center">4</h2>

The case of Walter Duranty of the New York Times is too complex for treatment in brief. I can no more than touch it. Unlike the others who took their line dutifully from the official viewpoints, he did not pretend to be favorably disposed to the enterprise or in the slightest interested in its ultimate success.

Mr. Duranty had that peculiarly disdainful attitude toward the masses that one finds among some middle-class Britishers—a kind of colonial distaste for "natives." I have already quoted his celebrated passage about Russians being fitted only for "Asiatic absolutism." The perpetual marvel, for him, seemed to be that certain Russians in power were fairly intelligent and almost human—despite the fact that they were natives. His readers overseas could not understand that his refusal to be perturbed by mounting horrors in Russia was at least in part an expression of his low opinion of the victims. At moments when the rest of us might be shaken by some calamity involving vast suffering, Duranty remained urbanely calm. He thus got himself a world-wide reputation as "a friend of the Soviets" based largely on his superior attitude toward the Soviet people and disinterest in the whole Bolshevik business.

His role as the understanding friend of the Bolsheviks had brought him fame, and he stuck to it. He was pretty candid on that score—none of your Fischer-Hindus type of identification with Bolshevism. The identification was purely professional. His own explanation for his failure to react to Russian horrors is that his war experiences had left him immune to such things. Curiously, though, he grew downright maudlin when those who suffered were people closer to his own kind—in the chapter of his autobiographical I Write As I Please, for instance, where he told in sentimental detail the tragedy of Isadora Duncan and the death of her children.

In the same book he took a crack at reporters who indulged in "moral judgments"—those who "prate of ruthless methods and the iron age and lament the brutality which drove through to its goal regardless of sacrifice and suffering." Duranty is too clever not to realize that ignoring ruthless methods or their consequences in human blood also implies moral judgments, though on another plane. If being moved by mass suffering is bad reporting, pretending to look upon it in terms of the vivisection of animals (as he did on page 304) seems to some of us even worse reporting.

"I'm a reporter, not a humanitarian," he boasted. "I had no intention of being an apologist for the Stalin administration," he added farther on. All the same, he admitted in relation to the iron age: "I allowed my critical faculty to lapse and failed to pay proper attention to the cost and immediate consequences of the policies that I had foreseen. . . . I had tried to make myself think like a true-blue Stalinist in order to find out what true-blue Stalinists were thinking, and had succeeded too well." In plainer English, his dispatches were written from the true-blue Stalinist angle. And the humor of it is that the most capitalist paper in America paid the cable tolls, and that the true-blue Stalinist version won a capitalistic Pulitzer Prize for foreign correspondence. . . .

In *I Write As I Please*, a book of over 300 pages, only about 30 pages are devoted to the crucial Russian years between 1928 and 1934, when it was written. Those were the most cruel, heartbreaking years; they comprised about half of Duranty's total Soviet experience at the time; yet he gave about 10 per cent of the space to it and the rest to the relatively pleasanter previous period. This lack of proportion, too, implies a moral judgment, if only negatively—a slurring over horror, whereby the true-blue ones are not too sharply discomfited.

Of all his elliptical writing, perhaps his handling of the famine was most celebrated. It was the logical extreme of his oft-repeated assertion that "you can't make an omelet without breaking eggs." Now he made his omelet by referring to the famine as "undernourishment" and to its consequences as deaths due to "the diseases of malnutrition."

Duranty's score on wrong guesses on Russia is exceeded only by people like Hindus, Fischer and Miss Strong. He began way back, in the earliest years, with those notorious dispatches out of Riga in which Lenin and Trotsky were shooting one another about once a week. He concluded with Dostoievskian explanations of the Moscow trials, when Stalin finally came around to making good on the Riga reports by really shooting a lot of Old Bolsheviks. In between he was the prophet of the chronic "improvement" and "progress" around the corner, which somehow never did turn the corner. Like Fischer, he went all-out in hailing the advent of "democracy" under the Stalin Constitution.

That document, he wrote in the Sunday Times of July 19, 1936, "is an outward and visible sign of an inward and spiritual change in the Russian people and its leaders. . . . In this nineteenth year of the Soviet State, there is introduced a new Constitution, under which the Russian masses emerge from their tutelage and are called upon to receive their rights and undertake their duties as a free and democratic people." This on the very eve of the bloodiest period in Russia's history and the final confirmation of Russia's emergence as a totalitarian state! "External enemies are no longer feared and internal enemies have been defeated and scotched, if not totally eliminated," he concluded. The "confessions" were being extorted in G.P.U. cellars while Duranty indited these words.

The Times paid the bill for this strange reporting. The mischief of it was that Duranty's dispatches, in all these years of the building of the great Russian myth, had a resonance and authority which they would have lacked in the Daily Worker. The liberals had in his true-blue reports clinching corroboration of their self-deceptions.

5

The astonishing opus by Sidney and Beatrice Webb, Soviet Communism, a New Civilization?, was not published until 1936. But the octogenarian authors had been at work on it for several years before that, and a note on it belongs at this point. It was the Third Period that they celebrated, even if the work carried over into the Fourth.

The aged couple presented the world with a veritable academic monument to the new Russia. Two volumes, nearly 1200 pages, thousands of footnotes and documentary citations, detailed analyses and the piling up of authorities. No wonder the liberal and even a few of the more conservative reviewers went overboard. Professor Counts spoke for them all when he called it, in the New York Herald Tribune,

"a work incomparably superior to anything else in the field . . . ju-
dicious, scholarly, wise . . . as near that unattainable goal of telling 'the
truth about Russia' as any work is likely to do in this generation." The
Webbs' book had a tremendous influence on the Red Decade, since it
provided a "professorial" refutation to the "libels" against Utopia.

But the Webbs' bulky treatise is as completely a work of the
imagination as Thomas More's or Bellamy's. In their old age the
couple apparently had decided to build themselves a cozy home for
their spirit. They used the raw stuff of official propaganda as bricks
and mortar and called the handiwork Soviet Communism. No communist in Russia would conceivably recognize the structure as more
than remotely related to his own country. But it was not written for
Russians—thousands of eager liberals in America and England were
likewise in need of spiritual vacations; they recognized it immediately
and took rooms under its capacious roof.

The Webbs had simply gathered all the official claims and documents and statistics, added the works of outsiders like Fischer, Hindus,
et al., thrown in a complete file of the Moscow Daily News, and organized it all into two huge tomes. They achieved a really impressive compendium of misinformation and ludicrous exaggeration on the subject
at hand. They "proved" that Stalin was not a dictator and his country
was not a dictatorship; that the deaths in 1932-33 were not "really" a
famine; that Russian villages enjoy "unprecedented freedom" not only
as compared to Czarist villages but to English villages.

Despite Stalin's own denunciation of brutal excesses in the liquidation of kulaks, the Webbs asserted coyly that "government persuasion"
and "something very like compulsion of hesitating peasants to join the
collectives" were used. They explained that "the only sanctions that
the [Communist] Party can use to control its members are those of
reprimand and expulsion; and these entail no legal disabilities." What
matter if the extra-legal sanctions include exile, imprisonment and
summary execution? Such things do not affect liberals afflicted with
"juridical cretinism." No Russian propagandist could have written
such a book. His sense of proportion would have acted as a brake.
The Webbs, writing honestly from the depths of their documented
and footnoted credulity, had no such inhibitions. They had the advantage of their high-minded innocence.

Imagine the shock to a fairly intelligent Russian worker were he to
discover that two reputable political economists treat the Tsik, the

Soviet "parliament," seriously as a governing body rather than a super-numerary rubber stamp. "In the end," the Webbs record of this legis-lative body, "the delegates unanimously give a general sanction to the outlines of policy and legislation expounded to them." Woe to the one delegate with a suicidal urge who dared vote "No" on those out-lines! The Webbs report of a "bill" that "it was enthusiastically adopted by the Congress, the whole of the delegates standing to give Molotov an ovation with no dissenting voice." If the day ever comes when a "dissenting voice" makes itself heard, the Webbs will have turned into prophets.

Perhaps the most precious remark in two volumes teeming with un-conscious humor refers to the appointment of a Constitutional Com-mission. It included, the authors say, Stalin, Kaganovich, Molotov, Litvinov, Bukharin and "other leading personalities of the Party, *rep-resenting all shades of opinion.*" The italics are mine, but they will be unnecessary to anyone halfway acquainted with the shadings of opinion in Stalin's party. The fact that about two-thirds of the members of the Commission have since then been liquidated by the firing squad or by exile may suggest the wide range of opinion allowed under Stalin.

Long sections of the "incomparably superior" masterpiece are given over to minute descriptions of administrative processes that exist only on paper and to rights and duties that had been dead letters for fifteen years. The essential facts—the sources of real power, the totali-tarian reality under the make-believe of constitutions, the effects of fear and hope—these the old couple did not even consider. "The control of party over the administration is not manifested in any commands en-forceable by law on the ordinary citizen," they let it be known. The fact that it is enforceable without law is presumably quibbling.

It is as though some foreign professors had made a minute ex-amination of government in New York in the period of Boss Murphy and limited their story to what they could learn from the charter of the city and the disclaimers of Mr. Murphy. To carry out the parallel the professor would have to go to documents written long before the Murphy regime, since the Webbs treat all laudatory books on Russia as applying currently, even if they were written in the pre-Stalin era.

The Webbs gave generous space to proving that the Soviet system represented "real" democracy, and stressed those features of Soviet-type elections which differentiated them from the bogus democracy of England and America. A couple of years later a new edition of their opus was issued. In the interim, that Soviet-type voting had been displaced by the bogus kind, with the exception that only one party appeared on the ballot. In the interim, too, the bloodletting of the purges had taken place, in the course of which dozens of the men and women praised by the aged authors had been officially murdered. Did all that affect their second edition? Yes, to the extent that they removed the question mark in the subtitle of their masterpiece, which now read Soviet Communism, a New Civilization. Period. The question mark had been washed out in blood. Lenin had spared no epithets in his day in belaboring the Webbs, whom he despised without restraint. Perhaps their book stands as an unconscious vengeance.

Faith in the Soviet Utopia has been the foundation of American Bolshevism. The Webbs, Duranty, Miss Strong, Fischer, Hindus and a host of other professional and amateur artisans collaborated to provide that foundation and to keep it in continuous repair, as shock after shock out of the Kremlin threatened to shatter the structure.

The latest artisan who deserves to rank with the fabulous Webbs, is Hewlett Johnson, the Dean of Canterbury. On the basis of tourist inspection, the good Dean wrote Soviet Power. He described a country "truly Christian in spirit"; a country of "complete equality," "new humanism," "a new form of democracy"; a country marked by "the absence of fear," where "prices steadily fall and wages rise." In that country every ruble is worth its official valuation of 20 American cents,* even if it can only buy two cents' worth. Every page of that volume attests the ecclesiastic's kind heart and strange mind. Considering the Webbs, the pro-Soviet Bernard Shaw and the Dean, can it be that extreme addiction to the Russian myth is a disease of the aged in England?

---

* For many years the Soviet Government insisted that its currency was stable, at about 50 American cents to the ruble and, after the devaluation of the dollar, at about 100 cents. But suddenly it "stabilized" its "stable" currency at 20 American cents.

Chapter XII

THE RED CULTURAL RENAISSANCE

1

IF A history of high-brow lunacies in these United States is ever written, it will of necessity devote a large part of its space to the strange career, roughly between 1930 and 1935, of Proletarian Culture, known familiarly to its caretakers as Proletcult. The noisiest of the litter were "proletarian criticism" and "proletarian literature," but there were also queer pups known as proletarian theatre, cinema, painting, sculpture, music, dancing, and so on. In this freehand sketch of their lives for the future historian I limit myself largely to the literary phase, because in the nature of the case it is the most readily accessible. But the pattern of shrill, bombastic and self-important make-believe holds no less true for the other "proletarian" arts.

What made them queer, among other things, was the fact that the proletariat was snugly oblivious to the whole pother. Indeed, it was oblivious to the fact that it was a proletariat. This made a lot of the middle-class converts sore and sad. Theodore Dreiser sneered in print at "a people that is almost wholly interested in ball games, golf, tennis, prize fights, the movies, flag-waving and bootlegging." Edmund Wilson noted "the ignorance, the stupidity, and the short-sighted selfishness of the mass."

The proletarian artists, however, made up for this lack by portraying—in paint, words, stage characters or dance rhythms—the idealized "workers" of their fond imaginations: tall men with immense biceps and squat women with buttocks like mountains, robust and rough-hewn and chanting of sweat and blood, of revolution and dialectics. Some of the artists went down to miners' districts and wrote angry poetry or prose about the horrible facts of life they were discovering so belatedly. Their work was not bad, on occasion, but the assumption that they were the first to discover poverty and inequality was, at least, extraordinary.

For all that, the artists, critics, professors and ballet dancers who

128

"went Left" in the proletarian epidemic were the same middle-class folk performing for the same middle-class audiences as before the great mass conversions. Many of them had been through fashionable types of exhibitionism in the previous decade—dadaism, surrealism, symbolism, lost-generation antics and what not. They had climbed into ivory towers fitted out with bars and seductive couches and looked down only to sneer at the madding crowd. They had defied the bourgeoisie with lower-case letters, stuttering sentences and chopped-up female torsos scattered on canvases. All of them now sensed the dissonance between their gin-drinking self-indulgence and the grim Depression world. Besides, mostly they could no longer afford that sort of existence; the bill collectors found them in the loftiest ivory tower.

So, singly and in packs they migrated from the Left Bank of Paris to the political Left of Moscow. They abandoned prosperity bohemianism for proletarian bohemianism. With the egocentric yowling of their species they rushed into intellectual slumming as heatedly as they had gone in for slummy intellectualism. A lot of humdrum novelists and academic grinds joined the general migration. Newton Arvin, Granville Hicks and other college instructors "discovered" the sociological approach to culture, though the approach had long been routine procedure on the Left. A lot of budding and a few overripe novel writers suddenly became interested in the plain people, and got all puffed up over their new virtue, as though Upton Sinclair, Jack London, William Dean Howells and a lot of others had never written. And above all Proletcult beckoned to droves of third-rate writers, singers, dancers, critics who recognized the drift as a short cut to recognition and ready-made audiences. Mediocrity for once seemed very like a special artistic merit.

Without doubt there were men and women of talent among the migrants. The fact alone that they counted John Dos Passos, Edmund Wilson, Waldo Frank, Sherwood Anderson, Theodore Dreiser, and younger men like James T. Farrell, Philip Rhav, Erskine Caldwell, etc., is proof of this. But the gifted were smothered by the proletarian phonies, by politicians legislating for artists, artists pretending to be "dialecticians," communist sycophants and logrollers. Despite the admixture of genuine artistic and moral values, it all added up to a noisy and nonsensical circus.

What made escape from reality to the Left easy—too easy to be genuine—was that it involved for the converts no exacting novitiate.

A mere declaration of faith sufficed to turn an intellectual playgirl into a proletarian prima donna. It was enough to "accept" communism or to "approach" the Marxian ideology, or simply to join up with a John Reed Club, a Theatre of Action, the Red Dancers or some other Proletcult catchall.

The overnight "proletarians" did not have to sweat or suffer over the creation of a philosophy or a new code of artistic conduct for themselves. Whether they joined the Communist Party outright, or attached themselves to its fringes, their "proletarian" instructions were waiting for them, worked out in elaborate "do's" and "don'ts" direct from Moscow. The "proletarian renaissance" was about as American as the rest of the "revolutionary upsurge" of these years. The same sort of Proletcult circuses, with the same tricks and the same ballyhoo, surged up at exactly the same time in Germany, France, England, Australia—wherever the Comintern had its branch offices—and in each place followed the identical zigzags of slogans and programs. That alone is proof that the movement was not indigenous to any of these countries.

More impressive and unlovely proof is provided by the spineless way in which the caretakers of Proletcult kowtowed to Moscow. Though individual fellow-travelers in the more distant fringes might not have been aware of it, the movement was as subordinated to the International Union of Revolutionary Writers as the TUUL was subordinate to the Profintern. In both instances all decrees were issued by Russians in Russia, without a legal appeal being left open to the non-Soviet Proletculters. The amazing story was told brilliantly in its day by Max Eastman in *Artists in Uniform*.

At the end of 1930 a congress of the "proletarian culture" crowd was staged in Kharkov, Russia. I have read its proceedings. The delegates, a few of them from the United States, took themselves very seriously, but saw themselves only as soldiers in the various campaigns ordered by the Kremlin—principally, of course, the campaign to "defend the Soviet Union" against "imperialist intervention." With masochistic relish they crawled on their bellies before the image of Stalin, as they pledged in chorus to obey the artistic edicts issued by his chosen literary mercenaries. Chief among the latter was a Comrade Leopold Auerbach, a third-rate journalist married into the family of the G.P.U. chief, Henry Yagoda, and behaving like a Stalin of the Arts.

The foreigners at Kharkov promised to "overcome their petty bourgeois character and accept the viewpoint of the proletariat," and to help others afflicted by the same disease to achieve a similar cure. They agreed that "art is a weapon" in the class war and that it should be used under the "careful yet firm guidance of the Communist Party." The proceedings were under the aegis of the Russian writers' organization, abbreviated as RAPP, which had for a great many years exercised a ruthless terror in the Soviet cultural fields. The delegates scattered to bring the glad tidings of RAPP and its creed of soldier-artists to their respective countries. The American contingent, captained by one Michael Gold, a slightly hysterical editor of the New Masses, went home with what they described as a "Program of Action for the United States, intended to guide every phase of our work." The cream of the jest is that a large number of otherwise sane writers and critics promptly put themselves in the RAPP harness and thrilled to the sensation of "collective" reins.

2

Did Edmund Wilson, Waldo Frank, Clifton Fadiman, John Chamberlain, and a lot of others know what they were affiliating with when they put on the harness? The fact that they wriggled out of it in time is circumstantial proof that they were innocent. The same can scarcely be said for Gold, Joseph Freeman, A. B. Magil, Granville Hicks, Isidor Schneider and others in the inner circle of communist "guides" of the proletarian renaissance. These must have known that RAPP, which dominated the whole world-wide Proletcult racket, had for many years and with increasing brutality crushed the spirit and even the lives of Russian writers and artists.

Here is what one of the Kremlin's most enthusiastic friends of the time, Louis Fischer, had to say about RAPP in the New York Herald Tribune, November 27, 1932:

If RAPP frowned on a writer, his career was crippled. It persecuted the fellow-travelers, or popuchiki, with a bitterness and relentlessness which merely indicated that it had no respect for art. . . . RAPP drove brilliant literary figures into silence. . . . Literature, and the cinema and theatre too, were paralyzed by the reign of RAPP. . . .

And this was the master under whose whip the American pseudo-proletarian culturists placed themselves so joyously. The RAPP leaders were the ones who sent the "directives" from Moscow which became law for the American Leftist in the arts. Fischer's indictment is far from harsh. A number of the leading Soviet novelists, poets, playwrights and cinema scenarists were among my Moscow friends. I can attest personally that they lived in a state of continuous fear, squelched their creative impulses, waiting for the inevitable day when the artistic inquisition would pounce on them for some word or gesture and crush them forever. Only the expert sycophants and literary politicians knew how to pick the plums; persecution of their more honest and more gifted fellows was their principal occupation.

Mr. Fischer allowed himself to criticize the sacred Stalinist inquisition only after Stalin himself had done so. In the nine years before that, neither he nor any other Stalinist had opened his mouth in defense of the persecuted artists, some of whom were hounded literally to death. In abolishing RAPP, however, Stalin acted the absolutist tyrant no less than he had done in keeping it going. He consulted no one. Auerbach and the other sub-dictators did not know that the blow was descending until it came crashing down. The end of RAPP was as obscene as its life.

The American "proletarians" of the arts, who until April 17, 1932, had obeyed every Auerbach edict, now joined in calling him filthy names; ultimately they would join in acclaiming his execution. But the post-RAPP regime was as stupidly sectarian, as arbitrarily Russian, as the one it superseded. The change was largely in names. Having lived in Moscow throughout this time, I am able to confirm that honest writing or creative effort in any other art remained the equivalent of suicide. The foreign Proletcult legions followed blindly, parroting the meaningless slogans: "socialist realism," "red romanticism," "conquest of literature," "Magnitostrois of art," "Five Year Plan of culture," ad nauseam. The writer, as Farrell said in a satire after deserting the circus, had full freedom, except that he must be "a Marxist-Leninist-Stalinist-socialist-realist." Only the Moscow literary hierarchy had the right to judge whether a given writer was or was not within the hyphenated area, and the New Masses was its megaphone.

3

In undialectic defiance of the simplest Marxist precepts, the capitalist press gave the neo-proletarians the widest leeway in using their new "class weapon" to attack their employers' system. Whether it bespeaks obtuseness or excessive self-confidence on the part of publishers I dare not decide. The simple fact is that for many years the New York *Times*, the *Herald Tribune*, *Current History*, the *New Yorker* and many of the so-called class magazines used largely "proletarian" standards in measuring literature.

Lewis Gannett, John Chamberlain, Clifton Fadiman, Granville Hicks, Horace Gregory, Matthew Josephson, George S. Counts, Isidor Schneider, Max Lerner and any number of other converts to the "proletarian" cause had the run of book review areas; some of them conducted regular literary departments. (Fadiman and Chamberlain were among the first to regain their senses and confront Stalinism critically.) English and French literati like Harold Laski, John Strachey, Henri Barbusse, too, had ample space donated to them by their chosen enemy for delivering blow after blow. Since all of these gentry accepted approximately the same yardsticks and labels of approval or disapproval, the total effect was a kind of "proletarian" literary lobby. For any new or old writer the question became, in the main if not entirely, whether he "belonged" or was still among the unshriven.

Inept novels, like *Marching! Marching!* by Clara Weatherwax, dull theological stuff like *Proletarian Literature in the United States*, any prose chopped fine to look like verse and hailing the revolution in standard expletives, automatically rated raves in the class-conscious columns of the capitalist press. Indeed, anything that had the blessing of Gold, Freeman, Hicks, Magil and other *New Masses* stalwarts could not conceivably be ignored or belittled by more fashionable critics. Woe betide the "fascist"—or worse, the "social fascist,"—who took exception to the views of the commissars of letters.

"American literature, in the midst of its wanderings in the wilderness, has been struck by a proletarian bombshell," the late V. F. Calverton reported in his *Modern Quarterly*. Those struck showed all the effects of shell shock. They wrote long, complicated dissertations on the fine points of the creed: the proper and improper theme for literary treatment; the "up" books of hope and the "down" books of proletarian defeatism; art-as-propaganda and propaganda-as-art; the "individualistic" versus the "collectivist" hero; the "forward" novels and the "backward" ones. They guaranteed for themselves an enthusiastic critical reception by making their heroes miners or strike leaders and their heroines prostitutes. They demolished Thornton Wilder, H. L. Mencken, Sinclair Lewis and nearly everyone but their own coterie as dangerous carriers of the streptococci of "bourgeois ideology."

The pioneer of the critical "okies" was probably Edmund Wilson. Announcing that the Leftist intellectuals "must take communism away from the communists," he gave up his post as literary editor of the *New Republic*, a publication too bourgeois for his apostate's zeal. The irony of it is that he was succeeded by Malcolm Cowley, a man of lesser literary attainments who quickly became outspokenly Stalinoid. Long after Wilson had convalesced from the totalitarian rabies, Cowley was still under the affliction. In fact, he remained the Number One literary executioner for Stalin in America after the *New Republic* itself had edged away from socialism à la Kremlin.

It was an amazing show the circus put on, year after year. The *New Masses* oracles were ruthless to outsiders and firm with their own to keep them from straying. Dos Passos was reprimanded because he "has not sufficiently emphasized the strength of the working class." Caldwell was warned that he "very inadequately suggests the latent power of the Southern proletariat." Writers were condemned for "unconscious fascism" and conscious social fascism even when they thought they were doing all right.

Granville Hicks publicly did penance for having enjoyed Marcel Proust in the dark days before his conversion; in his new incarnation, he explained, such a thing could not have happened because "I feel within myself a definite resistance, a counter-emotion, so to speak, that makes a unified esthetic experience impossible" when confronted with a heretical author. Comrade Gold tried to crawl out of his infidel liking for Gilbert and Sullivan despite the fact that Gilbert was a Tory. "Such men," he admitted contritely, "are the 'cultural' pioneers of fascism." Donald Morrow reinterpreted Shakespeare to make him respectable in proletarian circles: "When all else is said of Shakespeare," he pontificated, "the fact remains that in expressing this class he belonged with the movement forward. His work, as the entire renaissance, was on the side of life." (This was after Russia had produced some of Shakespeare's works and thereby removed him from the *New Masses'* Index Expurgatorius.) Other classics were ruled out as on the side of death, though the less ruthless comrades found big-hearted formulas for recognizing Dostoievski and Wagner, Balzac and Goethe, though these were "reactionaries."

Musicians, like writers, had plenty to plague their awakened class consciences. Thus the *Daily Worker* brought to its readers the sad tale of one member of a symphony orchestra. In his own words, "what the hell is a poor musician going to do when he is a Bolshevik in thought and sympathy and a dumb director puts the score of *Life of the Czar* by Glinka on his stand for him to play?" This comrade knew, of course, that composer Glinka was a "bootlicker" of Czardom. To play him would be "siding with the Czar against Lenin." Of course he refused to betray the cause through his cornet—or kettledrum, or whatever it may have been—even if it cost him his job. Let the Glinkas and Tschaikovskys beware!

Overwhelmed by the shoddy stuff he must praise because it was 100 per cent proletarian, Hicks sought and found a consolation: "The reason why revolutionary writers so often seem clumsy is that they are trying to communicate the operation of what deserves to be called a new type of sensibility." But the reading public in its ignorance assumed that these self-styled revolutionaries seemed clumsy because they didn't know how to write. It did not occur to the Golds and Hickses that "revolutionary" is a misnomer for writers who meekly take orders from mentally underprivileged politicians acting as messenger boys for an uncouth Asiatic despot.

Once a little Soviet-bred girl visited my daughter in Moscow. She picked up one of those slick, beautifully illustrated American magazines. For a few minutes she gazed spellbound at the pictures of handsome men and beautiful women and American comforts in the advertisements. Then she closed it softly, pushed it from her, and avowed sadly, "I think I have petty bourgeois leanings." In just that spirit the militantly proletarian critics looked at works of beauty and pushed them away with Spartan self-denial for fear of "petty bourgeois leanings." With the same Spartan courage they praised dull stuff approved by the communists.

A poet, Freeman wrote, becomes more of a poet by writing about economic problems. Whether an economist becomes more of an economist by writing poetry he did not say. Jack Conroy told the world that to him "a strike bulletin or an impassioned leaflet are of more moment than three hundred prettily and faultlessly written pages" about society dames and their gigolos—evidently referring to Proust. Edwin Berry Burgum faced a poetic couplet by Stephen Spender in which the latter "watched the dawn explode like a shell around us, dazing us with its light like snow." And Burgum was moved to retort:

The passive position of watching the dawn is hardly fitting to the revolutionary; nor should the dawn daze like snow those who under self-discipline have known what to expect and are ready for the next move.

Robert Gessner's unpoetic verse in *Upsurge* was hailed as poetry because it adhered to the party line and ignored dawns and moods. As the aforementioned Spender put it about these critics: "If the writer is ideologically sound, they express naïve surprise that his book is not readable, coupled with heartfelt hopes that the proletariat will soon do better." The youthful Fadiman, on his proletarian way-station on the highroad to "Information Please," delivered himself of mouthfuls like this:

Mr. Wilson represents a small but growing class of bourgeois intellectuals who are gradually (with varying tempos) realizing that, outside the revolutionary movement, there is no place for them, either as wage-earners or as thinking men and women. . . . By temperament and training he is splendidly equipped to open the eyes of those members of his own class who are lagging behind him.

Henry Alexander greeted Robert Briffault's *Breakdown* rapturously because the author was "one of the first important scientists to go communist." Tangled in his rhetoric but righteous in his jubilation, Alexander went on: "By dint of sheer thinking and logic, Briffault, an intellectual descendant of the days of Herbert Spencer, has cut and arrived at a revolutionary position . . . etc." And the brave Briffault himself, in an article on "Fellow-Travelers" in the *Modern Quarterly*, attacked those who dared object to mass slaughter in Russia, shouting to all who would listen:

It scarcely becomes putative sociologists and economists whose achievements amount to exactly nothing but a pissmire of fatuous blather to affect airs of judicial superiority in the matter.

Some of his bile in the same article is unfit for quotation in a book that will be seen by proletarian typesetters if no one else. Stalin's neat way of killing off other revolutionaries, among them Bolsheviks, moved Dr. Briffault to such noble sentiments as these:

When theory passed into action most of those high-minded gentlemen, had, in self-defense, to be invited to take a bath in the Neva or to line up against a wall for liquidation in order to protect from their sabotage those noble sentiments they had been so eloquent in announcing.

The temptation is to go on quoting. But perhaps I have quoted enough to indicate, at least, the bigotry and the hopeless fatuity of most of the "proletarian renaissance." Some of those I have mentioned managed to creep out of the ideological mire. A few of them are still scraping off the dirt. But for every one that escaped a hundred others took the plunge and found the warm ooze of it all—the lusty war cries, the comradely huddle, the collective mayhem on heretics, the cheering for mass murders in a far-off land—wholly to their taste. Only the fact that it was labeled revolutionary and proletarian kept the more timid souls from joining them in the primeval muds of totalitarian art. They waited for the Fourth Period, when words like "revolutionary" and "proletarian" would be displaced by "patriotic" and "democratic," before turning "communist."

4

The Proletcult enthusiasts needed organizations and periodicals to channel their revolutionary energies. The Communist Party provided them in ample number. In addition to the out-and-out party organs and party organizations, over and above the purely political or social enclosures built up at this time, there were the following exclusively "cultural" setups:

The John Reed Clubs, The Pen and Hammer, The Workers Film and Photo League, The Anvil, The Partisan Review, Left, Left Front, The Magazine, Left Review, New Theatre, Theatre Union, Workers Dance League, Theatre Collective, Theatre of Action, Pierre Degeyter Club, Workers Music League, The Music Vanguard, Red Dancers,

New Dance Group, Theatre Union Dance Group, The *Partisan*, *Blast*, *Dynamo*, Workers Laboratory Theatre, Leftward, American Revolutionary Dancers, *New Dance*, Harlem Prolets, New Duncan Dance Group, Vanguard Dance Group, Rebel Dancers, League of Workers Theatres, Labor Sports Union, etc., etc.

Most of these are no more. Others which had their ideological day and faded out have left almost no record of their passing. The more fashionable ones, like the John Reed Clubs, tended to swallow the lesser organizational fry, until they were in turn submerged in some new and more inclusive front. The Left theatre movements at certain stages of their lives got tangled in monetary success or were bled of talent by Hollywood raiders.

The network of cultural activities, with overlapping memberships, interlocking directorates, approximately the same audiences, was stretched or contracted, revised and patched, depending on the funds available to the party people who managed them all and the latest "directives" from headquarters. But there was so much of it, so various in its attractions, that it satisfied the cravings of a lot of young people and some older ones for gregarious excitement and mutual admiration. The surface dusting of "revolutionism" was less to the point than the sense of belonging to a special fraternity, with its own passwords and symbols and the backing of a great nation on the other side of the ocean.

Each of the organizations, each of the magazines, was a "weapon in the class war" and in mobilizing fighters the bars against infidels were gradually lowered. More and more "petty bourgeois" and reluctantly fellow-traveling folk were involved. With the control fast in the grip of party stalwarts, there was little danger of trouble. (Sometimes, of course, socialists and even anti-Stalin communists got in and, knowing the tricks of the trade, did cause the Stalinists some grief.)

A nucleus of party and near-party names appeared in all the organizational and editorial lists. Around them were grouped names of successful or up-and-coming practitioners and hangers-on of the arts. Whether it was a play, a dance, a painting, a magazine—the basic lines of Moscow's Third Period propaganda were so obvious that they needed no Sherlock Holmes to trace them. The glories of Stalin's country were contrasted with the evils of American life; American "militarists" were stoned while the Red Army was praised for its expanding power;

the "reformist" trade unions were damned and the "militant" unions under communist guidance were blessed; art was not art unless it contributed to the worship of Russia and the mobilization against the expected imperialist intervention.

The tens of thousands of Americans in every town and city who yearn for a theatrical career were especially vulnerable to the blandishments of the comrades. The names of Tairov and Meierhold became familiar to "little theatre" outfits throughout the land—remained familiar, ironically, after the theatres of both those Soviet innovators had been "liquidated." There were for the eager actors and burgeoning directors such varied outlets as the New Theatre League, comprising the Theatre of Action, Artef, Theatre Collective, Chicago Group Theatre, New Theatre Players of Hollywood, Negro People's Theatre of the South.

A National Theatre Conference of Leftish and innocent little theatre groups, summoned by communist leaders, met in New York in April, 1932. It founded the League of Workers Theatres as the American section of the International Union of Revolutionary Theatres with headquarters in Moscow. Thus the familiar pattern, here, as in every other field of Muscovite penetration. The American section proceeded to publish a magazine, Workers' Theatre, which by 1934 was retitled New Theatre, representing the Workers Dance League and the National Film and Photo League as well as the theatre setup. It soon became focal center for a lustily Stalinist faction on Broadway and in Hollywood.

The New Theatre boasted what is probably the largest group of "contributing editors" ever published at one time. Besides the party wheel horses it included Anita Block, Hallie Flanagan (subsequently head of the Federal Theatre Project), Virgil Geddes, Paul and Mrs. Paul Sifton, Jay Leyda, H. W. L. Dana, Langston Hughes, Robert Forsythe (Kyle Crichton), Muriel Rukeyser, etc. To leaf through the magazine pages is like revisiting the Soviet theatre world, so dominant is the Moscow note—reference to Moscow plays, directors, ideas. In fact, the issue of January, 1935, was an all-Soviet number, carrying this inscription:

This issue was printed in Moscow by Jay Leyda, with the assistance of Pearl Attasheva; Heinrich Diament, President of the International Union of Revolutionary Theatres; Anatoli Glebov; Sergei Eisenstein;

H. W. L. Dana; Sergei Tretyakov; Erwin Piscator; Leon Moussinac, film critic of *L'Humanité*; and Chen Iwan, art director of the Moscow *Daily News*.

It was the group around this magazine which was soon producing the New Theatre League plays, by Clifford Odets and others; conducting a New Theatre School; and hatching one "socially conscious" theatre project after another. The whole complex quickly became fashionable, if not among proletarians, at least among the well-to-do and the arty sets.

The approach to dancers, sculptors, painters was no more difficult. All of them are notoriously neglected and eager for contacts and audiences, and few of them have the political acumen to understand what they step into. The Workers Dance League, later altered to read New Dance League, made only one demand—that the terpsichorean hopefuls unwind "social" themes. That required, normally, only the alteration of the name of the dance and a little more staccato in the flings. An article in the anti-Stalinist *Vanguard*, signed by "David Lawrence," asserts:

At the height of its success the New Dance League had 25 sister groups, with a school, a booking office, a section of *New Theatre* for its very own. . . . The booking office was jammed with requests for performances from workers' clubs. Joint recitals were held almost weekly to packed halls. . . . Great dancers like Martha Graham danced for them at benefits. . . . This was the peak of their popularity.

And thus each of the arts contributed to the sum total of Muscovite indoctrination of sectors of the American people. Since the channels of communication with "the masses" who figured in the art works were exceedingly few and narrow, the doctrines took root in the middle classes, among intellectuals and professional men, on the campuses and in the leisure groups. The Proletcult episode served its purpose. It plowed up America for the sowing of the succeeding or Fourth Kremlin Period.

CHAPTER XIII

MORE PLANETS ARE LAUNCHED

1

WE HAVE already watched the births of the Trade Union Unity League; the Unemployed Councils and the Workers Alliance in which they were merged; the League of Struggle for Negro Rights; and earlier creations like the Friends of the Soviet Union, the International Labor Defense, and the Anti-Imperialist League. But we need to consider in more detail the histories of several other crucial Innocents' Clubs—or "transmission belts," as the party bigwigs preferred to describe them—which had their start at this time, providing ready vehicles for the policies of the succeeding period.

Lenin himself had marked out the strategy. He declared that since the communists were the vanguard of revolution, they needed "belts to transmit power" to the backward masses. In the United States, where the very word communism was anathema to the overwhelming majority, this strategy of multiple disguises was especially useful. It enabled the "vanguard" to make contact with various layers of the population without revealing their own identity. "The proletariat," Stalin once asserted, "need these belts, these levers and this guiding force." The American application of the principle was explained by Comrade Hathaway in an article in the party press in 1931:

We must learn to set up and work through a whole series of mass organizations and in this way also develop our party work. Our chief error is failure to understand the role of and to systematically utilize mass organizations (TUUL, Unemployed Councils, ILD, WIA, LSFNR, etc.) as transmission belts to the broad masses of non-party workers.

"Workers" is a habitual manner of speaking. It does not, in the vocabulary of transmission engineers, exclude coupon-clippers, successful playwrights, "society" women or other "brain workers." Comrade Hathaway and his readers knew that the belts in question led

141

largely to upper and middle-class regions. This was, in the nature of the case, especially true on the cultural front. The most significant of the transmission instruments in that region, and one destined to a gloriously goofy future, was the League of American Writers, which arose on the ashes of two earlier cultural revolutions: the John Reed Club and the League of Professional Groups.

The John Reed Club, first American affiliate of the International Union of Revolutionary Writers, was started in New York at the end of 1929. It grew big and fat rapidly on Proletcult enthusiasm. From the start it had the support of nationally prominent people in the literary world. The more prominent the person, the easier to manipulate—that principle is basic in the business of putting up stooge-organizations. Successful men and women are too busy to bother with running clubs and leagues; the management is safe from their intrusion.

The John Reed outfits were safely in the hands of the Communist Party, under direct control of Browder and his associates, operating through party literary lights like Gold, Hicks, et al. At various times the Club issued local and national magazines—New Force, Left Front, Leftward, etc.—but its main mouthpiece was the New Masses, and the words the New Masses uttered were pious if often pied variations on themes issued by International headquarters in Moscow. The English edition of International Literature, published and largely written in Russia, was the final arbiter on questions of party line and other theological matters.

As late as November, 1940, I was astonished to find a California playwright of some reputation who still doubted that the John Reed Club, with which he had played along in its day, was really a communist subsidiary. But there were not many on that level of blessed innocence in the heyday of the club, which thrived beyond the hopes of its fondest fathers. It had thirty-two sections in New York alone and branches in over a score of other large cities. The communist orientation was not too well hidden. In the mood of that more candid and intransigeant era, the Daily Worker did not hesitate to talk turkey to the club. It conveyed instructions in accents of ownership. On February 21, 1931, for instance, it stated sharply that the John Reed Club—

should broaden and enlarge its present work along the lines of the

Kharkov conference of revolutionary writers. It should keep closer
contact with the life and everyday struggles of the working classes, giving more attention to the development of proletarian literature, to the
development of new worker writers and artists, as well as to the winning over of radicalized intellectuals. It should become a real force
in the struggle for racial equality, especially for the Negro masses, and
give greater effort to exposing social fascists, and petty bourgeois tendencies, to the fight against imperialist war and the defense of the
Soviet Union.

In short, the same litany of dedication to Moscow objectives that
one might have heard on that day, recited by each and every Muscovite
puppet. Capitalizing on the Leftward migration, the outfit was soon
publishing *Blast* and *Partisan Review* in New York; *Anvil* in Moberley,
Missouri; *Cauldron* in Grand Rapids, Michigan; *Left Review* in Philadelphia; *Partisan Magazine* in Hollywood. It was operating special
schools for writers, artists, dancers, and branching out in Cartoonists
Groups, Left movie undertakings, a dozen other activities. The organization, in its multiplicity, offered a choice of hobbies, warm companionship, and a sense of participation in something big, vague,
heart-warming.

Artists and would-be artists were too grateful for these boons to ask
questions about who pulled levers or where the power station was
located.

2

For the managers of the enterprise, however, life was not as smooth
as this recital might imply. They worked under the stern and jaundiced
eye of a cantankerous master. The *New Masses* brain trust might dress
down the reviewers of the capitalist press here and tell off best-selling
novelists with a few rough epithets, but they pleaded for mercy each
time they were notified by Moscow that they had once again exhibited
"a whole series of serious defects." In the proletarian homeland such
"serious defects" were punished by exile or worse. That type of literary
criticism could not as yet be enforced in America. But one could not
have guessed that from the behavior of the dressed-down editors. The
anxious servility of the John Reeders suggests that they were unaware
of their American immunity.

In a 1932 issue of *International Literature* a lady comrade, A. Elistratova, took the John Reeders to task in these words, whatever they may mean:

The insufficient politization of the work of the *New Masses*, the insufficient impregnation of the whole activity of the journal with the spirit of party militancy, leaves an impress on the whole of its literary production.

Having hauled the editors over the coals she insisted that their errors

are traceable to one underlying defect, i.e., the insufficient politization of the whole work of the *New Masses* . . . It is significant in this respect that the *New Masses* has not dealt with the historic utterances of Comrade Stalin in recent years. This, of course, is not accidental: it is entirely due to the insufficient politization of the whole work of the *New Masses*.

It goes without saying that the culprits beat their breasts, explained things privately to Browder, Stachel and the resident colonial governor or "Rep." They hastened to work up the proper politization, impregnation and militancy. In early issues they examined the historic utterances of Comrade Stalin and, believe it or not, found them flawless gems of wisdom.

Who was this mighty Elistratova from whom Waldo Frank, Theodore Dreiser, Sherwood Anderson and the rest of the neo-proletarians took their guiding principles via the *New Masses*? It happens that one of the John Reed officials, Leon Dennen, met her soon thereafter in Moscow. Dennen, having turned "renegade" in the normal course of events, later described the lady for other renegades as "a big buxom girl with red cheeks—all of twenty years old," who "could read a little English but had not the slightest conception of American life, tradition or literature." She complained to him, among other things, about the silly way in which John Reed cartoonists, for mysterious but surely un-Marxist reasons, portrayed the American capitalist parties as elephants and donkeys, thus blurring the fact that they were bourgeois bloodsuckers.

The Moscow comrades clearly regarded their American intellectual charges with deep disdain to entrust their education and chastisement to this girl. But stupidities were pregnant with mystic insights when they came from Moscow. Another specialist on American letters who

regularly lectured our Left literati on their shortcomings was Sergei
Dinamov, for a time editor of the Moscow *Literary Gazette*. I came to
know and to like Dinamov for his sweetness of character, but his ignorance of American culture was truly impressive. Yet his edicts were law
to the John Reed fraternity in matters literary and esthetic.

It was a national conference of the John Reed Clubs, held in Chi-
cago in January, 1935, which issued the first call for a Congress of
American Writers. The direct descent of that congress from its John
Reed predecessors is not subject to doubt.

While one sector of the intelligentsia was being rounded up
through cultural tricks, more of it was being drawn in through more
frankly political appeals. In connection with the 1932 Presidential
campaign, the Communist Party succeeded in rallying a large number
of intellectuals to the support of its candidates. The League of Professional Groups for Foster and Ford was launched in October with a
manifesto signed by more than fifty writers and artists. For a number
of them it was their first public association with the communist movement, with which they were to become increasingly integrated in the
following years. Others in the line-up broke away quickly and shunned
false fronts forever after. Still others in the list—James Rorty, Sidney
Hook, Felix Morrow, etc.—soon turned into bitter critics of everything Stalinist. No doubt some of those listed would be hard put to
it, in the perspective of time, to explain to themselves how they happened to be taking the ride.

After the election the "for Foster and Ford" tag was cut off and the
League continued to function for other purposes. It had its quota of
"renegades," whom the party press duly bespattered with muddy
verbiage. James Rorty and a few others tried, naïvely, to divert the
organization to activities outside the strict interests of the Communist
Party and were sent sprawling on the street side of the door. The
organization lingered on for some years. But its most active spirits,
along with the salvageable material in the John Reed setup, entered
into a bigger and better organization.

3

Only a congenital dunce can peruse the proceedings of the first
Congress of American Revolutionary Writers, which launched the

League of American Writers, and doubt that the show was carefully staged by the communists. Every slogan of the Comintern was woven into the design of the performance. Its fundamental assumption was the perfection of Stalin's Russia, including its new literature. Messages from Soviet writers threw the audience into spasms of orgiastic enthusiasm. Every address was a direct or indirect salute to the Kremlin.

Held in the New School for Social Research in New York, April 24-27, 1935, the congress occurred unknowingly on the very edge of the crumbling Third Period. But in its ignorance of the coming collapse the gathering still acted up to the mildewed theory of "revolutionary upsurge." Its Muscovite inspiration was not yet muted and camouflaged; the adjective "revolutionary" was not yet outlawed; the allegiance to Russia was not disguised. Such stratagems would confuse the issue in subsequent congresses and leave muddled literary people more muddled than ever. But now the affair was boldly communist. Browder was well to the fore in the organizational stages. The fat little man with the tiny, frightened eyes, Alexander Trachtenberg, head of International Publishers and one of the party leaders, was busy moving scenery and prompting the actors.

Michael Gold was greeted as "the best-loved American revolutionary writer" and accepted the accolade without protest. He boasted of the deepening cultural influence of the Communist Party, referring specifically to the success of the Theatre Union and the Group Theatre and to the dozens of revolutionary books rolling off capitalist presses. "Our writers must learn," said he, "that the working class which has created a great civilization in the Soviet Union is capable of creating a similar civilization in this country." He called on red writers to regard themselves thereafter as "artists in uniform."

Waldo Frank presided and was selected as chairman of the League. Corliss Lamont, whose gilded star was rising rapidly in the red firmament, brought greetings from the Friends of the Soviet Union. The Young Pioneers and the Communist Youth organization sent plenipotentiaries. The wonderful achievements of the First All-Union Congress of Soviet Writers were celebrated by Moissaye Olgin, and Matthew Josephson, suddenly emerging as an authority on Soviet affairs, enlarged on "The Role of the Writer in the Soviet Union." Malcolm Cowley, Hicks, Dr. Harry F. Ward, dozens of others mouthed the well-worn Comintern slogans.

But the center of the stage was held by the party functionaries—Gold, Hathaway, Freeman, Trachtenberg, Olgin, et al.—without the concealment which would later become compulsory. The resolutions voted by the congress followed the Moscow line as closely as any party manifesto. The main address, of course, was Browder's. "The Communist Party," he declared, "greets this historic Congress of American Writers. We are all soldiers, each in our own place, in a common cause. Let our efforts be united in fraternal solidarity." The remarkable fact is that an organization as frankly Muscovite should, within less than twelve months, dare pretend to be independent and non-partisan. Only one fact is more remarkable: that so many hundreds of writers throughout the country should have believed the outrageous lie.

Before the memory of the League's parentage is quite obliterated, let me list the founding fathers for the coming historian of literary curiosities. The call for the congress was signed by:

Earl Browder, Michael Gold, Granville Hicks, Theodore Dreiser, Nathan Asch, Lester Cohen, Edward Dahlberg, John L. Spivak, Nelson Algren, Arnold B. Armstrong, Maxwell Bodenheim, Thomas Boyd, Bob Brown, Fielding Burke, Kenneth Burke, Robert Coates, Erskine Caldwell, Alan Calmer, Robert Cantwell, Jack Conroy, Malcolm Cowley, Guy Endore, James T. Farrell, Kenneth Fearing, Ben Field, Waldo Frank, Joseph Freeman, Eugene Gordon, Horace Gregory, Henry Hart, Clarence Hathaway, Josephine Herbst, Robert Herrick, Langston Hughes, Orrick Johns, Arthur Kallet, Lincoln Kirstein, Herbert Kline, Joshua Kunitz, John Howard Lawson, Tillie Lerner, Meridel Le Sueur, Melvin Levy, Robert Morss Lovett, Louis Lozowick, Grace Lumpkin, Lewis Mumford, Edward Newhouse, Joseph North, Moissaye J. Olgin, Samuel Ornitz, Myra Page, John Dos Passos, Paul Peters, Allen Porter, Harold Preece, William Rollins, Jr., Paul Romaine, Isidor Schneider, Edwin Seaver, Claire Sifton, Paul Sifton, George Sklar, Lincoln Steffens, Philip Stevenson, Genevieve Taggard, Alexander Trachtenberg, Nathaniel West, Ella Winter, and Richard Wright.*

The National Council of the newly formed League—openly and proudly affiliated at this stage with the International Union of Revo-

* From published record of Hearings by Dies Committee on H. Res. 282, August 16-17, 1938.

lutionary Writers—included a batch of names not among these signers. For the sake of completeness they, too, are herewith recorded:

Michael Blankfort, Van Wyck Brooks, Harry Carlisle, Eugene Clay, Merle Colby, Leonard Ehrlich, Angel Flores, Sidney Howard, Moishe Nadir, Clifford Odets, Joseph Opatoshu, Rebecca Pitts, Agnes Smedley, and James Waterman Wise.*

There is no implication that all signers and Council members were communists. On the contrary, *the principal purpose of the undertaking was to involve non-communists.* The only certainty is that the organization was a "weapon" forged by the Communist Party for the Moscow regime and worked without a hitch as expected by the foreign overseers.

Hardly had the League been launched, when Moscow promulgated a new party line that made a monkey out of every participant of the congress and every member of the organization. All their brave revolutionism was discarded, their resolutions thrown overboard, their membership diluted with most unideological recruits from Hollywood, Broadway, and Park Avenue. But the League did not founder in this storm of violent change. The steering machinery was in trustworthy and capable hands.

4

In the spring of 1932 A. A. Heller, a wealthy chemical manufacturer who had been "angeling" International Publishers and other communist enterprises, was host in his home to some thirty persons. Among them were active communists like Donald Henderson, Michael Gold, Joshua Kunitz, Joseph Freeman, Oakley Johnson, Edward Royce and Belle Taub; prominent fellow-travelers like Malcolm Cowley and Bernhard J. Stern; and a batch of liberal "innocents." Roger Baldwin, founder and leader of the American Civil Liberties Union, who is not easily classified, was also present.

Most of Heller's guests represented communist fronts like the John Reed Club, the Friends of the Soviet Union, the National Student League, the Anti-Imperialist League, the Trade Union Unity League. The gathering, in other words, was a typical hand-

---

* *Ibid.*

picked nucleus for yet another planet in Kuusinen's solar system. Those present formed the American Committee for the World Congress Against War.

Behind this nucleus was a Moscow agent named Urevich, who had recently arrived in the United States. Ostensibly he was a German banker here for business. Actually he represented Willi Muenzenberg. Two French writers who had swung into the Kremlin orbit, Henri Barbusse and Romain Rolland, served as window dressing for a World Congress Against War—scheduled to take place in Amsterdam on August 27-29 that year—but the real organizer and wirepuller was the energetic and resourceful Muenzenberg. His plenipotentiary in America was assigned to scare up an American delegation. He carried out the assignment.

The nucleus committee held a public conference on August 8 which was undisguisedly communist in make-up. A number of delegates to the Amsterdam Congress were selected by the conference, and others were arbitrarily added later by Comrade Urevich. Most of the thirty-two in the final list were either party people like William Simons, Joseph Cohen and Joseph Gardner, or familiar fellow-travelers like H. W. L. Dana and Margaret Schlauch.

The Amsterdam Congress, of course, was a wholly Stalinist undertaking. The Moscow press—which I read daily at the time on the spot as a professional chore—did not try to conceal the fact. The Kremlin was thoroughly frightened by the advance of the Japanese into Manchuria and worried over Hitler's rising strength. With acute food shortage, industrial breakdown and general debilitation marking the windup of the first Five Year Plan, with peasant desperation in the "collectivized" areas becoming more ominous, Stalin had ample cause for fearing attack. The Soviet State was in a weaker condition than at any time since the end of the civil wars.

The maneuver at Amsterdam aimed to form a chain of national "anti-war" organizations under strict communist management pledged to "defend the Soviet Union" and sabotage war preparations in their own countries. The prestige of men like Barbusse and Rolland served to give the enterprise a cultural and independently idealistic veneer. The sheen was so lifelike that world personalities like Albert Einstein and the Indian leader Patel made the blunder of associating their names with the meeting.

But despite the attempts to lure innocent outsiders, the gathering was almost entirely communist in coloration. Of its 2,196 delegates, 830 were admittedly party people and the majority of the others had long been tied up with various Kremlin projects. The speeches were paraphrases of *Pravda* and *Izvestia* editorials. The formal resolutions were standardized communist "theses." *International Press Correspondence*, an official communist publication, summed up the purposes of the enterprise as "combating the danger of imperialist war" and "defense of the Soviet Union." Although the triumph of Hitler was only a few months off, the Amsterdam Congress paid little attention to him. It was more concerned, in line with the Third Period preoccupations, with lambasting the socialists and trade unionists in Germany and other countries.

The Congress established a World Committee Against War, and the delegates scattered to their native lands with orders to form national sections. In the United States, the first step was the formation of an American Committee for Struggle Against War. Of the seventy in the committee, at least forty were party members, among them four members of the party's Central Committee. Neither here nor in other countries was the "anti-fascist" phase of the undertaking mentioned at this stage, though fascism was spreading everywhere and had long been in the saddle in Italy. Not until Hitler actually took over the reins in Germany, and insisted on hurling threats in the direction of Moscow, was the anti-war movement enlarged to include a fight on fascism. It needs to be emphasized that it was not fascism as such, but simply the fascist threat to the safety of Russia, that alarmed the Kremlin puppet-masters.

The American Committee announced the First United States Congress Against War for the end of September, 1932, in New York. An "organizing committee" did the preparatory work. Dr. J. B. Matthews, a socialist professor who was rapidly becoming one of the prime "independent" decorations of various communist efforts, took the chairmanship of this organizing group on the personal urging of Earl Browder. He has since then revealed in detail the procedure for building what would in time become Stalin's most effective American transmission belt. While various Left and labor groups were invited to participate, the purpose was to expose and embarrass their leaders in conformity with the current "united front from below" tactics. From Dr. Matthews' subsequent disclosures, in his *Odyssey of a Fellow-Traveler*, I quote this telltale passage:

Donald Henderson . . . assured me that the communists already had several strategic men in important plants and industries where they would be in a position to sabotage vital processes in the event of war— just in case the United States should become involved in a war *against* the Soviet Union. In this connection, Henderson was especially boastful of a revolutionary nucleus in submarine plants in Connecticut and of the work of Harry Bridges in the shipping industry on the West Coast. They were, Henderson claimed, secretly allied with the American League.

The organizing committee was able to list forty-nine organizations on its letterhead. But thirty-four of these were communist fronts. Most of the others were drawn in innocently with the aid of their own boring-from-within fractions. The First Congress finally opened, with Dr. Matthews presiding. Only a few former party leaders, including Jay Lovestone, broke the Stalinist unanimity of the occasion. Henri Barbusse was present for the Amsterdam body. Earl Browder, Donald Henderson, and other prominent communist chieftains made speeches. Neither the direct descent from Stalin's all-communist Amsterdam show nor the domination of the American party could possibly be questioned.

The meeting spent three days on what was little more than a restatement of all the Amsterdam "theses." The chief difference was that the "anti-fascist" slogan was now hooked on to the anti-war slogans. And at least one purely American contribution was made to the hocus-pocus. At one session James W. Ford, the Negro communist leader, took the chair. Trusted delegates were deployed through the dingy St. Nicholas Arena. News photographers were warned to "lay off" and were watched to make sure they did. Then the great moment exploded:

A uniformed soldier came up the aisle, climbed to the platform and in behalf of his comrades in the United States Army pledged to defend Russia and to sabotage any American attack on Russia. Then he left as secretively as he had arived. The delegates went wild with joy. Here was the symbol of their hopes. Browder personally had arranged the little drama and boasted, in his next report to the Comintern, of his party's success in penetrating the armed forces of his country. He could not foresee, of course, that this boast would haunt him in the years to come, when he would be obliged to pose as an American patriot and lineal political descendant of Jefferson, Jackson and Lincoln.

That congress organized the American League Against War and Fascism. Although the anti-war ring of the name would ultimately serve to fool a good many genuine peace organizations, it decidedly was not pacifist. The only war it opposed was war distasteful to the rulers of Soviet Russia. The ten-point program adopted aimed openly at crippling American war industries and national defense and at rolling up every sort of support for Russia and its policies. Dr. Matthews was designated national chairman. Donald Henderson became secretary and Ida Dailes assistant secretary—as usual in false-front organizations, secretarial jobs were reserved for people close to the party. Earl Browder, and William Pickens of the National Association for the Advancement of Colored Peoples were made national vice-chairmen.

Not one of the founding fathers had the faintest suspicion that their organization was fated to become in time a real force in American life. Had the most optimistic delegate been told that in time to come members of the President's political and personal families would give aid and comfort to this progeny of the Amsterdam Congress, he would have considered the prophet loony.

In giving the periodical accounting of his stewardship to the Executive Committee of the Comintern, Comrade Browder reported that the American branch office under his management had "led a highly successful U. S. Congress Against War," and that "the Congress from the beginning was led by our party quite openly." Such unruly elements as had disturbed the serenity of the First Congress— the Lovestone intruders, for instance, and socialist hecklers—were safely eliminated when the Second Congress met in Chicago a year later, at the end of September, 1934. It was in conjunction with this Second Congress of the League Against War and Fascism that Browder made and published a confession that he could never thereafter live down:

In the center as the conscious moving and directive force of the united front in all its phases, stands the Communist Party. Our position in this respect is clear and unchallenged.

This was still a few months before the change of "line." The communists still crowed about matters which later they would deny with lugubrious vehemence. In his speech at the opening of the Second Congress, Browder did drop a few hints of coming changes. He used, for instance, previously off-color words like "progressive," and smiled tentatively at persons still marked with the social fascist brand. But the major Third Period policies were unaltered in his address and in the program and resolutions and propaganda literature that came out of the League meeting. Browder urged that the fight against war be carried "into the factories, especially munitions factories, docks, etc.," and attacked the New Deal for "carrying through the greatest war program ever seen in peace time."

Nothing in the whole story of American Bolshevism is less open to doubt than the Muscovite origins and control of the League Against War and Fascism, later rechristened the League for Peace and Democracy.

5

From the day of its formation the Communist International has aimed to indoctrinate the young. The Fascists and the Nazis were merely copying Bolshevik methods in forming special groupings for every division of youth, from the cradle to enrollment in the adult organization. Wherever there is a Communist Party there are always Young Pioneers, Young Communist Leagues or equivalent organizations. Like their elder national sections, they take their ideas, their songs, their changing program from the respective Internationals with headquarters in Moscow. And where the communist approach to youth could not be made openly, some transmission-belt device has been employed.

In the American colleges, the National Student League was generally and rightly identified as the communist campus vehicle, as distinguished from the Student League for Industrial Democracy, dominated by the socialists. Between them the two divided the tiny minority of radical youth on the campuses. The Depression turned college undergraduates—paradoxically, the wealthier and safer ones especially—to more serious thinking, or at least worrying. Old values and certainties had crumbled in their homes and in their minds. The fear of unemployment beyond college was translated into revolutionary urges among the more sensitive and more intelligent young people. The adherents of the radical organizations in the colleges began to grow in number and enthusiasm.

As a matter of form, for the record, the National Student League has always denied that it is communist. Neither the Stalinist press nor its own members, however, ever took the denial seriously. Its domination by the Young Communist League was open and complete. Merely to glance at its earlier leaders is to confirm that fact: Adam Lapin, who edited *The Student* and later served as *Daily Worker* correspondent in Washington; Joseph Starobin, subsequently *New Masses* foreign editor; Joseph Cohen of Brooklyn College, who under the name of Joe Clark became the editor of the Young Communist League *Review;* Bert Witt, editor of *College News* under the name of White and later national secretary of the American Student Union; Celeste Strack, destined to become high-school director of the Young Communist League. Anyone so unrealistic as to assume that such leadership was accidental will not be convinced by this or any other book.

In the last days of December, 1932, the communist National Student League staged a Student Congress Against War at the University of Chicago. The effort was a direct follow-up of Stalin's Amsterdam show, with many of the same leaders taking part; on the national committee were Henri Barbusse, George S. Counts, J. B. Matthews, Leo Gallagher, Donald Henderson, H. W. L. Dana, Corliss Lamont, Scott Nearing, Margaret Schlauch, Frederick L. Schuman, Robert Morss Lovett. The Congress was addressed by Earl Browder, Dr. Matthews, Joseph Freeman, Jane Addams and Upton Close—the familiar recipe of communist stalwarts with liberal innocents for sweetening.

Again it is well to note that the proceedings were absolutely parallel to all other "anti-war" meetings under Kremlin aegis, whether of adults or children. When Jane Addams spoke as a full pacifist, she was rudely admonished that wars for revolution and for the safety of Russia were noble—only "imperialist" and anti-Soviet wars must be condemned.

We come now to the birth of the American Youth Congress. Its origins have been shrouded in lies by the later attempts to hide the communist leading strings. But the facts of its founding are simple enough:

An energetic young woman named Viola Ilma promoted the idea

of a national federation of existing youth groups. Miss Ilma and her backers said they wanted to bring a measure of stability to the country's young people to offset cynicism and nihilistic disillusionment. The mistake they made, from their own vantage point, was to attempt the impossible job of federating everything from the Boy Scouts and Junior Leaguers to the communists. Theoretically this seemed generous and broad-minded. As a practical matter it meant that one tendency or another would seize control.

When the American Youth Congress met in New York, August 15-17, 1934, the more seasoned and dynamic politicians of the Left Wing promptly took over. The communists had packed the gathering with full-fledged delegations from chimerical societies. By combining with the socialists, they captured the Congress, kicked out Miss Ilma, and filled the official slates with their own people.

It now remained only for the communists to oust the socialists. The job took them several years but was in the end fully accomplished. At the Second national meeting of the Congress, in Detroit, Comrade Hathaway, editor of the *Daily Worker*, was the speaker who drew the largest ovation from several thousand delegates and visitors. The resolutions were absolutely in consonance with *Daily Worker* precepts of the moment. Already the American Youth Congress was—in its views, leadership, slogans and temper—indistinguishable from the various adult Innocents' Clubs. In reporting to Moscow headquarters on September 26, 1935, the American Young Communist League took credit for capturing the American Youth Congress, though (in line with the emerging united front policy) it shared that credit with the socialists.

It could afford to be generous. The socialist role on the campus was nearing its end anyhow. For some time its Student League for Industrial Democracy had held out proudly against communist demands for "amalgamation." In the spring of 1934 the two groups had collaborated in pulling off a "Youth Peace Strike" in many colleges. They also agreed in taking the Oxford Pledge, a pacifist gesture. But Joseph P. Lash, head of the socialist group, knew what the communists were after. "The Student I.L.D.," he wrote, "is convinced that the Young Communists in the National Student League envision amalgamation as a god-given opportunity to smash the influence of the socialist movement and the socialist ideas in the student field."

Nevertheless, only a few months after these knowing words were written, Lash and the elder statesmen of the Socialist Party capitulated to communist "unity" pleas. In the autumn of 1935 the two radical campus groups were merged and the combination retitled American Student Union. It was the kind of merger a boa constrictor makes with a rabbit. Lash and other socialists got jobs. In due course Lash demonstratively resigned from the Socialist Party, publishing his reasons—in the *New Masses.**

The complex campaign for dominance of the relatively small but influential portion of *organized* college students was over. Moscow had at its beck and call a communist-controlled American Student Union which, in turn, expressed itself through an American Youth Congress under its total sway.

6

There is space only for the bare mention of lesser luminaries in the communist universe. Some of them flared up only to die down quickly. Others survived under different names or flowed together with more durable organizations.

There was a Free Tom Mooney Congress under party domination held in Chicago in the spring of 1933, which led to the formation of a National Tom Mooney Council of Action. A National Scottsboro Committee of Action was launched; the communists had seized the Scottsboro case and were making political and financial capital out of it with small regard for the interests of the Negro boys whose lives were at stake.

After the Nazis came to power in Germany, the party here started a subsidiary of the Workers International Relief under the name of National Committee to Aid the Victims of German Fascism. "On this anti-fascist committee," Comrade Browder later wrote frankly in a book, "we placed Muste as chairman . . . merely as a 'united front' decoration." Communist candor in books not read by the general public is really startling. Literally thousands, ranging from the First Lady of the land to obscure ministers, would be utilized as "decorations" without fully suspecting their humiliating function.

---

* Following the conclusion of the Nazi-Soviet Pact Mr. Lash resigned from the American Student Union and became an officer of an anti-communist International Student Service sponsored by Mrs. Eleanor Roosevelt.

There were also the American Friends of the Chinese People. Dr. Matthews, active in its work at the start, has testified to personal knowledge of communist domination. The prominence in its work of Dr. Matthews himself and of men like Comrade Hathaway is impressive confirmation to those familiar with Stalinist methods; the activities of people like Winifred Chappell, secretary of the Methodist Federation for Social Service, proves nothing—unless it be the gullibility of liberals. Maxwell Stewart, an editor of the *Nation* and one of the most trusted of communist collaborators, ultimately became national chairman of the organization.

Every national or international event served as an excuse for yet another committee or league; for yet more publications, mass meetings, fund-raising campaigns, jobs for deserving party hacks. The existing Innocents' Clubs provided a ready-made foundation for every new club. Having been inveigled into acting as decoration for one group, the victim was automatically available for the same role in endless new setups; sometimes these victims came to like the noise, the lights, even the sense of martyrdom evoked by attacks and thus became perfect puppets for communist politicians.

Monies collected were technically accounted for by the high cost of collection—due to packing every organization with salaried comrades—and friendly party accountants in many cases did the rest. Sometimes the funds were sent on to international headquarters outside the United States, beyond which point, obviously, American contributors could not trace them if they wished. Besides, Americans join causes and contribute money without much thought of such matters. They leave it to George to do the dirty work. And in these organizations the Georges were party people under party discipline, undeterred by the dirtiness of the work to be done.

CHAPTER XIV

MOSCOW ADOPTS THE TROJAN HORSE

1

AMERICAN communism, all its political suburbs, and their whole sprawling periphery underwent a sudden climatic change in 1935. Violent revolutionism gave way almost overnight to a mellow affection for capitalist democracy. The icy blasts of class hatred tapered off rapidly to soothing zephyrs of loving-kindness. From the storm cellars of social destruction the Stalinist creed leaped at a single bound to the penthouses of respectability.

Now literally nothing new had happened in the United States to explain the meteorological miracle. The New Deal had been in progress since 1933. None of the reasons for revolt had been assuaged. True, many things had happened elsewhere in the world to recommend a reappraisal of communist tactics—especially the Japanese aggression in Northern China, the victory of the Nazi brand of fascism in Germany, Italian aggression in Africa, more and more tendencies of appeasement in France and England in relation to the aggressors. But those things had been happening at least since 1931. Why did the great change come only in 1935?

For a clue to the mystery we must study the political weather in Moscow. Anyone who has read this far will understand that no profound change in the temperature and wind currents of American communism can be explained without tracing it to the source in Russia.

In a startling editorial in the Moscow *Pravda* of June 9, 1934, the Soviet people were tipped off that it was respectable and safe again to be patriotic in the old-fashioned flag-and-soil spirit. The editorial used the word "fatherland" and made a fervid argument for love of country. It amounted to a formal recognition of a process under way for some years. Under the formula of "socialism in one country," love of the native land, its history, traditions, folklore and national heroes had been made acceptable. The internationalist phrases survived as a kind of abstract holiday decoration, but all the concrete, earthy local loyalties outlawed by Lenin's revolution were not merely restored but made obligatory.

Russia has ever been divided in its soul, torn between its Asiatic and its European impulses. Its history has been conditioned by vibrant tensions between the mystic Slavophiles and the rational Westernizers or "Europeanizers"; between Asia and Europe, to put it crudely. And always, after episodes of Westernism—in the era of Peter the Great, again in the Napoleonic era—Russia has turned inward, rejecting the blandishments of Europe more fanatically than ever. After the great revolution, the old dualism reasserted itself, though the thick layers of Marxist and economic verbiage have hidden the fact from most outsiders.

Reduced to its least common denominator, the struggle between Trotsky and Stalin was another version of that ancient conflict and the outcome was true to the ancient pattern. Trotsky, the intellectual steeped in European ideas, was grappling with Stalin, the provincial-minded Asiatic for whom the West was a hateful mystery. The slogans were new: on one side "world revolution," on the other "socialism in one country." But the quarrel was as old as Russia itself. When Stalin won out, Asia triumphed over Europe, Ivan the Terrible conquered Karl Marx.

After that, the sloughing off of imported "modernistic" accretions in everyday life and in art, the fanatic Stalinist revulsion against the intellectuals, were inevitable. The fostering of a fierce patriotism, the exaltation of all things Russian, the translation of every Marxist idea into purely Russian terms, were not deliberate decisions made in the Kremlin. Rather were they changes inherent in Stalin's ascendancy. They were a deepening mood more than a program, though the court theologians found holy writ to match the mood.

Internationally the tragic comedy of the business was due to the accident that a significant world movement, calling itself communism but miles removed from the original communist doctrines, was tethered to this inward-turning, greedily self-centered Russia. Stalin's country had gone National Communist in the sense that Germany had gone National Socialist, with the accent in both cases overwhelmingly on the "National."

The real differences between the two nationalisms were no longer ideological. They were political, territorial, economic, and hence subject to compromise. For years the chief objections of the Kremlin to the Weimar Republic had been its inclination to forgive and forget Versailles and find an amicable adjustment of interests with the World War victors. Stalin, like Mussolini, was among the revisionists; that, in fact, had long been one of the strong political bonds between Fascist Italy and Soviet Russia. Though the Hitler advance and the progress of other brands of intense nationalism may have been linked with a fight on "international communism," the Kremlin saw the development as in the first place anti-Versailles, anti-French, and therefore in line with Moscow's own passionate anti-French and anti-Versailles policies.

It was that among other common interests, of course, which made the Nazi expansion less alarming to Stalin than the world assumed. In the middle of 1931, upon direct orders from Moscow, the German communists had voted with the Nazis in Prussia against the Republic. The unrecognized fact is that Stalin was for letting Hitler in, as the lesser of two evils, between the Nazis and the bourgeois Republic. The communist alibi was summed up in the oft-repeated boast, "after Hitler—our turn!" When the collapse of the Republic came, the Stalinists of Germany were prepared to go underground—but they were not prepared to fight against the change.

In December, 1932, a few months before Hitler's victory, the editor of the Social Democratic Vorvärts, Dr. Friedrich Stampfer, invited the Communist Party to join the socialists in a united front against the Nazis. The communists ignored the proposal, and ridiculed it in private. In March of the following year, after the Reichstag fire and the outlawing of the Left parties, Dr. Stampfer went to the Soviet Embassy and urged a last-moment union of forces for a final stand. Again he was laughed into silence.

For at least eighteen months thereafter, the Communist International was still sticking to its appeasement guns. Stalin in his speeches was asking Hitler for his friendship—for "good relations" such as Moscow had long maintained with Mussolini. Though the press of the rest of the world was filled with atrocity tales out of Germany, the Soviet press kept silent about such things or told of them mildly. While Stalin's emissaries bargained for a formula of collaboration with the Nazis, the comrades were held in line the world over with cynical promises of revolution around the corner in Germany. The Comintern regarded the Nazi regime as a setback, but "that, however, did not imply the collapse of the process of the maturing of the revolutionary class" in the Third Reich.

The Social Democrats were being jailed and murdered along with the communists, but the Comintern continued to attack them as Nazi agents! As late as December, 1933, it was insisting: "Social Democracy continues to play the role of the main prop of the bourgeoisie also in countries of open fascist dictatorship. . . . ," which is to say in Germany and Italy. The International thundered against those German leaders who regarded Hitler's triumph as a serious matter.

Naturally Stalin and his associates did not believe this. They were playing for time in the hope of winning Hitler over to a neighborly and collaborative attitude against the West. The Kremlin's great disappointment was that the ultra-nationalist Nazis, instead of turning at once on the Versailles powers, as it had reason to expect, were making eyes at them. What followed was in effect a contest for Hitler's affections in which Stalin for the time being lost out. And it was as a consequence of this failure that Moscow was forced to woo other loves—reluctantly and in desperation it fell so low, in its own estimation, as to flirt with the democratic countries.

2

All nations have secondary policy lines to which they can fall back if the first line of defense fails. Soviet diplomacy early in 1933 began to edge closer to the Anglo-French group, by way of political insurance. The Moscow press, I recall, began to say pleasant things about Lenin's "thieves' kitchen," the League of Nations, even before it had begun to say unpleasant things about the new German government. In September, 1934, Hitler having refused to play with the Muscovites, they entered the League. In May, 1935, they signed a mutual defense pact with France. The People's Front epoch—the Fourth Period in communist history—was under way.

The same International which had refused to co-operate with socialists to head off the Nazis in Germany, which in February, 1934, had refused to co-operate with other Left groups in Paris to head off a threatened fascist coup, was now eager to co-operate with everybody except communists of the anti-Stalin variety. The united front they now offered was so broad that the socialists were outraged; so broad that on occasion it even compassed avowed fascists, if only they agreed to oppose Germany.

What needs underlining again is the record proving that Moscow did not choose its new "democratic orientation" because of a change of heart, but because of Hitler's refusal to have a change of heart. The breach with Germany developed slowly during two reluctant years, with Moscow doing its utmost to prevent it. *Sub rosa* military collaboration between the two countries, a fact since the Rapallo Treaty, continued for more than eighteen months after the Nazis came to power. Even after the new anti-Hitler pro-democracy program had been publicly adopted, Soviet leaders continued to seek some basis for an understanding with Germany.

Many tales out of school have been told in recent years by Soviet officials who fled the blood purges. All of them agree that Stalin never relinquished his hope of getting together with the Nazis. The late General Walter Krivitsky, for a time in charge of military espionage in Western Europe for the Soviets, was explicit on this subject. He quoted Stalin as saying at Kremlin meetings, though the Franco-Soviet Treaty was nearing completion, "And yet we must come to an understanding with the Germans." Krivitsky wrote in 1937, soon after his break with Moscow:

The *rapprochement* with France was viewed by Stalin as a means of strengthening his position in the expected negotiations with Hitler, who was given to understand—officially and unofficially—that Stalin is very much in earnest about a Soviet-Nazi deal.

The task of working out such an understanding presumably was not in the hands of the regular diplomatists, but entrusted to secret intermediaries. This may well be the missing piece in the jigsaw puzzle of the bewildering later "Moscow trials" and executions without trials. The hypothesis is fascinating; it makes comprehensible so much that is otherwise fantastic. Many of the defendants confessed to having carried on negotiations with Nazi leaders while Russia was officially at swords' points with the Nazi regime. We need only suppose—what Krivitsky and other ex-Stalinists claimed to be a fact— that these people were doing so at the behest of Stalin, rather than at the behest of Trotsky as alleged, and their strange stories are no longer strange.

It would scarcely be the first time that a government tried out a secondary diplomacy under the surface of the official policies, and ostensibly without the knowledge of the higher-ups. Nor would it be the first time that agents were conspicuously disowned by their principals when their secret mission failed, as it seemed to have failed at the time of the trials and purges. As it happened, the conspiracy worked out after all—when Hitler was ready to use the Russians for his own purposes in August, 1939—but by that time the secret emissaries were no longer among the living.

Until that consummation dear to Stalin's heart had been achieved, he remained frightened of a possible capitalist-Nazi-Japanese coalition against Russia. It was essential for the Soviet regime, under the circumstances, to do everything humanly possible to separate the so-called democratic countries from Germany. There, in the simplest form, is the whole reason for the "democratic" and "anti-fascist" line of the People's Front maneuver. Only the bottomlessly naïve believed that Russia was in those years of "democratic" ballyhoo concerned with saving democracy or defeating fascism. It was concerned with saving Russia and defeating Russia's potential enemies. From the vantage point of its own *Realpolitik* it was behaving logically and shrewdly. The blame, if any, belongs on the heads of those who, knowing the truth, yet pretended that Russia was the spearhead of a crusade for democracy.

The idea, now being propagated, that "everyone was taken in" by the Soviet maneuvers is largely myth. A few statesmen saw through the Soviet strategy and insisted, in the face of furious opposition, that Moscow could not be trusted. A number of journalists, the writer included, insisted that the "democratic" line was a blind and a fraud. Let me quote one of these journalists, a former communist and at one time editor of the distinguished Berlin periodical *Die Weltbühne*, Willi Schlamm. He saw through the comedy of Soviet-Nazi shadow-boxing so well that he was able to write, in a book written at the end of 1936,* these startlingly prophetic words:

The Third Reich is marching against Europe. When and as long as Stalin's Russia opposes its march, it will be attacked. When Stalin withdraws from France and the European democracies, he can count on Hitler's tolerance. The anti-Bolshevik crusade of the Third Reich

---
* *Diktatur der Lüge*, by Willi Schlamm, 1937, Zurich.

is designed to obtain not the Ukraine but parts of Western and Central Europe and colonies; it is designed to break not Stalin's regime, but the Franco-Soviet military alliance. It won't take long and the Führers will conclude a realistic non-aggression pact. The one will guarantee Stalin's nationalistic states, the other will leave Europe to a Hitler-fate.

Schlamm was viewing the picture from the German angle. From the Russian angle it looked no different. Stalin's anti-fascist crusade was designed not to defeat Hitler but to lure him into a united front with Russia. If it could not accomplish that, the Kremlin calculated, then Russia might be able perhaps to set Germany and its Western neighbors at each other's throats, while it remained outside the squabble. At the very worst, should Hitler, fearing to tackle the Western powers, vent his dynamism on Russia instead, Stalin could hope for democratic allies. It was a deep and—again when viewed from Moscow's corner—justified *Realpolitik*.

An about-face in its entire foreign policy became inescapable for the Comintern if it hoped to win friends and influence governments in the democracies. The "revolutionary upsurge" had to be outlawed. The social fascists must be reinstated in communist good graces. The talk about turning "imperialist war into civil war" must be erased from the record. Capitalist nations must be divided into peace-loving democracies and fascist aggressors. The class war must be shelved until the fascist danger was out of the way. Potential allies of Russia must be made militarily stronger, not weaker, wherefore the whole anti-militarist propaganda must be buried far out of sight.

Of all its political somersaults, this was Moscow's boldest and most dramatic. In one acrobatic moment yesterday's fire-eating communists the world over found themselves far to the Right of the socialists and reformists whom they had been belaboring as renegades. Millions of "sympathizers" in the murky haze of the periphery continued to fancy themselves bold revolutionaries, but the sudden mellowness of the cause they were trailing now made it safe for them to become "activists." Comrades who had put in years of conniving and exhortation against militarism and conscription now found themselves, metaphorically speaking, in recruiting sergeants' uniforms in all democratic countries, yelling for bigger and better armaments and instant war against the aggressor nations.

A lot of young socialists and communists in France failed to adjust themselves to the change and continued to prate of revolution. Whereupon Moscow sent two Russians to their meeting to inform them (and these are the precise words used): "If in this period you make your revolution in France, you are traitors." In every country there were such episodes of rebellion. But they were too few and too scattered to affect the International as a whole. Its discipline, enforced through a world-wide bureaucracy long trained to uncritical obedience of Stalin's orders, held fast. The 180-degree turn was accomplished without a serious hitch.

Russia's new nationalism had blotted out what faint markings of genuine internationalism there had remained in the world movement. A new era of collaboration with bourgeois governments and individuals was opened, *solely because it suited the foreign policies of Russia.*

3

The Seventh Congress of the International met in Moscow in the late summer of 1935. It was the first congress in seven years. It decided nothing. The Fourth Period was already in full swing. The gathering, under the chairmanship of Georgi Dimitrov, only confirmed bombastically a change already put into effect by decree and under way in all nations where communists had a foothold. While giving lip service to the internationalist and revolutionary abstractions, all the concrete slogans and methods were aimed to conciliate liberals and to convince democratic governments that Russia was now a cleaned-up and respectable mate in a marriage of convenience aimed to disconcert Hitler.

In all countries the communists' duty was focused down to the one task of building Popular or People's Front governments—and civil organizations—pledged to stop Hitler and to help Stalin if Hitler couldn't be stopped. After Italy and Japan joined the Berlin Anti-Comintern Pact, those countries were added to Germany as the unholy trio whose neutralization must come before class war, before communism, before everything except Stalin.

In laying down the new line at the Seventh Congress, in Moscow, Comrade Dimitrov disdained subtleties. He took nearly a whole session to explain the new tactics, but their import was simple enough. No ethical or "revolutionary" inhibitions must hamper the big job of lining up democratic nations for the great cause of pulling Russia's chestnuts out of the fire. Somewhere in the second hour of that discourse he bethought himself of ancient Troy and the celebrated trickery by which it was overthrown:

Comrades, you remember the ancient tale of the capture of Troy. Troy was inaccessible to the armies attacking her, thanks to her impregnable walls. And the attacking army, after suffering many sacrifices, was unable to achieve victory until with the aid of the famous Trojan Horse it managed to penetrate the very heart of the enemy's camp.

Then he went on to dot the *i*'s and cross the *t*'s. By making friends of everybody in their respective countries the Communist Parties represented at the congress must "penetrate the very heart of the enemy's camp." "We must," he said, "utilize anti-fascist mass organizations as the Trojan Horse. Whoever does not understand such tactics or finds them degrading is a babbler and no revolutionary."

The delegates understood well enough. Far from finding such tactics degrading, they found them precisely to their taste. The Fourth Period, which they carried back to the United States, to France, to the remotest colonies and outposts of civilization, has with ample justice been identified as the Trojan Horse Period. Everywhere, big and small Trojan Horses smuggled Stalin's subsidized agents and unpaid enthusiasts into great governments; into universities, trade unions, women's and youth movements; into the arts and literature, religious organizations, the press and radio, theatre and motion pictures; into old deals and New Deals, coalition Cabinets in some countries, conservative one-party Cabinets in others. In particular the Trojan Horse trick succeeded in capturing well-nigh a monopoly of honest anti-fascist emotion. Niagaras of indignation against the bestialities of the Nazi regime, all the geysers of fear and hatred and panic started by the aggressions and duplicities of the Hitler Axis, were channeled off into communist-controlled reservoirs.

Comrade Dimitrov knew his people. They were the sort of "revolutionaries" for whom Trojan Horse tactics would have an irresistible fascination. For more than a decade and a half they had been applying the dictum that the end justifies the means. The squeamish had long ago dropped by the wayside or been hounded out of the ranks. Those who survived in the leadership had developed a passionate relish for the methods of disguise, duplicity, multiple moral book-keeping. Most of them had come to care more for the thrills and rewards of conspiracy than for the supposed revolutionary objectives of the conspiracy.

Boring from within, then united front from below, had given wide scope for sharpening talents for righteous deception on the grindstone of experience. But those were narrow outlets compared with what the new dispensation offered. Now the anointed could "penetrate the very heart" of an infinite number of institutions, under an unlimited number of masks. The sky was the limit for the exercise of their talents for intrigue.

Thus the meteorological miracle—the mellow democratic weather and the soothing zephyrs of all-embracing popular fronts—manifest in America had its origins in Russia. From this point forward our narrative is concerned with the adventures of the Trojan Horsemen in the United States, but it must be remembered throughout that their fellows were following the same course in other countries.

4

In Soviet Russia itself an extensive refurbishing of the externals of the regime seemed desirable to facilitate the tasks of the Trojan Horsemen. In reality the period was harsher than any that went before. It included the world's most extensive political purge, beginning with the wave of official murders after the assassination of Sergei Kirov at the end of 1934 and persisting until it had decimated the ranks of the Russian Communist Party itself, the Red Army officers' corps, the industrial elite, the new intelligentsia. A slight economic improvement in the middle 'thirties was followed by new industrial and agrarian setbacks and as always more brutal police measures were needed to hold down the lid.

Yet it was a period camouflaged with pseudo-democratic paint, forcible chanting of hymns to "the happy life," the pretense that "the final victory of socialism in one country" had already been accomplished. They were the years of the apotheosis of Stalin. The Revolution had been reduced to one man; Marxism, Soviet style, was just another name for the whims and blunders of one man; the Communist International and all its myriad appendages were literally nothing more than his private racket.

As part of the refurbishing, the hated G.P.U. was renamed Commissariat for Internal Affairs. But the dread three letters could not be eradicated from everyday usage. Under its new name, moreover, the police arm of the regime was as merciless and as greedy in its thirst for blood as under the old. No one inside Russia, except foreigners, took the relabeling and the new mock-democratic phraseology in earnest. But the paid propagandists, the fellow-travelers outside Russia, the self-deluded tourists and economists did handsprings of joy in their gurgling admiration for "Soviet democracy," for "the most democratic country in the world." Not even the blood purges could dissuade most of them. Not even outright attacks on democracy by Stalinist spokesmen could disillusion them. For some, not even the crowning betrayal, the alliance with Hitlerism, would suffice to dampen their infatuation with Soviet "democracy."

The greatest ballyhoo of all was touched off by the so-called Stalin Constitution—"the most democratic constitution the world has ever seen," as the sycophants described it. Hundreds of articles, an entire book by Anna Louise Strong, and endless lectures celebrated the genius of this document. Its verbatim publication—indicating clearly that the democracy was fake, with all power reserved for a single party and that party subservient to a centralized absolutism—did nothing to tone down the adulation. Long after the principal authors of Stalin's Constitution had been slaughtered by the glorious "rifle squads" and sent for their reward to heaven, their document was still held up as a model for the barbarian states not under Stalin's blessed tutelage. Only the first actual "election" under the Constitution caused a minor abatement of the madness abroad. It turned out to be a few grades less democratic than equivalent elections in Hitler's country.

My favorite Soviet author, Louis Fischer, was among the shrillest hallelujah-shouters for the Stalin Constitution. Through the pages of *Current History* for September, 1935, Fischer transmitted to America the glad tidings that "The Bolshevik dictatorship is slowly, almost imperceptibly, abdicating. When the change to democracy is completed, the world will wonder how it happened." The world, alas, never had the chance to wonder. "The Bolshevik dictatorship," he continued, ". . . is often cruel, ruthless and anti-democratic. . . . And yet in the full bloom of its youth this dictatorship is making ready for its own demise." To reinforce this idyllic picture he added that arrests were falling off "because there are no longer any large disloyal groups in the country." I am not insisting that Stalin, in unloosing a few months later the great purge that took tens of thousands of lives, was out to spite the Fischers, Strongs and Webbs. But the effect was the same. The "loyalty" of such people survived the insult. They could take it, no matter how much blood was shed for the glory of the Stalin Constitution.

And there we have the crazy pattern of the Fourth Period: Communists championing democracy in their own countries in the interests of a Russia increasingly totalitarian and brutalitarian. Now let us examine some of the details of the design in our own country.

CHAPTER XV

COMMUNISM BECOMES AMERICANISM

1

EARL BROWDER was summoned to Moscow in December, 1934, at the peak of the ultra-Left Third Period. He departed these shores a properly red-hot revolutionary, committed to violent conquest of our capitalist state for its impending Soviet destiny. The echoes of his speeches reviling the "fascist New Deal" and its social fascist henchmen had scarcely died down. The ink was still damp on articles in which he ridiculed capitalist democracy and denounced national defense efforts as "imperialist war preparations." In short, he was as union-splitting, Roosevelt-hating and uncompromising as any of the registered rebels or camp trailers of his movement.

During the months of his absence, American communists, blissfully ignorant of the new line of goods being handed to their pilgrim father, continued unabatedly intransigeant. They reveled in the leather-jacket, meet-me-on-the-barricades temper of the time, and kept their eyes fixed on the revolution around the corner. There was no letup in the abuse of "rotten liberals," "petty bourgeois" writers and artists, socialists, churchmen, the A.F. of L., John L. Lewis, collective security "war mongers," advocates of labor parties, and other familiar figures of Stalinist demonology.

At the moment, for instance, when Browder was hurrying to the fountainhead, Comrade Robert Minor was giving both barrels to a prominent California social fascist named Upton Sinclair. That gentleman's EPIC schemes, Minor wrote in the party press, "are the most reactionary that have been made by any politician during the economic crisis . . . the most cold-bloodedly pro-capitalist and reactionary proposals that were offered by any candidate in any election in the United States in a decade."

Sinclair was typical of the liberal-radicals whom the comrades would soon conciliate with amazing facility under the new dispensation; he would, in fact, soon shine as a star of the first magnitude in

170

the Stalinist heavens. His EPIC was typical of the reformism, even unto Dr. Townsend's panacea and California ham-and-eggism, which they would soon cement into united fronts. But at this juncture neither such men nor such movements were spared. The candidates for speedy liquidation, come the revolution, were legion.

They were saved from that dire fate in the nick of time. Browder raced home with a wholesale reprieve—the news that the revolution had been called off on account of Hitler weather. In Moscow, of all places, he had made the startling discovery that he was an American, that his party was the first line of defense for bourgeois democracy, and that those gadgets on the social fascist demons were really wings, not horns.

Straight from the New York dock he rushed to Washington. He had his orders. There was not even time enough to discuss the change with foremen, let alone innocent subcontractors. One of those fly-by-night "fronts" was meeting in Washington: a National Congress for Social and Unemployment Insurance. Earlier in the evening, in another place, a number of Lovestonites who were handing out leaflets calling for a Labor Party had been beaten up by communists for such social fascism. Now Browder took the platform at the Congress—and spoke up for a Labor Party!

This does not sound dramatic. The Labor Party issue may not affect your pulse one way or the other. But recall that this reformist heresy had been for years among the deadly Stalinist sins. To the assembled delegates and to all the communist cohorts among whom the news spread, it was as if the bishop had come out for Satan. For the time being the shock remained largely within the comradely fold. It was clear to the insiders from the one sample that a new "line" had been adopted. For outsiders, the change had to be staggered to dull the shock. What they saw was a somersault in slow motion. The complete convolution took approximately six months—from this Browder bombshell to the time Dimitrov talked Trojan Horse sense to his foreign agents.

Adjective by adjective the *Daily Worker* and the dozens of other party organs moved away from the lingo and viewpoints of the Third Period. To their own and their readers' amazement, William Green and Norman Thomas ceased to figure as "fascist agents," and F. D. R. was no longer a "fascist tool of Wall street." On the positive side, there was a sudden fondness for words like "democratic," "pro-

gressive," "anti-fascist." Stalinist propaganda, above all, became im-
measurably anti-Nazi and anti-fascist, making up in vigor for previous
evasions and confusions on the subject. No longer were all capitalist
countries lumped together, but fascist wolves among them were told
off from democratic sheep. The whole technique of the united front
from below was scrapped. Appeals—first shy, then shameless—were
now addressed to the leaders of all possible organizations (except
anti-Stalinist communists, of course) for a united front from above.

By late summer the maneuver was complete. The years of "revolutionary upsurge" might never have happened, even rhetorically. Down
through the pyramided organizations went the new party line—to
trade unionists, writers, students, Negroes, unemployed, peace enthusiasts, etc. They all accepted proudly the news that the communists
were champions of democracy and liberty. They did not even con-
cede—such is the power of faith—that they had ever thrown brickbats
at the Statue of Liberty. Just bouquets disguised as brickbats, they
explained. All the rash talk about taking power by violence had been
a little misunderstanding which now, thanks to Stalin, was finally
adjusted. A "comic misunderstanding," Stalin himself called it a few
years later in an interview with publisher Roy W. Howard.

"The Communist Party," it was in due time announced, "opposes
with all its power, and will help to crush by democratic means any
clique, group, faction, circle or party, from within or without, which
acts to undermine, overthrow and subvert any democratic institution
of the American people." The touch about "crushing by democratic
means" must be rolled on the tongue and savored, if you are a gourmet
in the matter of irony. As the communist enthusiasm for democracy
gained momentum, the American Legion and the D.A.R. were left in
the lurch.

Yesterday's perfervid internationalists now discovered America in
a big way, too. "Communism is the Americanism of the Twentieth
Century" became the most popular slogan for everybody concerned.
That disreputable line out of the past—"Workers of the world unite,
you have nothing to lose but your chains"—was quite forgotten. Previous standard party versions of American history were scrapped. Just
as the Kremlin had reinstated Peter the Great and Prince Vladimir,
so its American followers revised their verdict on national heroes and
events. They claimed Thomas Paine, Thomas Jefferson, Andrew Jackson, Abraham Lincoln as glorious forerunners. George Washington

remained under a cloud, along with Alexander Hamilton and other Tories, but judgment was not too harsh. Benedict Arnold and Aaron Burr, as every schoolboy should know, were simply Trotskyists and Bukharinites. Lincoln was the favorite prototype for Stalin and Browder.

The comrades went out of their way to demonstrate that they had become an indigenous American party. Good Anglo-Saxon names were favored for important party positions and as pseudonyms for *New Masses* editors. "We are an American party composed of American citizens," Browder proclaimed to a mass meeting. "We view all our problems in the light of the national interests of the United States." His comrades described themselves modestly as "political descendants of traditional American democracy as founded by Thomas Jefferson." More than that, as Browder was fond of explaining, the Communist Party "by continuing the traditions of 1776 and 1861 . . . is really the only party entitled by its program and work to designate itself as 'sons and daughters of the American Revolution.' "

We shall explore the ramifications of this new incarnation as we go along. For the present, suffice that there was scarcely a tenet of the Third Period which survived unchanged into the Fourth. Only the motivations and allegiances remained the same: defense of the Soviet Union and allegiance to its interests.

2

In American terms, the effects of the new party line were far-reaching. The effects were felt by classes of people which to this day do not know that a Moscow zigzag impinged on their lives. As a matter of fact, the vast majority of those drawn into the orbits of the new communist dispensation, having been unaware of the movement and disinterested in Left politics before that, did not suspect that Browder's party had ever been anything but democratic, progressive, non-violent and patriotic. The suggestion that it could ever abandon this character seemed to them self-evident prejudice if not outright red-baiting. For these novices the historical horizons of American communism swept back majestically a full year or two, to 1935.

What were the consequences of the new line? To begin with, a reconciliation with the New Deal, its leaders and its program was now possible. The love that swiftly flourished between them, to be sure, was rather one-sided. The Stalinist courting was torrid, public and thrived on snubs. The New Deal, in its official character, rejected the party's attentions; on various occasions President Roosevelt disassociated himself conspicuously from communist endorsements. In its unofficial character, however, the New Deal became deeply polluted by Stalinist infiltration. The economic dilettantism and the panicky zeal of the New Deal made wonderful breeding cultures for the Fourth Period germs.

The expanding paternalism of the Federal government, in particular, lent itself to Stalinist Trojan Horse skill. There was the proliferating bureaucracy, a large part of it new to Washington, new to the intoxication of authority. There were the teeming boards, commissions, agencies. Old-line politicians were out of the picture. Among the new crowds elbowing for the jobs, the organized communist minority—shameless in its political nepotism—had a distinct advantage. Whatever the President might do about it personally, his regime could not avoid communists. After all, it was filled with precisely the kind of people who, in all other walks of American life, were falling hard for the Moscow democratic and anti-fascist pretensions.

Frances Perkins, Harold Ickes, Leon Henderson, Robert H. Jackson, Eleanor Roosevelt—merely to read off their names is to characterize the type of Americans most readily misused as "decoration" for phony Left causes. It is not strange that Federal officials, from Cabinet members down, were soon addressing Stalinist-inspired mass meetings, helping fund-raising campaigns, collaborating more or less innocently in endless other Muscovite schemes. The First Lady of the land became almost standard equipment in setting up any new Innocents' Club or in bolstering the prestige of an old one; her sympathetic heart, social-worker enthusiasm and ideological naïveté made her a perfect subject for communist hoaxes of the Fourth Period. In the inner circle of activists, I was told, she was regarded as one of the party's most valuable assets.

The altered line on international relations, naturally, made a deep imprint on American policies. Moscow's party was now the most energetic and articulate element in America in support of strong measures against Italy, Germany and Japan, the aggressor nations. Through its open and secret friends in the press, the Administration, in its own as well as other people's pressure groups, it could and did promote the collective-security theme—the policy of a united front of democratic nations against the expanding totalitarian powers. That in turn meant demands for greater armaments, larger armed forces and big-stick attitudes by the State Department.

In the labor field, the communists once again were under orders to crawl back into the existing organizations. But they came now, ostensibly, not to bore from within but to co-operate with the conservative leaders. Many of the independent TUUL unions gave up the ghost, their members filtering back into the "reformist" parent organizations. Only those in industries where there were no A.F. of L. unions remained alive, but sought affiliation with the Federation on the solemn promise to behave. The revised trade-union line in a few years gave the party more tangible strength than it had dreamed of achieving so soon.

The schism in labor, with John L. Lewis heading up the insurgents through his C.I.O., gave Browder's crowd their largest and headiest draught of real power. The United Mine Workers' chief, until recently the most hated and vilified labor man in communist mythology, decided he could use their energy and their agitational talents. Bygones were bygones and the C.I.O. quickly became saturated with Stalinist organizers, communist ideology and Muscovite strategy. Lewis' boast that he could free himself of their influence when it suited his purpose was rash. After a while, in the complicated game of labor power-politics, the one disciplined bloc in the C.I.O. became too strong and therefore too useful to be dispensed with. The mechanic became the creature of his tools.

The new attitude on political coalition, too, had practical results for the nation. While retaining its political identity and in most cases presenting its own candidates, the Communist Party threw its weight into such efforts as the American Labor Party in New York State, the Farmer-Labor movement in the Midwest, the Lewis political machine known as Labor's Non-Partisan League. It was no longer above making deals with Republicans, Democrats, Fusionists. In California, where communist political maneuvering was most successful, Stalin's party worked openly through the Democratic Party. In Chicago it helped elect Mayor Kelly. In New York it electioneered vehemently for Mayor LaGuardia. In a number of places it made blocs with Townsendites and other pension promoters.

The curious and little recognized fact is that though the communists might not be able to roll up votes under their own banner, they were beautifully equipped for mobilizing support under other banners. As the most thoroughly organized minority in the nation, with a reservoir of crusading zeal to draw upon, they could conjure up an atmosphere of "progressivism" around some candidates and smear others with the colors of "reaction" and "red-baiting" and "fascism." Tens of thousands who would not dream of voting communist voted unknowingly under communist guidance.

All of these changes were simply variations on the main theme of union now with nearly anyone willing to oppose fascism and advocate collective international action against fascist nations. The platform was broad enough to accommodate everybody but out-and-out advocates of some brand of fascism, extreme isolationists, and of course—former communists now divorced from Moscow. All roads were therefore open to the Communist Party and its periphery contingents to approach for their variegated causes such diverse groups as church organizations, orthodox art societies, patriotic bodies, philanthropic outfits. The more successful fronts, such as the League Against War and Fascism, managed to obtain the affiliation of everything from Methodist organizations to bowling clubs. The combinations were so bizarre that even the inclusion of Father Divine, the Messiah of Negro Harlem, and a battalion of his "angels" in the line-up in May Day parades ceased to be news.

Not even the Catholic Church was spared the trouble of rejecting communist love-making. Browder in a number of speeches sought to demonstrate that the new party line ran parallel to Catholicism. In a letter to a Catholic prelate, William Z. Foster described his organization as "a party which stands four square for full freedom of worship," and solemnly called attention "to the tradition of primitive communism during the first three centuries of the history of the Catholic Church—traditions for which the Christian martyrs were crucified by the wealthy Hearsts of their day." In the sweet reasonableness of the new communist climate, the Vatican's uninterrupted war on the Moscow creed was conveniently forgotten. The same political amnesia made Stalin's business agents in America accessible to deals with anybody and everybody.

From one frontier of the American Bolshevik empire to the other, the sectarian spirit of previous years was dropped. "Proletarian" culture was killed off and denied the compliment of decent burial. It was displaced by "people's" and "democratic" arts. The practition-

ers of literature, theatre, the dance, music and the other cultural callings were freed from the necessity to treat only "desirable" subjects
in the approved style. So long as they joined the American Writers
Congress, the Friends of the Soviet Union or some other Innocents'
Club, they could count on tolerance and, at times, logrolling enthusiasm from the comradely fraternities. No longer was it indecent to
admire sunsets, Proust, Gilbert and Sullivan or low-brow movies.

In its new context the idea of the proletariat embraced everyone
from the lowliest sharecroppers to the wealthiest shareholders. Where
a brave dozen might reasonably have been expected to fall into step
on the uphill road to a sectarian Proletcult, thousands could join the
picnic parade of a chummy and vaguely progressive revolutionism. It
promised rewards—in emotional comradeship, the benefit of critical
doubts, ready-made audiences, an inside track on jobs in a string of
Federal cultural projects. And it asked few if any sacrifices in return.
The parade became almost a stampede.

3

Previous communist reversals of policy had involved, for Moscow's
faithful, certain physical discomforts and hazards, even a measure of
social ostracism. There are people with an esoteric taste for martyrdom. The sense of standing alone against the world, of being hunted
by the law but beloved of God (or in this case, History), has its psychological compensations. But the number of men and women with such
specialized tastes is in the nature of the matter limited.

The present reversal, on the contrary, offered release from risks
and a chance to "belong." It offered the sweets of respectability and
the comforts of conformity. After all, it is easier to go to bourgeois
cocktail parties than to jail. In America the Trojan Horse tactics
meant identification with the main trends in the national government,
with the vaporous surge of a strange new liberalism.

By the simple process of sloughing off its revolutionary past and
muffling its revolutionary future, American communism could now
become a mass movement. Not as measured by actual membership—
since that still called for considerable personal sacrifice and still involved some possible social if not legal disabilities; but as measured
by the size of an unaffiliated but profoundly devoted following, by
patronage in government and private undertakings where fellow-

travelers had influence; as measured, in particular, by the Communist Party's capacity to whip up feelings on any issue and to raise money for its teeming causes.

In the dawn of the Fourth Period the party had perhaps 30,000 dues-paying members; by 1936 it claimed for the first time to have passed the 50,000 mark; at the high noon of the Red Decade, about 1938, the leaders claimed 100,000 in expansive moments and compromised for 75,000 in private. But these figures do not suggest the magnitude of the influence. Several million Americans were consciously participants in a network of communist enterprises; and millions more took part, at one time or another, with only a hazy notion, if any, of what it was all about.

Arithmetic is the worst possible yardstick in such matters. A tiny group, rigidly organized and disciplined and guided by experts, can dominate a vast "independent" organization. A single person in a key position can set the tone of a large institution. In penetrating the American world, the communists were an army with banners and trained generals against a disorganized and leaderless rabble.

Of course, the cleaned-up patriotic version of Bolshevism did not go down easily with some of the old-timers in the ranks. Some of them departed in disgust. If this was revolution and Marxism, they said, then they might as well have joined the Democratic or Republican Party. Yesterday's moderate socialists now sneered at the watered-down brand of revolution. They even composed an ironical song:

> United fronts are what we love,
>   Our line's been changed again—
> From below and from above,
>   Our line's been changed again.
>
> We must appear to be sedate,
>   Our line's been changed again—
> The revolution? That can wait,
>   Our line's been changed again.
>
> Imperialist wars we once attacked,
>   Our line's been changed again—
> But since the Franco-Russian pact,
>   Our line's been changed again.

On and on in this ribald vein.

As for the excommunicated comrades of past days, Trotskyists, Love-stonites and the rest, they shouted derision. Stalin, as one of these purgees phrased it, "was selling the workers' cause on the diplomatic auction block." Arnold Petersen of the Socialist Labor Party pointed a disdainful finger at their "uninhibited orgy of opportunism." The anger and the contempt of the Left for the new Muscovite line, it is certain, were shared by the more principled of Browder's associates. They must have accepted the change with heavy hearts as an unavoidable compromise to save beloved Russia from the Nazi wolves, even as an honest woman might surrender her body to save someone she loves.

These were the exceptions. As a whole the communists took to the new respectability with yowls of joy. What were the sneers of Trotskyists against the cheers of liberals, college professors, $2,000-a-week Hollywood proletarians and Junior Leaguers who now flocked to communist organizations? In a *Saturday Evening Post* article Stanley High reported that "communism presses its pants." He was right, in a literal as well as a metaphorical sense. Romantic shabbiness was abandoned for Rotarian conventionality in dress no less than in thought. The barricades manner was given up and the comrades were soon draping themselves on penthouse bars among wealthy converts like veterans. They carried hardly a trace of the soapbox manner into the pulpits and into the college lecture halls where they now preferred to hold forth.

The artists in their midst began to shave more regularly and to put creases in their pants. A simple housewife married to a party leader told me subsequently that it was then, in line with Moscow's new attitude toward the bourgeois family, that her husband finally decided they could have a baby. A fanatic girl communist of my acquaintance had disdained the cosmetic wiles of bourgeois females, but now she combed the untidy knots out of her hair, used lipstick and rouge, and went in for permanents. The whole Stalinist movement, so to speak, went in for permanents. As long as it was wooing the working class it did not have to dress up. But now that it was selling its favors to, and seeking favors from, the upper classes and capitalist governments it had need for pomades and perfumes.

One day a base informer in the enemy camp whispered excitedly in my ear: "You'll never believe it—Mike Gold has put up curtains in his apartment!" Gold was columning for the *Daily Worker*. Any doubts I might have had on his unprincipled capitulation to curtains were dissipated when I came across a column of his defending the sanctity of the home and the joys of domesticity. I might have suspected he would end up badly when he came out in the *New Masses* not only praising the French *poilus* but comparing them to the Red Army soldiers! There is no telling what people of extremist temper will do when they get moving in any direction, even in the direction of conformity. In Gold's case it led him to such shameless admissions as this in his column of July 10, 1939: "After spending a week-end at one of the summer camps around New York, I returned to the city with the profound and novel conviction that it is only love that makes the world go round." Marxists, please note.

Earl Browder himself was in his proper medium at last. The book-keeper in his soul had never really adapted himself to the revolutionary climate. He could not quite learn how to wear clothes, but he tried hard. In the photographs of this period he looks like a shopkeeper on Sunday. The Jeffersonian democracy and New Deal reformism which he now preached suited his Midwestern voice a lot better than quotations from Marx and Engels. Behind his desk on Thirteenth Street, he felt himself the executive of a prospering business—a wholesaler in the democracy and anti-fascism line. The portraits of Washington and Lincoln, now hung along with those of Marx, Lenin and Stalin, must have given his Kansas heart the thrill of a homecoming.

Along with other party orators, he now made speeches on the Fourth of July and on Thanksgiving Day, as well as on May Day and November 7. They even hunted up more obscure patriotic anniversaries and celebrated them with red-white-and-blue trimmings. Communists and their friends staged a festival, for instance, to mark "the one hundred and fiftieth anniversary of the founding of the American Constitution and the fifteenth anniversary of the founding of the Communist Party."

On February 22, 1937, George Washington finally achieved publication in the *Daily Worker*. A streamer across an entire page featured the fable "Communism Is the Americanism of the Twentieth Century," with "The Spirit of '76" in the background center, Old Glory on one side and the Soviet flag on the other. Washington's picture dominated the page and an article by Führer Browder was titled "Communists the Heirs of the Revolution of '76." Harrison George also contributed an article on "George Washington— American Revolutionist." A leaflet announcing a party mass meeting for a Labor Party, before me as I write, divides the space on a colored front page between a drawing of Lenin and a drawing of the fife-and-drum trio of '76.

Where hundreds of Depression communists had come into the Innocents' Clubs before, their hordes had to be counted in thousands now. The meek ones, too, among schoolteachers, dentists, ministers of the Lord, Broadway producers and newspaper men, dared to sign up in Stalinist causes. And why not? The objectives were in general respectable: democracy and freedom, face-making at Hitler and the Mikado, culture for the masses, social reforms no more exorbitant than President Roosevelt's, hymns for "the most democratic nation in the world." Now they could be revolutionaries and patriots, communists and respectable, among the saved in a Marxist hereafter without relinquishing savings in the here and now.

The cult of Russia-worship was basic to the business. That sometimes caused misunderstandings. But Russia was conveniently far away. Even its more annoying peculiarities—such as show trials and blood purges and persecution of composers or theatrical producers—could be washed down with a few cocktails. The conversation could always be switched to sharecroppers and Sacco and Vanzetti. The least practiced of dialecticians could use Hearst as a lightning rod to divert indignation from the G.P.U.

So the existing planets in the Kuusinen solar system grew and new ones were launched almost daily. The liberal weeklies needed no longer to be ashamed of their Stalinism. They continued now and then mildly to reprove Stalin and his American agencies, but supported Stalinist enterprises here and defended Stalinist brutalities at home "despite everything." "It would be well to remember," the New Republic wrote of the new line, "that a sinister ulterior purpose that remains hidden away in a dark closet is reasonably sure in the course of time to wither and die of neglect.... When the communists come to the aid of what we regard as a worthy cause, we propose to welcome their help as we would that of anyone else."

The men who wrote such Pollyanna trash were too intelligent to believe it—they would hardly have accepted the help, let us say, of the German Bund or Father Coughlin for a worthy cause. This double book-keeping, however, was typical of nearly all the liberals. Secretary Ickes, for instance, let it be known that:

So far as the present is concerned, fascism is the deadly and insidious foe that we must prepare to combat without loss of time. For this reason I suspect either the motives or the intelligence of those who would have us marshal our forces against a barely imaginary danger of communism while fascism thunders at the gates of our citadel of liberty.

Mr. Ickes spoke for tens of thousands who likewise played into the hands of the Stalinists with such sophistries. Their tolerance was Browder's chief strength. Liberals of the Ickes type, it should be emphasized in their defense, simply did not understand the machinations and the motives of the communists whom they now helped. It required the tragic events of the Second World War, on the heels of Stalin's alliance with Hitlerism, to shock such people into an elementary awareness of their mistake in nurturing one variety of totalitarianism to offset another.

Meanwhile those who warned them were ignored. Max Eastman, for instance, tried to tell them that in dealing with the communists they are dealing with a "secret society" having plans and purposes not revealed to the fellow-travelers. "Americans who really believe in democracy," he wrote, "are entitled to know that the heads of this secret society were designated by a foreign dictator, are removable by him, and take orders on all vital questions from his headquarters...." But neither Ickes nor the *New Republic* groups, nor a thousand other groups busily engaged in doing jobs for Stalin, would listen.

The communist influence became literally inescapable. Like the maggots in a cheese, the fellow-travelers and stooges and innocents flavored American life. Their professional vocabulary—transmission belts, fronts, fellow-travelers, party line, liquidations, etc.—filtered into the nation's speech and thought. It added up, indeed, to an incredible revolution. Started by Moscow, ended by Moscow when no longer needed, conducted in absolute compliance with rules laid down by Moscow—but draped in the American flag, involving directly or indirectly millions of Americans and the government itself, it was by all odds the most extaordinary hoax ever perpetrated on our country by a foreign government.

CHAPTER XVI

THE INCREDIBLE REVOLUTION SPREADS

1

THE attempt to record chronologically expansion of that curious "communism" in "democratic" war paint under ultra-patriotic banners breaks down at this point. One can follow the windings of a stream or a dozen streams. But how follow the onrush of a tumultuous flood? We can merely look at it, here and there, almost at random, to note how it uprooted lives in one place, inundated another, destroyed a third.

Between the Seventh or Trojan Horse Congress in Moscow and the signing of the Soviet-Nazi Pact in the same city four years later almost to the day, Stalin's old and new fringe organizations grew in riotous luxuriance. Between one congress and the next, some of them were able to measure their enlargement by millions of affiliated memberships. Having dazzled a few clergymen or professional pacifists, the progeny of that far-off visit of Comrade Urevich, Comintern agent, could announce truthfully the addition of another million or two Americans to its roster by this Pied Piper technique. The rapprochement with the New Deal enabled the more important fronts to dress their windows with names sacred in Washington lobbies and living rooms. Transmission belts without greetings from the President of the United States or the personal participation of his busy spouse could consider themselves slovenly performers.

Take a copy of The Daily Worker, the New Masses or any other trade journal of the Stalinist invasion in the years 1936, 1937, or 1938. Gone is their old dog-in-the-manger growl. Theirs is now the arrogant and possessive bark of the favorite house dogs. They command and scold, bare their teeth to public enemies of Russia, and wag their tails at the rest of the world, including the most fantastic assortment of fellow-travelers among the rich and the socially elite.

They are no longer the voice—however hypocritical—of the have-nots and disinherited. They now "have" plenty and to spare and are mighty cocky about their new prosperity. They have the inside track on certain government jobs, a dominant role in the powerful C.I.O., special hand-tooled organizations for women shoppers, lawyers, artists, movie stars, teachers, writers, Federal employees, municipal employees, relief investigators, a hundred crisscrossed and overlapping categories. Their newspapers, like their multifarious groupings, exude an aroma of smug and comfortable self-esteem.

Their success, of course, cannot be compassed by mere listings of thriving organizations or prominent fellow-travelers. These were only the solid substances crystallized out within the new social atmosphere. It became increasingly "smart" to be red, now that red had lost most of its former political off-color connotations. Where the incredible revolution was most pervasive—in New York, Washington, Hollywood, certain college campuses, certain intellectual and social strata—one either conformed or remained outside the main trends. A species of intellectual ostracism was the price of rebellion against the pressure groups. Tens of thousands "belonged" automatically—they never joined; it simply caught up with them and saturated their lives. For hundreds of college professors, New Deal officials, book reviewers, columnists, liberal divines and undifferentiated liberals, show of resistance would have meant virtual isolation from their friends and families and associates.

A strange new code of conduct became routine among these people. It turned quickly into habit, unrelated to reason. There were key words that touched off their anger: Trotskyist, fascist, Hearst, petty bourgeois, red-baiter, Franco spy, Mayor Hague, etc. And there were key words that no less automatically touched off sizzling enthusiasms: Russia, Five Year Plans, anti-Nazi, sharecropper, social consciousness, Loyalists, picket, etc. In the same speech, on the same page, people defended executions and concentration camps in Russia and went purple denouncing the same phenomena in Germany. They condemned the burning of books in Hitlerland and hurrahed for the burning of authors in Stalinland. Hundreds among them denied vehemently that they were communists, though they were members under false names. Lying and cheating for the cause seemed to them noble and self-sacrificing. And in all this there was no contradiction and no trickery, since it was all on a plane way beyond logic.

Only the genuine radicals—socialists, libertarians, I.W.W.'s—were immune to the ideological contagion. They could not be stung into joyous frenzy by a few polished slogans. "Socialism" was not a new word to them, as it was to the poets, painters, millionaires' sons, dyspeptic clergymen and frustrated females who flocked to the Innocents' Clubs. They could not be knocked cold with a column of Soviet statistics or bluffed into silence by threats of the fascist bogeyman. This history of the Red Decade would not be complete without a tribute to the authentic Left; their publications, through all the lunatic years of the Muscovite obsession, stand as a record of courage and good sense in the midst of intellectual panic.

The mere summation of the main regions of American Life inundated by the Stalinist flood is no mean task. The literati, I suppose, deserve first place. Small in number, their impact on a nation's mind is subtle and incalculable. They set the styles in not-thinking. Their submission to Moscow influence was a species of moral surrender. Some were mobilized through national and regional congresses of the League of American Writers, others through the communist-dominated American Newspaper Guild, many through both and through involvement in stablefuls of specialized Trojan Horses not directly concerned with the writing craft. The converts ranged from humble book reviewers to best-selling novelists and playwrights; in time the sawdust flavor of Hollywood scenarists became the strongest in the stew.

In Hollywood and on Broadway, as we shall see, the incredible revolution swept important producers and modest extras alike off their feet into the comradely whirl of activities. Neither strip-tease gals nor cinema tough-guys, neither play producers nor publicity folk, were immune to the drive and drag of it all. Marx and martinis, bridge and dialectics, social consciousness and social climbing were all mixed up on the banks of luxurious private swimming pools.

In the national capital, a kind of social lobby composed mainly of the wives of prominent New Dealers gave the tone to the strange movement. The most ludicrous of fellow-traveler hoaxes could count on the mansion of some grand New Deal lady for hospitality, and a few dozen shining lights of the Federal government for embellishment. The administration of relief and the made-work projects were honeycombed with Stalinists; the trade unions in these fields were openly dominated by them; the communist factions treated the whole ramified structure as their private and almost exclusive domain. Potentially fine plans in writers', theatre, painting and other cultural projects were distorted for strictly Stalinist purposes and killed in the process.

College teachers slanted their lessons to match the latest views out of Moscow, and met with the communist faction among their students in conspiratorial caucuses. Press reporters smuggled "the line" into their copy. Scientists banded together to justify Stalin's execution squads. A hundred cocktail parties to raise funds for causes approved by the Thirteenth Street junta were often in progress on a single Saturday evening. Those who ran afoul of the revolution were made to feel the full weight of their crimes; they were ostracised socially, handicapped professionally and not infrequently stripped of their jobs as well as their reputations for ordinary decency.

It was a great and glorious, a gaudy and cockeyed period. I despair of doing more than suggesting its magnitude and savor. I can merely consider a few of its more notable, or more grotesque, manifestations almost at random.

2

Among the strangest of these manifestations was the adoption of the Cause by the swanky and the well-to-do. Caviar and vodka displaced the hammer and sickle as emblems of proletarian rebellion for these gilt-edged recruits. They fairly glowed with enthusiasm for their own speedy liquidation, and denounced "the system" that paid for this mock-revolutionary self-indulgence.

Not one in a thousand among them sensed the contempt with which they were regarded by the less debauched of the communists. The outward flattery, the sensation of being let in on a conspiracy, went to their heads. For a growing number of ladies of leisure, and for some of their menfolks, communism took the place of mahjong as a favorite parlor game. They threw parties—for this or that cause. R.S.V.P. black tie, Archie dear . . . yes, I've been promised a *real* proletarian . . . so don't fail to be there.

Mink and ermine and starched shirt fronts became a matter of course at openings of plays endorsed by the *New Masses* and the *New Theatre*, and at dance benefits for Stalinist causes. Limousines with liveried chauffeurs delivered earnest ladies to the picket lines, sometimes in strikes against businesses which helped pay for the limousines; they combined revolution with slimming exercises. A communist gathering without its quota of banker and broker sympathizers, fabu-lously paid script writers and "socialites" was considered a flop. Soviet holidays saw the Russian Embassy in Washington and Consulates else-where jammed with the kind of people whose bloody extermination was being celebrated. The Washington Bureau of the Baltimore *Evening Sun* was able to report, on November 8, 1937:

Wearing a black ensemble with orchids at the shoulder, Mrs. William A. Becker, national president of the Daughters of the Ameri-can Revolution, attended the reception at the Soviet Embassy last night to celebrate the twentieth anniversary of the Russian Revo-lution.

The revolution had more trouble making the news pages than the social columns.

The impending doom of the bourgeois order, whose wicked bless-ings these people enjoyed, filled them with an illogical but honest elation. Ignoring the minor circumstance that they were destined to be the victims, they already assumed a little of the swagger of com-missars and executioners. Their disdain for those who had not yet "found" communism was boundless.

In my own mind these economic masochists came to figure under the label of "penthouse Bolsheviks." The private christening derived from an exclusive penthouse party—exclusive in the sense that only true-blue admirers of the Soviets were invited. The opulence of the setting, the abundance of eats and drinks, the presence of well-groomed Soviet diplomatists, even the presence (for atmosphere) of a few unkempt specimens from Union Square—all of it composed into a delightful burlesque on revolution. Fortunately there were a few clear-eyed skeptics in the gay, self-satisfied crowd to relish the spec-tacle. Wonderful, thus to acclaim the "inevitable" collapse of the system incarnate in the hosts and most of their guests in warm com-radeship up there above the New York skyscrapers. . . . It was all so cozy.

One evening I was invited, by a fluke, to a farewell dinner for a de-parting Soviet official, at the home of a wealthy New Yorker who hoped to do business with the Soviet Union. The guests represented an aggregate of many millions of dollars—manufacturers, financiers, political bigwigs—with only myself and the Russian official to pull down the average. I shall never forget how the poor Russian fidgeted and looked to me for moral support as these men, one after the other, praised the land of proletarian dictatorship in unrestrained language. In the flush of the oratory they invoked the help of the Almighty for the success of atheist Russia. A former United States Senator put it on so thick that the Russian blushed under his neat beard.

The fascination of the "revolution" for a type of rich man was not entirely new in American history. Before the first World War there had been a batch of "millionaire socialists." What was new was the number and variety of those who now were attracted to Browder's standard. They were not intellectuals with money but just folks with money—simple-minded bankers, fluttery dowagers, smart debutantes who couldn't spell "proletarian" to save their lives. There was something richly satisfying about this game. Not only were they championing the downtrodden, but merging themselves with a powerful nation on the other side of the globe. They were descending among the lowly and ascending among the mighty in one simple operation and it was a thrilling feat. It had charity teas beat a dozen ways.

In relation to the whole periphery these diamond-studded fellow-travelers were, of course, not many. But their aggregate wealth made them an important division in the line-up. In one way or another they paid for the privilege of mixing with their future masters. A few of them were literate enough to take posts of leadership in Innocents' Clubs, and paid for this distinction by making up various party deficits. A few others backed communist periodicals, shows, congresses. Most important, the antics of these socially elite fired the imagination of middle-class imitators. They set a fashion. For every "cause" cocktail party in a millionaire mansion there were a hundred in middle-class apartments. The women who, in less ideological years, might have taken up table-rapping or theosophy, now took up the Friends of the Soviet Union or some equivalent excitement.

Under the heavy-sugar crust there was the filling of recruits from less opulent levels: small businessmen, professional classes, social workers. For some reason the self-righteous excitement had a particular fascination for doctors, dentists, actors and overpaid script writers. I leave it to psychologists to explain why. My own modest guess has to do with the fact that these are among the callings where exceptional skill has no relation to exceptional intelligence. All these good people needed a safe and steadying belief beyond logic, and the

Soviet paradise was far enough away to serve as a symbol of their yearnings. Rarely before had their kind been able to enjoy the thrill of conspiracy without the risk of punishment—indeed, with a heightened social éclat. Because rarely before had a "revolution" been dedicated wholly to the unrevolutionary purposes now demanded by the new Comintern credo.

I do not imply for a moment that these people did not have their hearts in the right place. At worst they were socially ambitious, at best they were chronic do-gooders. They bulged with good will to refugees, victims of Japanese and Italian aggression, political prisoners in all countries except Russia, and suffering peasants (including sharecroppers) everywhere but in Russia. If they were a bit bloodthirsty in their feelings for Trotskyists, critics of the G.P.U. and other counter-revolutionaries, they should be forgiven—they had not the remotest idea of what these words connoted. They were only hating Evil, as defined by comrades in the know. Not their hearts, but the organs located in their skulls, were at fault.

3

How did a small political party, without real roots in American life, succeed so conspicuously in attracting, organizing and milking a vast number of Americans? How did they manage so easily to permeate diverse social and professional strata in American life?

Certainly the answer is not to be found in the brilliance of the party leadership. In February, 1939, the Daily Worker published an intimate telegram, greeting William Z. Foster on his birthday. Only the first names of the signers were given. An expert on party personnel, however, filled in the missing family names for me. In the main the list represents the crème de la Kremlin of American Bolshevism in the heyday of its most successful period. Here it is, a kind of inner circle:

Earl Browder, Jack Stachel, Alex Bittelman, James W. Ford, Roy Hudson, Charles Krumbein, Gene Dennis, Rose Wortis, Robert Minor, Harry Gannes,* Ella Reeves Bloor, Gil Green, Clarence Hathaway, Irene Browder, Fred H. Biedenkapp, Rebecca Grecht, Steve Nelson, V. J. Jerome, Avram Landy.

---

* Gannes, foreign editor of the Daily Worker, died early in 1941.

I know most of them well enough to guarantee that the average—as measured by brain power, oratorical gifts, literary talents, erudition—would be somewhere on the nether side of mediocrity. The Beloved Leader himself has not been accused by anyone except his devotees of a better than average mind. Comrade Jerome, who passed as the party's chief "theoretician," is a dull, bookish person with a good memory or a good filing system. Comrade Ford's chief claim to leadership is that he is black, a kind of symbol of the Negro race. Comrade Bloor is an aged and sharp-tongued woman with a colorful career, but far from exceptional mentally. A few of these leaders have courage, most of them have enthusiasm. Yet all their virtues combined could not account for 1 per cent of the party's triumphs.

The clue to their success, it seems to me, is to be found in the conjuncture of circumstances. What such leaders did possess in superlative measure was a technique of connivance. The mere fact that they survived in a movement where purging is continuous and ruthless, is proof of their mental and psychological agility. Machiavellism is in the marrow of their bones, in the fiber of their minds. Given a favorable opportunity, they were perfectly equipped to make the most of it. They had discipline, fervor, a catechism. There were no ethical or democratic brakes on their methods, while dealing with people muscle-bound by liberal and democratic inhibitions. Their advantage was enormous.

And the opportunity was favorable. The new "democratic" anti-fascist slogans corresponded to realities in American life and emotion. Great sectors of the American people had been cut adrift politically and spiritually. They had lost old faiths and craved new ones. The assumptions of the pre-Depression years were bankrupt. The heroes of prosperity days had become ridiculous. Hopes and fears multiplied. Along came the communists with concrete slogans, a set of new heroes and new devils, large promises for small investments. And they succeeded beyond their fondest expectations.

Brutality and horror were rampant abroad. The ugly face of Hitlerism, in particular, was becoming more visible. It is impossible to over-estimate the role of anti-Nazi emotion in inflating the communist periphery. Any organization that put up an anti-fascist, anti-Nazi signboard packed its ranks with Americans too furious at Hitler to ask questions. They would have been willing to play along with Satan, let alone Stalin, against Hitler. Browder's agents exploited this state of mind to the utmost for Stalin's benefit—and, ultimately, by the in-escapable logic of such cynical alliances, for Hitler's benefit.

At home, indigenous brands of intolerance gave ample ground for fear and sympathy and indignation. Unemployment and uprooted farm population grew. Only the communists, directly and through an endless number of subsidiary enterprises, seemed to offer even the semblance of solutions. They were fitted by fifteen years of organ-izational experience to syphon off emotions into activities. Leagues. Congresses. Mass meetings. Collections. Manifestoes. Picket lines. Cocktail parties.

You joined one of their fronts—Friends of This, Congress of That—and your days and nights were suddenly brimful of action. There was no more time for moping. Soon, almost without knowing it, you were meshed in a dozen other fronts, caught up in the noise and gregariousness of it all. In a time of head-splitting questions, the com-munists offered answers. Incomplete, contradictory, often deliberately fraudulent, yet they seemed better than no answers. Every event, every complaint, from "okies" to the Spanish civil war, from China to the next election, had its counterpart in some Innocents' Club or special campaign.

Besides, though the core of the movement, the party itself, was small, it had behind it the prestige and resources of a powerful nation. The cult of Russia had been spreading. As a supposed counter-weight to Nazi Germany, the Soviet regime had become more popular than ever—outside Russia, that is to say. The American liberals and jittery conservatives needed a myth to sustain them. The meekest commissar from Union Square faced a Hollywood group or a batch of New Deal hopefuls or a roomful of New York book reviewers with a certain arrogance—he spoke with the voice of a nation holding one-sixth of the world's real estate. He was listened to less for himself than for the "revolutionary" Russia behind him.

The myth of a "victorious socialist nation," the failure of any other group in America to dramatize and sloganize solutions to obvious problems and threats, the surge of anti-Nazi feeling—these, rather than any innate genius in the Communist Party, account for the extraordi-narily successful permeation of American life by a foreign nation through a small but closely-knit and hard-working group of agents. Others lost out by default.

The new Stalinist line, it must also be recalled, was in the Leftist

reform spirit of the New Deal. The conspiracy thus had the tolerance, if not the actual backing, of our own government to supplement
the backing of a foreign government. The loose talk about Mr. Roosevelt and his associates being communists is nonsensical. It oversimpli-
fies a psychological relationship. The picture was more complicated.
The New Deal personnel as a whole was drawn from the kind of people
most vulnerable to communist penetration. It was as naïve and in
some respects as muddled as the most trusting clergyman roped in to
support an anti-religious campaign under a properly religious banner.
To explain the far-reaching saturation of various Washington bureaus
and departments with fellow-travelers is no harder than to explain how
lifelong pacifists lent themselves to organizations like the League for
Peace and Democracy, whose purpose was to help start its own kind of
war.

The colossal irony of the situation was that the fellow-travelers,
having thrown themselves into some stooge movement, really fancied
themselves revolutionaries—precisely when Moscow communism had
ceased to be revolutionary. They fancied themselves knight-errants of
anti-fascism—while championing a special brand of fascism. But
enough of the brave old nomenclature remained, enough of the revolutionary swagger, to give the mixture a beguiling shimmer of social
daring. It was a perfect recipe for those Americans who wanted the
thrill of revolutionary forms but none of their substance in blood and
death and sacrifice.

4

A large proportion of those who lent themselves to Trojan Horse
activities, it must be underlined, were not only innocent but high-
minded, idealistic, eager to be useful. Their anti-Nazi emotions were
utterly genuine, even if the organizations that exploited those feelings
were frauds. The boys who volunteered their lives to save Spain, and
the kind ladies who volunteered their apartments to raise money for
Spain, were the victims, not the authors, of a Muscovite "tactical maneuver." True, many innocents in time developed a taste for the game,
once they found themselves in the surcharged atmosphere of communist scheming. But the great mass of those involved, even those
who realized that the machinery was controlled in the Kremlin, did not
plumb the depths of the chicane in which they were implicated.

The point is that the incredible revolution was irrational. It was closer to a religious revival, in its mood, than to a new philosophy. The proof of this is glaringly evident in the ease with which the entire periphery discarded the extreme "views" of 1929-35 for the moderate slogans of 1935-39. It was not simply a dilution of a set of principles. The Third Period attitudes were not merely toned down. The principles and the attitudes were discarded and displaced by their exact opposites. Yesterday's enemies were today's friends, yesterday's virtues today's vices. With equal ease they would, at the appropriate time, discard and outlaw the new policies.

Such transformations, unrelated to American facts, might logically be expected to alienate those drawn into the movement in the preceding years. Yet nothing of the sort happened. They not only remained, with few exceptions, but dragged all their friends and relatives into the circus. The same "intellectuals" who were hot for revolution before the Seventh Congress in Moscow were now hot for evolution—and not one of them knew why, except that the "line" had been mysteriously changed by someone, somewhere, without the decency of consulting them. The same crowds who had cheered Mr. Strachey's or Comrade Browder's visions of barricades and bloodletting now cheered them as champions of democracy and the *status-quo-with-modern-improvements*.

Lincoln Steffens had been challenged by Professor Sidney Hook in the *Modern Quarterly* to explain rationally his defense of the Soviet dictatorship. The challenge did not perturb the grand old liberal journalist. He replied blandly, in the same journal, that he had given up the effort to think such things out; he simply "feels" that the communists are right. In the same vein, having become religiously communist on his road to adopting Catholicism, Heywood Broun boasted in a syndicated column one day that he did not care to argue about Russia. He "believed" it was going places, despite everything. For Steffens, Broun, thousands of their kind, it was merely "petty" and "haggling" to wonder whether the executed Old Bolsheviks were really guilty, or whether a nation with five million political prisoners was really socialist.

For those of us who had seen the symbol of their faith in close-up, the way that such people ran for their lives at the first sign of doubt of Soviet perfection was a continuous psychological miracle. I have told in another book how the editors of the *New Republic*, having invited me to a staff luncheon to discuss Russia, changed the subject when my views became unpleasant listening. People shut their eyes and their ears and their minds to anything which might reflect on their new religion. Supposed "intellectuals" were sure they were demolishing detailed reports on Russian realities by insulting the authors. I shall have more to say about the arts of character assassination as practiced against infidels. The process served essentially as a psychological trick for ignoring their views with a clear conscience.

One day an apologetic stranger came to see me. He told me a heart-rending tale. It seems that his wife, a high-strung and warm-natured woman, had devoted years of ardent effort to the communist movement. Several weeks before, she had heard me speak at a forum meeting at the Community Church of New York. What I had to report on Russia had shaken her faith. She came home that night and suffered a nervous breakdown. Now her husband came to plead that I go to the hospital and assure the woman that I had lied, that everything in Russia was lovely. . . .

I became familiar with high-pitched, hysterical hecklers; with insulting letters. As I came out of the auditorium after talking to a few hundred schoolteachers gathered at the Ethical Culture School on a Sunday afternoon, a wild-eyed, dark-visaged woman shouted obscenities at me and tried to scratch out my eyes. She was one of the "activists," I was told, of the communist local of the New York Teachers Union.

And my own experience was mild compared with those of dozens of others who dared to tell aloud what they knew of the bogus Utopia. Eye-scratching and name-calling and sneering were in the temper of the Red Decade. The methods seemed even less edifying when disguised as "literary criticism" in the New Republic or as "economic analysis" in the Nation, or as slapstick humor in a column by the late Heywood Broun.

CHAPTER XVII

AMERICAN LEAGUE FOR SOVIET WAR MONGERING

1

IN RETROSPECT, the impassioned disputes, in the press and outside it, as to whether the late unlamented League for Peace and Democracy was communist-controlled seem ludicrous. Those who had forgotten the circumstances of its birth at the Amsterdam Congress, were reminded by the circumstances of its death. With the outbreak of war, the need for defending peace and democracy, it would seem to simple undialectical minds, was greater than ever. It was precisely then, however, that the League committed suicide, leaving its vast membership orphaned.

For a few months after the brown and red dictatorships had made their alliance, the League gasped for breath and stalled for time. Then seven of its bosses met in a downtown New York cafeteria and called the whole thing off—without consulting those millions of affiliates of whom they had boasted. The chief stock-in-trade of the League, its anti-fascist fervor, was ordered back to the stock-rooms; Moscow was no longer attacking fascism. What was a weapon of Soviet foreign policy had suddenly become an embarrassment. The Rev. Harry F. Ward, head of the League, and his lieutenants had to choke it to death, and did.

Its demise, like its life, was thus correctly on the party line. The mechanism of this largest and most successful planet in the Comintern solar system was never especially mysterious. Repeatedly the communist press, in unguarded boastfulness, had revealed the party control. In November, 1935, the *Party Organizer* stated that the League—along with the International Labor Defense—must "be guided by the higher committees of the party." Browder had stated that the party's position "in the center as the moving and directive force" of the League "is clear and unchallenged." At all times the League bureaucracy showed the familiar animosity toward "detractors" of the Soviet regime. Analyses of the organization's affiliates and delegates had again and again revealed that the majority were paper and stooge-organizations under Communist Party management. Dr. Hillman Bishop of the College of the City of New York, who made the most detailed study, estimated that no less than 70 per cent of the delegates at an annual meeting were communists, although some of them represented non-communist groups. Men and women who had been close to the organization and told what they knew after breaking with it confirmed unanimously that the League was a communist creature.

Yet our Secretary of the Interior greeted the League 1939 Congress—the last, it happens, before it merged in the Soviet-Fascist-Nazi world front. Governor Benson of Minnesota marshaled one of the League parades. Several of the country's largest religious bodies associated themselves with its work. Four Congressmen served on its executive and national boards, as did a bishop and nine other clerical gentlemen. Harold L. Burton, Republican Mayor of Cleveland and a prominent local commander of the American Legion, welcomed a Congress of the League with an official address in January, 1936; he gave the organization the use of the city auditorium and advertised their confab in the city-owned streetcars. The Cleveland session listened to speeches by Major General Smedley D. Butler, Bishop Edgar F. Blake of the Methodist Church, Rabbi Barnett R. Brickner and other good "decoration" guests. Whether they were chagrined by the longer and louder applause drawn by Comrades Browder, Hathaway and other party chiefs is unrecorded. For the good of their souls, however, we trust they remained to hear the Rev. Mr. Ward's invocation, since it included this:

A good many times our constituent forces and those who come to our meetings ask: "Is the League Against War and Fascism anti-capitalistic?" Of course it is. How, otherwise, could it stop war? We try to show people in our propaganda that today the economic causes of war are rooted in capitalistic economics.

The Rev. Mr. Ward spoke as head of the organization. He had displaced Dr. J. B. Matthews when the latter proved difficult for Browder to handle. The Rev. Mr. Ward, by contrast, was easy. An obstreperous delegate at Cleveland offered a resolution condemning all dictatorships, including the Russian version. It was neatly referred to committee and was never heard of again. The organization at that time claimed that it represented 992 groups, with a total membership just under 2,000,000. The claims were stepped up to 5,000,000, then to 7,500,000, in subsequent national gatherings. Discounting duplications and biased book-keeping, it still adds up to a lot of Americans trailing a Muscovite band wagon. Before Stalin voted it out of existence, the League claimed its top figure, with 1,023 separate affiliated organizations—among them sports clubs, life insurance groups, churches, schools, trade unions and communist setups in all their rich variety of disguise.

At the Fourth Congress of the League, held in Pittsburgh in 1937, the spoor of its "revolutionary" past was so deeply buried that no trace was visible to the naked eye. Everything possible was done to broaden the deception. "Against War and Fascism" was changed to read "For Peace and Democracy." The Communist Party ostensibly withdrew as an official affiliate. "I do not think it necessary for me to say," Comrade Browder explained in a speech, "that this does not mean the withdrawal of communism. . . . We are perfectly satisfied to have our representation through those who are elected as representatives of non-party organizations." In other words, a withdrawal pro forma, the better to befuddle simple-minded bishops and pacifists and anti-Nazi know-nothings. Browder himself remained in the organization, no longer for his party but as delegate of his hand-tooled insurance and burial society, the International Workers Order, headed by Max Bedacht, a member of the Communist Party Executive.

The gathering called on all countries to "proclaim the invader of another nation the enemy of mankind," and "Hands off Poland!" was one of the peace cries of the occasion. In retrospect these sentiments bristle with irony. The Rev. Mr. Ward demanded a crusade to save democracy in the same breath that he extolled the dictatorship in Russia. The League now advocated peace by demanding that the United States take strong measures against Japan in the Far East. The communists had become blatantly jingoistic, and the League followed suit.

Nevertheless, more and more legitimate peace organizations joined the ranks. They never paused to ponder the import of words like these, uttered by Browder, the real boss of the League, in a report to his party's National Committee at the end of 1938:

We can no longer dismiss the armaments question with the old answer. We cannot deny the possibility even the probability that only American arms can preserve the Americas from conquest by the Rome-Berlin-Tokyo alliance. . . . The Atlantic ocean is transformed from a barrier to a broad high-road for the aggressor powers. The Pacific may soon be the same. . . . It will be necessary to clear away all remnants of the pacifist rubbish of opposing war by surrender to the war-makers. . . . Norman Thomas, in common with most reactionary ideologists in the country, propagates a most vicious form of this pacifist degeneracy when he argues . . . that in the very effort to defend itself democracy is transformed into fascism. This pacifist defeatism was made to order for the Rome-Berlin-Tokyo alliance; if they could only persuade the rest of the world to agree with Norman Thomas, their job would be done.

Such candor did not stem the tide of pacifist adhesions. Until the hour of its death, the League pounded the war drums in the name of peace. When Harry Elmer Barnes, historian and long useful as window dressing for the organization, revealed that he intended to attack *all* war at a demonstration in 1939, and not only wars that were disapproved by the Kremlin, he was immediately deprived of his baton as Grand Marshal of the day's parade. The most astonishing fact about the episode is that the erudite gentleman seemed astonished. Only when it has congealed as history will historians, I suppose, fully recognize their own naïve role in the incredible revolution.

In the Indian summer of its life the League had become a political force to reckon with. Among pressure groups in Washington it probably led all the rest. Certainly politicians could not ignore it, and a good many advanced their careers through its comradely co-operation. Behind the wizened little chairman stood husky comrades who knew what they wanted, having received their instructions without embellishment direct from headquarters. The vice-chairmen of the organization included the Rev. William B. Spofford, of the Church League for Industrial Democracy (Episcopal); A. F. Whitney, president of the Brotherhood of Railway Trainmen; Howard G. Costigan, boss of Washington State's important Commonwealth Federation; and Robert Morss Lovett, ubiquitous "decoration" for endless communist fronts and later secretary of the Virgin Islands.

The organization was called "Stalin's Great American Hoax" by Herbert Solow, a labor journalist who was present at that far-off house party where Comrade Urevich started the whole show. Browder confirmed the designation, except that he called it the Communist Party's "most successful application of the united front." In the more private party circles it was treated as strictly a communist racket; the *Party Organizer* gave many pages in issue after issue to detailed instructions for the work of the League.

In eight years of existence under changing names this League probably reached more Americans with its propaganda than any other foreign agency in the whole history of our country. By a generous definition of the "democracy" it ostensibly defended, the organization worked busily with all other communist stooge groups. This process of mutual help expanded the clamor and impressiveness of the incredible revolution immensely—a sort of multiple-mirror trick. The League published a monthly magazine, distributed millions of pieces of literature, staged scores of parades and mass meetings, lobbied for legislation, sent its speakers into hundreds of clubs and churches, promoted plays and motion pictures in line with its policies, and developed hundreds of contact points in our Federal and local governments.

In all this lusty career it was never guilty of a single word or act deviating from the foreign policies of the Soviet Union. Not even by accident.

2

The telltale difference between the Third and Fourth Periods of world communism lies in their contrasting attitudes toward war. Before the Trojan Horse session of the Communist International in 1935, no fine distinctions were made among non-Soviet nations. They were lumped together as potential enemies of the "socialist fatherland" whose military might must therefore be sabotaged, whose foreign wars must be converted into civil wars. We have seen that in American terms this meant penetration of munitions factories, communist "colonization" of the armed forces, unceasing agitation against "militarists."

Now the whole propaganda was in reverse. In the words of D. Z. Manuilsky, Stalin's trusted man in the International, "Now there are not only imperialist states, but imperialist states which have established a fascist regime, which are trying to impose this regime on other nations by force of arms, and which are acting as instigators of wars of plunder." Not only did he "divide wars into just wars and unjust wars," but

proved to the gullible comrades' satisfaction that this is "in conformity
with the teachings of Marxism-Leninism." He called on them to
"support a war that speeds the defeat of world reaction, and of its
shock troops—Germany, Japan and Italy."

The American comrades came through gloriously. Democrats and
patriots by Muscovite fiat, they now outdid all the maligned "militarists" of yesterday in a chant of blood and iron. Again and again the
Daily Worker thundered editorially, as it did on August 3, 1937: "Is it
not time for all the democratic nations to join hands with the Soviet
Union in issuing a word of warning to these mad dogs of fascist aggression?" The Central Committee of the American party did not
beat around the bush in telling how to meet fascist threats:

This problem will be solved in the first instance by breaking down
the conception of isolation and neutrality as the road to peace and by
preparing the masses for active collaboration with the peace forces
of all the world. . . .

In short, the policy that became popularized as collective security.

The armies and the navies of the democratic nations, formerly
symbols of imperialist villainy, were transmuted into symbols of anti-
fascist righteousness. Frederick L. Schuman, who was then vehemently Stalinist, explained in the *New Republic* that "The League
[of Nations] of today is not the League of Wilson, nor yet of 'Poin-
care nor of Streseman and Briand.' It has become a grand alliance of
liberalism and communism for mutual defense against fascism." Such
wishful thinking was typical. The overstimulated liberals took the
Kremlin's make-believe at face value. Little did they suspect that at
that very moment Stalin's agents were shuttling between Moscow and
Berlin on errands of friendship and mutual help. Those who sought
to warn them were, of course, hooted into silence.

Basically Moscow's strategy was to involve the rest of the world
in a war from which it would then, itself, withdraw in high-minded
and hypocritical disdain for "imperialist squabbles." Thus, while itself
supplying Italy with coal and oil for the war on Ethiopia, the Kremlin
tried furiously to set France and England into action against the fascist
aggressor. The comrades in America managed to justify the sale of
Soviet war supplies to Mussolini while clamoring for an American
embargo on such goods to Italy. The pattern of Kremlin behavior was

repeated in the tragic Spanish civil war. While limiting its own aid to the Loyalists, and supporting the non-intervention arrangement, and physically "liquidating" Loyalist leaders who refused to accept Stalin's yoke, Russia and its foreign legions of noisemakers did their shrill utmost to transform the Spanish war into an all-European war.

The strategy was especially shameless in relation to the Japanese aggressions in the Far East. Russia had permitted the Mikado to take Manchuria. Before launching its major drive on China, Japan had made a few explorative forays into Soviet regions, on the Amur and elsewhere. Only when Russia showed itself unwilling or unable to resist, did Tokyo feel free to pounce on its prey. While the invasion of China was under way, Moscow did not relax its efforts to obtain a non-aggression pact with Japan. But no stone was left unturned by the comrades in the effort to force a Japanese-American conflict.

No organ of finance capital was half as insistent on protecting "our investments" in China as the *Daily Worker*, the *New Masses*, the League for Peace and Democracy and all other megaphones of Muscovite policy. "CHINA TODAY—U.S. TOMORROW" an advertisement of a communist mass meeting in Madison Square Garden shouted. "When will America be attacked by these mad dogs?" Harrison George, *Daily Worker* columnist, asked. Comrade Hathaway warned us all: "We cannot avoid war simply by getting out of China—unless we want to be swallowed by fascism." The *Daily Worker* demanded instant punitive action against the Japanese: "But why wait, why not now—before it is too late. Must bombs rain on our cities before we act?" And again: "America will be living in a fool's paradise if it watches the war bullies advance step by step toward the inevitable explosion of a new world war without doing anything to stop it."

There was unconscious irony in the communist reiteration of the warning that Japanese aggression is "directed against the imperialist interests of the United States and Great Britain," and that "it is good business for the United States to keep China's vast but undeveloped resources out of Japanese control, despite the short-sighted attitude, from the viewpoint of their own self-interest, of some big businessmen in this country." The citations are from the *Daily Worker* and the *New Masses* respectively.*

---

* Quotations as given in *Pro-War Communism,* by Veritas, 1937, Advance Publishers.

It was, of course, America's safety and America's investments that worried the comrades, to hear them declaim. Nary a word about Russia's interest in embroiling Japan with America. In a published debate with Professor Charles A. Beard, Comrade Browder blandly denied that Russia was in any way menaced by her Eastern neighbor. In his best Fourth of July rhetoric he pictured instead the fair landscape of California desecrated by Nipponese invaders.

The signal for that brand-new solicitude for America's landscape and "imperial interests" had been given by Moscow. The signal to call off this comedy would be given in due time. The Soviet hope—quite justifiable from the angle of Russia's own *Realpolitik*—was to set Japan and the United States at each other's throats on one side; to get Germany and the Western nations fighting on the other side. But literally millions of Americans refused to see the obvious Soviet self-interests behind the thin pretense of anti-fascist posturing. It suited their anti-Nazi fervor to pile on the Soviet band wagon, only to be dumped in the morass of Hitlerism at the end of the wild ride.

And so they flocked into the leagues and congresses and committees under communist control. There they passed resolutions for collective security and staged demonstrations for stringent embargoes. In the war demands of these years by the League for Peace and Democracy, the American Writers Congress, the American Youth Congress, the Friends of the Soviet Union, the Hollywood Anti-Nazi League, the National Negro Congress and dozens of other outfits, there is scarcely any variation even in phraseology. The clamor mounted month after month—only to cease suddenly and startlingly on the day Russia, having made its bargain with fascism, could dispense with this maneuver. The longed-for-war having been started, Moscow could then wash its hands of the bloody business and return to its previous "anti-imperialist" line.

For twenty-two months thereafter the Comintern and its every appendage again ridiculed the distinction between democratic and anti-democratic capitalist states. Again they lumped all non-Soviet nations as "imperialist plutocracies." The value of those professions can be truly estimated only in the light of their own definitions and demands in the preceding periods. The shamelessness of the deception is explicit in such quotations as these, *both by William Z. Foster:*

This is isolationism pure and simple; it is the absurd theory that the United States can avoid the fascist aggressors by running away from them.—*Daily Worker*, October 4, 1937.

The war between the Allies and Germany is a struggle between rival imperialist powers, hence the workers have no interest in supporting either group in the contest.—*The War Crisis*, 1940.

Either of these statements may be defended. Both statements coming from the same leader of a political party constitute prima facie evidence of political trickery. Every participant in a communist meeting or resolution for collective security—whether a Cabinet member or a cabinetmaker, the wife of the President or the wife of a ditch-digger—was a dupe of the Stalinist collective security hoax. I do not for a moment argue that the collective security idea was itself a hoax. For all we know, the world would have been spared its present agony if fascist aggressions had been met with unmitigated force at the outset. I do mean that the Stalinist advocacy and leadership of the policy was fraudulent; and that insofar as the policy was predicated upon Russian co-operation and leadership, it was a delusion destined to end badly. Stalin's organizations were essentially engaged in priming the hoaxed millions for the planned betrayal that came, inevitably, in the Stalin-Hitler Pact.

The League for Peace and Democracy was the principal vehicle of the Kremlin's war policies. Its influence reached into the schools, the churches, the government, the arts. All its activities had the automatic backing of the whole array of other communist groups; and in turn it threw its weight into any job for Moscow undertaken by lesser innocents' groups. The integration of the whole system, with their interlocking directorates and their common domination, helps explain their amazing success.

Chapter XVIII

STALIN'S CHILDREN'S HOUR IN THE U.S.A.

1

IN OUR America not even Mother is more sentimentally idealized than Youth. The young men and women passing hazily and in a condition of glandular overexcitation through the difficult years between childhood and adulthood are credited with a sort of collective wisdom and competence, with special rights and special moral authority. "Student movements" and "Youth protests" are likely to be treated as serious expressions of opinion when they are, in large part, symptoms of a physiological condition—an aspect of growing pains. Parents, teachers, politicians genuflect before the altar of Youth. Organizations purporting to speak in the sacred name of Youth get hearings and privileges that would not, under similar circumstances, be granted to their elders.

This is especially remarkable because the same parents, teachers and politicians treat the same boys and girls—at home or in school or in industry—quite realistically. They recognize that individually these young people are far removed from the idealized version of Youth. Boy for boy, girl for girl, they are with few exceptions awkward, unstable, uncertain of themselves. They swing violently between the extremes of self-abnegation and greed, are insufferably frivolous or insufferably bookish. Even the most balanced among them are in danger of keeling over under the stress and strain of urgent physical changes.

Their opinions are more crudely colored by undefined emotional urges, at this stage of rapid adjustment, than at any other time in their lives. Because of immaturity and youthful eagerness they "follow the leader" more blindly than any other age group, and are perfect raw stuff for demagogic molding. Not one of them in ten thousand would conceivably be trusted to make policies for his community. Yet the ten thousand together, as Youth with a capital Y, influence policies, commanding attention beyond their numbers and without reference to their inexperience and peculiar psychological influences.

The glorification of Youth is a modern development. It puts a premium on lack of experience, mental fuzziness and intuition as against intelligence and maturity. I watched both Italian Fascism and German Nazism at close range in their formative stages. It is not generally appreciated to what a large extent they were both Youth movements. Demagogues who knew what they wanted used the energies and emotional drives of young people who had not the remotest notion what they really wanted. In both those countries, Youth was deliberately mobilized to beat civilization into a pulp.

Watching the Youth movements in this country against the memory of Italy and Germany, I have been struck by the similarity of the procedures. American Youth was no longer descriptive of an age group passing through adolescence—its organized and regimented minority had become a sloganeering political lobby, a bigger and louder pressure group, competing with elders for handouts and privileges as though it were a permanent class rather than a period of biological transition. The more articulate and capable were making professions and careers as Youth leaders. Partly through sentiment and largely for political advantage, politicians flattered the Youth lobbies and catered to their pretentious self-importance. It was inevitable that the most rigidly organized, disciplined and purposeful minority would take over this Youth racket and use it for its own purposes—and for a long time the elders, from the President of the United States down, were content to applaud the antics instead of exposing the influences and motives behind the whole show.

Those who should guide young people are content to follow, leaving that function to crackpot "champions of Youth" or political demagogues aiming to capture the campus and the youth. A lopsided liberalism has led teachers to believe that Youth must be given complete independence, that its preferences are inviolable. The result is that young people are set adrift just when they need and crave steering; the first group with a plausible and exciting program takes them over. Why the authority of a disinterested pedagogue should be evil and the authority of an interested demagogue good is beyond explanation. It is just another phase of the mythology of fashionable "modernism."

The practical effect is that the influence of teachers, parents and adjusted elders is displaced by the influence of ax-grinding outsiders and political charlatans. Men and women who have the prestige of important public positions are certainly doing America a disservice when they follow Youth groups instead of leading them—when they "play the game" with political minorities that have captured Youth organizations instead of siding boldly with the captives against these minorities.

The Popular Front and Trojan Horse techniques opened wide the gates of America to the Young Communist League no less than to its parent organization. There was no more need for sectarian exclusiveness or revolutionary hocus-pocus. The Y.C.L. leaders, prompted by the adult party, could now wave the American flag, outshout any jingo, join the Young Methodists in public prayers—anything to "broaden the people's youth front" and snare more unsuspecting organizations. Above all, they could now forget their communism and concentrate on Moscow's immediate objectives. The Yipsels—young socialists,—whom the junior Stalinists once derided as "reformists," now seemed intransigeant rebels by contrast.

The new tactics worked as well among young people as among adults; sometimes better. The American Youth Congress became another important instrument of the People's Front. Under the confusion of claims and counterclaims as to the control of the organization are the familiar and indubitable signs of party-line dominance. Whether Waldo McNutt, Joseph Lash, William Hinckley, James Lerner, Molly Yard, Joseph Cadden, Edward E. Strong, Jack McMichael and the rest of the top-shelf leaders were technically members of the Young Communist League or the Communist Party is an academic question. There was little doubt that they acted as good fellow-travelers would and were utilized by the East Thirteenth Street masterminds as mouthpieces. The Congress resolutions matched the official Stalinist line, year by year, even unto the sensational flip-flops after Stalin and Hitler got together and after they split again.

The totalitarian liberals, of course, sputtered with fury against those who claimed that the A.S.U. and its American Youth Congress were dominated by the communists. They cheered Mrs. Roosevelt's know-nothing championship of these organizations. But they came to know better, and in due time were to admit it. Writing in January, 1941, the Nation in an editorial casually would refer to "the communist leadership of the A.S.U. and the American Youth Congress" and the need "for a democratic youth movement to free itself" from this monitorship. The fact is that Stalin's fingerprints were all over these captive Youth organizations.

Yet the Administration in Washington went the whole hog in support of Browder's junior innocents' front. New Deal stalwarts like Aubrey Williams, Robert H. Jackson, Eleanor Roosevelt, Harold Ickes took the organization to their bosoms and defended it against "suspicions" of communist controls. The President repeatedly lent his name and the prestige of his position to the Youth Congress, and the Young Communists in its managerial setup used those political gifts to the limit.

But let no one throw stones at the New Deal without investigating the behavior of his own political and social colleagues. Young Republicans, just like Young Democrats, took part in Youth Congress shindigs. Among the Senators and Congressmen, dozens of them in the aggregate, who tried to make political capital out of flattering this Youth lobby, there were die-hard Old Democrats, and a number of Republicans, as well as New Dealers. College presidents, mayors, pious denominational Youth leaders joined the parade. The more that joined, the easier it was to inveigle others. In political and pressure-group band wagons, nothing succeeds like success.

As one reads Communist Party literature of these years, there is no evading the feeling that the comrades regarded the American Youth Congress as their private property. They treated it frankly as their baby, and boasted about what a good-natured and co-operative baby it was. Speaking in Moscow, the head of the American Young Communists, Gil Green, told how "we"—the communists—led the Youth movement and drew in ever more religious, liberal and other non-communist young people. The *Party Organizer* continually gave instructions about Youth Congress matters, as blandly as though it were another branch of Stalin's party.

At the celebrated Seventh or Trojan Horse Congress in Moscow, Comrade Kuusinen praised his American contingents. "Our American comrades," he informed the congregated delegations, "achieved a great success at this Youth Congress. . . . And when, somewhat later, a second general Youth Congress was held, our young comrades already enjoyed a position of authority in it." Browder confirmed the compliment. In his book *The People's Front* he boasted that "The Young Communist League with the assistance of the party has from the beginning played an important part in building the Youth Congress movement and formulating its program and activities." Which was putting the matter mildly, of course, for public consumption. In his book *Communism in the United States* he attested that in the American Youth Congress "the center of gravity is the work of the Young Communist League," adding: "Practically all the basic proposals and policy came from us and from those influenced by us."

"The utmost concentration is required for the building of the American Youth Congress," an official party resolution said in the first year of that Congress. The utmost concentration is what it received in all subsequent years.

By the time this superb innocents' front met for its fifth annual convention, in New York City over the July Fourth week end in 1939, its delegates claimed to represent 513 organizations with a total of 4,700,000 members. The figures can be halved and it would still be an exaggeration. Delegates listed organizations which had never affiliated. Shepherds maneuvered their organizations into the line-up without the knowledge or consent of their flocks. Young people who held memberships in a dozen groups thus had themselves tallied a dozen times. After every discount is made, however, it was still the largest aggregate of young people ever lured into one political enclosure.

About a hundred religious groups were listed by the meeting as participants—Evangelical, Methodist, Jewish, Presbyterian, Polish Catholic, etc. Along with the Young Republicans and Young Democrats, the Y.M.C.A.'s and Y.W.C.A.'s, there were (as the *New Republic* recorded) "young Coughlinites." The Townsendites had been in the fold for years.

Two months removed from the outbreak of the war, this last pre-pact convention still raged against fascism and Hitler, still hurrahed for the Roosevelts, still adhered to the full Fourth Period catechism of the Comintern. Neither the delegates nor the millions whom they professed to represent could guess that all their "views" would be canceled out so soon. If there was any margin of doubt as to who held the levers of this youth machine, it was wiped out by the Soviet-Nazi alliance. Automatically the American Youth Congress turned isolationist, exchanged its anti-fascism for "anti-imperialism," converted its approval of the New Deal Administration into fanatic hatred, switched from support of national defense to raucous attack on rearmament.

It did so at the same time and as arbitrarily as the League for Peace and Democracy, the Friends of the Soviet Union, the communist-controlled labor unions and every other Stalinist front organization here and abroad.

2

The strange case of Eleanor Roosevelt cannot be evaded. She has been the most conspicuous example of the curious liberalism which throws malleable young people to any demagogic wolves who manage to corner Youth movements. By this time it must be clear to the most sentimental victim of the mothering impulse that Stalin's children's hour was more sinister than it seemed. Mrs. Roosevelt led all the rest in siding with the Stalinist minority against the great captive majority within the Youth Congress. She had an opportunity to expose the technique of domination, but she chose not to interfere. Whatever it may prove about her sympathies and fine intentions—she deserves every benefit of the doubt—it does not lessen the magnitude of the mischief done.

Repeatedly the First Lady explained that she was defending the right of young people to think and act for themselves, even if they were communists. And she meant it from the bottom of her capacious heart. Unfortunately she was defending the exact opposite. In allowing herself to be used as respectable window dressing for the organization, she was really helping the Youth bureaucracy to prevent the young people from thinking and acting for themselves. She was in effect lined up with the canny leaders and their secret caucuses against the mass of members; with the political machine against the more naïve and unsuspecting religious and liberal and social affiliates. In a larger sense she was siding with the tiny organized lobby against the vast unorganized mass of young people. Like thousands of other mothers and teachers and clergymen Mrs. Roosevelt had unwittingly abdicated in favor of Browder, Gil Green and their henchmen, who took over by the default of the natural leaders.

The American Youth Congress and its controlling political junta, the managers of the American Student Union, represent the closest American approximation of the totalitarian leadership principle. These organizations have gone through several major policy somersaults; from the Oxford Pledge to intensive collective security to know-nothing isolationism. Such profound changes were made in every case suddenly, by edict from above, without mass discussion and

in obvious compliance with signals from a world-wide conspiratorial
movement. The young people did not "change their minds." Their
minds were not involved in the business. They merely "followed the
master," most of them scarcely aware where they were going, none
of them aware why. The more conscientious among them rationalized
the change of view afterward, but the change itself was mechanical:
a reflex of obedience and loyalty to leaders.

Mrs. Roosevelt—and scores of others who made themselves part
and parcel of the governing clique in the Youth organization—gave
the leadership principle the moral authority of their support. The
victims were left friendless. The duty of these adult patrons, it seems
to me, was to challenge the steam-rollering of programs and the camou-
flaging of motives.

They might have exerted their influence to force wide and unham-
pered discussion of policies. They owed it to the inexperienced younger
people in the rank and file to dig beneath the surface of pretenses, to
follow the leading strings to their source, to analyze the bureaucracy
and its secret purposes. Instead, they joined in the cheering and
snubbed the young socialists and others who tried to tell the truth
about the whole Stalinist deception. They sided with the Youth
bosses, with collective know-nothingism against democratic and intelligent exploration of facts.

It was not a question, as Mrs. Roosevelt insisted, of the American
Congress having the right to vote as it pleased. The problem—her
problem in particular, as uncrowned queen of the Youth Congress—
was to find out why the organization was voting in a particular
way at a particular time. Who had decided it? Did the politically
less-seasoned delegates and affiliated organizations understand the implications of the views forced on them? How many of the delegates
represented paper organizations? How many of the delegates from non-
communist groups were secretly in the Communist Party? It was a
question of leading a free examination of disputable issues in a democratic spirit; of defending the rights of non-conformist minorities
within the Congress; of guiding young people to think rather than to
shout hurrah on a cue from the rostrum.

The honesty of Mrs. Roosevelt's or Robert Jackson's intentions
does not make their role any the less culpable. They were typical of
hundreds of other politicians and educators and social leaders. Unknowingly, but in reckless disregard of warnings, they handed over

youth to political manipulators. Their blame must be shared by all the public officials, the college presidents, the well-meaning Youth cultists who abdicated their adult position as guides for the fun of trailing a gaudy band wagon. In supporting the tiny group that had maneuvered itself into control, they were playing false to the rest of the members, and to the millions of American young men and young women not represented at all in these highly centralized pressure groups.

When the Youth Congress, in alert compliance with the Kremlin's new marching orders after World War II got going, changed its foreign policy line, Mrs. Roosevelt should have suspected the inspiration of the change. Yet she sponsored their next gathering, held in Washington. Indeed, the arrangements were made in part directly from the White House, where Youth leaders were living as guests of the family. She swung her prestige to obtain special official privileges for the delegates. Her wards repaid the hospitality by staging one of the rowdiest attacks on the Administration in all its seven years. They booed the President, put on a roughhouse session in the gallery of the House, passed resolutions vilifying all those who sided with the Allies against the Nazis.

The First Lady gritted her teeth and took it. Not until a year later, February, 1941, did she finally refuse to sponsor or address the Congress. Unfortunately she did it without tearing the mask from her "young people." She disavowed any "disillusionment" with the organization, insisting merely that she did not see eye to eye with it on America's foreign policy. She could detect no wrong in their Communazi views on the war, but happened to disagree with them, that's all. In short, she continued to treat the organization as though it were an ideologically independent American body, thinking out policies in conformity with American interests!

Even in breaking with the group, Mrs. Roosevelt thus shielded it against the "slanders" of Kremlin control—slanders acknowledged as true by communist leaders and obvious to all but the most naïve victims of Stalinist hocus-pocus. After the long years in which she had thrown the cloak of White House patronage around this foreign agency, it was her moral right and her American duty to ask: "Why have you leaders of the American Youth Congress changed your minds on foreign policy? Why have you become so eager to prevent a British victory over Hitler? Why are you following a road in the very opposite direction from your previous, pre-pact destination?" Such questions, if answered boldly and honestly, would have made clear to the youth of America that this organization took its lead from a foreign tyrant.

Whatever her logic, the First Lady failed in her duty and her opportunity. She left the Young Communist League in a position to carry on its work of obfuscation. Mrs. Roosevelt represents the fellow-traveler type at its best—idealistic, emotional, stubborn in holding on to illusions. The Youth sponsorship was only one of dozens of activities in which she innocently contributed the glamor of her name, the weight of her position, the moral cloak of her good intentions to the Kremlin's American followers. A list of organizations in which she participated in one way or another includes the World Youth Congress, the Southern Negro Youth Congress, the Motion Picture Artists Committee, the China Aid Council of the American League for Peace and Democracy, the Foster Parents Plan for Spanish Children, the communist-dominated Local 5 of the American Federation of Teachers, the American Student Union, the Workers Alliance, the Southern Conference on Human Welfare, the American Communications Association, the National Negro Congress, the League of Women Shoppers, the Daughters of the American Depression, the Federal Workers School, the American Newspaper Guild, the American Rescue Ship Mission, etc. These organizations have in common the fact that they are—or were—under full or partial communist control.

Her failure to break sharply with the Youth organization is another demonstration of the psychological loyalties that still bind fellow-travelers to the Stalinist causes, despite outward disavowals. It makes them available for the support of every new hoax ordered by the Communist Party leaders.

3

Of the twenty 'millions who make up, roughly, what is called American Youth, about one million are in colleges and normal schools. The American Student Union never claimed more than 20,000 of this million. Its dues-paying adherents at the peak, in December, 1938, were put at 9,000. Of these, perhaps half were either members of the Young Communist League or wholly committed to its program and discipline. But the Y.C.L. had—and has—an absolute grip on the

A.S.U., which in turn plays the decisive role in the American Youth Congress, an organization claiming to represent more than 4,000,000 and to speak for all 20,000,000. It all adds up to a perfect demonstration of the capacity of a highly disciplined political machine to work its will on a millionfold amorphous mass of unorganized people.

From the beginning the A.S.U. was the intellectual spearhead and the dynamic political element in the Youth Congress. Of course, it always had the disciplined collaboration of delegates from the Young Communist League, the Youth Sections of the American League for Peace and Democracy, the International Workers Order, various communist-controlled C.I.O. unions, the National Negro Congress, the Workers Alliance and a long series of other specialized names for the same totalitarian machine. Against such a bloc—led by experts, functioning through caucuses, committed to concealment and duplicity as a matter of policy—the denominational religious groups, the Y.M. and Y.W.C.A.'s, the various liberal delegations, were utterly helpless. The plumbing of bloc control was concealed and the majority was scarcely conscious that it was being fooled.

The prestige of the A.S.U. on the American campus rose rocket-like with the spread of the incredible revolution to college professors. Always, thus, one department of the aberration dovetailed into another, multiplying the cumulative effect. In Brooklyn College as many as 48 teachers took part in Communist Party faction caucuses, out of a faculty of some 300. In dozens of other colleges, the condition was analogous. But large or small, these factions came in many places to dominate collegiate life since they acted together, supported one another, and could count on the acquiescence if not support of their own periphery of "liberal" fellow-travelers.

Contrary to the general impression, the Student Union often had a more difficult time of it in city and state colleges than in some private and more exclusive institutions. In places like the City College of New York or the University of Wisconsin the communists at least had to contend with radical anti-Stalinist students who understood their tactics and challenged their pretensions. Little if any such opposition could be expected on the more exclusive and well-to-do campuses. There the leap from indifference to pseudo-communism had been made by a large number of students and professors without intermediary stations, precisely as in other sectors of the middle and upper classes.

Nearly everywhere the Muscovite program took in men and women who should have known better. A.S.U. conferences now could count on the dean or president as chief speaker, along with some outside communists bringing greetings. The "peace strikes"—now a euphemism for collective security—could count in most places on faculty and administration support. Radical and liberal students and professors who saw through the fraud, who refused to join it or abandoned it in disillusionment, were persecuted as "Trotskyites," boycotted and subjected to filthy character assaults.

The Young Communist units among the students and the adult communists among the professors often caucused together. In many schools they were the real power behind the throne. Where they could not cajole an administration into toeing their line, they resorted to. browbeating, campus pickets, organized vituperation of faculty leaders, deans, presidents. They could always count on the unthinking support of liberal weeklies, sentimental columnists, Stalinist-led locals of the Teachers Union. Through ignorance or through fear, campus administrations in many places entered into silent partnership with the communist terror.

The whole story of that terror has not yet been told. It has barely been suggested in the testimony of the President of Brooklyn College, Dr. Harry D. Gideonse, before a State legislative investigating committee. He told how his efforts to break the communist grip on his college marked him for fantastic campaigns of picketing, a war of nerves by means of night-time telephone calls and personal insults, political pressures from fellow-travelers in all parts of the school system. A member of his faculty, Dr. Bernard Grebanier, having publicly broken with the communists, similarly found himself the target of carefully generaled attacks. He was ostracized by his former friends, snubbed by former admirers among the students, plastered with outrageous libels on his private life and character. For a time there were also open and partially successful boycotts of his courses.

Multiply this picture a hundredfold and we have an inkling of the incredible revolution on the campus—whence it made itself felt through Youth groups off the campus, by direct and covert control of the Youth Congress. Numerically negligible, the A.S.U. yet gave the color of its political views and social attitudes to college life and in large measure to Youth movements generally. It had become dominant, arrogant, fashionable. Its 1938 convention was addressed by

Mayor Fiorello H. LaGuardia of New York, by Dr. Ordway Tead, Chairman of the Board of Higher Education, and an array of other public figures. Messages of greeting were received from President Roosevelt, Governors, Senators, Congressmen, Republican and Democratic leaders. These were the "decoration." The lustiest cheering was reserved for Gil Green, Hathaway, Browder and for their standardized resolutions along the current party line.

Sensational magazines have attempted to explain the phenomenon of communist penetration of the colleges simply in terms of sex. The explanation is only partly true. Inevitably sex plays a great psychological role in any Youth movement. The unorthodox attitudes that go with radicalism helped to attract followers for the organization. But sex was only one element, and the smallest, in a larger cultural design.

The American Student Union gave its followers concrete and convenient answers to pressing questions, in years when Depression had stirred up fears and doubts. It gave them a sense of intellectual companionship, an exciting new "Marxist" jargon, a feeling for the validity and thrill of being alive and being part of an unfolding historical process. To put the matter bluntly, it gave these young people what a dessicated and routinized and excessively "modern" curriculum did not. In unit caucuses and "cause parties," in picketing and sloganeering, they found the stimulation which apparently they missed in classrooms. Like Mrs. Roosevelt and the politicians, our educators had failed to provide leadership and guidance. An international political party took their place.

The fault, surely, does not rest with the students. It rests with those who exploited their youthful zest for action and thirst for faith. It rests, even more, with the elders who relinquished the age-old function of *leading* Youth and were content to *follow* Youth.

4

In the summer of 1938 the American Youth Congress played host to a World Youth Congress at Vassar College, Poughkeepsie, New York. Unquestionably there were many innocents present, but the whole affair was fervently communist. The world organization had originated in a Student Congress Against War and Fascism in Brussels, Belgium, four years before. The first World Youth Congress, held at Geneva in 1936, was a typical Popular Front occasion under Comintern guidance. The fact alone that the second world gathering was being staged in the United States was high tribute to America's Red Decade by its absentee promoters.

Abroad, where governments and educators were less naïve about such proceedings, it was generally recognized as another of Stalin's fronts. The British Labor Party for that reason refused to take part. The Union of South Africa, branding the gathering as part of the Young Communist International, refused passports to delegates. The press in Moscow candidly played up the affair as a Popular Front triumph. In America, however, those who called this communist meeting by its real name were denounced as "reactionaries" by the "liberal" mud gunners. The President, Mrs. Roosevelt and the rest of the complacent wishful-thinking group whooped it up for the Poughkeepsie demonstration with all their might.

The most active organizational backing in this country for the Vassar congress came from the Young Communist League, the American League for Peace and Democracy, the American Student Union, the National Negro Youth Congress—different names for the same clique. The loudest press support came from the *Daily Worker*, the *New Masses, Fight, Champion of Youth* and other party papers. The American delegation was, of course, the largest. It was so preponderantly communist that no one familiar with the Left could have doubts about the color of the enterprise.

The delegation counted James Lerner, Marian Briggs, Joseph Lash, Edward F. Strong, Leon Straus, Joseph Cadden, William Hinckley, and a dozen other followers of the party line of that period.* Americans acting as representatives for international bodies included Celeste Strack of the Young Communist League. The foreign delegates were for the most part the Gil Greens of their respective nations—Communist Youth leaders like Raymond Guyot of France, Dave Kashton of Canada, Ernesto Guidice of Argentine, and John Gollon of England. The visitors' sections were constantly jammed with well-known American comrades. And, of course, the resolutions finally adopted were the routine Fourth Period formulations on everything under the sun.

But none of this sufficed to warn well-meaning dupes. The Presi-

---

* Some of them, of course, have since then repudiated Stalinism.

dent of Vassar, Dr. Henry N. McCracken, in a press statement made the ludicrous estimate of 5 to 10 communists present. He must have felt himself betrayed when the International Secretary of the gathering, Betty Shields-Collins, herself admitted that among the delegates were "21 representing communist organizations." Running one's finger down the list of delegates, it is easy enough to spot ten times as many as Dr. McCracken estimated.

Mrs. Roosevelt, in her daily column, cited the fact that the conference opened and closed with a prayer as proof that it was not communist-controlled. Had she investigated these matters on which she acted so impulsively, she would have learned that prayers were specifically included among the Trojan Horse tactics taught to comrades. Browder's "democratic front" was making eyes at the Catholic Church just then, let alone the liberal Protestant denominations, and a few prayers were the least of the concessions they were ready to make.

The First Lady and the President of Vassar were demonstrating how easy it was to take in such innocents. Their behavior provides the most impressive answer to the question: How did the communists manage to put it over? The answer is less in their own talents than in the eager gullibility of the victims. Most of the Youth Congress literature and letterheads were printed on the same presses as the Communist Party's literature. Comparisons of Congress pronouncements with those of the party on the same subject reveal startling similarity not only in content but sometimes in phrasing. These were matters spread on the record and easily subject to checking.

Yet the Administration and various Congressional Committees continued to treat the heads of the American Youth group as the voice of young America instead of the voice of old Moscow. It was no secret that the Young Communist League was paying railroad expenses for delegates to conferences to swell the ostensibly non-communist representation. Before the Third Congress, the national officers of the Y.W.C.A. felt it necessary to warn their local organizations against being bribed by such subsidies. That, however, did not deter Mr. Roosevelt from sending his fraternal love to the meeting, or various Democratic and Republican organizations from following his lead. In that particular session, the *American Socialist Monthly* estimated, "of the eleven hundred delegates about seven or eight hundred were communists . . . about 100 were socialists and trade-unionists, the balance were liberals and church groups."

In a carefully documented pamphlet, Murray Plavner proved the communist domination of the Youth Congress to the hilt.* The self-appointed champions of that cumulative deception of American Youth did not reply to the challenge. They simply ignored Mr. Plavner, thus implying that the communist insults against him were deserved. His was the fate reserved for all who tried to bring facts and logic to bear against unthinking fervor. But his record stands as a reproof to the twittering and self-righteous patrons of Stalin's children's hour. The years since the publication of his exposé have merely confirmed overwhelmingly his every charge.

The controversy around the political identities of the American Student Union, the American Youth Congress and their associated fronts cannot be dismissed lightly. The communist strangle hold on Youth movements has left deep imprints on American life and thought. It is perhaps the strongest ingredient in that skepticism and disillusionment which is now making so many of our undergraduates indifferent to the fate of democracy. Thousands of those who were indoctrinated with communist amoralism will help to shape our American life of tomorrow. Many of them are today in places of strategic importance in our national life. Having regimented a sizable sector of our youth, the communists had no trouble in switching them from one political position to the exact contrary position. The Kremlin had obtained a significant leverage in manipulating our youth.

The educators and political leaders and others who collaborated to make this possible can now make amends in only one way. It is by helping expose Stalinist penetration, despite the fact that the exposure will leave indelible stains on their own records for good sense and sound judgment.

------

* *Is the American Youth Congress a Communist Front?* by Murray Plavner, 1939.

CHAPTER XIX

STALIN MUSCLES IN ON AMERICAN LABOR

1

SCAB and assassin were among the standard descriptions of John L. Lewis, President of the United Mine Workers of America, current in good communist society before the flowering of the Popular Front. Lewis, who is no slouch in name-calling himself, paid back in full measure. He carried his ranking as Number One communist-baiter with a swagger, proud of merit recognized. As long ago as 1924 his union financed and published an·earnest if slightly hectic study entitled *Attempt· by Communists to Seize the American Labor Movement*.

"The communist organization on the American continent," it asserted, "is composed of more than six thousand active leaders and lieutenants, and approximately one million members," whose purpose it is to capture trade unions "as a strategic instrument in fulfillment of their revolutionary designs." The Hon. Henry Cabot Lodge made the charge official record by presenting it to the Senate. Two years later Mr. Lewis declaimed before a convention of the American Federation of Labor:

> We are fundamentally concerned, however, when that interest which now exerts a dictatorship over 130,000,000 people in Russia systematically and persistently attempts to impose their philosophy and impose their theories of government and impose their own particular machinery and their own specific ideas upon the workers of all other countries of the civilized world. . . . For years past, our union has been subject to their deceitful attacks, to their intrigues and to their conspiracy.

His harangues on the subject, in fact, became familiar convention fare. In kicking out John Brophy, Powers Hapgood and other rebels from his organization, he branded them one and all as communist stooges with the sizzling irons of his special vocabulary for the subject.

Such was the background for the love affair between Lewis and the Stalinists which suddenly turned the beetle-browed ogre into the hero of the Communist Party, its friends within the New Deal, and its whole empire of front organizations. The formation of the Committee (now Congress) of Industrial Organization within the A.F. of L. late in 1935 coincided with the launching of Moscow's "democratic popular united front." The comrades had cast off the last lingering inhibitions about working with "reactionaries." Under the banner of communism-is-twentieth-century-Americanism there was room for Lewis, Father Divine, the Catholic Church, the Social Register and Mayor Kelly of Chicago. Everything went.

On his side, Lewis needed men skilled in agitation. His imagination was aflame with the vision of millions of unorganized men and women in the mass-production industries enrolled in a great horizontal labor federation under his command. The job was too urgent for squeamishness in choosing organizers and leaders.

While there were plenty of unemployed trade-union organizers of more temperate stripe available, they had not been so effectively conditioned to hating William Green and the American Federation of Labor as the foot-loose communists. Besides, the communists had for many years sought to obtain a grip on many of the very industries which Lewis now aimed to organize. Although their efforts had been consistently sterile, they did have the skeleton of an apparatus in the fields of steel, electricity, transport, machinery, automobiles, shipping. They had men like Jules Emspach and James Matles on hand in the electrical industry, Wyndham Mortimer in the Detroit automotive area, John Santo in the New York transport system, a lot of well-entrenched stooges among maritime and dock workers. Lewis sensed the potential value of this embryonic apparatus, now his for the taking. He took it. What if their allegiance lay beyond our American shores? He would straighten out such details later.

In his characteristic arrogance he never doubted he could keep them under control. "It's a good rule to work with anyone who will work with you," he said when questioned about the growing number of known communists in his officers' corps. At another time he remarked, "Who gets the bird, the hunter or the dog?"

He undervalued Stalin's dogs. Nor did it occur to him, in the pride of his leadership, that he might be the bird and that the hunters were working from a Union Square cover. In any case, he opened wide the gates of the C.I.O. to outright and thinly disguised communists, hundreds of them. Now that reality had caught up with his exaggerated figures of a decade before, he made peace and a partnership with "their conspiracy." He welcomed back dozens of organizers whom he had himself repeatedly accused of being tools of Moscow. When the C.I.O. had broken away from the A.F. of L., he put many of Browder's favorites, men who were familiar figures at party mass meetings and in party Innocents' Clubs, in critical positions on his organizing staff. But he kept them out of his own United Mine Workers union as rigidly as ever in the past—he wasn't making any experiments with his own baby when there were so many orphaned industries to work on.

There is little doubt that Lewis intended to use the communists and discard them, or at least to tame them to his purposes. There is less doubt that they entrenched themselves to a degree that gave them the upper hand. There is even ample room for suspicion that the hunters got their bird.

What else could explain Lewis' seemingly slavish adhesion to every change in the official communist policies dictated from the Kremlin? The old maestro turned on the President and the New Deal about the time that all of Moscow's agents did so. He dropped his fight on Hitlerism for support of the party's isolationist slogans, and "imperialism" displaced fascism in his vocabulary when the war started.* He has sided invariably with the Stalinist factions in the multitudinous union disputes. He has not even scrupled to go far beyond his constitutional powers to nullify an important regional meeting whose actions were not to the taste of the communists.

The desperate attempt to keep him in the presidency, notwithstanding his public promise to resign if Wendell Willkie were defeated, was conducted by all the unions in the communist bloc; strong representation on the C.I.O. Executive was their compensation for agreeing to Philip Murray as Lewis' successor. Since then their hold on the C.I.O. machinery has been powerful enough to keep Lee Pressmen, Len DeCaux and other favorites of the party-liners in office under the new administration. When the Amalgamated Clothing Workers Union, headed by Sidney Hillman, and other independent unions accepted Murray as Lewis' successor, the tacit understanding

---

* Whether and how Mr. Lewis will adjust his isolationism to the new situation created for so many of his associates by the Nazi attack on Russia in June, 1941, is not yet clear at this writing.

was that the totalitarians would be restrained if not expelled. In practice Murray has ignored that understanding. At every crucial juncture he has placated the comrades in his entourage. Instead of a new president, the C.I.O., it soon appeared, merely had a proxy prexy.

The launching of the C.I.O. met a definite need for the horizontal or industrial type of all-inclusive unions. The old craft unionism was narrow and outmoded for industries where specialized craftsmanship was at a minimum. It coincided also with the Wagner Act, the apparatus of the National Labor Relations Board, and a mighty impulse toward labor organization. The C.I.O., and its Stalinist sectors in particular, had the tacit collaboration of the government and the frank support of key people in key places like the N.L.R.B., the Maritime Labor Board and the La Follette Civil Liberties Committee. It moved forward by huge leaps.

Workers in the automobile, steel, rubber, shipbuilding and a score more industries accepted the new leadership. They neither asked nor cared about the politics of the men they followed, and no one in his senses can blame them. The blame rests elsewhere. Ben Gold, the only communist labor leader who admits it, took his fur workers into the C.I.O. The late Heywood Broun, then in the flush of his communist incarnation, led the American Newspaper Guild into the fold. Nearly all other Stalinoid unions abandoned the A.F. of L. for the C.I.O. By late 1937 Lewis stood at the head of an organization that claimed over four million members and was conceded three millions by neutral labor journalists. The C.I.O. was as large as the parent federation and apparently destined to outgrow it.

Then it began to slide. A series of unauthorized wildcat sit-down strikes dealt the organization serious blows. These strikes were claimed as victories for communist tactics by Browder's press, in tones which left small margin for doubt as to who fomented them. Stalinist control grew at the cost of general organizational unity. Internal schism shattered promising unions. Rule-or-ruin struggles for control frittered away endless opportunities. C.I.O. membership fell off below the two-million mark. Investigations and other public pressures curbed N.L.R.B. support. Lewis was obliged to remove himself from open leadership, to operate behind the wings through Philip Murray and others.

The federation seemed definitely on the downgrade when history intervened. After some hesitation, America undertook all-out defense and aid-to-Britain programs which vastly stimulated just those industries where the C.I.O. was at work. Bethlehem Steel, Ford Motors, the Southern coal operators and other great industrial groups knuckled under. By mid-1941 C.I.O. membership was at a new high, probably over 4,000,000. Because it was entrenched in production fields closest to national security, its significance for American life was far greater than that of the American Federation of Labor.

The communist cancer in the C.I.O. grew in malignancy with every passing month. Precisely in the period of the federation's greatest expansion, Soviet contractual obligations to Nazi Germany called for strikes in defense industries which embittered American opinion against the organization and deepened the festering political enmities and contradictions within the C.I.O. (We shall look more closely at those strikes in another chapter.) No matter how big and strong it may become, its unity and its very life will be continually in danger by reason of this alien element in an American labor body.

For the formal record, there are no communists and fellow-travelers at the helm; not even Harry Bridges, West Coast director, who was active in communist work years before the C.I.O. was born; not even Michael Quill of the Transport Workers Union or Joseph Curran of the Maritime Workers Union; not even Wyndham Mortimer, who was known to fellow-members of the Communist Party as George Baker. The public can be confused by such quibbling. But in the unions the Stalinists are known at once to all but the most naïve by the policies they follow with such amazing unanimity, the political company they keep, even by the epithets they apply to opponents.

In dealing with the period of C.I.O. decline before its wartime revival, Benjamin Stolberg, one of the ablest labor journalists in the country, wrote in the *Saturday Evening Post*:

There is one basic reason for the disintegration of the C.I.O. All other reasons flow from it. The Communist Party, which penetrated the C.I.O. from the beginning, has increasingly dominated its policies, subverted its purposes, dissipated its energies and disrupted its unions.

The truth of his judgment has been confirmed repeatedly since then, notwithstanding the numerical expansion of the organization. Until the Nazi war on Russia changed the picture, the issue of defense strikes racked the whole C.I.O. and at times threatened its life.

Fantastic though it sounds to the uninitiated, a foreign government and foreign issues are far more important in the life of a great American labor federation than any purely American considerations! Local and national gatherings of C.I.O. units are primarily arenas for fratricidal conflict over the twisting Moscow party line.

In every such conflict the division of forces is as good as a roll call. The unions notoriously under Stalinist influence—such as longshoremen, transport, maritime, newspaper, communications, furriers, government employees, woodworkers, cannery workers, office employees, die-casters, aircraft locals, etc.—operate as a tight, disciplined bloc. It was by discipline of their minority, acting always together in conformity with caucus-made decisions, that they obtained disproportionate weight in the C.I.O. It is by the same methods that they intend to hold it, whatever the cost in terms of labor unionism.

2

Practically everyone mentioned in this book would not hesitate, under oath, to deny that he is in fact or by conviction a communist. Such denials are part of the Kremlin code. We are dealing with a conspiracy, rather than an open aboveboard political movement. Although so many carry red cards in their wallets or their hearts, we can only describe their behavior, which can be proved, rather than their membership.

Having made this acknowledgement, the fact remains that a great many C.I.O. union officials and organizers have consistently followed the Moscow policies for foreign trade unions; that these gentry have played together against the rest of the world in defense of those policies; and that their loyalty has been hailed and supported by the communist press and other Stalinist agencies. Witnesses before the Dies Committee have listed over three hundred alleged communists in important places in the C.I.O. Whatever the tally, the description, as cautiously defined above, certainly fits men like Harry Bridges, Donald Henderson, Philip M. Connolly, Joseph Curran, Michael J. Quill, Ben Gold, Marcel Sherer, Morris Muster, Milton Kaufman, Wyndham Mortimer, Mervyn Rathborne, Lew Michener, Frederick N. Myers, Morris Watson, Reid Robinson, Meyer Adelman, Lewis Allen Berne, Harold Christoffel, Abram Flaxer, Lewis Merrill, O. M. Orton, Joseph Selly and dozens of others. Whether or not they are technically communists, they deserve plots on Red Square on the basis of their services. The veils of mystification around the whole business are being increasingly lifted by C.I.O. leaders themselves— by Sidney Hillman, R. J. Thomas, Gustav Strebel, etc.—as the inner struggle to rid the organization of the men of Moscow gains impetus.

Two men at C.I.O. headquarters who have richly earned special mention in any discussion of fellow-travelers in the setup are Lee Pressman, the powerful general Counsel for the organization, and Len DeCaux, publicity director and editor of the official organ, *C.I.O. News*. Pressman is known to exercise an influence far beyond his formal standing as attorney. He has held New Deal posts at various times, was especially close to those members of the N.L.R.B. who were publicly charged with communist leanings, and has been a sponsor or speaker for numerous Popular Front enterprises. He is generally regarded as the closest advisor of Lewis. As to DeCaux, a casual perusal of his paper and his publicity output discloses a curious bias in favor of precisely those people and unions generally believed by the rest of the C.I.O. to be friendly to the Browder boys. The long hand of planned coincidence.

We have already touched on the rise of the Maritime Workers Union. We have seen the unobtrusive clubs for seamen on the water fronts of this country spreading the Muscovite doctrines, the development of the Marine Workers Industrial Union and its transformation into the National Maritime Workers. From the start there was an active opposition, but it has been slowly chipped away by all the methods of union terrorism including goon squads and fake votes. Joseph Curran was pushed forward as spokesman for the Left Wing organizers of the enterprise and is today among the half dozen most influential leaders of the communist-inspired sector of American labor. Both the *Saturday Evening Post* and the *American Mercury* have devoted detailed articles to the communist orientation of the union and its leaders. The latter include graduates of a special Communist Party school for marine organizers.

Curran's jurisdiction dovetails with the longshoremen's domain under the generalship of Harry Bridges, the International Longshoremen and Warehouse Workers Union. Both strategists have been working hard to put their political friends in control of the warehouse workers—the struggle for domination is in progress furiously at this writing—which would round out their transportation empire.

The American Communications Association, a C.I.O. union of telegraph and radio operators, has traveled consistently on the party line. Mervyn Rathborne, for many years its president, surrendered his post to become secretary of the San Francisco C.I.O. Industrial Council—the general belief being that he was thus being tactically stationed to replace Bridges should the latter be ordered deported. His successor as president is Joseph Selly, who has also been on display in fellow-traveling undertakings.

Obviously the radio and telegraph operators fit nicely into the complex of transport and communications. It means that a segment of America's industrial life essential to its existence and its military safety is in large measure in the hands of friends of a foreign dictator! The enormity of this fact, unfortunately, has not yet been grasped by the American people. It does not call for any special powers of imagination to recognize the sabotage-potential represented by pro-Soviet union leaders in shipping, warehousing, radio and telegraph communication. And it is on record that Joe Curran once boasted, at a union meeting, that his maritime organization could "dictate when and where the government could ship munitions."*

The automotive union was stalled, after a brilliant start, by communist attempts to monopolize its jobs and power. A battered fragment was led into the A.F. of L. by Homer Martin, and is now virtually extinct. The rest has been mushrooming under the impulse of war production, but it is racked internally by the communist disease. At one end, its president, Roland J. Thomas, is vociferously anti-communist. At the other end, various locals, especially in the airplane construction industry, are under the Muscovite brand of leadership, defiant of union orders, and sustained (from all appearances) by the toleration or outright support of Lewis, Murray, and all their Left Wing C.I.O. units.

Homer Martin, the first head of the C.I.O. effort in the automotive field, was a confused and temperamental amateur in union matters. He let himself be guided by a few people closely connected with the expelled Lovestone group of communists and blundered into endless trouble. The Lovestone tie-in suited the orthodox Moscow crowd even less than if Martin had been an ultra-conservative trade unionist. Stalinists colonized his locals so thoroughly that Martin could not keep

---

* Quoted in article on the Maritime Workers Union by Charles Yale Harrison in the *American Mercury*, October, 1940.

them out of important posts, especially as they had the help of Lewis. The famous 1937 sit-down strikes, carried out against Martin's orders but with the tacit blessings of the Lewis machine, gave the communist elements additional leverage. It was during these outlaw strikes that Wyndham Mortimer—later notorious as leader of defense-industry strikes in California—first acquired prominence.

The communist ganging-up on Martin grew into one of the most complex and violent factional wars in the history of the American labor movement. By 1939 Martin had been ousted, to the jubilant hurrahing of the Communist Party press. But this accomplished, some of those who had played with the communists now turned against them, and R. J. Thomas, an honest anti-Stalinist and a bona fide trade-union leader, became president. There was much talk to the effect that the automotive union had been purged of Moscow agents. Far from being finished, however, that task has scarcely been started and its completion has been hampered by influential leaders at C.I.O. headquarters. The truce with Stalinism encouraged by the Russo-German war makes the confusion more confounded.

Pro-communist infiltration remains very strong in the Detroit area, which is the solar plexus of the automotive industry; although the comrades probably do not control the larger aggregates, such as the Ford and General Motors locals. They do seem to exercise a decisive weight in the Milwaukee area, where Harold Christoffel is head of the Allis-Chalmers local as well as of the Milwaukee Industrial Union Council. Communist leadership, as outlaw strikes have demonstrated, is also dominant on the West Coast, where Bridges runs the show, and where men like Lew Michener and Wyndham Mortimer have been active in the airplane organizational drives. Attorney for the auto workers' union is still Maurice Sugar, a Detroit man who sued for libel when branded as a communist—and lost in a jury trial.

The rock-bottom fact is that communists are so firmly planted in many sections of the automobile and airplane unions of the C.I.O. that an earnest attempt to oust them might endanger the life of the union. In a larger sense that is true of the C.I.O. as a whole—the cancer has gone too far to be operated upon without real risk to the patient's life.

Another citadel of the C.I.O. totalitarians is the Transport Workers Union, headed by Michael Quill, Austin Hogan, John Santo and other party-liners. The union was born in 1933-34 at 80 East Eleventh Street, New York, a structure housing a horde of communist front organizations at that time. Its first publication, the *Transport Workers Bulletin*, was printed on a Communist Party press. Its first president, Thomas O'Shea, was a member of the party, according to his own testimony; he resigned soon thereafter and has fought the Stalinists lustily ever since. O'Shea testified before the Dies Committee that the union had been built and controlled by the communists.

While enthusiastically supporting Quill and his union, the communist press has in the last few years disclaimed ownership of the Transport Union by the party. In earlier years, however, it had not been so modest. In March, 1935, the *Party Organizer* gave a four-page report on organization of transport in New York, in which it recounted proudly how "comrades" had been successfully "concentrating" on that industry. "During the entire process of organization," the report concluded, "there has been careful and planned united activity of the [party] section and the Union." A virtual official claim of possession was also made by the national convention of the party in 1938. It awarded a wreath to Rose Wortis, chairman of its trade-union section in New York, for her good work in organizing transport. The only transport organized in her territory had been the union headed by Quill.

Recently the New York *World-Telegram* brought documentary proof that Austin Hogan, president of the New York section of the union, had registered as a communist in the elections of 1933 and 1934. The power behind Quill's throne from the start has been John Santo, once editor of the Hungarian language communist organ, *Uj Elore*, published at that time in Cleveland. The Dies Committee has on file a typed party document headed "Control Tasks Adopted by Enlarged District Committee Meeting March 8, 1936." At one point it says:

Especially we did make headway . . . in traction, where the Union, built and led by our comrades, has grown to the strength of 5000 members.

The C.I.O. union of agricultural workers—the United Cannery Workers—is headed by the same Donald Henderson whom we met repeatedly in the launching of Innocents' Clubs.

The United Electrical, Radio and Machinists Union had a large concentration of communists almost from the beginning, among them veterans of Foster's TUUL like James Matles and Jules Emspach. A personable young leader, James B. Carey, became president—he was for years more than willing to string along with the comrades, fronting for a number of their fellow-traveling organizations. In the end, however, Carey became fed up with the Muscovite stew and recently has been fighting the cooks in his union.

Communist domination of the American Newspaper Guild has long been matter for national scandal. But the grip of the comrades seems to have been slowly pried loose; optimists aver that the capture of the organization by non-communists is inevitable.

The fact that the National Association of Die-Casters is lined up with the communist-dominated wing is something that should—but apparently doesn't—worry the country. Small numerically, the union controls an industry which is in the truest sense a "bottleneck" of national defense production.

But the story is too long to be told in full. Where the communists do not control, they frequently constitute a minority strong enough to need appeasing. Their principal spheres of operation are in industries of primary importance to military security and defense output. Anyone in the least acquainted with communist history knows that the Kremlin has repeatedly issued instructions for exceptional efforts in muscling in on just those spheres.

The most serious aspect of this picture is its threat to the labor movement itself. Stalinist penetration of the N.L.R.B. nearly wrecked the Wagner Act. Such penetration of the C.I.O. turned a promising unionizing effort into a chaos of political wrangles and a focus for public resentments. The activities of communist minorities are providing anti-labor groups with a powerful weapon with which to beat all labor organization. The plague cannot be cured by pretending it does not exist. On the contrary, it must be exposed wherever the infection shows itself, and the task is above all one that challenges the good sense of labor itself.

Among unions which (at this writing) are suffering from the infection—where pro-communist and fellow-traveler leadership is influential if not actually dominant—are the following:

> National Maritime Union
> Transport Workers Union
> Aircraft and Machinists Divisions of the United
>   Automobile Workers
> Die-Casters Association
> American Communications Association

Maritime Federation of the Pacific
International Longshoremen and Warehouse Workers
International Woodworkers Union
American Newspaper Guild
United Electrical, Radio and Machinists Union
Farm Equipment Workers Organizing Committee
State, County and Municipal Workers Union
United Tannery Workers Union
Packing House Workers Organizing Committee
Mine, Mill and Smelter Workers Union
United Office and Professional Workers Union
Book and Magazine Guild
Quarry Workers Union
Fishermen's Union
Furniture Workers Union
Sections of the United Federal Workers of America
Fur Workers Union
Sections of the Aluminum Workers
Federation of Architects, Chemists Engineers and
    Technicians
Artists Union
United Shoe Workers
Retail and Wholesale Workers, Local 65
Inland Boatmen's Union
Marine Cooks and Stewards Union
United Cannery, Agricultural, Packing and Allied
    Workers of America
C.I.O. Industrial Councils of Greater New York,
    Queens, Chicago, Cleveland, Milwaukee, Seattle,
    Portland, San Francisco, Los Angeles, Bridgeport,
    Baltimore, etc.; also State Industrial Councils
    (C.I.O.) of Connecticut, California, Wisconsin,
    Texas, Washington
Alabama Farmers Union
Local 5 of Teachers Union, A.F. of L. (expelled)
Local 537 College Teachers Union, A.F. of L. (ex-
    pelled)
A.F. of L. Painters District Council No. 9, New
    York
Workers Alliance
Gas and Chemical Workers Union

3

The long-drawn hearings, in the summer of 1939, to determine whether or not Harry Bridges is a communist would be comic if they were not symptomatic of the general muddleheadedness of our country and our government in relation to the Stalinist threat. Fortunately for Mr. Bridges, his case headed up at that time to a Federal department with a typical starry-eyed liberal as its Secretary. The hearings were turned over to another of the same breed. Frances Perkins, Dr. James McCauley Landis and their kind are admirable in their place. Whether that place should include assignments calling for tough, hardheaded, clear-eyed leaders is not even open to question. People less suited to deal with foreign conspirators and subsidized muscle-men in a time of world crisis can scarcely be imagined.

Madam Perkins seems to live in dread of criticism from the Left. She can take lambasting from the Manufacturers Association and enjoy it. But reprimands from writers in the *New Republic* and the *New Masses* worry her deeply. While saving face for the law by various devices, she permitted Comrade Bridges to function without interruption year after year. It all went under the head of "liberalism"—and the country later drew dividends on the investment in the form of strikes on the Pacific Coast. Then her department staged his hearings in a fashion that gave Bridges and his friends the chance to laugh at her publicly instead of merely privately. The deportation action was initiated in the autumn of 1937. It was allowed to drag until the summer of 1939. In a letter to Edward J. Shaughnessy of the Department of Labor, written by R. P. Bonham of the department's West Coast office on September 23, 1937, there is this cute information:

I believe it is proper that I acquaint the Central Office with the fact that when I interviewed Mr. Bridges some time ago on another matter he boasted that he had seen the Central Office file relating to himself and also that they had an excellent "intelligence" organization of their own that kept them well informed of what was going on.*

Mr. Bridges had not made an empty boast. His intelligence service may have had nothing to do with it—but the Central Office docu-

* Quoted in the *Congressional Record*, January 24, 1939.

ments in question *disappeared from the Department of Labor file* during the following months!

In March, 1939, Bridges appeared at the Immigration Service in Baltimore accompanied by Lee Pressman and was released on his own recognizance. Between that time and the actual hearings more than a year later, Madam Perkins and her associates were under the relentless pressure of organized appeals in Bridges' behalf.

The selection of Dean Landis was a product of that moral intimidation. Every line of his verdict in Bridges' favor attests to a charming complacency about the charges under consideration. The decision to hold the proceedings at Angel Island was made at the insistence of Mr. Bonham, who urged that in San Francisco it would be impossible to avoid "communistic demonstrations" and "intimidation of witnesses." Dr. Landis was authorized to issue passes "as he saw fit." He saw fit to issue them to Donald Ogden Stewart, Ella Winter and other well-known Stalinists, thus helping convert the occasion into a pleasant and comradely little comedy. His attitude may have been big-hearted, but it was politically frivolous.

A booklet about the case—enthusiastically pro-Bridges—was published by Modern Age Books, whose list is loaded with Stalinoid literature. The author, E. E. Ward, writes: "Time and again Bridges had Dean Landis chuckling. . . . By this time Landis and Bridges were chatting as two men would before a fireside. . . . That drew Landis and Bridges into the subject of the Soviet Union." Comrade Bridges thereupon explained to the Harvard professor how much better off Soviet sailors are than their fellow-workers in other lands and also enlarged on the special beauties of civil liberties under Stalin. Throughout, the booklet reveals Dean Landis as incredibly childlike in treating seriously the standardized communist hokum which even Park Avenue hostesses no longer believed.

He remained blissfully innocent of the forces at work behind the case, and the Department of Labor did not disturb its files to educate him. He knew nothing, for instance, of many letters containing data such as this (from Mr. Bonham on the Coast to Mr. Shoemaker in Washington, March 29, 1938): "Confidential information has also reached me, which appears to be very credible, that the same group of communists that handled the propaganda and intimidation program in the Earl King *et al* murder case, has been detailed for the same purposes in the Bridges case." On April 11, 1938, Arthur J. Phelan had conveyed information from San Francisco to the effect "that Bridges had already told his 'beef squad' to get in a lot of practice because after his hearing is over there will be a lot of 'work' for them to do on witnesses to appear against him."*

The citations could be continued for pages—pages which Dean Landis never saw. The department instead made a laughing stock of the whole affair and, as Mr. Ward puts it, gave Bridges "a gigantic sounding board." . . . "Bridges literally embraced the opportunity with a wrestler's clutch." The Landis verdict for Bridges is no more remarkable, come to think of it, than the fact that so many others of his general psychological make-up were enlisting in the Trojan cavalry. It was, indeed, a segment of the same picture. The scholar generously went beyond the immediate issue to assert that the communists may have given up their former violent manners anyhow. This he figured out on the basis of the "democratic line"—a couple of months before it was withdrawn!

Despite the hearings and the verdict, the presumptive evidence of Bridges' affiliation with communism is overwhelming. He first came into the national spotlight as leader of the San Francisco shipping strike for which the communists have openly claimed credit. Ex-communists in a position to know intimately—among them Benjamin Gitlow and Joseph Zack, top-rank party men in their day—testified that he had been one of them. Bridges had taken direct part in or sponsored numberless Stalinist undertakings. For years he has been the center of hope and adulation in the communist press. His defense attorneys have included people specializing in the defense of communists, making him part of an exclusive clientele that includes Browder and Mrs. Browder. The Bridges Defense Committee was a typical Stalinist front. Bridges himself testified that he solicited and received the help of the party and its official organs. His political opinions have coincided at all times with the opinions prescribed by Moscow—and have changed when the prescription changed.

None of these things, standing alone, is decisive. All taken together present a picture which only eager and willful sophistry can smudge. Dean Landis, now that it is all over, may hatch the suspicion that Harry Bridges is a communist. In the light of events after the Stalin-Hitler partnership was announced, he may even revise his views on the com-

---

* *Congressional Record,* January 24, 1939.

munist "reformation." Perhaps he will go as far as to ask himself whether, all technicalities aside, Bridges is really a safe man to be entrusted with a strangle hold on a large sector of American shipping, particularly when other sections are controlled by his friends and political allies.

Whether Dean Landis asks these questions or not, the American people scarcely can avoid doing so sooner or later, and insisting on realistic answers.*

---

* In February, 1941, the Department of Justice—now in charge of immigration matters—reopened the Bridges deportation case. Naturally, all the totalitarian liberals instantly shrieked "red-baiting!" and charged an "anti-labor" move. The implication that labor is interested in perpetuating Moscow's right to control the American water front is wholly unjustified.

CHAPTER **XX**

RUSSIAN PURGES AND AMERICAN LIBERALS

1

ONCE again we must pause to consider the course of events inside Russia. The pro-Soviet obsessions in the United States make no sense without continuous reference to their point of origin. The whole Popular Front and each of its embodiments in leagues, congresses and cocktail parties rested in the final analysis on the myth of triumphant socialism and the happy life in the Soviet realm.

That myth was subjected, from the beginning of 1935 forward, to a series of body blows as the bloodiest political purge of modern times unfolded in Stalin's land. It was official carnage unprecedented for size and imbecilic in detail. Before it ran its sanguinary career, a whole generation of Soviet leaders—the generation that had made the Bolshevik Revolution—was slaughtered; at least fifty thousand communists, officials, professors, economists were killed without the formality of trials; the country's foremost generals, admirals and marshals were executed and four-fifths of the higher officers' corps, about 30,000 Red Army, Navy and Aviation specialists, were "liquidated" by exile, demotions and execution; a terror more frightful than anything in a thousand years of Russia's sanguinary history swept through the country, leaving mountains of corpses in its wake.

For the outside world and the Soviet population itself the process was dramatized in a succession of "show trials" in which the heroes of the revolution, group after group, "confessed" to hideous duplicity, treason and bloodthirst. Not a shred of honor or idealism was left for the Russian Revolution by the time its most renowned architects, "confessing" to the impossible and the incredible, had revised their own biographies in the glare of these fantastic trials. Half-truths and palpable inventions were blended in supreme insanity to the music of rifle squads and the groans of the dying, while mass suicides and almost daily announcements of liquidations behind closed doors provided a sinister backdrop. Had some satanic enemy of the Russian Revolution, its founders and its traditions, aimed to defile its memory and destroy its living witnesses, he could not have done the job more thoroughly. The only hypothesis, indeed, on which the cumulative obscenity of death and dishonor can be explained is that Joseph Stalin was moved by a pathological hatred of the revolution he had captured from its original fathers.

The outside world was chiefly aware of "the Moscow trials" with their bewildering pattern of self-accusation, seemingly unmotivated treachery, crude lies and devious inner contradictions. There was the fascination of ultimate horror about the proceedings, a macabre quality that left the world gasping. The assumption that every one of the actors in the sinister melodrama was telling the truth explains nothing; if they were a hundredth part as depraved as they claimed, this final act of contrition after twenty years of criminality and political perversion would be ludicrously out of character. The opposite assumption—of an elaborate, confused and ill-fitting police fabrication to which several score aging men were forced somehow to lend themselves—leaves much unexplained, but it at least meets the minimum demands of common sense.

I shall not attempt to summarize, let alone analyze, the nightmare in a few pages. But a few significant facts usually ignored in discussing the horror must be set down.

The most crucial of them is this: *That only those fully prepared to confess were brought to public trial.* For every important Bolshevik "confessing" and prostrating himself before Stalin, hundreds were disposed of in the dark, dozens took their own lives, refusing to give themselves to Stalin's show trials. Presumably they died defiant. The impression was manufactured that all those accused admitted guilt and saluted the master of the Kremlin. The terrifying truth is that only those willing to go through the mummery were brought to trial. Whatever the pressures employed in months and years of solitary confinement, whatever transpired in the torture chambers of the G.P.U., only those who succumbed totally were exhibited to the world. The pre-condition for exhibition was their consent to play an assigned and rehearsed role. Not until the archives are thrown open by Stalin's successors will we know precisely what terrible pressures could have extracted such terrible sacrifices. For the present we know only the obvious: that bargains of self-immolation had been struck.

The world thus saw only one tiny facet of the picture, a facet painstakingly stage-managed. The rest was invisible. In elementary justice to the greatest single event of our epoch, the Russian Revolution, we must assume that thousands of others died nobly, protesting their innocence and accusing their killers. Among them were men and women of top rank in the story of the revolution—General Tukhachevsky, General Yegorov, Abel Yenukidze, Karakhan, Mdivani, Tomsky, Gamarnik, a hundred others. Had such people been willing to play the strange game of public executioners of their own reputations, would Stalin have spared them the final humiliation? If the whole story is ever known, what was exhibited to the world as gibbering depravity may prove to have been merely a device for concealing an episode of massive sacrifice for honor and revolutionary integrity.

A second point of the utmost importance must be kept firmly in mind. In the great mass of so-called evidence piled up in the trials, year after year, only a few scattered items were subject to independent checking. Those were the incidents alleged to have taken place *outside Russia*. And in every instance that evidence turned out to be false.

There was, for instance, the supposed meeting between one of the trial defendants and Leon Trotsky in a Copenhagen hotel. Investigation disclosed that the hotel in question had been razed years before the rendezvous! Defendant Piatikov "confessed" to having flown from Berlin to Oslo for a secret meeting with Trotsky. Check-up of the respective airfields and Swedish police records for the period in question—Trotsky was under continuous surveillance, his every visitor a matter of record—canceled out that story completely. A witness claimed to have delivered a message to Trotsky at a rendezvous in Paris—at a time when Trotsky was demonstrably hundreds of miles from Paris, guarded day and night by the police. Another piece of testimony revolved around the delivery of a letter to Trotsky at a specified date—but he was then in mid-Atlantic on his way to Mexico!

Thus episode after episode, where neutral confirmation was physically possible, was exposed as pure invention. The circumstance that we cannot explain as yet why these unhappy creatures lied against themselves in the face of certain death does not alter the fact that their testimony was fraudulent. At the very least it throws a pall of doubt around all the rest of the testimony—wholly undocumented, based only on self-accusation, mutually contradictory and impossible of independent examination.

A third aspect of the trials that is usually overlooked seems to me especially revealing. I refer to the fact that *each successive batch of prisoners told precisely the story most useful to the Kremlin at the moment of the trial.* Deliberately they took upon themselves the blame for economic disasters, political excesses and other causes of popular discontent. They were fashioning alibis for the Kremlin in matters which cannot reasonably be blamed on "plots"—in matters which continued to plague the country long after the supposed plotters were dead. Every trial served to divert the people's anger over specific troubles from the rulers to a group of appointed scapegoats. But this matching of political needs and confessions was even more startlingly artificial in connection with foreign relations. The crimes to which the defendants so volubly confessed may have dated back ten or twenty years, but miraculously they coincided with the policy needs of Stalin's government at that particular juncture. There had been a kind of considerate and prophetic foresight in their sinning.

Let me illustrate. The 1937 trials implicated Germany, Japan and Italy, even in allegations harking back to the first years of the revolution. Those were the nations with which the Old Bolsheviks about to die claimed to have connived to betray their country and their life's work. Neither France nor England was accused. By March, 1938, when the third of the great show trials was staged, Russia's relations with the Western democracies had taken a sharp turn for the worse. Anthony Eden had been ousted and appeasement was in the ascendancy. Soviet propaganda the world over was beginning to prepare lines of retreat from the democratic front. And the Old Bolsheviks now on display, it turned out, had plotted not only with fascist nations, but with Western democracies!

I submit that this miracle of coincidence constitutes presumptive proof of doctoring of the trials, revision of the "confessions," collaboration between the accusing state and its puppets on trial. Such crude reconditioning of the past "crimes" to suit current policy gave away the whole macabre deception.

2

Above all, however, let us remember that the trials were only a negligible fraction of the whole blood purge. They monopolized attention beyond their deserts—which is exactly what the directors of the affair intended. Even in the perspective of the years, these trials in the forefront cut off an unimpeded view of the thousandfold greater bloodletting behind them. The elements of bewilderment in the trials shed their confusion on everything else and prevent an understanding of the bigger situation which, divorced from the mystery of the trials, seems much more logical and comprehensible.

In previous nationwide purges the victims had been remnants of the former pre-Bolshevik upper and educated classes. They had been old-time engineers, conservative professors, ex-members of former anti-Bolshevik parties; in short, actual or potential enemies of the Soviet State. In the greatest purge of all, however, the victims were overwhelmingly the natural friends of the Soviet idea—prominent Bolsheviks, high officials, the upper crust of the Red Army, the leaders of minority-nationality Communist Parties, communists all. The situation adds up essentially to a planned and ruthless blotting out of the Bolshevik heritage. Deep changes in Soviet policies and Soviet attitudes had transformed Russia beyond recognition by its revolutionary founders. The physical extermination of those whose loyalties were still attached to the heritage and of the younger people who had become infected with such loyalties was an inevitable part of the process.

I have already indicated in broad outline elsewhere the far-reaching revision of the revolution: the revival of nationalistic patterns of thought, the retreat from advanced ideas in everyday life and culture, the expunging of the last shreds of workers' control in industry, the virtual substitution of the ruling party by a ruling bureaucracy. Stalin was the consequence as well as the author of these changes. For lack of a more precise word I can only describe the slow but thorough revision as the *fascization* of Soviet Russia. It was a process that left Russia different from Germany, even as Italy is different, but identical at their core, in moral temper and intellectual outlook. Only the fact that the labels remained the same—that there was a continuity of the governmental machinery and external trimmings—hid from the world what was apparent to a few students of Russian affairs: the triumphant counter-revolution.

The great slaughter of 1935-38 was the confirmation of that counter-revolution in terms of human beings. The actual and potential opposition to the change were eliminated in the only way that dictatorship knows, by death. Had the changes in the character of the state and the murder of all those tied to the displaced order been achieved by an outsider, the fact of the counter-revolution would have been obvious to a child. Because it was accomplished from the inside by insiders, even erudite historians failed to recognize the reality.

Stalin did the job of wiping out all nuclei of possible revolt against the fascization with a profligacy of brutality in the tradition of Ivan the Terrible and Peter the Great. Practically all who remained of Lenin's closest comrades were slaughtered: Zinoviev, Bukharin, Rykov, Kamenev, Serebriakov, Smilga, Smirnov, Tomsky, Yenukidze, Krestinsky, on and on into the dozens and the score. (Only the chief figure, Leon Trotsky, evaded that fate until 1940, when a G.P.U. killer finally cornered him in Mexico and literally dug out with an *alpenstock* the brain that Stalin feared.)

Most of the surviving heroes of the civil war were killed off, along with the officers who might still retain some affection for the revolutionary past of the Red Army and for the executed generals and admirals. Among the major Soviet diplomats, only those who had never been too close to the Bolshevik Party or had actually served on the other side of the political fence—including Mensheviks like Maisky, Troyanovsky, and Suritz—remained alive. The heads of all the autonomous national republics were either executed or driven to suicide. The men who drew up and carried through the Five Year Plan were destroyed. The very G.P.U. chieftains who organized the earlier installments of the gigantic killing were themselves thrown on the altar of counter-revolution by their successors. At least two-thirds of the Tzik Committee which had drafted the Stalin Constitution were liquidated.

Over and above the men and women whose names are imbedded in Soviet history, there was of course the destruction of great masses of the lowly communists, minor officials, economists, professors, writers. There is no way of overestimating the magnitude of the "cleansing." Imagine a new government taking over power in a great nation and expelling all those suspected of lingering sympathy for the ousted regime. That is what happened—except that the expulsion was permanent, through physical annihilation.

Whatever else may come of the Russian Revolution, it has at least set a new low for official sadism, a new high for official murder, for modern times. Ivan and Peter seem restrained in their orgies of carnage compared with their present successor in the Kremlin.

3

A species of panic was produced among foreign fellow-travelers by the repeated shocks of the Russian slaughter! Here and there individual communists in America and elsewhere went through a revulsion of feeling. But by and large the periphery of "sympathizers" and secret communists and vague camp-followers swallowed the blood purge as their forerunners had gulped down the man-made famine. It was in the midst of the purges, in fact, that the liberal middle and upper-class conversions to the Comintern religion had their greatest growth. No stronger proof can be adduced of the irrationality of the whole business. It thrived on blood. It derived a certain ecstasy from the continuous spectacle of human sacrifice. Nor is it the first time in the history of pseudo-religious obsessions that blood played this role of heightening emotion.

To the so-called communists of this period, 99 per cent of them new recruits, ignorant of revolutionary history, the names of the Old Bolsheviks who were being killed off meant nothing. There was for them no magic in names like Zinoviev, Bukharin, Rykov, Rakovsky, Tukhachevsky, Sokolnikov. They felt no sense of horror and sacrilege in the shooting of the authors of a revolution with which they had identified themselves twenty years too late and in its period of degradation. Indeed, at bottom it was the new, know-nothing, tough counter-revolutionary character of the Soviet regime which attracted them. The erasure of a lot of polysyllabic and unpronounceable names associated with a long-past and essentially disreputable affair back in 1917 involved no psychological violence for the fellow-travelers.

The years of apologetics for the bloodletting in the parlors and penthouses of a hundred thousand comfortable American homes, among the intellectuals and artists and scholars of our country, represent the lowest ebb of American "liberalism." It had lost its instincts of fairness and its natural revulsion against large-scale brutality. It had become essentially totalitarian in its reflexes, siding automatically with power—with the executioners against the victims, with the police against the terrorized.

I have before me as I write a file of *Nation* and *New Republic* editorials and articles on the Moscow trials. An aroma of decay seems to me to pervade them all. Here and there, toward the end of the horrible process, there are expressions of "regret" and appeals to Stalin to shut off the taps of death. But the mass of words as a whole is putrescent in its eagerness for alibis for the killers and insults for the killed. The same editors and writers who once spoke up for Mooney, for Sacco and Vanzetti, who presumably cherished the memory of the world response to a Dreyfus or Mendel Baylis case, now gave every benefit of the doubt to an omnipotent state and its firing squads, rather than to its victims.

Without exception the Cowleys and Kirchweys and Blivens fussed over the details of this or that trial, steadfastly refusing to assay the whole chain of events, which alone might have given them the clue to the tragedy. It suited their belated inside-out revolutionism to tell themselves that this was a mere accident, an unhappy interlude, rather than an expression of a deep intrinsic change in the nature of the Soviet regime, or the consequence of Leninist amoralism. If only they could convince themselves that Zinoviev did poison the soup in a factory kitchen, that the ascetic Bukharin had "sabotaged" something somewhere, they could reconcile themselves to the slaughter of a hundred thousand and the conversion of all the makers of the revolution except Lenin and Stalin into a band of money-grubbing cutthroats. In their sad "admissions" that something must be amiss the Stalinoid liberals were even more pitiful than in bold apologetics, since they dared not follow the logic of their admissions, but invariably ended with a pious "nevertheless" and "despite everything."

What was the Nation's first reaction to the announcement of the initial "Trotskyist" trial? Not even decent astonishment. "It was to be expected that under the velvet glove of the New Soviet constitution," it wrote, "there would still be the firm outlines of the iron hand. There can be no doubt the dictatorship in Russia is dying and that a new democracy is slowly being born." The impending death of thousands of communists was thus another confirmation that the dictatorship is dying! Proof? Why, "Louis Fischer, in his article published in this issue, says that the constitution marks the abdication of the dictatorship and the inauguration of a new era in civil liberties." What other proof is needed? The start of the appalling purge and the abdication of the dictatorship all in one package!

As that new era of civil liberties really got going, with hundreds of executions weekly and the spread of a terror more total than the world had yet seen anywhere in modern times, the Nation continued to take its moral bearings from the same man who had tipped them off on the abdication, with reinforcement from the dispatches of Walter Duranty.

The gallant New Republic in its first reaction blandly assumed that the fantastic charges compounded by the G.P.U. were true. "Perhaps the deepest lesson to be learned from the Russian trial," it declared, "is the profound, unchangeable stubbornness of human nature. From the standpoint of practical expediency, these men had little to gain and much to lose by their effort to bring down the Soviet state in ruins." Thus an offhand assertion that the police claims elaborated by cornered and terrorized men were true! This sort of big-hearted considerateness for the Stalin tyranny marked all the "liberal" comment. It was so complacently understanding of the domestic difficulties, so forgiving of the minor peccadilloes of a hard-worked dictator!

Mr. Duranty, of all people, had been rushed by the New York Times to cover the trial. He acted as a lifesaver for embarrassed Stalinists here by evolving the theory of a special Russian psychology to explain everything. I can readily imagine the twinkle in his eye and the bulge in his cheek as he offered this consolation to the faithful abroad. The victims, said he, were just a lot of Dostoievsky characters enjoying self-torture and indulging their Slav souls! Never mind that Zinoviev, Kamenev, Radek and dozens of others had about as much Slav blood in their veins as Duranty. Never mind that other Slav revolutionaries in other times had exhibited their Dostoievsky streak by defying the Czar and his Okhrana in open court, by fanatic heroism rather than fanatic self-abuse. The "liberals" would not spoil a soothing alibi by too much testing.

Duranty, the New Republic was pleased to announce to its readers, "has apparently been forced to the conviction that the confessions are true." The word "forced" is an exquisite touch. Messrs. Cowley, Bliven, et al, knowing how consistently Mr. Duranty had resisted the temptation of saying anything pleasant about Stalin, could see him struggling to expose the trial but finally being forced over the line by the overwhelming and irresistible proofs. "And it seems to us," they added knowingly, "that the weight of the evidence supports Mr. Duranty's view." Thus everything was neatly ironed out.

In editorial after editorial the liberal weeklies "suspended judgment." In one instance the Nation conveniently suspended it for a hundred years. With each successive trial this Olympian aloofness became more difficult to maintain. But, to quote the *New Republic* on the last trial:

At the same time we must not, Hamlet-like, contemplate this tragedy so exclusively that we misjudge the USSR in its present strength. There is no real reason to believe that it has been seriously weakened by recent events in a military sense. . . . The USSR is in many respects the strongest nation on earth—as Japan and Germany may find out to their cost.

Not until March 16, 1938, did the *New Republic* come around to conceding that "Moscow loses caste." But the years of equivocation, apology and complacent suspension of judgment had helped the incredible revolution absorb the purges, to emerge stronger after the invigorating draught of blood. Moreover, the magazine's literary editor, Malcolm Cowley, having assumed the functions of a legal expert merely because the trial transcripts were between book covers, continued to find the proceedings fair and the evidence true. This he achieved by carefully passing over teeming inner contradictions and obvious falsehoods and by refusing to place the purges in their larger setting of changing Soviet attitudes. Even after the voluminous records had been carefully analyzed and digested by a committee headed by Professor John Dewey, revealing the absurdity of the confessions, neither Cowley nor his journal had the humility to face their mistakes. Throughout their pro-Soviet years the liberals were more concerned with saving face than facing facts.

When the *Modern Quarterly* posed the question whether "Trotsky is guilty of the charges listed in the indictments," a profound jurist like Leo Huberman needed only one word to settle the matter. "Yes," he replied—neither more nor less, just "Yes." Another expert, Theodore Dreiser, found the trials confusing, "But somehow they seem characteristic of what might be called the Russian temperament. . . . The trials represent a real triumph of the spirit of self-abnegation. . . . As for Trotsky, I believe that he is guilty of all the charges made against him."

Others may have retained an edge of doubt or a fringe of confusion, but not Russian experts like Sherwood Eddy. The mounting piles of dead communists in every corner of the Soviet realm were no problem for his big-hearted erudition. "In my own mind," he informed the impartial *Daily Worker*, "after reading the reports of these two trials, the guilt of treason on the part of those who were sentenced, and the double guilt of Trotsky as the archconspirator, is now thoroughly established." And that was that. . . .

Maxwell Stewart, one of the *Nation* editors, returned from a visit to the Soviet Union during the slaughter years with glad tidings for friends of the executioners. He had learned, and now transmitted the news solemnly, that the blood purges were really an expression of new Soviet democracy. The masses, he explained, were now killing off unpopular leaders; cleaning house, so to speak. Discontent which "had been festering for some years" now "only belatedly made itself felt. . . . The motive force of the purge has come almost exclusively from below." The people, Stewart discovered, "particularly resented the special privileges acquired by the new class of bureaucrats"—hence the purge to soothe their resentment.* Stalin, Yagoda, Yezhov and Vishinsky were mere tools in the hands of an aroused democracy.

There were no intellectual acrobatics which the fellow-travelers would not undertake to save their lovely faith in Russia. Year after year they had accepted and explained away horror and super-horror: falsifications of history, corruption, terror, man-made famine, the death penalty for minor thefts, the punishment of relatives for alleged crimes committed by members of their family thousands of miles away, capital punishment for young children, concentration camps with a population running into millions. They had developed a set of card-indexed formulas of rationalization for washing out such minor blemishes on the beloved dictatorship of the proletariat.

The Kremlin's solar system of "mass organizations" abroad prospered enormously despite the purges—perhaps because of them. The liberals' betrayal of their heritage and their conscience stands stark and ugly on the pages of recent history.

---

* *Nation*, December 17, 1938.

CHAPTER XXI

HOORAY FOR MURDER!

1

A DEFINITIVE judgment of the Moscow trials, and of the mass killings without trial behind them, calls for a profound knowledge of the Russian Revolution, its leaders, its ethics and motivations. As a minimum it presupposes a thorough study of the trial records, the literature of exposure outside Russia, an intimate familiarity with the life stories of the Old Bolsheviks actually on trial. The materials of the tragic episode, we may be sure, will be examined and analyzed by generations of historians and jurists.

But there were some 150 Americans for whom the problem was easy as pie. They saw in it neither mystery nor confusion. They knew and proclaimed their knowledge. With a sweeping self-confidence that savors of higher revelation they diagnosed the Russian purges and made their findings public. Those findings were not tentative, allowing for the remote possibility of doubt. No, theirs was an unqualified and unequivocal verdict justifying Joseph Stalin and his overworked executioners.

The bold assurance of long-distance experts on Soviet history and jurisprudence is the more remarkable when we realize that they were not professional students of world affairs nor specialized legal savants. Truth to tell, few of them could even pass a test in pronouncing the names of the dozens of Russians upon whose liquidation they placed the seal of their collective approval. They were, to quote the proud announcement of the phenomenon in the columns of the *Daily Worker*, merely "movie actors," "Broadway figures," "composers" and the like. Let that brave newspaper (April 28, 1938) tell the astonishing story in its own modest fashion:

Nearly 150 prominent American artists, writers, composers, editors, movie actors, college professors and Broadway figures yesterday issued a statement in support of the verdicts of the recent Moscow trials of the Trotskyite-Bukharinite traitors.

246

That traitors are guilty of treachery is scarcely an exciting discovery, but the clumsiness of the announcement may be blamed on the zeal of the *Daily Worker*. The paper went on to quote the statement itself. The amateur jurists gave it as their solemn and considered, nay impassioned, opinion that the trials "have by sheer weight of evidence established a clear presumption of the guilt of the defendants." They even went beyond their moral and juridical verdict to warn that "the preservation of progressive democracy" in our own country makes it necessary for democrats and progressives—that is to say, themselves—to "support" Stalin's policy of blood purges.

Who were these specialists in history and Soviet law? The miracle of such certainty on perplexing matters of revolutionary facts and ethics flourishing all unsuspected on Broadway and on Hollywood lots is an American phenomenon worthy of note outside the *Daily Worker* and the *New Masses* to which the glad news was at that time confined.

Only 123 of the 150 were named in the communist press. The missing 27 must therefore be deprived of the immortality of these pages. Those in the published list included such famous Russian and legal authorities as Lionel Stander, Muriel Draper, Dashiell Hammett, Dorothy Parker, Philip Loeb, Harold J. Rome—which is to say, comedians, lyricists, actors, society ladies, fiction writers. But the list also included scholars and scientists. That, perhaps, is even more extraordinary. Surely men like Dr. Henry E. Sigerist, Paul de Kruif, and Professor Jerome Davis in their own fields of knowledge apply rigid scientific criteria of judgment. Would Dr. Sigerist diagnose a case of smallpox, let us say, on the third-hand assurances of an agent perversely interested in the spread of smallpox? Would Mr. de Kruif think of making such sweeping judgments on a question of medical history, intuitively so to say, as he did in this matter of political history?

The variety of the signers of this amazing whitewash of Stalin prepared by movie actors and scientists must stand as a symbol of the Red Decade. Its insanity was surpassed only once, fifteen months later, by four hundred experts who publicly denied the possibility of any common ground between Russia and Germany—nine days before the two nations made their alliance in the Kremlin. Here, for the record, is the distinguished list, exactly as published by the *Daily Worker* of April 28, 1938:

Arthur Arent
Nelson Algren
Beril Becker
Thomas B. Bennett
Arnold Blanch
Marc Blitzstein
Roman Bohnen
Millen Brand
Phoebe Brand
Dorothy Brewster
J. R. Brown
Edwin Berry Burgum
Alan Campbell
Morris Carnovsky
Vera Caspary
Si-lan Chen
Haakon M. Chevalier
Ch'ao-ting Chi
Harold Clurman
Robert Coates
Merle Colby
Jack Conroy
Curt Conway
Ted Couday
Malcolm Cowley
Bruce Crawford
Kyle Crichton
Robert M. Cronbach
Lester Cole
H. W. L. Dana
Jerome Davis
Stuart Davis
Paul de Kruif
Muriel Draper
Robert W. Dunn
Dr. Garland Ethel
Phil Evergood
Guy Endore
Louis Ferstadt
Frederik V. Field
Elizabeth G. Flynn
Jules Garfield

Hugo Gellert
Robert Gessner
Harry Gottlieb
Emmett Cowan
B. D. N. Grebanier
Richard Greenleaf
Dashiell Hammett
Abraham Harriton
Henry Hart
Lillian Hellman
Granville Hicks
Langston Hughes
Rolph Humphries
Leo Hurwitz
Burton C. James
Florence B. James
Joe Jones
V. D. Kazakevich
Adelaide Klein
H. S. Kraft
John Howard Lawson
Corliss Lamont
Catherine Lawrence
Melvin Levy
Jay Leyda
Philip Loeb
Louis Lozowick
William C. Macleod
Albert Maltz
V. J. McGill
Selden C. Menefee
Alfred Morang
Elizabeth Olds
John O'Malley
A. L. Ottenheimer
Samuel Ornitz
Raymond Otis
Dorothy Parker
Paul Peters
John Hyde Preston
Rebecca E. Pitts
Samuel Putnum

Charles Recht
Wallingford Riegger
Lynn Riggs
Holland D. Roberts
Anna Rochester
Harold J. Rome
Henry Roth
Paul Romaine
Margaret Schlauch
Morris U. Schappes
Edwin Seaver
George Seldes
Howard Selsam
Irwin Shaw
Dr. Henry E. Sigerist
George Sklar
Harry Schlochower
Bernard Smith
E. Tredwell Smith
Jessica Smith

Hester Sondergaard
Raphael Soyer
Lionel Stander
Bernard J. Stern
Housely Stevens, Jr.
Philip Stevenson
Maxwell B. Stewart
Paul Strand
John Stuart
Genevieve Taggard
Nahum Tschabasov
Ethel Turner
Keene Wallis
Max Weber
George T. Willison
Frances Winwar
Martin Wolfson
Richard Wright
Victor A. Yakhontoff

A more curiously assorted jury has rarely sat in judgment on a set of complicated facts. Many of them, of course, have since then publicly denounced their own frivolity in thus endorsing official murder; but this is a history and the record stands. For piquancy this list of American apologists for the G.P.U. methods is exceeded by only one other document in connection with the same miracle of instinctive knowledge. It is the letter soliciting signatures to this whitewash sent out several weeks earlier (April 2) by a committee of five self-identified "liberals and progressives." Their names should be enshrined in some museum of political curiosities: Robert Coates, Malcolm Cowley, Stuart Davis, Marc Blitzstein and Paul Strand.

The combination of liberalism, progress, Stalin's staged trials and executions without trial is sufficiently astonishing. But it pales before the context of the letter itself. These gentlemen argued that the gory Russian doings were really brilliant maneuvers for freedom, democracy and a superior kind of justice. The logic might be roundabout and obscure, but to these five sponsors the business was at bottom a defense of individual rights and cultural liberties. Those honored with an invitation were apprised:

Your voice . . . will lend even greater weight to the worldwide defense of the right of the individual to speak, write, create, and otherwise engage in cultural activity in complete freedom.

When I first saw this letter I thought it a hoax played on the five men. I took the trouble to tip off Mr. Cowley that his name was being used on a fantastically preposterous circular letter. It was not easy to believe that Americans in their right mind and without G.P.U. compulsion would recommend cultural freedom of the kind vouchsafed to Old Bolsheviks and Red Army marshals before they are shot. But it was no hoax. The circular not only was genuine, but its crystal-clear logic went straight to the conscience of 150 scientists, artists and Broadway figures.

The strange document would not be worth notice if it were a grim but isolated stunt by 150 political illiterates. Unfortunately it was typical of the incredible behavior of the growing number of freshly minted neo-communists on Broadway and Park Avenue, in Hollywood and on college campuses. They indulged themselves gloriously in safe "ruthlessness" and stood ready to see Stalin through if it killed the last bloomin' Russian. At the bargain price of an occasional donation to the cause, an occasional signature on some outrageous statement, these bogus radicals fancied themselves brave souls defying the social order. They met the "best people" and exciting "Broadway figures," and looked down with a glow of condescension on humdrum neighbors who had not yet "found" the revolution.

The game was so patently phony that the average American confronted with a specimen of Stalinist hocus-pocus was inclined to remark that there ain't no such animal. But it was real enough in that political wonder-zoo inhabited by communists, fellow-travelers, stooges and innocents.

2

Leon Trotsky, the central figure in the lunatic tale told by the Moscow trials, was beyond the immediate reach of Stalin's police. One of his sons, working in Russia as an engineer, was put to death. The remaining son, Sedov, died of poisoning several years later in Paris, under circumstances which left no doubt in the minds of his friends and family that he had been "gotten" by Kremlin agents. Trotsky himself was finally assassinated, in 1940, after several abortive attempts. But throughout the course of the purge trials, he was at large, first in Norway and then in Mexico. His sharp commentary on the proceedings received some circulation, but not one-thousandth part of the notoriety given to the horrible charges against himself and against the whole Bolshevik revolution as dramatized by Stalin.

As the person most concerned in allegations which were keeping the Soviet executioners working overtime, the least he merited was a full hearing of his side of the story. Besides, each new trial brought into focus accusations which were open to neutral investigation abroad. The least that the outside world therefore could do—especially the portion of it to whom the tragedy was extremely vital in relation to their own social and political views—was to look closely at those phases of the testimony, as a sampling of the whole G.P.U. structure of evidence.

These minimal acts of decency and justice were undertaken by Professor John Dewey, America's foremost living philosopher, in association with other well-known liberals, labor men, progressives and radicals. Although the communist and fellow-traveler press instantly branded them as "Trotskyites," there was not a single member or supporter of Trotsky's wing of communism in the commission of investigators. In the American Committee for the Defense of Leon Trotsky, of course, there were followers of the exiled leader; it was only natural that his friends should come forward in his defense. But Professor Dewey and his fellow-commissioners were in no way responsible to anyone but themselves.

On the face of it, such an investigation, even if it failed to unearth new facts, could do no harm—after all Professor Dewey had no rifle squads at his command. Why should anyone object to an attempt to ascertain whether or not various supposed meetings between Trotsky and his self-confessed confederates had actually taken place? The claim that such an attempt would hurt the reputation of the Soviet Union and thereby "play into the hands of Hitler and Hearst" was palpable nonsense. Nothing any outside group might do could add perceptibly to the mountain of horror proudly displayed by the Kremlin itself. No report made by the Dewey commission could conceivably paint the revolution and its masters in more repulsive colors than the trials and the purges had already done.

But an amazing and ugly thing transpired. Scores of American men and women who had prated of justice all their mature lives now jumped with both feet on the octogenarian professor and those associated with him in the thankless undertaking. Only people aware of the social power held by the Stalinists on the Left at this time can appreciate the valor of that undertaking. Everyone who joined Dr. Dewey knew as a certainty that he or she would be denounced as a "Trotskyist"—a word that meant ostracism in that particular milieu—and smeared without mercy. They were challenging the best-organized, most articulate, least squeamish pressure group in American life, a pressure group backed by the total prestige and resources of a great foreign nation. Only those familiar with the realities of the incredible revolution understand that affiliation with the Dewey enterprise was an act of heroism.

Not only did the so-called liberal press fail to welcome and support the effort, but it joined lustily in throwing mud at it. Those who joined the defense committee were instantly buried under filthy epithets in the communist press. They were made the targets of organized campaigns of telephone calls—usually after midnight for more effective results in wearing down their nerves—and barrages of telegrams and letters. Many of them were visited by delegations. They were given to understand that they would lose their friends and in some cases their livelihoods if they persisted in the folly of offending the dominant communist opinion of their circles. Ugly rumors were set afloat reflecting on the private character of those who persevered in the undertaking, from Professor Dewey down. A few comrades joined the committee, it seemed, in order that they might resign publicly and smear the committee in the role of ex-members. A few were terrorized into resigning, a few others perhaps were honestly convinced that to expose the trials would "hurt the revolution."

The campaign against the Dewey proposal, too, produced its symbolic document. Eighty-eight open and covert communists and an array of gullible innocents published an Open Letter to American Liberals exhorting them not to help Professor Dewey. That letter deserves a place of honor among the curiosa of the Red Decade. It would be interesting to ask the signers now, in view of what some of them have since then learned about Stalin's Utopia, how they feel about their own role in concealing the truth about the purges.

Here were supposed liberals objecting to an outside investigation of a gruesome official crime, at a time when thousands were still being shot monthly by the Soviet government. Their principal excuse—defense of the "good name" of a dictatorship which was itself doing its utmost to blacken that name. They were demanding, in effect, that Trotsky be muzzled and that no steps be taken to check up on trial testimony even where such checking could not be stymied by the Soviet police. Not only were they objecting to Professor Dewey's committee—they were against any sort of investigation, since, they warned, it would "lend support to fascist forces." This was their reasoning:

Should not a country recognized as engaged in improving conditions for all its people, whether or not one agrees with all the means whereby this is brought about, be permitted to decide for itself what measures of protection are necessary against treasonable plots to assassinate and overthrow its leadership and involve it in war with foreign powers?

Consider the chicanery of this formulation. In the context of the question it is assumed that Stalin's victims were guilty of the charges against them. The implication is that the Soviet regime could do no wrong and must be its own judge of its own slaughterhouse procedures.

Only the ardor of blind faith or the naïveté of exceptional ignorance of political realities can explain the signatures. The fact that they included names like Lillian D. Wald is a commentary on the intellectual climate which prevailed in so-called progressive circles at the time.

I do not know how the innocents were cornered and high-pressured into joining the campaign for suppression of crucial facts on an affair of epochal importance. I do know that a large number were far from innocent—their names were standard on nearly all communist-inspired documents. Among those who escaped the communist contagion, the signatories acquired fame under the designation of the "stinkers' committee." Those who maneuvered them into signing the Open Letter clearly wanted to surround the investigation in advance with a bad smell. In any case, here is the list of signers* as attached to letters received by associates of Professor Dewey:

---

* Published in *Soviet Russia Today*, March, 1937.

John C. Ackley
Newton Arvin
Heywood Broun
Edwin Berry Burgum
Alan Campbell
Haakon Chevalier
Ethyl Clyde
Humphrey Cobb
Gifford Cochran
Malcolm Cowley
Addison T. Cutler
Jerome Davis
Dorothy Douglas
Theodore Dreiser
Mary Dublin
Guy Endore
Mildred Fairchild
Robert Gessner
Louis Fischer
B. Z. Goldberg
Alphonse Goldschmidt
Wyllistine Goodsell
Lillian Hellman
Granville Hicks
Arthur Kallet
Vladimir Kazakevich
Rockwell Kent
Paul Kern
John A. Kingsbury
Mary Van Kleeck
Corliss Lamont
Ring Lardner, Jr.
Max Lerner
Robert Morss Lovett
Katherine Lumpkin
Robert S. Lynd
William Malisoff
William P. Mangold
Naita Marburg
Elizabeth Dublin Marshall
George Marshall
Clifford T. McAvoy

John McAlpin Millen
Lewis Milestone
V. J. McGill
Carey McWilliams
Herbert A. Miller
Loren Miller
Edwin Mims, Jr.
M. Y. Munson
Dudley Nichols
Samuel Ornitz
Dorothy Parker
Walter N. Polakov
D. W. Prall
Samson Raphaelson
Col. Raymond Robins
Henry Roth
Margaret Schlauch
William Seagle
Howard Selsam
Arnold Shukutoff
Dr. Henry E. Sigerist
Irina Skariatina
Bernard Smith
E. Tredwell Smith
Robert K. Speer
Rev. William D. Spofford
Viola Brothers Shore
Tess Slesinger
Bernard J. Stern
Donald Ogden Stewart
Maxwell Stewart
Anna Louise Strong
Paul M. Sweezy
Lillian D. Wald
Mark Waldman
Eda Lou Walton
Lynd Ward
Clara Weatherwax
Max Weber
Louis Weisner
Nathaniel West
David McElvy White

James Waterman Wise   William Zorach
Art Young   Leane Zugsmith

The list is made up predominantly of writers, near-writers, teachers, social workers, with a few artists and clergymen for ballast. These classifications identify fairly accurately the chief areas of Stalinoid infection. Although some businessmen, a few millionaires' sons and a labor man here and there were swept up by the epidemic, it may be regarded primarily as a disease of the intelligentsia, hence properly the domain of psychiatrists. A journalist can only gather some of the raw materials, the symptomatic data, for the expert in pathology who will one day tackle this mass support of a far-off and bloodthirsty dictatorship by otherwise sane and largely well-meaning people.

Those associated with Professor Dewey on the investigating commission were John Chamberlain, Alfred Rosmer, Professor Edward Alsworth Ross, Otto Ruehle, Benjamin Stolberg, Carlo Tresca, Francisco Zamora, Wendelin Thomas, Suzanne La Follette, and John F. Finerty as counsel. A subcommission which gathered data in Europe was headed by the exiled Italian socialist leader G. E. Modigliani, and included Mme. César Chabrun, M. Mathe, Jean Galtier-Boissière, Professor Jacques Madaule and Maurice Delépine.

They worked for long months under the handicap of lack of funds, lack of authority, G.P.U. terrorization, and a crescendo of vilification in the Stalinist press the world over. Considering these difficulties, their achievement is truly amazing. The published volume of their findings is clear, detailed and to an unprejudiced mind utterly destructive of the whole police fabrication in Moscow. The job of analyzing the trial records, isolating the endless absurdities and contradictions, needed to be done. Even without the new information on dozens of disputed points the Dewey report therefore shed light on a matter steeped in darkness. In this book, however, I am less concerned with the results of their inquiry than I am with the incidental light that it throws on the temper of the Red Decade.

As a footnote to the story I offer in exhibit Mr. Waldo Frank. When Mr. Frank exchanged his private mysticism for the fashionable mysticism of the Muscovite aberration, he was hailed as a hero in the communist press. He was made chairman of one of the principal planets in Stalin's solar system, the League of American Writers. All went well until the Soviet bloodletting touched Mr. Frank's conscience. He wrote a letter to the *New Republic* suggesting an international labor and socialist inquiry into the whole matter. Immediately his services to the cause were forgotten and his name was mud. He had committed the deadly sin of doubting. When the next American Writers Congress foregathered, he was mysteriously missing. Let the innocent literati who continued to claim that the League and its Congresses were independent, explain the technique by which Waldo Frank was eliminated after his slip, and his place taken by one of Hollywood's best, Donald Ogden Stewart.

Chapter XXII

"FRIENDS OF THE G.P.U."

1

IN THE frantic campaign to smear and discredit the so-called Trotsky Commission headed by Professor John Dewey, the generalissimo was Corliss Lamont, one of the more pathetic figures thrown up to public view by the Red Decade. He spared neither his money nor his energy in defending the mass slaughter in Russia and in damning those who dared examine that horror.

The pathos of Dr. Lamont derives primarily from a circumstance for which he is not in the least to blame. I refer to the fact that he is the son of the multimillionaire banker and Morgan partner, Thomas W. Lamont. This gave his every Stalinist utterance and gesture an accidental melodramatic quality. By multiplying his Stalinism a hundredfold, his family connection somehow made it seem, like most things bigger than life-size, peculiarly grotesque. The comrades were not content to exploit his wealth for support of their many causes. They delighted in exhibiting him for his propaganda value as a front, rather like bigoted atheists exhibiting a renegade bishop. In time a patina of eccentricity came to cover poor Lamont's identity from head to toe.

He has also had the misfortune of tangling, again and again, with men of exceptional intellectual power: men like Professor Dewey, Sidney Hook, Max Eastman. His shortcomings have consequently been limned more clearly than they would have been had he, with more becoming humility, confined his attentions to members of his Friends of the Soviet Union. For instance, after the publication of the Dewey commission's report, Dr. Lamont had the temerity to rush to the radio with a reply. No one who listened to the two men that evening can forget the pathos of the contrast. Professor Dewey made a calm, carefully reasoned and scientifically documented report. He was followed by Dr. Lamont with a shrilly emotional "reply" that nowhere even touched the older man's charges and pleaded weakly for all-out faith in Stalin and in Russia.

But precisely because he has been accidentally "blown up" larger than life, it is easier to examine Dr. Lamont as a type—the upper-class near-intellectual driven perversely to assert himself by an extremist pose. If he had not been born into excessive millions, young Lamont might easily have grown into a drab but contented pedagogue. Or he might have turned into a clergyman—his first enthusiasm was for revealed religion. But the prominence of his father, the ease with which he could indulge psychological impulses, were his undoing. To be rich or to become richer would be no achievement but only a confirmation of his secondary role. He must have been under inner compulsion to assert himself in some way different from his father's —nay, in direct opposition to the things symbolized by his father.

This protest first took the form of frantic attacks against "supernaturalism," against the religion he had first championed. From there he went on naturally to attack bankers and capitalists. Surely, he may have felt inwardly, no one can doubt that I rose in the revolutionary movement on my own rather than on inherited values. He did rise— to the eminence of chairmanship of the Friends of the Soviet Union, an honored place on every list of innocents thrown together to cover up some new Russian atrocity, featured booking for endless communist publications and mass meetings. But I doubt whether he has really achieved the psychological catharsis which he sought. There must be moments in which he recognizes that even in the ranks of non-communist communists he rose so rapidly more by reason of his newsworthy name and his fat donations than through unadulterated ability.

The fact alone that he was selected to head the Friends—the least disguised of the Communist Party appendages—and not one of the teeming "cultural" fronts was a subtle insult. Less subtle was the fashion in which he was used continually as a publicity come-on, his name assuring attention where Joe Zilch could never obtain it.

In earlier years the Friends of the Soviet Union and its predecessors were headed frankly by party members. It was the "respectable" auxiliary of the party, but the intimate connection was not concealed. A reservoir for non-party sympathizers, its purpose was to make them over into party comrades. The F.S.U. literature read very much like the party literature. In the Third Period the membership card identified the Friends as "an international organization, with headquarters in many countries, devoted to developing the international solidarity of the working masses for the support and defense of the Soviet Union." At its national conference in Chicago, January, 1934, Comrades Minor, Hathaway and Trachtenberg spoke as "representatives of the Central Committee of the Communist Party." The F.S.U. magazine, Soviet Russia Today, would have had not the slightest trouble passing the most rigid Moscow censorship. Its editorial council, at the zenith of the Red Decade, included the usual amalgam of open and not-so-open fellow-travelers: Malcolm Cowley, Robert W. Dunn, A. A. Heller, Dr. John Kingsbury, Isobel Walker Soule, Maxwell S. Stewart, etc.

The fact that Dr. Lamont was raised to supreme command in the organization of "working masses" is typical of the humorless revision which produced the incredible revolution. He was the exaggerated equivalent of Congressman Vito Marcantonio, an alleged Republican, as head of the International Labor Defense—started by Willi Muenzenberg and in better years headed by party stalwarts like James Cannon. Lamont's name could not blur the essential continuity of viewpoint and objective between his Friends and its predecessor.

There is little to record of the Friends, since the activities of Lamont's organization were substantially an extension of the activities of Browder's organization. Its "respectability" merely enabled it to give larger banquets and to invite collaboration of Americans who would have shunned the official party.

The high point of F.S.U. achievement was the preparation of a Golden Book of American Friendship with the Soviet Union in November, 1937, to mark the twentieth anniversary of the Bolshevik Revolution. Several hundred thousand signatures were gathered for that book. In view of the fact that the Kremlin was then in the midst of bloody purges which will continue to horrify mankind for generations, the size of the Book indicates once more how extensive the Stalinist penetration of American life had become. At a gala meeting in Carnegie Hall, the Book was turned over to Soviet representatives, with hymns of praise being sung from the stage by an array of speakers that included James Waterman Wise, Dr. Henry E. Sigerist, Jerome Davis, Mary Van Kleeck, Frederick L. Schuman, Joshua Kunitz, Congressman Ernest Lundeen, Louis Fischer, Mauritz Hallgren, Harry W. L. Dana, Donald Henderson, General V. A. Yakhontoff.

Press reports of the occasion indicate that no one of them ventured to mention the heroes of the revolution they were celebrating. They had unfortunately just been liquidated wholesale by the sub-hero to whom they sent their *Golden Book of Friendship*.

2

The high point in Corliss Lamont's own career among the comrades was provided by his aforementioned command of the anti-Dewey campaign. An analysis of Lamont's curiously passionate defense of the purges was published at the time in the *Modern Monthly* (March, 1938) by Sidney Hook. I can do no better than to summarize and paraphrase it.

Dr. Lamont had no qualifications for the job other than enthusiasm. He knew no more about the Moscow trials than any other newspaper reader. His chairmanship of the F.S.U. scarcely left him open to the suspicion of unbiased judgment. But he rushed headlong into the job and, as might be expected, bruised his self-esteem and his reputation even among those who were willing to give him the benefit of the doubt.

The report of the Dewey Commission was extremely detailed. It demonstrated: *first*, that the structure of the charges in the Moscow trials rested on the claims of defendants who "confessed" that they had acted as intermediaries between Trotsky, his son Sedov and the alleged plotters in Russia; *second*, that in every instance these claims, being subject to investigation abroad, were proved false. It reached the conclusion that the exposure of these fundamental pieces of evidence invalidated the confessions as a whole. This was the story as told to the American people over the radio by Professor Dewey.

"Now the very least one could have expected from Lamont," Professor Hook wrote, "was an attempt to answer these damning revelations which made the front page of every important paper from coast to coast. But all Lamont could say—and mind you *after* he had read the Commission's abstract—was that he was 'convinced that the Soviet authorities acted in a just and proper manner.' And his reasons? 'The defendants openly confessed and pleaded guilty. . . .' Lamont had rushed to defend the Moscow trials without being able to answer a *single* point in the evidence which proved them to be frame-ups."

The most remarkable passage in his speech was this: "The Soviet regime and its achievements are indivisible; and we cannot believe that its system of justice is completely out of step with its splendid accomplishments in practically all other fields." Even without arguing the "splendid achievements," the logic of this argument is amazing. It simply meant that Lamont was disposed in advance to believing anything that came out of Moscow, because its virtue was "indivisible." Against reason and fact he brought to the radio his amazing plea that nobody should ask embarrassing questions about Stalin's acts because he, Lamont, knew them a priori to be perfect.

Dr. Lamont later pulled another boner that again left him sadly stripped to the public view. An American engineer named Littlepage wrote three articles on Russia for the *Saturday Evening Post*. In the second of these he said that sabotage and bribery and other skulduggery were rife in the new Russia—a fact which no one denied. Littlepage also told a strange anecdote intended to show that one of the trial defendants, Piatakov, had been implicated in a piece of sabotage which did not come off. Now the prevalence of sabotage in Russia no more proved that Rykov and Zinoviev and Radek had sabotaged than the prevalence of murder in America, let us say, proved that Lamont had murdered anyone. Littlepage's suspicion of Piatakov, even if it were true, proved nothing about the bigger charges against him and the charges against the thousands of other victims of the purges.

But Dr. Lamont proceeded to circularize the members of the Dewey committee with the second Littlepage article, claiming it as "new and concrete evidence of wrecking activities."

The logical *non sequitur* was turned into farce the following week, when the *Post* published Littlepage's third article under the title "The Serfs of the Soviets." Having played up the author as a reliable witness, poor Lamont now had to read this man's appalling picture of forced labor in Russia for millions of workers and peasants under horrible conditions. To sum it up: Dr. Lamont disdained examination of evidence because of the "splendid achievements" of Russia. Then he decided to advance one piece of evidence notwithstanding—and his sole witness proceeded to picture those "spendid achievements" as a peculiarly brutal type of mass enslavement. He had enough good sense, one hopes, to recognize the hopelessness of his own confusion.

No one has any warrant for doubting the sincerity with which such a man first entered the communist orbit. But politics has its own logic. Having lent himself to the machinations of the Browder boys, he sank deeper and deeper into their political swamps. By the time Stalin embraced Hitler, he was too profoundly compromised psychologically for retreat. He did not even have the courage to dissolve the Friends of the Soviet Union, but allowed it to expire without benefit of public notice.

Max Eastman once made an eloquent appeal to Dr. Lamont's conscience as a scholar and a human being. The tragedy of Corliss Lamont is summed up in a few paragraphs from that appeal:

You are not so blind to the rays of justice, if your eyes were not held shut, as to accept these show trials of a few dozen who were ready to "confess" as proof of the guilt, and justification for the murder behind closed doors, of hundreds, and indeed thousands, who were not. You are not so superior to the idea of mercy that you would naturally ignore the still unanswered question: What has become of the wives and children of these thousands of murdered communists? You would under normal conditions, sense the ugliness of your own position—the son of a leading finance capitalist engaging in a campaign of slander by private correspondence on engraved stationery against the executed leaders of the Russian revolution, a scion of the house of Morgan assisting in the process of their dishonor by circulating arguments from the *Saturday Evening Post* based upon the premises of black reaction. Surely you could find a more appropriate way to serve the cause of labor! And you would find it, if you were free from pressure, free to be your simple, chivalrous self. . . .

The one priceless thing you could have brought to the proletarian movement, coming from the source you do and with your education, was true knowledge and absolute principled integrity. Instead you are bringing a little money, a small gift even when it is large, and an increase of mental confusion and moral decay.*

3

The Littlepage "evidence" so avidly lapped up by Lamont and the *New Masses* recalls to my mind another piece of "evidence" which, at about the same time, was featured by writers in the *New Republic* and widely quoted in fellow-traveler circles to justify the Stalin murders.

An American engineer, whom I remembered rather vaguely from Russia, came to see me at my office. He had worked for the Soviets for eight or nine years. In the latter part of his sojourn he had married

---

* The *New International*, April, 1938.

a Russian woman to whom he became deeply attached. But when his contract was ended, the authorities had refused to let his wife accompany him out of Russia. He had been knocking at official doors, writing letters and cabling wildly in the hope of obtaining her release. It was a familiar story—dozens of foreign engineers, having taken Russian wives, tried for years to get them out of that country.

At the same time he told me in detail about his plans to do a book about his long residence in Russia. As he told it, his would be another gruesome record of chaos, injustice, starvation.

"Well," I asked him, "which interests you more—getting out a book or getting back your wife?"

"My wife, of course," he said. "I'm desperate. I'd do anything almost to rescue her."

"In that case," I smiled, "you are doing just the wrong thing. Don't for God's sake, come to visit people like myself, who are on the Soviet blacklist. And don't write or speak a word about these horrors. If such stuff reached the comrades, any remote hope you may still have for getting her out will be ended. On the contrary, you ought to convince the Russians somehow that you are friendly to them; otherwise your wife, just because you do love her, will be held as a sort of hostage."

The engineer left. I forgot about him. But five or six weeks later I was startled by a series of articles under his name in *Soviet Russia Today*. He had taken my advice rather literally. The articles were so contrived as to seem an indirect confirmation of the charges against the victims of the purge! Soon I was being confronted with this "evidence" by earnest fellow-travelers seeking to break down my disapproval of the Moscow trials. . . . I could not tell them what I knew, for fear of spoiling that bargain. I can only hope that Stalin came through at his end and that the ransomed wife is now in America. If she isn't here by now, despite those articles, her case is hopeless and this little tale can do no harm.

4

The International Labor Defense may be bracketed with Dr. Lamont's late unlamented Friends of the Soviet Union among the least camouflaged of Stalin's Trojan Horses. Its official organ, *Labor Defender*, repeatedly identified it as "the American section of the International Red Aid." In April, 1934, the magazine added: "It was under the banner of our parent organization that Dimitrov was freed; that the Scottsboro campaign became international."

But Vito Marcantonio, chairman of the I.L.D., cannot be bracketed with Dr. Lamont. He is a self-made man; the hammering of the process has been loud and discordant, the resultant carpentry pretty rough. The political opportunism of his every move has been exceedingly in evidence.

Marcantonio—merely by way of summing up his talents—landed in Congress under the joint auspices of the Right Wing of the Republican Party and the Left Wing of the American Labor Party; took part in Italian pro-facist meetings and communist meetings almost simultaneously; demanded national armament and soon thereafter opposed national armament with equal fervor; and to top it all, firmly denies all these facts in turn as called for by any specified occasion. He is by all odds the most "denyingest" politician in captivity.

Marcantonio has appeared as a speaker before the Leonardo da Vinci Art School, which Professor Salvemini has cited as a front for the Italian government's "cultural" work here. One of the chiefs of Marcantonio's Republican Club in East Harlem, New York, is Paolo Del Bagno, who was president of the Circolo Mario Morgantini, an organization named in honor of a fascist hero and on record as "loyal to the Duce."

But Congressman Marcantonio indignantly denies any sympathy for fascism.

Not only is he head of the Muscovite I.L.D. but his name has appeared on endless communist speakers' lists and documents. His election was the principal task of the pro-communist wing of the Labor Party. His works and words have consistently rung the bell of communist enthusiasm in the *Daily Worker* and other party papers. His views on public questions have run parallel to those of Browder, even unto his lone-wolf opposition to national-security measures in the House of Representatives. No one in the least familiar with the realities of American communism has any doubt that Marcantonio, without joining the party, served it extremely well.

But Congressman Marcantonio denies, no less indignantly, that he is a communist.

And he carries the passion for denial to the point of denying that the I.L.D. which he captains is a stooge Moscow organization—this despite the organization's own candor in the matter. The fact remains, all the same, that the I.L.D. is the legal defense arm of American communism. Occasionally it also acts in behalf of non-communists. But it has never spared an angry adjective in support of any labor or radical prisoner known to be hostile to communism. Indeed, the I.L.D. and its captain have not yet indicated publicly any awareness of the most prominent American labor prisoner—Fred E. Beal, victim of the Gastonia, North Carolina, textile strike situation. Beal, it happens, had forfeited comradely sympathy by denouncing the Soviet Utopia.

Such are Marcantonio and his American branch office of the International Red Aid. In 1937 it claimed 300,000 members, in 800 branches scattered through 47 states. If the figure was half correct, it must have meant something to a young ambitious politician. But we may assume he denies it.

5

In the preoccupation with the proliferating Innocents' Clubs and the unregimented sympathizers, we must not lose awareness of the machinery far behind the fronts. The official Communist Party, section of the Comintern, was always there, counting the "take," distributing the jobs and sopping up the Popular Front gravy.

The non-party masses and the American public generally saw Browder, Foster, Minor, Bedacht, Hathaway and the rest only on dress parade, so to speak, wrapped in American flags and singing *Yankee Doodle*. They watched Mother Bloor behaving like Barbara Frietchie, Minor as Massa Tom Jefferson, Earl Browder stretching to look like Honest Abe, and Mike Gold posing as a domesticated Tom Paine. But between the acts these people had a prospering party to manage, a party now expanded to Big Business scale. We must visualize the innermost administration of the incredible revolution, with its directives from Moscow, its decrees from Union Square. its thousands of caucuses and conflicts.

Factionalism in the open dog-eat-dog spirit of Gitlow's and Lovestone's days was no more, of course. Like its Soviet prototype, the American party was now properly "monolithic." Browder was the American equivalent of Stalin, James W. Ford was the Negro counterpart of Browder, the late Moissaye Olgin was the Jewish version of

Ford, and so down the line. Every race, city, category had its Beloved Leader in a hierarchy as rigid and venerated as in any church. A ritual of "affection" developed, closely modeled on the "affection" enforced for the Leader of Leaders in the Kremlin. The faithful even staged hurrahing receptions at railroad stations when the Beloved Browder returned from a propaganda tour. There was nothing like it in New York south of Father Divine.

Under the monolithic calm, however, there was plenty of competition for jobs and honors. As the Popular Front fleshpots grew more numerous and juicier, the contest for preferment tended to reach murderous intensity. Comrades spied on one another's conversations not only from zeal for the cause but, alas, from hunger for the erring one's lucrative post. There were trials and purges of every degree. Well-known comrades disappeared from the *Daily Worker* social columns, sometimes turning up in the Hearst publications. Scarcely a month went by without its quota of "fascists, Trotskyists and counter-revolutionists" read out of the party. I even heard the fantastic details of a purge trial in a New York high school against a little girl suspected of heresy.

A constant ferment of purging and smearing, spiced with confessions of sin and Muscovite rituals of self-degradation, provided the psychological element in which the higher strata of party people lived and worked and intrigued. And Moscow remained, now as in the lean and hungry days of yore, the final arbiter on all things in the American party. "Reps" of the International sat on the party executive and exercised veto powers. Messengers, duly equipped with false passports, came and went between Moscow and New York. Leaders from Browder down were subject to sudden and frightening summons from the Leader of Leaders, and the entire party held its collective breath until their return.

The notorious Robinson-Rubens case for a moment lit up the lurid tale of Stalin's "passport mill" in the United States. Adolph Arnold Rubens, a Latvian working for the Soviets, and his American wife were arrested in Moscow. The intrigue is too complex to be traced here. But in the following months it became clear that Rubens had operated in New York a communist mill for the production of fake American passports for the use of communist leaders and Soviet espionage agents the world over. Three of his minor confederates in May, 1939, received prison terms after conviction in a Federal court. According to Herbert Solow, who made an exhaustive study of the scandal, hundreds of passports had been manufactured in the preceding years. After the conviction of the three underlings, he wrote:

Behind their trial lies a sensational story of organized underground Soviet activities on American soil by agents sent from Russia to work in collaboration with American communists. The story shows that, just as Hitler utilizes his sympathizers in the German-American Bund and its auxiliaries to propagandize and spy for Germany, so Stalin utilizes members and hangers-on of the American Communist Party for the Kremlin espionage. . . . The central fact of the story unfolded here is that the American Communist Party, and its periphery of sympathizers and fellow-travelers, constitute a vast reservoir of spies for the Kremlin.*

Gitlow after his expulsion, head spy Nick Dozenberg, the late General Krivitsky, Jan Valtin in *Out of the Night*, and others have in recent years contributed to the picture of Soviet espionage in America. Anti-Stalinists have charged a lack of vigilance on the part of high authorities in hunting down such intruders. In any case, this network of Stalin's undercover agents is only an extension of the open party membership, and frequently it is difficult to know where one ends and the other begins. The fellow-travelers, whether in government or literature or labor unions, need not console themselves that they only worked with the "legal" end of the communist conspiracy. The whole Stalinist system is too well integrated for such divisions. At best they are labels to confuse the unwary.

A surface refurbishing of the American party was undertaken in these years to make the "democratic" hoax more credible. A new party constitution was adopted, for instance. The comrades dipped their pens in the ink and their tongues in their cheeks and wrote:

The Communist Party of America is a working class political party carrying forward today the traditions of Jefferson, Paine, Jackson and Lincoln, and of the Declaration of Independence; it upholds the achievements of democracy, the rights of "life, liberty and the pursuit of happiness," and defends the United States Constitution against its reactionary enemies who would destroy democracy and all popular liberties.

Not even the most rabid enthusiast for the Kremlin's execution technique could object to that; not aloud anyhow.

---

* *American Mercury*, July, 1939.

CHAPTER **XXIII**

COCKTAILS FOR SPANISH DEMOCRACY

1

A FTER the first hectic year of the Spanish civil wars, control of the Loyalist government apparatus was unified and systematized—in the hands of the communists and their creatures. Largo Caballero, having refused to outlaw the Leftist P.O.U.M. group and to surrender the War Department and his conscience to Stalinist dictation, had been ousted. Moscow's threat of cutting off completely the flow of outside arms and supplies gave the communist minority the upper hand. Dr. Juan Negrin, who had been carefully "built up" in the Stalinist press and was openly working with the Kremlin crowd, displaced the socialist trade-union veteran.

Thereafter the function of the Loyalist regime most rigidly supervised by Moscow's agents was propaganda in all its branches. The censorship was under the control of Constancia De La Mora and other trusted Stalinists. News out of Loyalist Spain was filtered through communist sieves, rigidly controlled and in part lavishly subsidized. Hundreds of thousands of dollars went through the hands of a single alleged "independent" American writer actually on the Loyalist pay roll—this according to affidavits from Loyalist leaders on file in official quarters here. In addition to paid journalistic agents, the totalitarian propaganda setup enjoyed the fatuous and enthusiastic help of neutral reporters too childish politically to see through the game. Excited literati from many countries had rushed to the scene. They failed to distinguish between the Loyalist masses—predominantly anarcho-syndicalist and socialist and ·plain democratic—and the communist bureaucracy that had blackjacked its way to control.

The result was that the outside world heard the Loyalist story only from the communist angle. Not one in a thousand supposedly well-informed newspaper readers even today knows that there was any *other* angle to the story. The suppressed and persecuted anti-communist *majority* never got a break. Only the generals in the Kremlin's

268

ideological livery were featured as heroes; magnificent fighters from the socialist, anarchist and other non-Stalinist ranks were loaded with blame and obloquy. The one man who came nearest to representing the overwhelming majority of the anti-Franco millions, Caballero, was systematically maligned in the foreign press. Stalin's horrifying methods in dealing with anti-fascists of other than communist persuasion were either ignored or blandly reported as "victories."

The calculated news succeeded in reducing the whole Spanish tragedy, from Franco's rebellion in July, 1936, to his final triumph in the spring of 1939, to a beguilingly neat black-and-red pattern. It showed a life-and-death struggle between fascism and democracy, with Hitler and Mussolini aiding the rebels and Stalin supporting the democrats. This was a fantastic simplification of a maelstrom of events and purposes—of revolutionary and counter-revolutionary impulses, greedy foreign self-interests, profound inner tensions within both the Franco and the Loyalist camps. The picture was false and contributed greatly to the collapse of the Loyalist cause.

Perhaps its most mischievous effect was this: that it threw the whole weight of world-wide anti-fascist emotion behind the totalitarian elements which had hijacked the Loyalist cause. A healthy and intelligent support from abroad might have given the anti-communist majority a fighting chance. But nearly every dollar of outside contributions, every ounce of outside sentiment, every volunteer for the fighting fronts, went directly to the Stalinists! Tens of thousands of Americans who thought that they were "helping the Loyalists" were only helping the Moscow gang in Spain to dominate the Loyalists.

The black-and-red simplification was the product of deliberate and expert propaganda. Its imprint is still so deep on the world's imagination, especially among liberals, that what I am saying here will sound to them like wild blasphemy. Yet only the most "religious" Stalinists and the hopelessly naïve could have failed to sense, by this time, that the picture was not quite so neat. They must have gathered, however vaguely, from the belated hints by Ernest Hemingway and the writings of Loyalist leaders in exile, that there was something mysterious and sinister in the business which they had failed to understand. They must be aware by now that thousands of earnest anti-fascists, from conservative republicans to ultra-revolutionary radicals, agree in blaming Russia's highhanded intrusion for the Loyalist failure. The mere fact that Russia does not give refuge to any of the Loyalists still cooped up in concentration camps in France holds significant implications.

Those who are politically more sophisticated may even have caught a glimmer of the idea that the Spanish people were the victimized pawns in a complicated international game of power-politics. Slowly but inevitably, the basic truth is emerging—the truth that Stalin, ostensibly the would-be savior of Spanish democracy, actually had other fish to fry. Ultimately it must become clear that the Muscovite dictatorship diverted, sabotaged, and demoralized the Loyalist strength in the successful attempt to grab total control. "The inner-line communist tactics of winning the upper hand paralyzed the military and political efforts necessary to beat the strong enemy," Luis Araquistan, the Loyalist Ambassador to France and a lifelong popular democratic leader, has stated in recording the blackout of freedom in his native land.*

Piece by piece the story has been coming out of the mists of propagandist verbiage—the story of how Russia "muscled in" on the Spanish revolution, capturing ascendancy by fraud, blackmail, and profligate violence. In the process it splintered and demoralized the anti-Franco masses, emptied the Loyalist cause of its emotional revolutionary driving power, and thereby in effect guaranteed the victory for the fascists.

Having hijacked the Loyalist regime, the Stalinists proceeded to capture anti-Franco sentiment the world over and to canalize it for their own political purposes. In this they had the co-operation, as I have said, of paid propagandists from many countries and volunteer innocents. We have seen how in relation to Russia itself hundreds of well-meaning liberals thought they were serving "progress" and even "democracy" by covering up and justifying Stalin's crimes and blunders. Even thus writers like Hemingway and Ralph Bates, André Malraux and Herbert L. Matthews, Jay Allen and Vincent Sheean, dozens from all over the world convinced themselves honestly that they were "fighting fascism" by explaining away the crimes and the blunders of Stalinist muscle-men in Spain. Too late most of them are now finding out that they had sided with a totalitarian invader against the Spanish revolution.

The Loyalist story, it bears repeating, was told almost exclusively through conscious or innocent communist mouthpieces. The rest of that story has appeared only in little magazines, in the labor and social-

---

* *New Leader*, June 3, 1939.

ist press, in flashes of truth here and there in recent novels about Spain. The reports of Spaniards and Americans like Araquistan, John Dos Passos, Largo Caballero, Sam Baron, Liston Oak, Anita Brenner—people whose deep loathing for fascism is beyond possible question—simply have not registered. They have been unable to break through the great falsehood about Russia's role "sold" to the world by a powerful government operating a vast agitational machine and disposing of unlimited fiscal and moral resources.

Many American volunteers in the Loyalist armies, though they proved their honesty by risking their lives, not merely dollars, have tried to tell the truth about the communist blight on Spanish democracy. They have been ignored. The stories by volunteers and the families of volunteers told before the Dies Committee and in various magazine articles have been brushed aside as "incredible" and "fantastic" merely because the truth was, indeed, incredible and fantastic. Disciplined communist organizations, abetted by silly women and gushing liberals who cannot see beyond an enticing slogan, have managed to tar and feather every critic of Stalin's policies in Spain as "Franco agents," "fascists" and "Trotskyists."

Nevertheless, the facts are emerging. Spanish leaders who collaborated with the communist invasion, through ignorance or cupidity or under moral duress, are beginning to speak out. The journalistic victims of the propaganda setups in Barcelona and Madrid are beginning, in the perspective of time, to recognize the contours of Stalin's real purposes. It took years for elementary truths about Russia under Stalin to seep through the thick layers of misconception and wishful thinking. It will take years for the elementary facts about Spain under Stalin to come through. But ultimately they will be known.

In February, 1941, for instance, one phase of the sad story, a phase especially interesting for Americans, was made public through the press by a prominent New York physician, Dr. John Jacob Posner. For six months he had been the chief oral surgeon for the American Hospitals in Loyalist Spain, an enterprise to which Americans contributed $1,756,000 through the Medical Bureau to Aid Spanish Democracy and its affiliates. He left in disgust, together with his technical assistant, Miss Martha E. Mitchell, and another American physician, Dr. Z. M. Stadt. They had found it impossible to work under a hospital regime which was more devoted to promoting Stalin's objectives than fighting disease.

On returning to America, the three volunteers placed detailed charges, backed by a mass of documents, before a subcommittee of the Medical Bureau. They showed that the American hospitals were entirely communist-dominated and served Stalinist rather than Loyalist purposes; in addition they showed how the management of "political commissars" caused confusion, inefficiency and the spread of disease. Having volunteered as Americans interested in relieving suffering, they had discovered that they were expected to behave like Russian communist agents. Robert Minor, one of the chief leaders of the American Communist Party, was the final authority on all matters in these hospitals sponsored innocently by people like Professor Albert Einstein, Paul Muni, Lillian D. Wald, Newbold Morris, Grace Abbott, Dr. Walter B. Cannon and hundreds of others. Naturally the complaints of Dr. Posner and his two associates were ignored. They had simply been hoaxed along with every man and woman who had contributed toward the $1,756,000.

Moscow's seizure of a monopoly of anti-fascist emotion was the major Stalinist triumph of these years. It gave the communists an absolute moral authority over millions of men and women throughout the world who, at bottom, had no real sympathy with the Russian tyranny. That, more than any other single factor, made possible the amazing growth of People's Fronts, Innocents' Clubs, mythical united fronts, and the Stalinist intellectual terror sketched in these pages. And it was the strangle hold on Loyalist Spain which above all gave the communists that monopoly. That is why this chapter is part and parcel of the history of Bolshevism in America.

The fight against Franco had become a symbol of democracy's struggle for survival—Stalin grabbed that symbol and turned it into a Soviet racket.

2

Irving Pflaum is an American who reported the Loyalist side of the civil wars from the start for the United Press. His bias was frankly and passionately against Franco and against fascism. Writing in the American Mercury soon after the Loyalist collapse, he began thus:

Three dictatorships are responsible for the destruction of the Spanish Republic. Italy, Germany—and Russia. Yes, Russia. When the story is finally told in full it will become apparent that Stalin's domination of the Loyalist regime since May 1937 was one of the most decisive factors in assuring victory for Franco. Now that the Loyalist cause is lost, silence on the subject can no longer be justified on any grounds.

Luis Araquistan is a true-and-tried socialist leader of Spain; he served the Republic as Ambassador in Berlin and later as Loyalist Ambassador in Paris. In analyzing the reasons for the debacle, he, too, stated unequivocally: "The chief responsibility goes to the Communist Party." And since the Spanish communists themselves were a negligible few when the fight started, he pointed out, the blame must rest squarely on the Soviet government.

Mexico had sent arms even before Russia had decided to do so. "Other countries in the later days of the civil war sold us important quantities of arms," Araquistan confirmed. But these neither demanded nor obtained control of the Loyalist government or army or press. Only Russia extorted not merely exorbitant cash payments in advance, but far-reaching political concessions. At a time when Spain, in its desperation, could not afford to haggle, this was plain blackmail. Control of arms and munitions, doled out parsimoniously at profiteering prices, gave Stalin a decisive weapon of bribery and blackmail. The communists—and this the world has not grasped—did not simply turn over their "aid" to the Spanish people. The fraction that did reach Spain was stored in communist-controlled warehouses and dispensed by the Stalinists, making and breaking generals at will by giving or withholding weapons and supplies. The very first boat loaded with supplies from Russia, reaching Barcelona, refused to unload until certain men known to be anti-communist were removed from the Catalonian Cabinet. The hard-pressed Spaniards yielded—and it was only the first in an endless chain of highhanded acts of blackmail.

Caballero told an American socialist, Sam Baron, in detail how such juggling of "aid" saved Franco from what might have been knockout defeats. At least three times during Caballero's term as Premier—at Guadalajara, Pozoblanco and Aragon—the flow of munitions was arbitrarily cut off by the communist managers of supplies just in time to save the fascist forces. "I believe the prolongation of the war was deliberate," Caballero charged. "Arms were held back until communist control over the army was assured."

The People's Front government which the communists had maneuvered into being, it had become clear even before the Franco *putsch*, was for them simply another "tactic," a piece of political legerdemain. It soon became obvious, Araquistan has written, that "they did not want a just, sane political power. They wanted complete control—the exclusion of all other political groups. . . . Democracy was only one of their political tools to unite the absolute power in their hands. . . . After the first twelve months of the coalition, it was clear to everybody that the so-called Popular Front conception was nothing else than a simple communist ruse."

It should be recalled that when the civil wars began, in the summer of 1936, the Kremlin was in the very midst of its ambitious "tactic" of lining up France, and if possible Britain and America, as allies in the event of a German-Japanese squeeze on Russia. Simultaneously it was conducting secret negotiations looking toward a possible pact with Germany. Spain, a thousand Spains, meant less to Stalin than the safety of his own political hide. Only befuddled comrades in New York and Los Angeles, Paris and London, took the revolutionary pretensions seriously. For Stalin, the interests of his dictatorship came first.

Once he had injected himself into the picture, he needed absolute domination and he proceeded to take that, at any risk to the Loyalist side. A republican victory would have been meaningless to him, even dangerous, if his political enemies, syndicalists and socialists—the only labor groupings that counted in Spain—remained in control. Rather the hazard of a Franco Spain, so far as Moscow was concerned! Moreover, control in Spain gave him bargaining power whether in relation to Hitler or to the Anglo-French leaders.

The Kremlin had hesitated for nearly four months before moving a finger in behalf of the Loyalists: the most crucial months of all in many respects. The legend that Russia hastened boldly to the defense of Spanish democracy is a silly later invention. André Gide, the French novelist, happened to be in Russia during those months. In his book on that visit he tells of his consternation in finding Russians, high and low, indifferent to Spain, embarrassed when he mentioned the subject; they had not yet been instructed how to think and feel on Spain.

When Stalin finally decided to enter, it was on terms fatal to Spanish democracy. In the first place, he made little secret of it that nothing less than totalitarian control over the stricken nation would satisfy him. In the second place, he quickly indicated that he would stand for no revolutionary nonsense!

Strange as this may sound to people who regarded Russia as "revolutionary," its self-imposed function in Spain at that juncture was to head off any real Left revolution against landlords and industrialists. The Soviet State was eager to demonstrate to capitalist democracies whose favors it was seeking that it had renounced its former revolutionary policies. It was also hoping to promote the Spanish "dress rehearsal" into a full-fledged all-European war between the Rome-Berlin Axis and the democracies, itself retreating to the sidelines. It could hope to do so only by making sure that the Loyalist cause did not get out of hand in a genuine social revolution which would frighten off France and England.

For the same reason that in America and everywhere the communists had suddenly become ostensible supporters of the bourgeois *status quo*, they would not tolerate an anti-bourgeois revolution in Spain. With communist ascendancy came the organized smashing of farm and industrial collectives, the repression of workers' militias wherever possible, the persecution of Left movements.

The communist muscling-in consequently took the form of violent attack against the non-communist Lefts. More than 95 per cent of the organized masses, at the outset, were under the leadership of non-communist labor and political organizations like the C.N.T. and the U.G.T. In undertaking to disrupt and remove this leadership, Stalin in effect declared war on the Loyalist masses. Some middle-class, dilettante and even semi-fascist elements flocked to his standard, if only because they were frightened of the deeper revolutionary rumblings. It is one of the major ironies of our time that Soviet Russia, by the logic of its self-interests, became the spearhead and organizer of counter-revolution in Loyalist Spain. It is a role which the selfsame logic may impose on Russia again and again in the future.

In curbing the revolutionary impulses of the masses, Stalin did more for Franco than Hitler and Mussolini combined. Something more than an inert conscripted army was needed if the superior military forces of the fascists were to be overcome. The boundless zeal of millions of simple men and women had to be galvanized into heroic action, into a do-or-die guerrilla spirit, into the kind of romantic and desperate resistance which, back in 1918-21, enabled the Russians to defeat immense armies in the civil wars of those years. That spirit was choked off violently by the Stalinist dictatorship. The communist role was to squelch the ardor, jail and murder the people's trusted leaders, and give the Loyalists a choice only between a Spain under Franco and a Spain under Stalin.

Russia possessed the resources to enable the Loyalists to make short work of the rebels, had it so desired. But it would take no chances of offending the ruling classes in France and England. Neither would it risk breaking irretrievably with Italy and Germany. All through the Spanish wars Russian oil, by way of Italy, helped to fuel Franco's planes and tanks. Some Spaniards even insist that Stalin sought to make a deal with Hitler at Spain's expense, but that Hitler was not yet ready to play that particular card; in the light of the subsequent Soviet-Nazi alliance these charges no longer sound as farfetched as they once did. However that may be, Stalin certainly was carrying out a devious and complicated policy—with the fate of "Spanish democracy" the least of his concerns.

Just as it had continued to sell oil and grain to Italy while pretending to oppose the Ethiopian aggression, so Moscow now restrained the Loyalists while pretending to help them. First Stalin wanted to make sure that he ruled the roost—and that he had the blessings of Anglo-French leaders. He maneuvered, played a cat-and-mouse game, doled out supplies where they would help entrench communists. Perhaps he hoped for the ultimate defeat of Franco—but only if he were certain Spain would then fall supinely into Russia's lap.

3

The methods whereby Moscow hijacked control of Loyalist Spain provide some of the grimmest and bloodiest pages in the history of this epoch, which is saying a lot. On December 17, 1936, only two months after the Kremlin had sold its first armaments to Spain, the Moscow *Pravda* wrote editorially:

As for Catalonia, the purging of the Trotskyites and the anarcho-syndicalists has begun. It will be conducted with the same energy with which it was conducted in the U.S.S.R.

The significance of this statement cannot be overemphasized. Already Russia was speaking of Spain as though it were just another Soviet province!

The Spanish communists claimed only some 10,000 members when the war started, compared with millions organized in other labor and radical groups. They had only one deputy in the first Republican Cortes, only a dozen out of 50 in the last Cortes just before war broke out—and those through a deal, as a gift, and not on the basis of voting strength. Yet Stalin had the gall to threaten purges!

What is more, he carried them through "with the same energy with which it was conducted in the U.S.S.R." His agents moved in and did their stuff. They used their control over the trickle of Soviet supplies, and beyond that they used ordinary gangster methods. Stalinist agents by the thousand descended on bleeding and prostrate Spain from all directions, but chiefly from Russia. They deliberately battered down the organizations of Spanish labor, ousted and murdered leaders whom they could not flatter or buy into stooging, and started an open and secret terror that did as much damage to the Loyalists as Franco himself.

The communists developed an extralegal G.P.U., their own secret prisons, off-record tribunals, torture chambers and execution squads. Anti-fascist leaders refusing obedience to Stalin were cornered and murdered. Scum elements were mobilized and subsidized for special tasks—not against the fascists but against socialists, anarchists and other radicals. Even from far-off Cuba the secret Cheka imported gangsters, brothel-toughs, passport forgers, pathological sadists, according to revelations in Cuban labor papers. (Nice ladies on Park Avenue and movie queens in Hollywood contributed their homes and their money to finance this noble work. . . .)

In short, twenty years of Russian practice in terrorism were visited upon the Spanish labor and republican movements. Those who talked out of turn, Spaniards or foreigners, were imprisoned and in hundreds of instances assassinated. Certainly there were fanatic communists among these intruders, but they drew to themselves adventurers and careerists of every variety. They had the jam pots of power and money and the insects flocked to them. (The secret G.P.U.'s in Madrid, Toledo and other centers, it developed at one point, were doing a lucrative trade on the side in releasing fascists for a consideration.)

Caballero was a thorn in the side of the communist invaders. As early as January of 1937 the "build-up" of the obscure professor, Dr. Negrin, had begun. In May the communists goaded the Barcelona workers into a desperate anti-communist revolt and drowned it in blood to serve as the ready-made alibi for eliminating the workers' leaders and organizations. When Caballero refused to outlaw anti-communist labor groupings, his fate was sealed. "There is no reason whatsoever to dissolve a legal Spanish workers' party," he protested. And the socialist *Adelante* of Valencia wrote (May 11, 1937): "A government composed in its majority of people from the labor movement cannot use methods reserved for reactionary and fascist-like governments."

Two months later Louis Fischer, whose views normally reflected official Stalinist views, wired to the *Nation:* "Anarchists are being eliminated as an active factor. The Caballero socialists, if they persist in their present tactics, may be outlawed within five months." *Nation* readers were not informed that this meant the purging of an overwhelming majority by a tiny minority which was seizing control by violence and trickery.

It was Caballero's refusal to turn over control of the military machinery to Moscow's henchmen which was the immediate cause of his expulsion. At a meeting of his friends in Madrid he thundered, "They demand that I turn over the Ministry of War to the communists, with which they shall do as they please. Never, never, never!" The "nevers" did no good. He was forced out and Dr. Negrin was installed in his place. From that day to the end Stalin was boss.

The "liberal" and "anti-fascist" press and organizations the world over obediently attacked Caballero, the syndicalists, anyone whom the professional and amateur finger-men pointed out. A "unified command" was imposed—not the unified command representing all factions which everyone favored, but a single all-Stalinist generalship. Officers who demurred were deprived of arms. Local newspaper editors were imprisoned if they refused to color the news to match the communist line. Only trusted communists were assigned as "political commissars" at the fighting fronts, which meant that "undesirable" soldiers and officers by the hundred were soon being liquidated or put in the most dangerous and exposed positions. The volunteer system was abolished in favor of a "disciplined" conscript army. Enthusiasm was displaced by whips and firing squads.

A semblance of coalition government remained, of course, as a political stratagem. But the key posts—especially control of the press, the army, censorship, communications—were held firmly by Stalin's agents and those who, for various reasons, played with them. Late in

1938 the pathetic President Azaña tried to break the G.P.U. throttle hold on his country by dismissing Negrin. He failed. Negrin threatened to put himself at the head of communist divisions to fight the ouster, and Azaña yielded.

In the outside world, the simplified black-and-red pattern was imposed on the faithful. The Stalinist overlordship was presented in the glowing colors of a "defense of democracy." Naïve or cynical foreigners, including a batch of Americans, pitched in to reinforce the deception from Madrid and Barcelona, even as their kind had done for years from Moscow. Some of them, in fact, were merely continuing in Spain the volunteer press-agenting jobs started in Russia.

As early as September, 1937, a detailed account of Soviet "Chekist" methods behind the Loyalist lines was offered to the American public by Anita Brenner in a long documented study in the Modern Quarterly. No one paid any attention—the liberals and caviar communists were too busy pouring cocktails and dancing "for Spain" to know or to care. The spectacle was ghastly. Men who went to Spain for the Communist Party but could not "take" the Stalinist horrors tried desperately, on getting back here, to let the deluded ones know—they were only told off as "fascist spies" for their pains.

With every month of communist domination the chances of a Loyalist victory receded. Popular hatred for the communist masters could no more express itself in Spain than in Russia. Only in the last catastrophic weeks, when the rotten structure began to collapse and the Soviet big shots fled in shameless panic, did the repressed hatreds burst to the surface. Even Fischer was obliged to cable to the Nation (March 13, 1939) that " a powerful hatred of communism had developed in Spain" and that "the communists made many enemies by their irritating attempts . . . to control important institutions."

Belated though this admission may have been, coming from a Stalinist it gave a hint of the truth so long suppressed. As Irving Pflaum put it, "When General Jose Miaja early in March turned his guns against the communists in the Madrid area, the deep contradiction between Spain and its Russian saviors became obvious to the world."

Unfortunately it became obvious to only a few in the world. Thousands of Americans have still to realize that they were co-operating with the betrayers of Loyalist Spain under the tragic delusion that they were helping Spanish democracy. With the intolerance of new converts, they had stoned those who tried to save them from their folly.

4

Referring to Spaniards rather than foreigners, Luis Ariquistan later wrote:

I must mention an important group which partly innocently contributed to our downfall. I am speaking now of the so-called "communist sympathizers," the fellow travelers who were so active in giving the Spanish communists the power and influence they actually had. . . . They were astonishingly numerous among our bourgeoisie where they formed large and influential groups. Writers, journalists, artists and professionals. . . . I am mentioning the unhappy part this group played in Spain because I happen to know the great influence similar groups are exerting in France, England and the U.S.A. One of the reasons why I am giving this résumé of Spanish experiences is to teach them this lesson.*

It was precisely among such people that the "Spanish aid" rackets had their glorious success. In every large American city the communist-controlled committees for Spain raked in fortunes in contributions that went to fertilize communist activities here and abroad. The innocents relished the thrill of being fleeced and resisted every effort to disclose communist control or to investigate the destination of the millions flowing into Stalinist coffers.†

---

* *New Leader*, June 3, 1939.

† In a report issued in April, 1940, the Committee for Cultural Freedom offered the following sketch of communist-dominated Spanish relief organizations: "The original communist-dominated organization was the Medical Bureau to Aid Spanish Democracy. There followed The North American Committee to Aid Spanish Democracy. In 1938 the two were merged and renamed, Medical Bureau and North American Committee to Aid Spanish Democracy, into which was later incorporated The American Friends of Spanish Democracy. After the civil war had ended, in April, 1939, a new organization was formed, The Spanish Refugee Relief Campaign, from which Socialist and Communist Party representatives were asked to drop out. A crisis was precipitated within the organization in March, 1940, when unauthorized statements were issued from the Campaign offices and when, to protest a forged government 'decree,' communist members ordered the picketing of the French Consulate. The chairman, Francis J. McConnell, and the secretary, Herman F. Reissig, disassociated the Spanish Refugee Relief Campaign from all responsibility for the demonstration and wrested the national body from control of the communists. The New York section, however, remained in communist hands and was temporarily called The Emergency Conference to Save Spanish Refugees. Its 'permanent' name is now The North American Spanish Aid Committee. Overnight there sprung up Dorothy Parker's Spanish Children's Relief Fund, with headquarters in the offices of The North American Spanish Aid Committee."

No one has estimated how many "Spanish cause" parties took place during these years, but without doubt they came to tens of thousands. Cocktail parties, bridge and roulette sessions, garden and swimming pool parties, theatre benefits, raffles, street collections, mass meetings, little private dinners at a hundred dollars a plate, dansants, musicales—with a communist trusty always on hand to carry off the "take." There were cocktail parties in penthouses and aristocratic mansions, and fifty-cent-admission evenings in middle-class flats.

The whole underlying assumption—that Loyalist Spain needed cash—was a fake to begin with. Spain needed the right to import arms and supplies across embargo barriers, but it had plenty of money. Spanish credits in vast amounts were available in France at the disposal of the Loyalist leaders. A vast gold horde was transferred to Russia— more than half a billion dollars is the estimate given by Loyalist leaders like Araquistan and confirmed by former Soviet agents like Krivitsky. From all indications the gold has remained there as Stalin's loot. Only minute dribbles of the millions gathered in by the Stalinist commit- tees ever reached Spain. Even the portion which was transferred abroad merely went into the central treasuries of international com- munist committees. The funds served to support bevies of communist bureaucrats and to pay for the costs of hoaxing the contributors. The fund-raising also provided a technique for pepping up the newly faith- ful and expanding the whole incredible revolution.

Out of curiosity I attended a number of the Spanish fund-raising parties. One of them was in a swanky mansion on Manhattan's fash- ionable East River fringe. All the guests were in dress clothes and there was a shimmer of jewels. Four floors were jammed with New York's social and literary elite, spinning the roulette wheels, playing blackjack, shooting craps, buying drinks, playing bridge, raffling off trinkets . . . the house taking a generous cut for the cause and a few comrades on hand to take over the proceeds. A good time was had by all despite some obstreperous drunks. In a West Side apartment the prices were cheaper, the guests in mufti, but the temper was no less bizarre. A great crowd danced to the radio, drank bad punch at a quarter a throw, made love in corners—all for the Loyalists.

Multiply these and endless other varieties of cause gatherings a thousandfold and you have some notion of how the racket prospered during any week end straight across the country. It prospered so well, indeed, that the Communist Party issued manuals to guide its army of collectors. I have one of those before me as I write: *Give a Party for the PARTY* it is called, and it is inscribed "Issued by New York State Committee, Communist Party." The causes for which these gatherings were given might be grim enough—civil conflict in Spain, the sufferings of sharecroppers, the dying Chinese—but the pamphlet is gay and blithe. The cover cartoon, by A. Redfield, shows a pair of dice prancing, young people in the throes of the Big Apple, a jazz band in full blast. The contents are in the same character.

Fun and frolic for the revolution, boys. "Have a 'guest book' to register names and addresses. This makes a mailing list afterwards," the manual instructs. "For entertainment call the Party Entertainment Committees. . . ." "Add refreshments, dancing, mix well and dish out!" "For beer parties, comrades, remember that pouring in the middle gives more foam and less liquid—stretches each barrel further." For the lucrative game of Definitions, "Get a copy of *L is for Labor* by Leane Zugsmith, issued by the League of Women Shoppers." Also, comrades, "Don't forget periodicals and subscriptions for them. *State of Affairs, Daily* and *Sunday Worker, New Masses, Health and Hygiene, China Today, Moscow News, Science and Society Quarterly, The Communist*, etc."

Loyalist workers and peasants were dying by the hundred thousand. G.P.U. squads were "liquidating" socialists and syndicalists and just people. Barcelona and Madrid were being bombed out of shape. What better excuse for dowagers and simple *Hausfraus* to give gay parties? The lunacy went on month after month, year after year. Even after the collapse, the racket was not called off. Now the refugees became the focus of fund-raising enterprise. One of the five hundred millions in gold purloined by the Soviets from Spain might solve the problem. But Russia was not admitting even the volunteers it had itself lured into uniform! At this writing Stalinist committees are still gathering in shekels under promise to place Spanish refugees in Mexico, in other countries—everywhere but in Russia, which will have none of them now they have been used and discarded.

Fatuous American liberals worked with the party stalwarts to recruit volunteers for the communist-controlled foreign armies in Spain. They got the thrill of safe vicarious heroism by sending high-spirited, idealistic boys to their deaths. Of the thousands recruited here, not more than half returned. Most of them died in battle, the rest died at the hands of Stalin's firing squads. Those who enlisted for definite periods, usually six months, were not allowed to leave when the term ended. All American passports were confiscated and are even now being used by Soviet espionage operatives all over the globe.

Hundreds who were quickly disillusioned and dared to indicate it were "liquidated" or merely sent to spots where their liquidation by Franco was certain. Not a fraction of the ugly story has as yet been told. In line with the Fourth Period technique, the Stalinist volunteers were camouflaged with names like Abraham Lincoln Brigade—one can see Stalin smiling through his mustaches at the cynical trick. Dozens of these boys, having been alien residents in America at the time they joined the Brigade, could not return and are still languishing in concentration camps. The survivors who got back, penniless, often crippled, were helpless; through economic pressure many of them continued to play the roles of heroes for the comradely committees and a percentage of the collections. Those who refused were smeared in the party press and among their friends as spies or "Trotskyites."

But little things like that could not be allowed to interfere with penthouse parties. The racket went on long after democratic Spain was dead. High-minded liberals still gave their impeccable names as decoration for "rescue ships" and other gadgets which only the willfully blind could fail to recognize as communist stooge setups.

I have no more than hinted at the obscenity. Stalin's crime against Spain—and the joyful participation in it by gullible herds of Americans—cannot be compassed in a chapter or a book. But even this sketchy outline may help us understand the Red Decade. The emotional leverage of Spain, the heroic symbolism of the struggle there, were forces utilized by the communists in America, as elsewhere, to penetrate deeper and still deeper into American life.

Chapter XXIV

REVOLUTION COMES TO HOLLYWOOD
AND BROADWAY

1

A HOLLYWOOD party has been described to me in such hilarious detail by one of those present that it sticks in my memory. It was on New Year's Eve in one of those palatial Beverly Hills homes, and only true-blue reds were invited. There were bigwigs of the League of American Writers, activists from the Hollywood Anti-Nazi League, officials of the Motion Pictures Artists Committee. The well-heeled proletarians—average salary $1,000 a week—were doing nobly by the food and liquor. Liveried butlers moved about silently distributing champagne and picking up broken glasses. On the stroke of midnight the guests rose to their feet, a few of them unsteadily but all of them solemnly. They raised their champagne aloft, the organ went into stride and they all intoned the "Internationale":

> Arise, ye prisoners of starvation;
> Arise, ye wretched of the earth . . .

Hollywood, belching with satiety, in the role of a prisoner of starvation! It was cozy and crazy and heart-warming. It was Hollywood, where "colossal" is a diminutive. Perhaps it was no more than appropriate that the make-believe revolution of Moscow's Fourth Period should find one of its most bizarre embodiments in the world's capital of make-believe.

The revolution that came to the town was on the munificent scale of its salaries, its race tracks, its swimming pools: "the goofiest era in cinema legend—a compound of high ideals and low I.Q.'s; party lines and just parties; noble slogans and ignoble political rackets." The quotation is from an article in the *American Mercury* (February, 1940) by William Bledsoe, who edited the *Screen Guild Magazine* and saw the wonders in close-up. He grows rhapsodical in the telling:

I saw the Celluloid Uprising in its most fantastic hours. . . . I witnessed the revolt of the Hollywood wage slaves and the Stalin putsch. I saw Social Consciousness quicken and come to a boil in actors, writers and directors whose names rival Rinso and Camels as household words. I followed the insurrection mass meeting by mass meeting, cocktail party by cocktail party, until many a Big Name was more or less secretly enrolled in the Communist Party or tagging along solemnly in one of the "front" leagues and committees. The political pig-Latin of class struggle, anti-fascism, and revolutionary tactics rippled around swimming pools and across dance floors. Five-thousand-dollars-a-week proletarians rattled their gold chains of servitude as Russia, Spain, the sharecroppers, China and the New Masses were saved anew and defended once more.

In the heroic early days of the Russian Revolution, when being a Bolshevik meant social ostracism and real sacrifice, Hollywood was aware of it only as an occasional theme for slapstick comedy. Now that the revolution had degenerated into a dictated slaughterhouse, the cinema capital went whole-hog on the idea. Glamour girls and scenario maestros took personal credit for everything Lenin had done (though they remained extremely vague as to what it was) and threw in the French Revolution for good measure. It was not the first time, of course, that a comfortable upper class had revolted vicariously for the lower orders. But (as Morrie Ryskind pointed out once) there was this difference: the Hollywood rebels, with their genius for pretending, actually felt that they were in person the downtrodden, the wretched, the prisoners of starvation. They were titillatingly sorry for themselves.

It is credibly reported that one of the comrades, having read The Grapes of Wrath, was so moved that he broke into his producer's office to demand a $500 raise, crying, "You can't do this to me!"

It is Mr. Bledsoe's theory that Hollywood is a city of "unhappy successful people" and that "communism with two butlers and a swimming pool" gave them at last "a Reason for Living and an alibi for living so absurdly well." Which perhaps is not so different from my own theory. Watching the great pilgrimage of glamour to the shrines of the Muscovite cult, I felt that the converts were being chased not only by aching inferiority complexes but by aching consciences. In a time of general unemployment and misery, it is not altogether comfortable, psychologically, to enjoy a six-figure income. The watered-down communism of the Popular Front gave them an identification with the miserable herd, without interfering with their incomes. The consolations of political religion, as dispensed by the local commissars of the Communist Party, fitted their souls exactly; it was an unguent and deliciously perfumed. They loved it, they paid for it, they lived it more earnestly than any other fad that had come their way.

The earnest part of it needs emphasis. Let it be understood that the impetus behind the goofiness was fine and noble. The overtones of sadism were worked off on Hitler, *kulaks* and Trotskyites; for the rest of humankind there was only loving kindness. The cinema rebels were genuinely angry at the Nazis and genuinely concerned for Spanish democracy, Spain's orphans, Chinese freedom, and sharecroppers. They had not the remotest idea what communism was in terms of economic structures or political superstates. For nearly all of them it was an intoxicated state of mind, a glow of inner virtue, and a sort of comradeship in super-charity.

Many, if not most, of those who swelled the Communist Party's treasury and frolicked at its do-good shows and dances and signed shrill manifestoes for infinite causes did not know specifically that they were being taken in tow by the communists. They were not "plotting." They were just doing emotional calisthenics. Few of them bothered to wonder where their contributions were going, how their names were used to cover up monstrous terror in Spain or Russia.

A few dozen Hollywood names appeared on almost all communist listings between 1936 and 1939 when the Red Decade caught up with the movies. Innocence so long maintained is a kind of achievement, since there must be a point at which even cinema stars become aware of the difference between political love and political rape. The majority were well-meaning and befuddled.

They were led by their heartstrings into blind alleys of political skulduggery, slugged with slogans and made to shell out. The political "commissars"—whether Herbert Biberman and Sam Darcy locally, or emissaries like V. J. Jerome from Thirteenth Street—worked on the simplicity of the Hollywood peasantry. Once a *Daily Worker* interview with a male glamour lad, written by Beth McHenry, unconsciously betrayed the contempt in which the comrades held the easymarks. "He strikes you," she wrote of the actor, "as both healthy and intelligent and it's only incidentally that you remember he is an artist."

Variety and *Film Daily* might continue to cover the drab workaday Hollywood, but the *Daily Worker* increasingly reported the soul of Hollywood. There you found the record of the ideological emanations of the awakened conscience of the movie capital—its collections for "progress," the blossoming of ever new organizations, the special showings of Spanish propaganda films, the gay parties and publicity stunts for the cause. There you read interviews with Clifford Odets, William Dieterle, King Vidor and any number of others whose opinions, by some coincidence, fitted into the current drives backed by the *Worker*. Above all, Stalin's trade journal carried the day-to-day story of the generous cash contributions by stardom; business is business under any regime.

One estimate has it that the Stalinists milked the colony for at least two million dollars in the heyday of the Red Decade. Biberman deposited $89,892.51 in a local bank for just one front, the Anti-Nazi League, between May 14, 1936, and August 16, 1939. The neo-Bolsheviks, Hollywood model, followed the new political scripts as blindly as any that fell to their share on location. But let us pick up the compassionate Mr. Bledsoe again:

> The Communist Party traded on this emotional stew and cashed in big. . . . A lot of unrealistic, naïve, sometimes not overly bright people looking for something to hold on to were sucked into a political racket. Moscow agents stumbled on Hollywood about the middle of 1936, and found it colossal—Big Names with magical propaganda-carrying power. Barrels of money . . . Only one thing surprised the pioneering communists prospecting in them thar Beverly Hills: the speed and size and ease of their strikes. . . . The decisive battles of the Hollywood Revolution were fought in the living arena of mass meetings, boycotts, benefits, leagues, committees, congresses, conventions, speeches, relief money, telegrams, protests, pamphlets, parades, picket lines, pictures, parties, politics, pledges, petitions, dinners, dances, slogans and all the rest of the effects that made up the united-front show. . . . Fans and autograph hounds in the know didn't waste time hanging around the Brown Derby or Trocadero. The real pickings were at the mass meetings in the Shrine and Philharmonic Auditoriums and the Hollywood Legion Stadium.

> It was at one of these meetings that Gypsy Rose Lee chided her audience to this general effect: "I have not come to lift my skirts, but to lift the embargo on Spain!" It was all most thrilling. At the Holly-

wood Health Cafeteria, in a hygienic vegetarian setting, screen folk
discovered yet another Marx in a sort of informal workers' school
under the tutelage of Biberman, Sam Ornitz, Lionel Stander and
others. James Cagney was said to be among the brightest of the earlier
crop of students. Class-conscious wage slaves in dress clothes made
dialectic noises in the lobby of Filmarte Theatre every time a new
Russian picture came to town. Pardon me, not Russian but Soviet.
One of the sins of the new dispensation was to call Russia otherwise
than the Soviet Union.

Fred Keating wrote a torrid piece entitled "Are We Laborers?"
He demonstrated nicely that notwithstanding their $100,000 incomes
and showy estates they were, like the horniest-handed proletarians,
slaves of The System. Frank Sculiy publicly posed this question: "Is
the Middle Class in the Middle?" He decided thus: "If the middle
class wants to get rid of its white collar of servitude, it had better get
its picket lines in order."

It was loony but wonderful—the proletariat, the middle classes,
the enlightened capitalists and Browder's boys all in one big happy
family, making faces at Hitler. Somehow it did wonders for the taste
of Astrakhan caviar and the feel of Russian sables.

It did wonders, too, for the self-esteem of men and women who
were at bottom ashamed of their status as intellectual slavies of the
movie moguls; who dreamed of writing a great novel or taking Broadway by storm, but meanwhile had to be content with dunking in
swimming pools. For years they had smarted under the jibes of envi-
ous but superior "intellectuals." Now they were not only accepted by
the intelligentsia but made to feel equals. Perhaps a few of them did
realize that they were merely buying that bogus equality with cash
contributions and contributions of their advertising value. But the
rest glowed with a new self-importance. The Red Decade gave a lot
of self-conscious low-brows a chance to pose to themselves as heavy
thinkers. They paid for the privilege, and gladly.

2

"In the studio labor organizations," Bledsoe writes, "the comrades
had only mixed success." The painters' union went over to the side
of the revolution. The Screen Writers' Guild joined the Popular
Front, despite brave attempts of the Authors' League of America to

wrest the Hollywood section from the Stalinist grip. In the furious fight against the "fascists"—meaning anyone who objected to communist domination—Donald Ogden Stewart acted as generalissimo, with such fine lieutenants as Dudley Nichols, Francis Hackett, Humphrey Cobb, Dalton Trumbo, Irwin Shaw, Tess Slesinger, Sam Ornitz, Frank Scully, Oliver H. P. Garrett, Lillian Hellman, Boris Ingster, John Howard Lawson, Lester Cole, Joel Sayre, Madeline Ruthven. Many of these, of course, "hadn't been shown the script and doubtless are still innocent," as Mr. Bledsoe puts it. The point of the story, throughout, is that the innocents trailed along and joined the shouting, enticed by "progressive" labels on totalitarian goods.

The Screen Actors Guild, however, succeeded in fighting off the tender attentions of the overzealous "progressives" in their midst. It remained independent despite its Left Wingers. For a while the Left Wing succeeded in steering the Guild into the wide-open arms of the gallant Willie Bioff, by linking it up with the Federation of Motion Picture Crafts and the communistic studio painters' union. After a great tussle, however, the Guild shook off most of the Bioff crowd.

Hollywood needs to be seen in the larger setting of California. The Stalinist comrades had taken over the remnants of Upton Sinclair's EPIC, the scattered Democratic Party units, and welded it all into a New Deal party which carried the state. The new Governor, being an old-fashioned liberal, was fractious but Lieutenant Governor Patterson moved pretty consistently along the party line and many State offices, especially in the relief setup, were jammed with comrades. In Los Angeles itself the party gave its helping hand to a reform administration and sat pretty politically. The C.I.O. under Harry Bridges was bossing the coast and a great many interior industries.

To merge yourself with Stalinism, therefore, was decidedly not a form of self-abnegation. It was a species of social climbing. In California at that time it meant the inside track in local cocktail society as well as government, labor, the New Deal. The Hollywood Anti-Nazi League claimed 4,000 members. The Motion Picture Democratic Committee, a front for Stalinist fund-raising, had no trouble rounding up 1,700 members. The cultural sensation of one year—the year, alas, when the revolution hit the rocks and turned mysteriously anti-Roosevelt in the impact—was a show with the theme song *Mr. Roosevelt, Won't You Please Run Again?* This plaintive sentiment was embedded in the first production of the Motion Picture Guild, a one-reeler called *A Message from Hollywood*, music by Jay Gorney, words by Henry Meyers, directed by Herbert Biberman and Frank Tuttle. It was no fault of the President, of course, that these enthusiasts did not know where the New Deal ended and Stalinism began. For that matter, they did not know where intellectual clowning ended and grim reality began. Anyhow, everybody was most embarrassed.

Under the tomfoolery there was plenty of tough self-interest. For the younger members of the colony, avid for the fatter fleshpots, Stalinism became the shortcut to success. At "cause parties" they rubbed shoulders and bosoms with big shots they could not have met otherwise. Those who tried to detour the revolution, unless they were stars well fixed in the firmament, found themselves slipping from favor. It was at once a movement and a lobby, a religion and a racket.

3

There was no dearth of committees to channel off the amorphous and puerile enthusiasms. Messrs. Biberman, Jerome, Lionel Stander, J. Edward Bromberg, Melvyn Douglas, Donald Ogden Stewart and the others needed only to touch buttons marked "Spain," "China," "boycott," "children," "anti-fascist," and new organizations leaped into being. Those not bold enough to join the more openly Stalinist League for Peace and Democracy, found sanctuary in the Hollywood Anti-Nazi League, which did a good job of hiding its connections with the Los Angeles branch of the mother-league. Those hesitant about affiliating showed that their hearts were in the right place by signing a few resolutions, taking part in floor shows, joining welcoming committees for Spanish Loyalists or contributing to the series of film-making enterprises and film-promotion projects started by the fellow-traveling gentry.

There was the Theatre Committee for the Defense of the Spanish Republic, started in the East in August, 1936, which found Hollywood boosters quickly. Among its original officials and sponsors were George Abbott, Heywood Broun, Rex Ingram, Albert Maltz, Herman Shumlin, Albert Bein. A few months later American Labor Pictures, Inc., was founded to make a special picture. "Money for the film," the *Daily Worker* reported, "has been supplied by some of the more prominent movie men with Left-Wing tendencies." Anonymity was rapidly thrown to the winds, however, as the fashion caught on. By the time the communist-controlled Scottsboro case formed its Hollywood committee, it could announce Robert Benchley as chairman over ninety-six "swell names" from the studio rosters.

A few months thereafter the Hollywood Citizens Committee for the Federal Theatre could proudly list, along with more familiar fellow-traveler names, also Helen Gahagan, Gilbert Gabriel, Anthony Veiller, Joseph Santley, Viola Brothers Shore, Sylvia Sidney, Alan Campbell, etc.* Films for Democracy, a little farther in the career of the revolution, was able to offer the world an Organization Committee and Advisory Board which were perfect blends of political Stalinists and glamorous celluloid names; a mere sampling, herewith: Ned H. Dearborn, Helen Hall, Dudley Nichols, Gardner Jackson, Lee Pressman, Herman Shumlin, Percival Wilde, Ordway Tead, William E. Dodd, Frank P. Walsh, Irene Lewisohn, Libby Holman, Walter Wanger, Jerome Davis, and Morris U. Schappes.† The executive secretary was one of the most complacent Stalinist fellow-travelers, Sam Rodman, a former Moscow correspondent who should have known better. In 1939 the Motion Picture Guild was launched to produce Erika Mann's *School for Barbarians*. The fact that Biberman and Tess Slesinger were to do the scenario, that the sponsors included Lillian Hellman, Sidney Buchman, Joris Ivens, Irving Reiss and other standardized names indicates its temper.

The childishness of many of those who flocked to these enterprises is illustrated by an anecdote told by Morrie Ryskind:

> Some six months ago one of our more prominent stars, enthralled by the league pamphlets, corralled a dozen cynics for lunch in an effort to induce us to join. After a heated discussion in which he pooh-poohed our objections, a bargain was struck: the star said he would get the name changed to the Hollywood Anti-Nazi and Anti-Communist League provided we would thereupon join. He left us, promising he would have the transformation complete within an hour. As I said, that was six months ago.

In the tons of resolutions and pamphlets ground out by the Hollywood organizations, not a syllable can be found that reflects on Russia—that is, on the Soviet Union. The country figures extensively

---

* *Daily Worker*, February 19, 1938.
† *Daily Worker*, November 26, 1938.

but only as the most democratic, most anti-Nazi country in the world and the sole true friend of peace and freedom. And as already noted, Hollywood names led all the rest on statements "supporting" the democratic achievements of Moscow's firing squads and political kangaroo courts.

After the retreat from the gritty literary ideals of Proletcult, the League of American Writers was increasingly diluted with the pseudo-writers of Hollywood. The displacement of Waldo Frank, a novelist in the higher artistic brackets, by Donald Ogden Stewart, a Hollywood punster in the higher financial brackets, as head of the organization tells the story. The literary average took a nose dive, but the income and publicity average skyrocketed. The annual exodus from Hollywood to New York for the Congress of American Writers was an affair of great social éclat. But there were also local shindigs such as West Coast Writers congresses.

At one of these I was singled out for attention. Harcourt, Brace & Co. had announced *We Cover the World*, a book by foreign correspondents, with myself both editor and a contributor. Although the book had not yet been published, the Hollywood literati resolved sight unseen to warn the world in a press release that what Lyons said about Russia in that volume was unworthy and a lie. Alas for their dignity, when the book appeared it turned out that Lyons had not written about Russia at all but about Persia! An editorial in the *Saturday Review of Literature* ribbed these protesters-in-advance-by-intuition.

Influenced perhaps by the pseudo-Spanish architecture of the cinema studios, the colony fell especially hard for the Loyalist cause as interpreted and exploited by the communists. The *Daily Worker*, in reporting that every Loyalist meeting in Hollywood brought from five to eight thousand dollars into the comradely coffers, added, "Think of that, you New York provincials!"

The whole approach to the problem was exceedingly coy and sociable. Dances, swimming pool parties, moonlight romance for the victims of bombs in Barcelona. When André Malraux, then still a leading literary communist, reached the movie capital, he was greeted by a committee headed by Franchot Tone and filled with gilt-edged star names. Everybody had lots of fun buying, equipping and autographing two ambulances for the Loyalists, among the announced donors being Fred Keating, Franchot Tone, Guy Endore, Herbert Biberman, Sidney Buchman, Humphrey Cobb, Lewis Milestone,

Gale Sondergaard, Dudley Nichols, Stella Adler and, of course, Donald Ogden Stewart.* Later a stamp sales campaign was launched by the comrades in connection with Spain, with Edward Arnold, Richard Arlen and Florence Eldridge among the easy-marks. But the story tends to get repetitious.

The sudden prominence of Gypsy Rose Lee in the Loyalist ranks has its satirical overtones. In the autumn of 1936 she was still a symbol of bourgeois decadence in Moscow's eyes. Thus the *Daily Worker*, under a picture of the gal: "A young lady who proves that the capitalist system is in the last stages of very beautiful decadence. . . . She is what is quaintly known as a strip-teaser, an art which has blossomed under the Depression whilst all else declined." But soon she was so active in the cause that she practically formed an undraped front in herself. Exploiting the decadent bourgeois appreciation of shapely and unimpeded flesh, the comrades made the young lady chairman of a committee to gather clothes for the Loyalists. The advertisements for "any old clothes" were illustrated with a scantily clad Gypsy.

4

Herbert Biberman, whose wife is Gale Sondergaard, is a tall, heavy, bespectacled person who was once a director on a movie lot. In the goofy era he developed into director of the larger make-believe covering the whole Hollywood area. He has been in the foreground of the Celluloid Uprising, recruiting shekels for causes and members for all Stalinist booby fronts and encouraging American lads to fight in Spain. He is also credited with the lead role in the creation of a new declaration of independence, as of 1938. Only Hollywood could have doped that one out, but the scenarists must be ashamed of themselves over the exceedingly unhappy and absurd ending.

The declaration called for nothing less than the immediate breach of all economic relations with Germany. Nearly all Hollywood clamored for the honor of signing, for the most part neither knowing nor caring that it was at bottom another communist fund-raising and propaganda stunt. Unluckily only fifty-six had signed the original document in 1776, wherefore no more could endorse the new one. Among the lucky ones to rate as Hollywood Hancocks were: Joan

* *Daily Worker*, August 26, 1937.

Crawford, Myrna Loy, Paul Muni, John Ford, John Cromwell, H. M. Warner, Walter Wanger, Edward G. Robinson, Roland Young, Gloria Stuart, Melvyn Douglas, Rosalind Russell, James Cagney, Gale Sondergaard, Donald Ogden Stewart, Kenneth Macgowan, Josef von Sternberg, Carl Laemmle, Henry Fonda, Jack Warner, Rosemary Lane, Fay Bainter, Herbert Biberman, Priscilla Lane, Nunnally Johnson, Frank Tuttle, Bette Davis, Groucho Marx, George Brent, Ben Hecht, Joan Bennett, Bruce Cabot, Elliot Nugent, George O'Neil, Ann Sheridan, Dick Powell, Charles MacArthur, Claude Rains, Miriam Hopkins.

The list is proof enough that the enterprise was innocent so far as most of the signers were concerned. One signed because the others did, because it was the fashion of the moment to join that parlor game. Celluloid revolution was in the atmosphere; the Bibermans and Tuttles led, the rest followed like so many sheep.

The actual signing took place at the Beverly Hills studios of Twentieth-Century Fox, with floodlights blazing and cameras grinding. If only the Founding Fathers back in '76 had had such advantages! As the ceremony proceeded, the year 1939 came over the horizon, but none of the actors could guess that it held anti-climax for their venture. The scheme unfolded in the next months. "Committees of 56" were organized in other cities, and it was announced that twenty million subsidiary signatures to the declaration would be gathered, for presentation to Congress to force a break with Germany. The New York 56'ers, the *Daily Worker* apprised, would be captained by Dorothy Parker, Sylvia Sidney, Frances Farmer, Dashiell Hammett, John Garfield and others.

The gathering of the signatures was still under way with Biberman touring the nation when Stalin shifted into reverse. He made friends with Hitler and left poor Hollywood holding the bag, wherein the declaration and subsignatures and newsreels on the subject bulked large and uncomfortable. The drama had turned to farce. Biberman apologized for having been temporarily a war monger and the declaration was hurried out of sight if not out of mind.

To complicate matters the Hollywood Anti-Nazi League had elections scheduled for September just after Stalin had got the war started. Before decisions could be made to abandon the anti-Nazi label, the meeting was upon them. A plenipotentiary from New York hailed the Soviet-Nazi Pact as a glorious contribution to world peace and described the war as an "imperialist" one for division of spoils. Only the most pure-minded and the truest of the brethren would have stuck out their necks at this time. Those who went along after this date presumably represent the *crème de la crème* of Hollywood Stalinism.

The officers elected at this meeting are therefore a kind of honor roll: President, Donald Ogden Stewart; Vice-President, Frank Tuttle; Secretary, Dudley Nichols; Treasurer, Bern Bernhard; Executive Board, Milton Merlin, Edward Chodoroff, Professor Byrne, Marion Spitzer, J. E. Bromberg, Marvin Harris, Charles Katz, Mrs. Beatrice Buchman, Maxwell Shane, Donald Rose, Herbert Biberman, Francis Faragoh, Ira Ratner, Mrs. Charles Page, Hy Craft, Jay Gorney, Frank Scully, Mrs. Jerome Sackheim.*

The Stalin-Hitler Pact, here as everywhere, spelled catastrophe. While a larger number than most movie-goers suspect held on grimly to the party line, learned to curse Roosevelt and to bless isolationism and to avoid harsh words about Comrade Hitler, the glow had departed. As the useful Mr. Bledsoe wrote early in 1940: "What Stalin is doing to Finland is nothing compared to what he has done to the innocent, high-pitched, hypnotic faith of Hollywood. For once the city faced Reality, and it turns out to be just another piece of make-believe." Alas, movie stars upon whom Jerome and Biberman once could count implicitly now visited Congressman Dies to deny it all. Melvyn Douglas accepted the lead in such sacrilegious pictures as *Ninotchka* and *He Stayed for Breakfast*, swore off communist organizations and even began to write for the anti-Stalin *New Leader*. Some of the babes in the Hollywoods are still rubbing their eyes and wondering whether it really happened. In a whisper for those who may query me or assail me on the subject: "I'm sorry, but it did happen. And how!"

5

Broadway was a pale reflection of Hollywood. It could no more compete with the celluloid industry in revolution than in other types of amusement. But it tried hard and chalked up some notable victories. The ultra-Left days of the New Theatre League had petered out though the ermine and chinchilla ladies were still available for

---

* *Daily Worker*, September 29, 1939.

proletarian drama openings. But a Theatre Arts Committee—TAC for short—had come into being as catchall for comradely activities. The magazine *New Theatre* folded the same month TAC, with its own magazine, was born. TAC had been sponsored by the ubiquitous League for Peace and Democracy in the spring of 1937, but it grew so lusty that it could go on by itself. It sprouted branches in Hollywood, Washington, Chicago and other cities. But the fruits of the New York mother-tree are best recorded.

Among the prominent theatrical and cinema folk who have had places on the TAC executive board are Robert Benchley, Remo Bufano, Constance Cummings, Jane Dudley, Angna Enters, Frances Farmer, John Garfield, Lillian Hellman, Rex Ingram, Fred Keating, Edward Kern, Philip Loeb, Robert Reed, Herman Shumlin, Virginia Stevens, Mrs. Donald Ogden Stewart (she functioned thus or under the maiden appellation of Ella Winter, as need required), Paul Strand, Martin Wolfson. While we instantly recognize names familiar on all Stalinist lists, the percentage of genuine innocents is larger. Why should anyone expect theatre people to look below the surface of political make-up, and understand what they saw any more than college professors or clergymen?

TAC raised money for all the causes O.K.'d by the commissars. It did so directly and by providing artistic talent to front organizations. One Christmas it even put up a huge Christmas tree on Columbus Circle, New York, with receptacles for contributions to the correct causes. . . . Stalin in the role of Santa Claus, no less! TAC put on skits and sang songs absolutely parallel with the party line: promoting collective security, attacking fascist aggressors, extolling the Soviet Union's peace and democracy. Unaware that it would soon have to take an impassioned stand for isolation, against Finnish relief and for aid and comfort to Hitler, TAC in its glory whooped it up for the very opposite of these sentiments. In November, 1938, its official magazine wrote: "Pro-fascist interests in America are pleading isolation at this crucial time. Isolation is a prelude to catastrophe, not only for Europe but for America." In the following month TAC petitioned President Roosevelt for an embargo against Germany. In April, 1939—three months before it realized that Hitler was just another imperialist like Roosevelt and Churchill—TAC told the theatre world:

We wholeheartedly believe that the United States must take a leading part in the bloc of democratic nations which are organizing to resist Hitler. WE MUST STOP HITLER.

The members of the organization, five hundred strong, showed they meant business by marching in the following May "Stop Hitler" Parade.

A theatrical setup is perfect for luring the unsuspecting. There is about it an aura of the play world and childlike innocence that defies suspicion. Only that can explain the circumstance that TAC fund-raising for comradely coffers on occasion ensnared the help of people like Brooks Atkinson, Helen Hayes, Lee Simonson, dozens of others. Glamorous play-acting names on the billboards of drives and com-mittees—party stalwarts in the wings to direct the work and rake in "the take." It was a perfect division of labor, if rather imperfect divi-sion of spoils.

The counsel of TAC was Harry Sacher, who used to teach at the Communist Workers' School in Chicago, and was also legal advisor to Quill's Transport Workers Union. Its financial adviser was Bernard Reis, whose name appeared on various "front" lists. Every TAC activity automatically rated full coverage in the *Daily Worker* and glowing reviews in the *New Masses*. Of the TAC board of twenty-eight, twenty had been affiliated with the New Theatre—the continuity of these efforts is truly remarkable and reveals the unsubtle hand of the stage managers.

The Thespians, playwrights, scriptwrights, directors, strip-tease artists, etc., functioned both through their own Broadway and Holly-wood organizations and through the more generic organizations. They were at once a source of income to the communist movement and an invaluable decorative element. The certainty of meeting one or another of the effulgent ones was among the lures held out by money-raising cocktail parties, mass meetings, and even picket lines.

With the change in the party line after the love fest with Hitler, the best days of the Hollywood-Broadway-Moscow Axis were over. Yet enough of the Axis remained to support Stalin's "liberation of Finland" and to throw monkey wrenches into the machinery of our own national rearmament and our own national morale. However innocently some of them may have started out in playing with totali-tarianism, its fumes penetrated their minds and hearts too deeply for easy fumigation.

CHAPTER XXV

AMERICA'S OWN POPULAR FRONT GOVERNMENT

1

THE main purpose of the Comintern in its fabulous "democratic" period, of course, was to establish People's or Popular Front governments in as many countries as possible. The Popular Front idea, however, must not be confused with the run-of-the-mine coalition government. Its distinguishing mark was the inclusion of the communists—not so much as a domestic political element but frankly as agents and spokesmen of Soviet Russia.

In France, where the Popular Front regime under Leon Blum offered the clearest exemplification of this unique political instrument, everyone concerned took it for granted that the policies of the French communists on every issue, domestic and foreign, were decided in Moscow. A proper definition of the Popular Front government, therefore, would be: *a coalition government with representation for Russia.* Such inclusion of a foreign government in a sovereign domestic cabinet is sufficiently bizarre. Its equivalents were provided later in somewhat different form by puppet regimes in which Germany participated through local Nazi parties.

Where the Comintern could not achieve actual participation in united-front governments, it exercised political pressure through its bloc of communist deputies in various national legislatures. But in England and the United States, where political communism is a negligible force, it could only operate indirectly through fellow-traveling, "sympathetic," totalitarian-liberal organizations and individuals. It did so with extraordinary effectiveness.

We witnessed the unfoldment in this country of an amazing *unofficial Popular Front government*—unrecognized, unadmitted, independent of the Administration, yet operating energetically within the New Deal framework. It added up to the most potent and ubiquitous

298

influence in Washington, a half-clandestine government-within-the-government, arrogantly open in some spots on some occasions but conspiratorial in essence. The Roosevelt Administration was aware of the intrusion and never quite happy about the embarrassing collaboration. Now and then it made face-saving but futile gestures to shoo off the intruders. But with every passing month the penetration was deeper, the entanglement closer. The leaders of this sub rosa power were for the most part not in office themselves, but worked through hundreds of big and little officials deployed through the length and breadth of the mushrooming New Deal bureaucracy.

Perhaps I can make the picture more comprehensible by describing it in more familiar American terms as a super-lobby, bigger than all other lobbies rolled together. It is the routine technique of great lobbies to angle for supporters in high places, to smuggle their creatures into every government department, to exploit the social as well as political focuses of influence, to disguise self-interests as urgent popular causes. The Soviet super-lobby merely followed this time-honored technique. The thing was extraordinary only in the size of its success and in the fact that the ultimate control of the ambitious undertaking rested at all times in the fists of a distant dictator.

Most of those in official and semi-official circles who lent themselves to the scheme, we may grant, were ignorant of its inspiration and its implications. They had—and mostly retain to this day—a confused sense of their own virtue and bold "liberalism" as champions of glittering causes. They resented and still resent being reminded that they had been manipulated by G.P.U. and Comintern operatives. Certainly all but a few of the upperbracket New Dealers who were maneuvered into giving aid and comfort to this foreign lobby were merely victims of their own high-minded enthusiasms. At worst they were dupes of an amateur Machiavellism which reconciled them to any associations for noble ends. The Stalinist slogans of the period were so beguiling that the more befuddled officials—like the professors and literati and penthouse rebels—saw no harm in tagging along. The New Deal doors, politically and socially, were thus opened wide to the temporary Kremlin-democrats.

The sub rosa Popular Front government was bodied forth in the flourishing Washington chapters of all the party setups—the League for Peace and Democracy, the American Youth Congress, the International Labor Defense, the League of Women Shoppers, the National Lawyers Guild, various Spanish Aid outfits, Films for Democracy, the Workers Alliance, etc. It functioned through a system of what might be called ideological nepotism, guaranteeing a host of little jobs in strategic offices for comrades and their sympathizers. It made itself manifest in that endless chain of garden and cocktail parties, intimate do-good and serious-thinker conferences and other social functions— in the homes of New Deal big shots, down to the chintzy rooms of humble stenographers with sex appeal.

The Popular Front prospered in Washington through the snob appeal of the New Deal intelligentsia, and subcontractor brain-trusters and pseudo-intellectual lawyers and writers-turned-politician. Certain Congressmen and especially the bored wives of politicians were thrilled and flattered by friendship with the polysyllabic sophisticates scattered through all the new bureaus, agencies, projects. It all fitted into the amorphous crusading fervor of the New Deal era. Political patronage was being lapped up greedily by boys and girls who talked Veblen, Spengler, Marx and the party line as glibly as the morning's news. The whole show was a godsend for up-and-coming young lawyers, fluttery social workers and capital ladies of a restless ripeness of years. They plunged into the ideological lingo and activities—all so excitingly unorthodox, edged with conspiracy yet seemingly harmless.

The truth is that despite its flashy pseudo-intellectualism and its pose of social consciousness, New Deal Washington was infinitely naïve and infinitely bewildered. The communists gave some direction and consistency to a vague do-good itch. In fact the more sincerely reformist the new officials were, the easier marks they proved for canny, disciplined comrades acting as a unit, all relentlessly pushing the same line of goods with the benefit of caucuses and "directives." New Dealers like Leon Henderson, William O. Douglas, Harold L. Ickes, Mrs. Roosevelt, Frances Perkins, Robert H. Jackson, J. Warren Madden, etc., each competent in his own sphere, were as helpless in the practiced hands of the comrades as any parlorful of aging ladies being instructed in how to save the world.

The success of the Browder boys in Washington is really no more remarkable than their success on the campus, among writers, among movie actors, among liberals generally. The Popular Front government-within-the-government was only a section of the larger Fourth Period pattern.

2

At the risk of minor repetitions, let us sum up again the three stages of the communist relations with the New Deal. What needs noting is that the initiative at each turn was taken by the comrades on explicit instructions from the Comintern bosses. There was no basis for the changes in specifically American events.

1. *Until late 1935.* The communists were shrilly hostile. F.D.R. was a "fascist . . . financial dictator . . . imperialist," given to "shameless demagogy" and "drastic attacks upon the living standards of the masses . . . terrorization of the Negro . . . systematic denial of civil rights." These are only mild samples of Stalinist appraisals of Mr. Roosevelt's government.

2. *From 1935 until the Soviet-Nazi alliance.* Without so much as a decent interval of transition, the President emerged in communist circles as the doughty savior who was "keeping our country on the path of progressive and democratic development," to quote Comrade Browder. The hosannas for the New Deal in the Muscovite press here and in the resolutions of all the front organizations became frenzied. Pages could be filled with Stalinist hymns to Roosevelt which not even his explicit rejection of their support could squelch for a moment. The party did its best in 1936 and in subsequent elections to roll up votes for the New Deal through Labor's Non-Partisan League, the American Labor Party in New York and other channels. Doubt of the New Deal or any of its projects—including the Supreme Court enlargement scheme, the nomination of Justice Black, the reorganization bill—was accounted counter-revolution in the remotest reaches of the periphery. Perhaps the International Workers Order, headed by an executive member of the Communist Party, bestowed the supreme accolade when it listed Mr. Roosevelt's birthday alongside of Lenin's in its annual calendar, among the notable events in human progress.

3. *After the Moscow-Berlin Pact.* Love for the government, born miraculously without a period of gestation, expired abruptly without an interval of ailment. Pretending that F.D.R., rather than the party line on F.D.R., had suddenly changed, the comrades announced that he had been "transformed almost overnight . . . from a New Deal, progressive administration . . . into the leader and organizer of all reactionary forces in the country," co-operating with "the Wall Street

camp" in "spreading the war," guilty of "scrapping the New Deal social legislation, curbing and weakening the labor movement and oppressing the Communist Party." The quotes are from Browder. Every one of the organizations which the Presidential private and political families had long graced with their patronage—including a few which Mrs. Roosevelt, Mr. Jackson, Mr. Henderson and others continued stubbornly to patronize even after this—now discovered unanimously that Mr. Roosevelt was a "war monger" and, of all things, an Economic Royalist.

The illicit partnership had been started by the Comintern and called off by the Comintern. It was neither more nor less than a Kremlin "tactic." Many of those in Washington who fell in line with the tactic may have kidded themselves that they were using the communists. By this time they know, one hopes, that they were being used—and despised for their innocence. The bitterness of the later communist attacks on the New Deal was a measure of the disdain in which the dupes had been held all along.

3

The New Deal, genuinely interested in promoting labor unionization, was playing with the C.I.O. The C.I.O. in turn was playing with the Communist Party. An increasingly close and overlapping contact among the three groups was therefore inevitable. The co-operation was fairly obvious in places like the Department of Labor, the National Labor Relations Board, the Maritime Labor Board.

No one in his senses would suspect the prim and high-minded Madam Perkins, Secretary of Labor, of being a communist. The idea is ludicrous. Yet her awed respect for "liberal" opinion, her intimidated meekness as against the beetle-browed Lewis, her confused eagerness to do the Left thing, made her putty in Stalinist hands. They stocked her department with "dependable" comrades. The Dies Committee was able to list fifty-six League for Peace and Democracy transmission-belters in Madam Perkins' bailiwick, many of them communist activists. The Harry Bridges crowd, as we have seen, boasted of its access to Labor Department files, and its influence sufficed to turn a deportation hearing into a farcical whitewash.

Madam Secretary's confidential filing clerk was a woman who later married the notorious and self-confessed Soviet spy, Nick Dozenberg, recently released from Federal prison. One of the party's most useful "decorations" in the national capital, Merle D. Vincent, became Director of Hearings in the department's Wage and Hour Division. His high and delicate office did not deter him from sharing the platform with Elizabeth Gurley Flynn and other ranking communist leaders—even after the Administration of which he was part was being brutally lambasted by the communists. One of Harry Bridges' close friends, Dr. Louis Bloch, was appointed to the United State Maritime Labor Board, a position in which he had to make important decisions involving not only Bridges' unions but also Joe Curran's National Maritime Union. And those are only peak-points; the penetration became more extensive the deeper one went into the lower strata of the bureaucracy. A newspaperman has told how, during his visit to the Department of Interior building, he heard the elevator boy in cynical jest call the floors "Second Soviet," "Third Soviet," etc. On being questioned, the boy explained that there were so many communists on certain floors that the help around the building referred to them as Soviets.

A Congressional investigation has uncovered some of the communist influence in the National Labor Relations Board, as well as its consistent loading of the dice in favor of the communist wing of the C.I.O. Unfortunately official stupidity took its first revenge not on a communist but on the very man who had for years been combating Stalinist influence, Dr. David Saposs. He had been a thorn in the flesh of the party bloc in the N.L.R.B., which cleverly directed the Congressional lightning against him, of all people. The fact that honest American radicals and liberals are made to suffer for the machinations of Stalin's foreign agents is one of the tragedies of the situation, but decidedly it does not relieve them of the duty of exposing those agents. The communists know the ancient "Stop thief!" device and use it unsparingly.

In the first years of the life of the Labor Board, its reigning triumvirate consisted of Edwin S. Smith, Nathan Witt and Thomas I. Emerson—all of whom, it goes without saying, deny that they are in any sense communists. The chairman of the board at the time, J. Warren Madden, was no match for his associates. There is evidence to the effect that Nathan Witt, secretary of the board, has been extremely close to pro-communist trade-union officials. Mr. Emerson, assistant general counsel of the board, was, along with Witt, among the founders of the National Lawyers Guild and leaders of its extreme pro-communist faction. Both remained in the organization after it had been publicly denounced by Adolph A. Berle, Assistant Secretary of State, as communist-dominated. Both of them are familiar figures among the sponsors of other Stalinist Innocents' Clubs.*

Edwin S. Smith came to Washington as the protégé of Mary Van Kleeck, founder of the communist-sponsored Interprofessional Association and passionate champion of the party line. He took a prominent place in the Stalinist social lobby and became an executive member of the Washington League for Peace and Democracy. His name has been attached to at least fifteen transmission belts. In 1938 he accompanied Miss Van Kleeck to Mexico City for the conference of the International Industrial Relations Institute—to taste its published proceedings is to recognize the acrid Muscovite flavor. Mr. Smith was active in the Washington Friends of Spanish Democracy and later in the National Conference on Constitutional Liberties, both transmission belts. If he is not a party-liner, then there is no such animal.

Supported by an assortment of office workers, lawyers and minor job holders who for reasons of faith or reasons of career followed the party line, the triumvirate had the run of the board, despite the spirited opposition of men like Dr. Saposs and Dr. William M. Leiserson. Applicants for jobs came to know—as such things are always known in political life—that the best way to get into the N.L.R.B. was to play the Popular Front game. Even casual inspection reveals that the board's decisions were crudely weighted in favor of the C.I.O. in general and the Bridges-Curran-Pressman wing of the C.I.O. in particular.

When Mr. Berle resigned from the National Lawyers Guild on June 5, 1940, he explained that "it is now obvious that the present management of the guild is not prepared to take any stand which conflicts with the Communist Party Line." It was a kind of confession since a man of his perspicacity might have discovered the conspicuously obvious before that. Like Tom Corcoran, Attorney General Jackson, Nathan Mangold and other New Dealers, he waited until the Hitler-Stalin alliance hit them before disowning this fellow-

---

* Both Witt and Emerson resigned, along with other fellow-travelers on the Board, when Madden was replaced by Harry Millis. Although the F.B.I. was at the time investigating Emerson's activities, he was appointed to an important post in the Department of Justice.

traveling organization. The guild is an offshoot of the International Labor Defense, American section of MOPR with headquarters in Moscow—the section headed by Congressman Vito Marcantonio. All the pro-communist and prominently fellow-traveling gentry in the legal profession had been in the forefront of the guild. Those familiar with the Stalinist apparatus had long identified the lawyers' front as part of the machinery. But even the belated identification by Mr. Berle did not budge Merle D. Vincent, who remained at the head of the Washington chapter, and dozens of other government officials. Secretary Ickes, stubbornly refusing to ascertain the character of his hosts when accepting invitations, made the opening address at one of the Guild meetings!

Mr. Ickes has for years been wheeled into position, like a bulky stage prop, on all sorts of ideological occasions. Verbally or in person he provided the opening invocations for sessions of the League for Peace and Democracy, the National Negro Congress, the Negro Youth Congress, to name a few. The American Student Union, as we have already indicated, for years made capital out of President Roosevelt's generous support. His wife keynoted at the World Youth Congress. The prestige of the White House, indeed, was until recently the most valuable asset of the communist leadership in the American Youth Congress; the conversion of that Innocents' Club into an instrument for blackjacking the New Deal foreign policies added a dimension of irony to that tragi-comedy of the First Lady's noble blundering. Two New Deal officials, Aubrey Williams and Robert Bulkley, opened a congress of the Workers Alliance, an organization some of whose former leaders (now that they have broken with the party) have denounced it as Moscow-dominated. The Southern Conference for Human Welfare started proceedings with Presidential blessings. Secretary (now Vice-President) Henry A. Wallace made the opening address for the Consumers National Federation. The list could be extended for pages. These organizations were all communist transmission belts.

The Administration's unbridled attacks on the investigations of the Special Committee on Un-American Activities, headed by Congressman Martin Dies of Texas, was a clear-cut function of the Popular Front. Every ounce of available fellow-traveler pressure throughout the country was mobilized to blast the committee and its chairman. Men and women in all walks of life, writers, officials, movie stars, playboys purchased reputations as "liberals" and absolution for past anti-liberal sins at bargain prices—by merely throwing another bucket of muddy water at the Dies Committee. Time has more than justified the committee's work. Supported by a tiny margin in the House at the outset, the committee's most recent appropriation was made by an almost unanimous vote. The very man put into the committee as a liberal counterweight to the Texas chairman, Congressman Jerry Voorhis of California, became more and more convinced of the reality of the menace under investigation and became increasingly energetic in his co-operation.

This is not to say that the Dies Committee has a perfect record. Its first months of activity were decidedly blundering. The chairman's blasts continue occasionally on the flamboyant side. The committee members were bewildered by the overabundance of evidence and its teeming inner contradictions. The fact is that they had barged without preparation into a field that called for immense knowledge and fine discrimination in judgment. Its handicaps were multiplied a hundredfold by nationwide attacks against the undertaking and the readiness of the Administration, the press, the pulpits, nearly everybody to exploit the committee's every mistake or political gaucherie.

But the committee learned as it went along. For all its errors of judgment and occasional boners, the Dies investigation has done an outstanding job that needed doing. The same people who damned Dies when the machinations of Moscow agents were exposed praised him when the exposure was directed against Nazi and Fascist, Silver Shirt and other native know-nothing agents. In the end, by sheer industry in piling up volume upon volume of detailed evidence, the Dies Committee succeeded in demonstrating that all these movements and phobias were, at bottom, part of a single totalitarian, anti-democratic pattern. Had the Administration been more co-operative with the Dies Committee, it would have had less of a headache in later years from communist-led strikes against the defense program and less to fear from communist Fifth Columnists deep within the government departments.

An enterprising research man will one day make a detailed study of the nationwide drives to kill the Dies Committee. It may reveal what is perhaps the most intensive campaign of this kind in American history—a campaign supported by every brand of totalitarianism, by a misguided liberalism and by the government, and ranging from ordinary calumny to attempts at frame-up. While there were strong Nazi and Fascist ingredients in the anti-Dies concentration, it was overwhelmingly a Popular Front exploit, unrestrained and desperate.

4

This must suffice to indicate the boldness of the party-line brigades and their success in involving popeyed neo-liberals and overnight social revolutionists in their work. It is perfectly obvious that most of these New Deal leaders either had no understanding of the super-lobby, or reasoned that its activities were not harmful. The cumulative effect of this complacency was to give Stalin's cohorts the inside track in our capital. Here, as in Hollywood, the pig Latin of the cause caught on. It was open knowledge that the shortest route to a government job was through Thirteenth Street or its Washington representatives.

The social lobby, in which the women played the leading roles, was in many respects the most effective mechanism in the Popular Front. The lists of the Washington collaborators of the League of Women Shoppers, for instance, sounds like a who's who of New Deal society: Mrs. Roosevelt, Mrs. Morgenthau, Mrs. Pressman, Mrs. Ezekiel, Mrs. Witt, Mrs. Gifford Pinchot, etc. Yet the files of the Philadelphia Communist Party listed this league as a "party organization." No one familiar with the Innocents' Front personnel can possibly doubt this. In nearly every city its main administrative jobs were in the hands of party members. Helen Kay, a party activist, was its first executive secretary. The *Daily Worker* and other party papers reported this League's activities with that intimate solicitude reserved for party fronts. Mrs. Aline Davis Hays was the New York chairman of both the League for Women Shoppers and the isolationist pro-Stalin American Peace Mobilization.

In the *News Letter* of this organization as late as May, 1940, "a gay carnival" to raise funds is described. We learn from it that Supreme Court Justice Douglas awarded the prizes and that high credit for the gaiety must go to "the psychic Abe Fortas; to Leon Henderson whose love potion of suffrage transformed Betty Vinton; to Metcalfe Walling and his *Post* boy, Gardner Jackson." Under the title "It is Cricket to Picket," the *Letter* reports a "spirited talk" by Mrs. Pinchot, after which "25 volunteered to picket the next Wednesday at the Press

Cafeteria." That celebrated authority on civil law, Miss Dorothy Parker of Hollywood and all Innocents' Clubs, presided at the league's panel discussion on "Labor and Civil Rights."

One of the goofier episodes was provided by the communist-staged assembly of what was called the "Daughters of the American Depression." Without inquiring who was behind the gathering, who staked the unemployed women who came to Washington, who stage-managed the whole show, droves of New Deal ladies gave their names as sponsors, among them Mrs. Roosevelt, Mrs. Henry F. Grady, Mrs. Ickes, Mrs. Thurman Arnold, Miss Josephine Roche, Mrs. Robert H. Jackson, Mrs. Edwin S. Smith, and Mrs. Aubrey Williams.

In Washington, no less than in Hollywood, the Spanish Loyalist cause was misused with amazing success to channel off emotion and dollars. Leon Henderson was especially prominent on this front, remaining inaccessible to counsels of caution. He headed two of the Spanish Aid outfits whose activities have been denounced by dis-illusioned veterans of the Loyalist fighting lines as well as by radicals and liberals acquainted with the Muscovite techniques. He acted as chairman of a Stalinist meeting in New York on the Loyalist theme after the whole business had become a stench in the public nostrils. The Washington Friends of Spanish Democracy, heavily colonized by the comrades, counted among its sponsors: Dr. Louis Bloch, John Carmody, Murray W. Latimer, Robert Marshall, Edwin S. Smith. It was an organization highly regarded and continually praised by the communist press.

The women in particular provided the heavy social artillery for the Loyalist fund-raising campaigns. Bridge parties, garden shindigs, cocktail parties for the Loyalists—all money going into coffers presided over by communists and their agents—were legion. The Popular Front made itself at home and plotted its moves and cemented its "contacts" in some of "the best homes" in the capital.

Thus in a thousand devious ways the Stalinist influence seeped into the New Deal and its intricate bureaucratic extensions. The fear of being called "red-baiter" prevented some of those who understood what was happening from speaking out. The pervasive feeling that the comrades had powerful support in exalted places curbed the dis-sidents and helped regiment the meek ones and the greedy ones for the super-lobby. It is impossible to trace the exact channels of influence, but somehow foreign communists obtained visas for the U. S. A. more readily than non-communists; somehow party members had an easier time obtaining a place at the public feed trough; everywhere those known as anti-Stalinists felt themselves intruders.

Communist-controlled or influenced unions, like the Workers Alliance and the United Federal Workers, gave additional leverage to the faithful and helped trip up the infidels. True, the President might sometimes take a crack at the comrades, but "it wasn't done" to attack them; there was the risk of "red-baiting" and "fascist" tags. Though the American Youth Congress in its rowdy demonstration for the newest party line booed the President and jeered at Congress, Mr. Jackson still took the trouble to kowtow to them. "My embarrassment in speaking to you tonight," he said on February 9, 1940, "is not from a sense of being holier than thou but from a sense of inferiority." Like the First Lady before him, Mr. Jackson preferred to humble himself before that regimented know-nothing meeting instead of exercising his prerogative as a mature human being to talk turkey to the gathering. It never occurred to him to inquire, for instance, why the Congress had suddenly reversed its views on nearly everything, including the New Deal of which he was such an important part.

Mr. Jackson at the Youth gathering was demonstrating that "hangover" of the Popular Front government which is still discernible nearly everywhere in Washington. Men and women whose co-operation with the Muscovite lobby continues as before are still holding appointive government jobs. Every new Stalinist front—the "peace mobilizations," the "Rescue Ship Mission," the phony new "civil liberties" outfits—can still count on New Deal officials and New Deal ladies. An understandable sense of guilt and humiliation still obliges many former stooges, now that they have understood and ended their stoogedom, to denounce anyone who alludes (as this book does) to their gullibility. Washington official and social life remains deeply infected with the Muscovite virus. The totalitarian liberalism of some, the complacency of others, the power of the C.I.O. unions of Federal employees, the presence of outright communist agents in all government departments—all these factors are still at play. They distort thinking on all matters affecting Russia and other communist interests.

Half a century ago one of the prophets of Russian Bolshevism, Nechayev, in his celebrated *Catechism of the Revolutionist* gave this formula for using "liberals of every shade":

One may conspire with them in accordance with their program, making them believe that one follows blindly and at the same time one should take hold of them, get possession of their secrets, compromise them to the utmost, so that no avenue of escape may be left to them, and use them as instruments for stirring up disturbances.

Nechayev's prescription may well be inscribed on the monument to the unofficial Popular Front government in Washington, now officially outlawed but unofficially still ubiquitous, vigorous and effective.

CHAPTER XXVI

THE TYPEWRITER FRONT

1

A PARDONABLE glow of boastfulness lit up Earl Russell Browder's voice when he explained to the Dies Committee in Washington how his beloved party had put its stamp on the "cultural life" of these United States.

"Well," he said, "we communists pride ourselves on the influence we have had in the cultural life of America. It has been one of the influences of communism, the communist influence, that stimulated the arts; rather there has been a renaissance of American drama and literature."

Stalin's branch-office director could hardly have referred to any Periclean flowering of artistic creativeness, because there had been no such thing in the Red Decade. First-rate books and stirring plays were written. Some exciting things were spread on walls and canvas. But there was no opulent eruption of talent, no great burst of genius or even originality to set the 1930's off from other decades. Its literary and art movements, especially the much-touted Proletcult and its toothless successor in "people's culture," were raucous but sterile. The enduring things produced in the decade were with minor exceptions outside the polluted waters of stormy polemics.

What Comrade Browder alluded to, we happen to know, was the noise, the mass meetings, the sloganeering that filled the world of art so full there was no room left for creation and artistry. He had in mind the huge standardized stockades into which his lieutenants had succeeded in herding men and women in the cultural crafts, his leagues and congresses for writers, painters, actors, movie people, dancers. His amazing "renaissance" expressed itself in the production of resolutions rather than art works. The practitioners and hangers-on of culture, especially its second-raters and Bohemians, went political with a vengeance. Artists and writers are normally temperamental and individualistic. But suddenly, frightened by gathering social storms the

311

world over, they huddled together like scared sheep and bleated slogans. Sheep-critics hailed the bah-ing as a renaissance. If it was "anti-fascist," if it was party line, then it was art by fiat. It was as though all of them had given up the effort to think and to feel for themselves, sinking themselves in a panic of moral surrender in congresses and resolutions.

Unquestionably the communist movement left its imprint on American culture. The bookstalls are heavy with "socially conscious" tripe. Acres of government-owned wall space are smudged with resolutions in colored symbols. Undigested political notions rumbled through the viscera of plays and movies. Education was saturated with formulas that short-circuited thinking. There had been other "intellectual" fads. But this one was backed by a political party and an international power machine, engineered consciously in the interests of the Soviet dictatorship. Its popularity consequently was on a larger scale.

Among writers the sudden but virulent affinity for the revised and perfumed "democratic" Fourth Period became epidemic. Thousands in and near the writing craft plumped for the revelation though they had remained indifferent—or even hostile—to the Stalinist catechism in the years of fighting phrases. And the definition of "literature" was expanded to include half-literate society ladies, Hollywood script girls, press agents, advertising copy writers, nearly anyone willing to bleat in unison.

The spread of the disease made a fascinating spectacle. You knew writing men and women as sober-minded, realistic, tolerant human beings. A few months later you met them accidentally and recognized at once that the contagion had caught up with them; they had broken out in a rash of Stalinist clichés and in their delirium talked fevered gibberish under the sick impression that they were making sense. Overnight they had moved from the private cynicism of lavatory humor to the collective cynicism of defending execution squads. They were ready, nay eager, to liquidate the last literary *kulak* in their vicinity. And magically, their own writing, which until then had been ignored or brushed aside as "petty bourgeois," suddenly began to evoke rave notices in the press, from Browder's *Daily Worker* to Ogden Reid's *Herald Tribune*. From that point forward you looked for their names on all the mushrooming united-front idiocies and, sure enough, there they were!

2

Take the case of George Seldes, celebrated in the ideological history of the period. As a reporter for the Chicago *Tribune*, he had been to Russia in its earlier, milder and more idealistic years and had been duly expelled. For twelve or thirteen years thereafter he devoted himself to exploding the myth of Soviet socialism, before Stalin and after. In a series of books, in endless lectures and articles, he consistently bracketed Bolshevism with fascism and never tired of warning his countrymen against the threat of Bolshevik intrusion in American life. He was among the foremost anti-communists in the first half of the Red Decade.

But suddenly, around 1937, George popped up far inside the communist orbit, a regular contributor to Stalin's American press, gunning for the hides of colleagues who were quoting his own stuff on Russia. What had happened to explain the mysterious conversion? Certainly the Russian terror had not subsided and Stalin's regime had not become any less dictatorial. Every impassioned indictment of Bolshevik horrors set down in *Can These Things Be!* and his other books still applied—only a hundred times more so. He had not revisited the scenes of his former disillusionment nor even, as far as I am aware, publicly repudiated his own reports on the mess. Unlike political neophytes such as Dorothy Parker or Gypsy Rose Lee, he could scarcely have become so belatedly aware of fascism and the Depression, matters he had been reporting in detail for a great many years.

No, there is no clue in logic to the change. The transformation had clearly occurred on a level beyond logic, beyond common sense. George, poor boy, had caught communism as one catches the flu in an epidemic. At this writing he has not yet convalesced, and even if he survives the long siege there will be permanent scars on his mind and soul. Currently he is editing a pro-Soviet, party-line sheet called *In Fact*; until the breach between Russia and Germany, it was loudly anti-British and opposed to our defense efforts.

Or take the interesting clinical case history of Frederick L. Schuman, now professor of government at Williams College. The professor went to Moscow. If he had been overwhelmed by the glories of Soviet life and thought, he concealed that fact very effectively. Yet by 1932 he had associated himself with the League of Professional Groups for Foster and Ford. Later, testifying at an official investiga-

tion of the faculty of the University of Chicago, he "flatly denied that
he had any ideas which were in any way radical." With something less
than magnificent courage he even denied signing that Open Letter for
Foster and Ford.

"In my public address and publications," he swore, "I have repeatedly pointed out that the liberal and radical critics of our present
economic and social order have been short-sighted or dishonest in
failing to recognize that extensive governmental interference with
profits and property rights can only lead to chaos or to socialism."

Despite this public repudiation of socialism, he was soon showing
up, as inevitably as fate, in Stalinist groupings for the literati and the
campus comrades. "Underneath their skins," he now confided to the
New Republic, "communism and liberalism are blood brothers." The
same profound discovery he shared with clients of the distinguished
Southern Review. "Bolshevism at the end of its second decade," he
proclaimed, "is building a great community not less democratic in its
values than those of Western Europe and America and not less devoted to those values which liberal Western culture has long cherished." These words must be placed against the background of the
blood purges then at full tide to savor their quintessential absurdity.

Nine days before Hitler and Stalin got together, Dr. Schuman
joined Max Lerner, Corliss Lamont, Vincent Sheean and the rest in
tarring John Dewey and Ferdinand Lundberg and John Dos Passos
as "fascists and allies of fascists" for daring to call Russian culture
"totalitarian." Soon thereafter the professor was lustily assailing
Stalin. An exchange of letters between Dr. Schuman and Lawrence
Dennis recently put the finishing touch on the professor's mental portrait. Dennis, who is a brilliant exponent of the fascist viewpoint,
wrote to Dr. Schuman: "It takes clear thinking and writing to formu-
late debatable issues between us when we have so much in common in
method, attitude, and conclusions." The italics are mine.

There is a world of difference between the political somersault of a
Seldes—go-to-hell cynical in its offhand irrationality—and the elaborate
mental acrobatics of Dr. Schuman. But both cases are expressions
of the same elephantine confusion. The infection spread to the remotest corners of the American cultural world. Bukharin, Rykov,
Rakovsky, Smilga, Radek, Tomsky, Serebriakov were being liquidated
as "fascist spies," but no matter—new proletarian leaders like Dorothy
Parker, Dashiell Hammett, Van Wyck Brooks, Lionel Stander, Rock-

well Kent, Paul de Kruif, Corliss Lamont, Muriel Draper, et al., stepped forward to take their places in the trenches of a musical-comedy class war.

Anyone who doubts that the process had in it an element of real religious hysteria—turning it into a kind of political children's crusade—need only read Dorothy Parker's confessions of faith. Beating her bosom, she renounced "the gallant and hard-riding and careless of life" in favor of Stalin's Utopia. There is not the remotest indication that she knew what she was accepting as she exclaimed, "There is no longer 'I', there is 'WE'! The day of the individual is dead." Somehow it made it all right, after that, for any number of individuals to be put literally to death by the individual in the Kremlin in the name of "We." Only this is more lucidity than the high-pitched converts normally attained. After that the spectacle of Father Divine's angels marching shoulder to shoulder with the novelists and jokesmiths of the League of American Writers in a May Day parade was merely in the character of the delirious mishmash. It was the stuff nightmares are made of.

I have before me some political writings of a gifted literary historian. It is hard to believe that the same mind conceived these and, let us say, *The Ordeal of Mark Twain*. Dr. Van Wyck Brooks discovered, all in a frenzy, that the Founding Fathers of our Republic were really collectivists at heart. "The Declaration of Independence," he propounded to a writers' conference in Connecticut, "speaks in the name of 'all men.' Is there not something collective in this conception?" Karl Marx and Lenin turned in their grave and showcase, respectively, as Dr. Brooks proceeded to define collectivism as "government of the people by the people."

The naïveté of this neo-collectivism may be surmised from the fact that he placed before his "communist fellow-members" in the League of American Writers this profound riddle: Did they think that they would have freedom if we Americans had a Stalin? He described the league—so carefully organized and manipulated by the Communist Party—as "a product of spontaneous combustion." He even had it figured out that the Yankees "also produced modern Russia"—a libel for which the Yankees should have sued him. Later he addressed a "personal statement" to the league wherein, in his political innocence, he listed Trotsky along with Lenin and Stalin as the "John Browns and Garrisons for our younger people, who had no Browns and Garrisons to contemplate at home." The comrades must have suffered a thousand deaths at such blasphemy.

I cite Dr. Brooks precisely because he is a man of honest instincts and a great writer. He could not possibly have been subverted by the crude flattery and cruder logrolling which helped draw in literary failures or Hollywood wisecrackers plagued by inferiority complexes. The ideological puerilities of such a man are impressive symptoms of the fevered atmosphere. It at least exonerates the nobodies who entered the sheep-pens partly to be in his distinguished company.

3

But I do not have to rest my diagnosis on my own researches. We have ready to hand an expert judgment by a specialist and a leader on the typewriter front of the Red Decade. The commissar for the herded intelligentsia was one V. J. Jerome. It was he, along with Comrades Trachtenberg, Gold, Schneider, Hathaway, who had achieved the "spontaneous combustion" and kept it combusting through the People's Front years. What did these comrades really think of their literary fellow-travelers? When the wild ride was over—when the "democratic" hokum had been dumped overboard—Comrade Jerome finally *told*. He proceeded to reveal the limitless contempt in which his crowd of insiders held their "cultural" dupes.

At the end of 1940 Jerome published a pamphlet lambasting the intellectuals who had formerly played in his yard, exempting, of course, the "good" intellectuals who were still playing there—their turn will come later.* It was calculated to make every last member of the League of American Writers, every last literary enthusiast for the Kremlin's blood purges squirm in humiliation.

Those people, Jerome says candidly, never understood "the democratic tactic." In other words they thought it was really democratic rather than a temporary tactic. They "joined the party because of their social milieu," he charges, "finding that this made them socially acceptable among people of living culture." In plain English, they were doing some social climbing among the ideological elite and, Jerome sneers, had the gall to look on themselves "as guests of honor. . . . These pseudo-Marxists did not see integration with the

---

* *Intellectuals and the War*, by V. J. Jerome, 1940, Workers Library Publishers.

working class [read Browder and Jerome] as a privilege; they came like arrogant slummers. They looked upon the working class as a pedestal on which to rise. They saw an opportunity to 'cash in' on the publicity that the movement accords to those who join with the forces of progress."

The double-talk about forces of progress does not obscure the charges of social climbing and publicity seeking. That is what the comrades really thought about Van Wyck Brooks's variety of collectivism, Dorothy Parker's orgiastic "We," the rest of the literary stooging for Stalin's causes—despite the comradely embraces in the pages of the communist press. Among those he considers beneficiaries Jerome specifically mentions Archibald MacLeish, Vincent Sheean, Lewis Mumford, Malcolm Cowley, Granville Hicks, John Strachey, Harold Laski, André Malraux. (He does not mention "renegades" like Louis Fischer and Maurice Hindus, apparently disdaining to class them among the "intellectuals.")

These writers, as Jerome puts it, "did not perceive the tactical line of the People's Front in real relation to the basic strategy of the revolutionary working class for the attainment of power." And that, it may readily be conceded, isn't one-half of one per cent of what they did not perceive. Unfortunately for their human integrity, Comrade Jerome waited until the "tactic" had been abandoned to help them perceive these things. Until then he and his associates were dedicated to the job of preventing the literary fellow-travelers from perceiving and understanding their function in the "democratic tactic."

Comrade Jerome is not too gentle with his cultural dupes, but no one can object that they do not merit the spanking. In Comrade Jerome's "spiritual fatherland" they would not have got away with a mere spanking. They would have faced their beloved firing squads.

4

It might all have been harmless insanity, except that it provided the instruments for an intellectual terror against those who retained some sanity. Many a writer joined up and went through the motions of ideological schizophrenia to avoid ostracism. Anyone who dared point out in that period what even the embattled Malcolm Cowley would ultimately admit—that the communists ran the show—was treated like a leper guilty of matricide.

The central mechanism of that terror was the League of American Writers comprising the national body and an array of regional setups. Lillian Symes tells how she was invited to join the Sponsoring Committee of one of the Writers Congresses, on the West Coast: "It was after both Leon Blum and Herbert Hoover had been suggested as honorary members that my nerves gave way and I nominated Colette and Leon Trotsky. The fellow-travelers have never recovered from the shock." Prospective members at that time had to sign a statement agreeing to the principles of the People's Front in the United States and throughout the world. Not all of them realized, of course, that they were signing a blanket endorsement of the current Kremlinesque "tactic." Like most Stalinoid organizations, the league never published a roster of members; the vagueness added vastly to the impressiveness. But it is safe to say that a good majority of the outstanding American writers at one time or another participated in league activities even if they did not sign on the dotted line.

The initial congress which launched the league, as we have already recorded, was frankly communist in its temper. Among the signers of its call were Comrades Browder, Alexander Trachtenberg, Gold, Moissaye Olgin, Joseph North, Joseph Freeman and other undisguised communists. The call for the Second Congress, held in New York on June 4-6, 1937, omitted such names. It was garnished more discreetly with non-political names, in line with the new period. The signers now were Newton Arvin, Van Wyck Brooks, Erskine Caldwell, Malcolm Cowley, Paul de Kruif, Waldo Frank, Langston Hughes, James Weldon Johnson, John Howard Lawson, Robert Morss Lovett, Archibald MacLeish, Claude McKay, Vincent Sheean, Upton Sinclair, George Soule, Donald Ogden Stewart, Genevieve Taggard, Jean Starr Untermeyer, Carl Van Doren, Ella Winter and Lewis Mumford.*

Certainly Dr. Brooks was not the only one among them who thought it was all "spontaneous combustion." It was a typical Fourth Period manifesto, devoted to "a rebirth of the American labor movement," related to "the new stirrings in literature" and dedicated, among other things, to "freedom of thought and expression." Those who tried to exercise such freedom at the Second Congress were given the works. Dwight MacDonald, in telling of his own experience in trying to speak out of ideological turn, subsequently wrote:

---

* As published in the *Nation*, May 8, 1937.

My politically sophisticated friends warned me that the congress was merely a maneuver of the Communist Party, and that I was naïve to expect any such discussions—since discussion implies the possibility of disagreement. . . . The congress assumed a *priori* agreement on Stalinist policies, despite the failure of the call to mention any such thing and despite the fact that the signers of the call were practically all non-communist liberals. . . . The congress was one long "pep talk" reminiscent of the rallies I used to attend at Phillips Exeter Academy on the eve of the annual football game with Andover. . . . A great many intensely earnest people told us over and over that we must lick fascism, but as to the strategy—that was entirely up to Quarterback Stalin. Anyone who criticized his tactics was a Trotskyite wrecker and assassin (read: "lacking in school spirit").*

Führer Browder appeared as the leading speaker at the opening session—as was only fitting at a national conference of American literati—and applied himself to America's principal literary problem of the moment: the Trotskyist threat to American culture. Although Waldo Frank, previous president, had been among the call signers, he lost the presidency—punishment for suggesting that the Moscow trials needed investigation. That distinction fell—and I use the word advisedly—to Donald Ogden Stewart. The breadth of the united front may be surmised from the participation of men like Thornton Wilder, Ernest Hemingway, Marc Connelly and others who had been favorite examples of "petty bourgeois mentality" in the previous period.† Strangely enough, not a single novelist, playwright, journalist or Hollywoodian who was publicly critical of the Russian paradise happened to have been invited. The wonders of coincidence!

Archibald MacLeish presided at a meeting dedicated largely to glorification of Russia's role in Spain—G.P.U. methods and all. Hosannas to the Kremlin were sung at various sessions and in various keys by Walter Duranty, Albert Rhys Williams, Joseph Freeman, Cowley, Hicks and a great many others. The standard party-line resolutions on Spain, China, anti-fascism, the W.P.A., defense of the Soviet "peace policy" and all other subjects were duly passed. A book summing up the proceedings was later published. Whatever 1937 may mean to others, it was identified in the introduction to this book as

---

* The *Nation*, June 19, 1937.
† These, and many others, have since then made clear their disapproval of Kremlinesque communism.

"twenty years since the Russian people established their Soviet republic." A more curious chronological system for a "non-partisan," spontaneously combusted meeting of American writers would be hard to invent.

The league's Third Congress was held two years later, on June 2-4, 1939. The closeness to the approaching catastrophe of the next August, when von Ribbentrop would be the guest of the Kremlin, makes the congress, in retrospect, an Alice in Wonderland performance. Its call listed prominently among the league aims: "Co-operation of this country with other nations and peoples opposed to fascism—including the Soviet Union, which has been the most consistent defender of peace." The secret negotiations between Moscow and Berlin were coming to a head as these words were penned.

Of the seventy-two signers of this call, at least fourteen were generally known to be members of the Communist Party. The others were names that had become fixtures on Stalinist manifestoes and whitewash documents. The whole list* merits enshrinement in these pages, being one of the last of the People's Front demonstrations before Stalin pulled the props from under it:

Benjamin Appel	Guy Endore
Newton Arvin	Henry Pratt Fairchild
Albert Bein	Francis Edwards Faragoh
Aline Bernstein	Kenneth Fearing
Millen Brand	Arthur Davison Ficke
Bessie Breuer	Marjorie Fischer
Dorothy Brewster	Joseph Freeman
Van Wyck Brooks	David Fuchs
Sidney Buchman	Mauritz Hallgren
Kenneth Burke	Henry Hart
Erskine Caldwell	Lillian Hellman
Katherine Garrison Chapin	DuBose Heyward
Humphrey Cobb	Eugene Holmes
Lester Cohen	Arthur Kober
Malcolm Cowley	Jess Kimbrough
George Dillon	Alfred Keymborg
Muriel Draper	Joshua Kunitz
Philip Dunne	David Lamson

* *Direction*, official organ of the League, May-June, 1939.

Jesse Lasky, Jr.
John Howard Lawson
Meyer Levin
Helen Merrell Lynd
Albert Maltz
Bruce Minton
Ruth McKenney
Carey McWilliams
Harvey O'Connor
Dorothy Parker
S. J. Perelman
Frederick Prokosch
Lorine Pruette
Samuel Putnam
W. L. River
Ralph Roeder
Harold J. Rome
Muriel Rukeyser
Budd Wilson Schulberg
Vida Scudder

Edwin Seaver
Irwin Shaw
Vincent Sheean
Viola Brothers Shore
Upton Sinclair
Philip Stevenson
Leland Stowe
Tess Slesinger
Donald Ogden Stewart
Irving Stone
Genevieve Taggard
Jean Starr Untermeyer
Louis Untermeyer
Carl Van Doren
John Wexley
William Carlos Williams
Ella Winter
Richard Wright
Stanley Young
Leane Zugsmith

The congress was largely another communist mass meeting, with the usual greetings from the writers of Russia (those not yet liquidated, that is), praise of Moscow's "anti-fascist" leadership, resolutions embodying every inch of the party line. The Soviet message, we may note for posterity and the current party-liners, said: "*The attempt to hide behind neutrality, non-intervention or isolationism has become a mockery.*" There had been a batch of defections before the opening. Babette Deutsch and Frances Winwar, among others, had resigned, protesting communist domination. But new innocents by the dozen and the score took the place of the "renegades." Thomas Mann was inveigled into a front place in the show window, and even Louis Bromfield, who is normally less gullible. Behind such names, the old crowd pulled the strings as in the preceding session.

Sylvia Townsend Warner spoke up for the British equivalent of the League; Ralph Bates held forth for something called the International Association of Writers for the Defense of Culture; Frederico Mangabas brought the blessings of the Philippine Writers League. It was a high-spirited and warmhearted and optimistic gathering. It was the Indian summer of the Red Decade, had they only known it, but Stalin had not taken Browder into his confidence, let alone Thomas Mann or Heywood Broun. The Stalin-Hitler nuptials soon unveiled the real character of this, as of most other, communist Innocents' Clubs.

No less an authority than Cowley reported sadly by 1940: "Half a dozen members withdrew from the executive board of the league. In a sense these resignations were only the latest in a long series that included the honorary president, Thomas Mann, and four of the ten vice-presidents. They meant . . . that there was no longer any hope of changing the league's policy." What was that policy that Cowley wanted to change? And why was there no hope? In tendering his own resignation, he answered these questions—and incidentally admitted in substance what had for so many years been so vehemently denied: that the communists dominated the league!*

Naturally, being so deeply involved in the long-drawn deception, he could not make the admission straightforwardly but only by unmistakable implication. He described an attitude on the European war "which is now the general line of the Communist Party," adding: "The league is not a communist organization, but this is the line it has chosen to follow." Then he continued blandly on the assumption that the league represented the new communist line and charged it with following the new Comintern theory "that fascism is really a movement forward, the next step along the road to universal socialism." "Their present theory," he wrote to the league, "about the 'imperialist war' is plausible enough to persuade women's peace societies and kiddie-book writers, but it has little relation to what is actually happening in Europe. And in any case, the league is not supposed to be an organization devoted to the world proletarian revolution." The upshot of the matter was that Cowley—not the communist partyliners—had to resign. It was his admission that the Stalinists had a death grip on the machinery of the organization.

Only the fear of expanding this book to encyclopedic proportions prevents me from tracing the same pattern of Muscovite domination in the other "cultural" planets in Kuusinen's universe of dupes and dopes, innocents and not-so-innocents. There were special fronts for painters and sculptors, with their own congresses. There were notable

---

* *New Republic,* August 12, 1940.

muscling-in proceedings in the field of documentary films—with Nelson Rockefeller and Jock Whitney paying the bill! Even the musicians were mobilized under the prescribed Fourth Period slogans.

Comrade Browder, in short, had ample cause for pride in his "influence . . . in the cultural life of America." That cankerous influence is still gnawing at the heart of American art and letters.

CHAPTER XXVII

INTELLECTUAL RED TERROR

1

A N INTELLECTUAL and moral "red terror" spread through the areas under the influence of the incredible revolution, which meant particularly in New York, Hollywood, Washington, many college campuses and the more infected social sectors in all large cities. I am conscious that this charge will sound extreme to people without direct experience of the reach and fire-power of the terror, and I do not know how to make it credible to skeptics. Only those who have been targets of the concerted and stubborn attacks, month after month, year after year, will know what I mean. But the terror was no less real because it was underground, underhanded and in the nature of the thing not readily subject to proof.

It was a terror directed in general against critics of Russia and of its foreign activities. But the fullest force of its mud gunners, character assassins and poison-gas brigades was reserved especially for "renegades," meaning people who were at one time in the political environs of the Communist Party but had shaken off its authority. I have known men and women so frightened by the certainty of persecution from the Left that they hid their doubts and disillusionments like criminal secrets. The prospect of being branded, a thousand times, over a fascist, Trotskyite, Franco spy, agent of Hitler and Japan, tool of Hearst, lackey of Wall Street and the Liberty League has kept hundreds of comrades toeing the party line long after their faith had turned to ashes.

They knew that the vilification would not be limited to political name-calling but would spread into fantastic personal smearing with whispered accusations from simple embezzlement and pimping to subtle corruptions even unto murder. They knew—and that was the most efficacious part of the business—that thereafter they would automatically be ostracized not alone by former friends and comrades but by that whole broad social, literary and intellectual periphery. They would become aware of mysterious pressures against them even on the most conservative newspapers, in seemingly uninfected government bureaus, in solid publishing houses, wherever the party had fellow-travelers or outright agents in key positions—which in these hectic years meant approximately everywhere.

A break with the party meant subjection to vast and ingenious strategies of slander. If the responsible leaders suspected a cooling of affections and an incipient case of "renegacy," they might begin the barrage even before the break, on the theory that a vigorous offensive is the best defense. The Communist Party, in fact, does not recognize or accept resignations. It expels the dissident with appropriate notice to his erstwhile colleagues of trumped-up reasons ranging from "petty bourgeois" mentality to high crimes of Trotskyism.

But the procedure is not restricted to backsliding party members. It is applied with no less energy to people who were merely sympathetic and co-operative. Their desertion cannot, obviously, be left unpunished. They must be turned as rapidly as possible into hideous moral lepers, intellectual perverts and the germ carriers of fascism, Trotskyism, etc. In the first place, it ended the need for replying to anything the culprit may say in private or in public by demonstrating that he had "sold out" or been "exposed" or even been "caught with the goods." Secondly, it served as a wholesome warning to others of waning faith or crumbling enthusiasm. For every disillusioned comrade who dared speak out and take the consequences in the coin of personal abuse, there were dozens crushed into silence by the prospect. Men and women who returned from Russia or Spain heavyhearted with disenchantment often could not muster the courage to make their feelings public.

Let no one suppose that the calumny was casual, a mere flare-up of righteous indignation. On the contrary, it was a strategy developed and systematized by the party chieftains and applied with scientific care. Unable as yet to destroy chosen enemies physically, as in its Russian homeland, they aimed to destroy their reputations and influence. I know of special secret conferences of party writers and agitators called to decide how most expeditiously to "destroy" some critic; the details of such a conference about myself, held in the Soviet Consulate in New York, were confided to me by a participant.

Planned defamation brought the party some famous victories. Having demolished the character of a critic, his opinions could be dismissed by all the faithful—and especially by the *Nation-New Republic-Writers-Congress-cocktail-hour* crowd of liberals—with a sneer and a shrug. Self-righteously the part-time revolutionists could shut their minds against the writings of moral monsters and turncoats like John Dewey, Max Eastman, Benjamin Stolberg, Liston Oak, John Dos Passos, Edmund Wilson, André Gide, James Rorty, Boris Souvarine, Walter Krivitsky, Sidney Hook, James T. Farrell, Sinclair Lewis, Suzanne La Follette, William Henry Chamberlin, Charles Rumford Walker, Charles Yale Harrison, V. F. Calverton, Lillian Symes, Benjamin Gitlow, Evelyn Scott, Isaac Don Levine, Ferdinand Lundberg, Eugene Lyons, Leon Dennen, Harry D. Gideonse, John Haynes Holmes, Ludwig Lore, Claude McKay, Morrie Ryskind, to mention a few who at various periods incurred communist disfavor.

The part that I cannot induce the uninitiated to believe is how effective the terror could be. When you first met a particularly far-fetched libel on your character, it merely seemed funny in its absurdity. Then it became a haunting refrain, its total effect depending on your nerves and your reservoir of self-esteem. The same fantastic inventions in approximately the same words bobbed up in all parts of the country among the most diverse kinds of people. They were shouted at you from the floor of lecture halls and echoed in book review and gossip columns. Your friends assured you that of course *they* didn't believe such nonsense, but what was the low-down? Did you really operate a brothel in Moscow? Did you really conduct a lucrative Black Bourse? And what about your career as a contrabandist? Ten thousand well-meaning people co-operated innocently with the official poison-gas brigades.

And you were lucky if you had the talent or the personal prestige to weather the onslaught. When the victim was a meek and friendless creature he might find himself stripped of a livelihood along with his good name. For a known "renegade" to crash one of the cultural Federal projects—literary, theatre, art—was a feat more difficult than passing that camel through the eye of the needle. Wherever he moved there were manuscript readers, casting directors, book reviewers who—consciously or by a sort of pack instinct—took their prejudices ready-made from the Popular Front comrades.

If you think I exaggerate, seek out some member of the Abraham Lincoln Brigade who dared to tell the truth about G.P.U. corruption and brutality in Spain. Corner some college professor who broke relations openly with his communist unit on the campus. Find almost anyone who has written an article or a book attacking the Soviet Utopia. Have him convey to you what it means to have your private life maligned, your every word and act twisted out of shape, your every piece of work automatically condemned by party-line judges in the most unexpected places.

He may give you some inkling of the intellectual and moral red terror. It could bar you from house parties on Park Avenue, jobs in Hollywood, places on the relief rolls of your city, fair treatment in the columns of great conservative papers, a hearing before supposedly broad-minded public lecture forums, access to Federal projects. It could hold the threat of this power over the heads of doubters and backsliders. To the conformists, by the same token, it offered the joys of logrolling, the publicity of endless committees and causes, the benefit of every doubt in any number of professional columns of criticism and review, a sense of belonging to a social and intellectual elite that combined the fashionable with the self-righteously virtuous.

2

As recently as 1936 our most distinguished philosopher, Professor John Dewey, still rated high in the American communist press. He had written warmly about Soviet education and loaned his name to communist-controlled organizations. Soon, however, few names were more abominated in respectable communist-liberal circles than Professor Dewey's. He drew the lightning of Muscovite damnation by heading the inquiry into Stalin's charges against Leon Trotsky. The Daily Worker instantly excommunicated him and nullified all his good works for the communist cause. It described him as "a Charlie McCarthy for the Trotskyites" wallowing in "a swamp of filth," who "has become the puppet of disruption in America's liberal and progressive movements . . . has wiped out his standing as a liberal" and become "a tool of reaction." This estimate of the philosopher's character appeared under the caption "American Labor Has a New Enemy"—clearly the main concern of American labor was to protect the G.P.U. against Professor Dewey.

The diurnal onslaughts were reinforced by sniping in the weekly New Masses, with columnist Robert Forsythe manning the mud guns. Along with Michael Gold, Malcolm Cowley and the Heywood Broun of that period, Forsythe held the first line of offense in the campaigns on individual nonconformists. He deserves a paragraph of close-up:

His prosaic workaday identity is Kyle Crichton, long the theatre and movie writer for *Collier's*. He is a tall, stooped, spectacled, rather professorial or clerical looking gentleman. The last thing you would guess him to be from his looks and talk is the author of a weekly chunk of creampuffery for the masses—press-agent gurglings about Hollywood starlets, vaudeville comics, theatre hopefuls, skating queens and the like. The man and his work are so ludicrously at odds that it is a safe guess he despises his hacking and hates himself for it. The first time I looked at this dignified person I felt I could understand the bitter and uninhibited name-calling in his romantic communist incarnation as Robert Forsythe. The *New Masses* Forsythe, I felt, was trying to prove in issue after issue that under the surface of *Collier's* Kyle Crichton there was really an audacious fellow with a mind and a soul and, above all, literary guts. Precisely because his *Collier's* stuff was so sickly saccharine, his defense of the Kremlin's tortuous line had to be written in gall and bile. The sardonic Burton Rascoe hit the nail on the head when he disposed of Crichton-Forsythe with the phrase, "So red the pose."

And so, in hurling a lot of bold epithets at a real thinker like John Dewey, poor Mr. Crichton, we can assume, was merely avenging the fate that forced him to compose drooling-sweet articles about glamour girls. In any case, while plunged in his brave Forsythe saga, he posed the question in the *New Masses*, "Is John Dewey Honest?" and worked his way gleefully through a pageful of abuse to a negative answer. Professor Dewey, he found, "is a most disarming old gentleman who is capable of great viciousness." The "viciousness" of the "old cuss"—Forsythe's elegant phrase—lay, of course, in his attempt to get at the truth behind the Moscow purge trials. "Mr. Dewey has ceased being disarming and pathetic," Mr. Crichton decided, "and is now graduated into dishonesty. . . ."* This by the man who, as Crichton, reviewed a book by "Forsythe" for the old *Life* and found it exceedingly good!

The abuse of Professor Dewey was echoed in all other communist and near-communist publications. Heywood Broun took some hefty wallops at him on his *New Republic* page. The news that the philos-

---

* *New Masses*, January 4, 1938.

opher had gone "fascist" and "Trotskyite" was spread diligently through the whole world of "sympathizers," middle-class sensation-seekers, pseudo-intellectuals and other innocents around the Communist Party. The propaganda to the effect that Professor Dewey was "doddering" was rather badly confounded by the publication of his book on *Logic*, one of the most impressive jobs in his career. One of the damning crimes charged against a comrade being investigated on suspicion of heresy—I happened to see a part of the recorded proceedings—was his reported remark that "John Dewey is an honest man." The professor's name could no longer be mentioned in good fellow-traveler society without some scurrilous adjective. Consorting with him came to rank among the unpardonable sins for a "friend of the Soviet Union." Even the pseudo-scientific writers in outright communist magazines and in communist-dominated publications like *Science and Society* suddenly discovered that Professor Dewey's philosophy was worthless. Dr. V. J. McGill wrote under his own name in *Science and Society* and under the name of Philip Carter in *The Communist*, thus getting in a double-header assault on Professor Dewey. Penthouse parties thereafter shuddered at the mention of the "renegade."

Or take the great ganging up on Max Eastman. His character has now been under siege for more than a decade, so that he is by this time a living compendium of all known iniquities and infamies and a few rare ones to boot. In 1927, although he was already loud against Stalin, the *New Masses* still announced proudly that he would contribute to its pages. "What the *New Masses* needs is a Max Eastman!" the editors quoted readers as saying and promised to meet this demand. The American comrades were still hesitating as between Stalin and Trotsky. Then the die was cast, and immediately the thesaurus was sacked for adjectives of abuse against Eastman.

The polite designation "bandit of the pen" or "gangster of the pen," later a generic term for all writers disavowing the authority of the Kremlin, was tailored in Moscow especially to Eastman's measure. A dispatch from the Soviet capital to the *Daily Worker* on April 4, 1937, recorded Stalin's reference to hostile journalists in America as "a notorious gang of writers . . . headed by the notorious crook Max Eastman." Five days later, in Moscow again, Earl Browder echoed: "The Trotskyite wreckers have their reserves. Among their reserves outside the U.S.S.R. no small place is taken by the American bandits of the pen. . . . At the head of this gang of bandits is the notorious swindler Max Eastman." The gang leader's achievements as "crook" and "swindler" would not quite place him in a class with Al Capone, being on the politico-ideological rather than on the commercial level. For instance, he was the first to make public in America the full text of Lenin's famous Last Will, in which the dying Father of Bolshevism called for the removal of Stalin.

The well-known labor journalist Benjamin Stolberg won his titles as enemy of the people and bandit of the pen by the fact alone that he participated in Professor Dewey's investigation of the Moscow trials. Even that faded by contrast when he dared, in articles and a book, to expose the tactics of the Stalinists in the C.I.O. Though he defended the C.I.O. against the Machiavellian connivers inside and outside—a warning which, had it been heeded, might have saved the organization from its later troubles—the liberal and communist press treated his writings as an "attack" on the C.I.O.

"That stool-pigeon of the pen, Benjamin Stolberg, has hit the front-page again," the *Daily Worker* apprised its readers. The editors of the paper, who exhibit a peculiarly intimate knowledge of the most ancient trade and its lingo, called him an "ordinary low-priced street-walker ready to peddle himself in parks, alleys or hallways to any chance customer." Broun joined the attack, and the admirable Crichton-Forsythe, of course, contributed his handful of epithets.

That sort of thing could be shrugged off by men like Stolberg, Dewey, Eastman, but it put the fear of God into meeker men. The discrediting of the immediate victims was only a part of the objective—intimidation of fellow-travelers generally was the main purpose.

3

First place among the objects of planned calumny belonged to a category in which I enjoyed a considerable place: the authors of books telling too much about Russia. In April, 1933, the *New Masses* said of the great French writer, André Gide: "Nothing is so odious to him as the lie. He would not resort to mendacity even if it could 'prove' what was most dear to him." Four years later the same magazine flayed M. Gide as a liar and added innuendoes about his private life; the same whisperings were soon to be heard at every "cause" cocktail party. The Frenchman, of course, in the meantime had published a brochure accusing the Soviet regime of "oppression of the human spirit." All over the world, and especially in his own country, the novelist was subjected to unprincipled persecution.

The comrades picked on a German novelist of great talent but tragically limited political understanding, Lion Feuchtwanger, to make the official reply to M. Gide. They took him to Russia, entertained him to the point of ego-inflation and let him float loose. For years after—even after the Stalinists had made common cause with the Hitler who drove him to America (not to Russia, be it noted) as a refugee—Herr Feuchtwanger was still playing the Muscovite game, knowingly or in childish innocence.

An American worker, Andrew Smith, went to Russia in 1932 with the intention of settling there. An official recommendation by an American Communist Party agent praised him as a loyal comrade and an "expert machinist." A few years later Smith returned to tell what he had experienced in Stalin's realm, in a book he called *I Was a Soviet Worker*. It was as realistic and horrifying an account as had come out of Stalinland. The capitalist press was almost unanimous in ignoring that book, though it gave attention as a matter of course to any volume of praise of Russia—but that's another story. Mr. Smith was immediately smeared in the comradely press as a "Hearst tool, a traitor to the working class" who "after a long career of trickery has found his proper place with the fascists." Even his standing as a workman was impugned: he was now "a poorly skilled worker."

A most striking example of "character murder" on the Left is provided by communist treatment of Fred E. Beal, leader of the celebrated textile strike in Gastonia, North Carolina, in 1929, now serving a ten years' term on charges growing out of that strike. It was in the direct service of the Communist Party that he led the strike and drew the sentence. He had been advertised for years as its great labor martyr. Yet the communists not only do nothing to help him but denounce the trade-unionists who seek his release! Though he is the most prominent and most clearly victimized labor prisoner in America—now that Mooney and Billings are free—the misnamed International Labor Defense, headed by Vito Marcantonio, does not recognize his martyrdom!

Why? Because while still a communist hero he skipped bail (with the blessing and very likely, as he claims, on the order of the party) and fled to Russia. There he was revolted by the misery, injustice and terror. Risking imprisonment, he left Russia for the life of a fugitive from justice at home, determined to tell what he had seen. He succeeded in publishing articles and a book, *A Proletarian Journey*, before he was apprehended. His martyrdom quite forgotten, the machinery of communist abuse was set to work on his reputation. Though communist pamphlets had once described him as "one of the most courageous leaders," an article in the *Daily Worker* by Harrison George now accused him of cowardice and demanded in effect that he be allowed to rot in prison despite his innocence.

It is easy to imagine what a great national noise would be under way in Beal's behalf now, how many thousands of liberals would be converging their energies on North Carolina if he had not made the fatal blunder of attacking communism. Collection boxes would be rattling on street corners, cocktail parties would be under way, mass meetings and parades would be staged. But he offended the Stalinists, so not even Mrs. Roosevelt seems to have recognized this particular and especially striking case of social injustice. I can think of few greater proofs of the power of Stalin in America than the fact that he holds Beal—whose innocence few doubt—in an American prison!

William Henry Chamberlin, a newspaperman of academic temper, covered Moscow for over twelve years for the *Christian Science Monitor*. In his early years he was widely quoted by the communists. But after the advent of Stalin he became more critical, his dismay finally finding expression in *Russia's Iron Age*. Whereupon he was branded in American fellow-traveling circles as an agent of Hitler and the Mikado. The story was spread diligently and is still circulating that Chamberlin began attacking Russia after he married "a Russian princess." His wife, whom he married before they ever went to Russia, is a New York high-school teacher of Russian descent.

During the first Five Year Plan, hundreds of American engineers had been drawn to Russia. With few exceptions they returned home with a deep contempt for the Bolshevik pretensions of glory. The process of discrediting these engineers, if they happened to talk too much in public, became a ludicrous routine. When we who were living in Moscow saw a "job" being done on some repatriated American, we knew that he was writing a book or making speeches unfavorable to the Stalin regime. The Moscow *Daily News* was the normal instrument of offense. An article would suddenly appear attacking a given American engineer as a drunkard, a rapist, an embezzler and a phony in his profession. The charges would be supported by affidavits by his former secretaries, interpreters and assistants—as though Russians could refuse to make such affidavits when ordered. The American comrades would be duly notified of the culprit's evil ways— and his reports on Russia could thus be brushed aside.

One reason why the comrades here could operate without the risk of libel laws was that they had the Soviet police force behind them. Anyone who had sojourned in Russia could be accused of anything from murder up, since the G.P.U. would have no trouble manufacturing any number of affidavits and other "proofs" if needed. Beyond that, the communist press managed to juggle its ownership and finances to make a financial threat useless. On the contrary, they usually relished libel suits as an excuse for "defense committees," fundraising and frenzied outcries of "red-baiting."

William G. Ryan of Milwaukee, then a member of the party, enlisted in the International Brigade and fought for the Loyalists in Spain for eighteen months. On several occasions he was cited for valor; he was mentioned in a New York *Times* dispatch as an American hero of the war. But he was gradually revolted by the communist murders of his fellow-volunteers, by the G.P.U. theft of American passports, by the refusal to release men after the expiration of their enlistment periods. Ultimately he escaped from Spain at the risk of his life. When he arrived in New York, the Spanish committee that had recruited him nearly two years before offered him this alternative: either to tell their story, in which case he could have a job and a percentage on collections; or to tell his own story, in which case he would be smeared as a spy and worse. Here is what he wrote later:

Prior to going to Spain, I had never been accused of any crimes or misdemeanors, not even so much as a traffic-law violation. Since my return, I must admit I have been accused of a great many—drunkard, wife-beater, forger, liar, coward, deserter, Hitler spy and, most devastating of all, red-baiter. Strangely enough, I developed all these vicious characteristics in Spain after attaining the age of thirty-four years. By a remarkable coincidence, the deterioration in my character began immediately after I became critical of the murderous methods employed by the Stalinist regime in Spain.

Liston Oak, once editor of *Fight*, the official organ of the League for Peace and Democracy, and long active in other communist work, went to Spain to direct English-language propaganda for the Comintern. What he saw caused him to turn against the Stalinists. When he returned to America the legend that he was a "Franco spy" was already deeply planted. For a long time the comrades succeeded in keeping him off the New York Federal Writers' Project, thus imposing an economic blockade on him. Only his fighting spirit and their fear of a public scandal finally opened the project to him; even then he was allowed to join the Workers Alliance only after a trial *in absentia* by Stalinists in the Alliance—and a warning not to carry on his spying and Franco propaganda!

The same ugly labels were plastered on Sam Baron, a well-known socialist who returned from Loyalist Spain critical of the dictatorial ruthlessness of the communists.

A veteran of the Russian adventure in Spain sat in my office. He was distressed nearly to hysteria. "If I come out and tell what I really think about the Spanish affair," he said, "I'll be called a traitor, a fascist, a spy. I'll be shunned by my friends and avoided even by some members of my own family." At that time he was still making speeches for a Spanish aid committee under Muscovite control.

One of the signers of the notorious document whitewashing the Moscow trials, Dr. Bernard D. N. Grebanier, having finally freed himself of the communist obsession, revealed part of the compulsion under which fellow-travelers lived. In a letter to the *New Leader* (September 9, 1939), he referred to himself bitterly as "one of the fools who signed the statement whitewashing the Soviet treason trials." He did it, he explained, despite "gravest doubts as to Stalin's integrity." He was terrified by the prospect of being called a "Trotskyite," a veritable mark of Cain in the milieu in which he lived and worked.

"Out of a desire to avoid that dreadful stigma myself," he wrote, "when I was asked to sign that statement and knew that some of the signers had doubts equal to my own, I put my name on it. Only those who have been allied to the communists can have any idea of the weapon they wield in being able to brand as a disciple of Trotsky anyone who takes exception to Stalin."

4

We have seen how Waldo Frank was reduced from the chairmanship of the League of American Writers to an outlaw status among its members for one slip off the party line. The same general fate, embellished with bad language and repulsive rumor, awaited anyone who ran afoul of the comrades. The operation of the character assassins was wondrous to behold. They seemed to relish the work. They put their hearts into it. Both Westbrook Pegler and Harold Ickes could take lessons in vituperative letters from practitioners like Gold, Forsythe, Harrison George. Here is a sample of communist rhetoric, excerpted from the *Daily Worker*, directed against some hapless excomrade, as far back as 1924:

One particularly loathsome specimen of that type [renegade radical] ... is X. Y. Physically he is a big chunk of animated protoplasm who wears a 22-inch collar and a 6¼-inch hat. The brain capacity of a moron, with the neck of a gorilla. ... The political pus that flows from the social excrescence which is personified in X. Y. finds its way into the organs of big business. ...

Many of those who later became useful stooges of the party went through their own baptism of mud at the hands of the comrades. In 1934 a *New Masses* cartoon showed Upton Sinclair as an insect on the boot of a capitalist marching straight for fascism. He expiated his sins when he joined the Popular Front of know-nothing defense of the Stalinist terror and thus won immunity. The apex of his glory as a Muscovite megaphone was reached when he spoke by direct wire from Pasadena, California, to a mass meeting in New York in fervid approval of Stalin's "liquidation" of the Old Bolsheviks. He certainly had traveled far since the days of *The Jungle*, since human slaughter could leave him so beautifully untouched.

Heywood Broun, too, had tasted communist abuse. "A scabby rat becomes a desirous household pet," the *Daily Worker* said editorially on May 5, 1934, compared to a journalist like Broun, the "fat, bloated enemy of the heroic Toledo strikers." But bygones were bygones in the years when Broun, cagily through his capitalist daily column, without restraint in his weekly *New Republic* piece, acted as Browder's hatchet man against infidels.

James T. Farrell, the author of *Studs Lonigan* and other novels, was among Broun's favorite targets. At one time he described Farrell as conducting a "one-man picket line" against the Writers Congress—a pure invention, of course. Although once he had championed plain speaking in literature, he now attacked Farrell as a "reactionary" who sought "escape . . . in a swamp." If this were simply one columnist's change of mind, it would be meaningless. But it was only a strand in an elaborate pattern of calumny against the novelist since he had turned against Stalinist hypocrisy and power-politics. In February of one year the *Daily Worker* had reckoned Farrell in "the ranks of the outstanding young writers of fiction," but by October it described him as "standing still, ideologically." A few months later it had stripped him of every vestige of talent. The *New Republic* (January 12, 1938), indeed, had the ill grace to publish a round robin signed by twenty-five people attacking Mr. Farrell in slimy language. The publication of such a gang-up letter against a recognized novelist was, to put it most mildly, an extraordinary and unprecedented procedure.

It was the price men of talent paid for refusal to play the Stalinist game. The price could not deter a Farrell or a Dos Passos. It did keep scores of lesser literati in line.

The one word "GREATNESS" headed a review of a book by John Dos Passos in August, 1936. His skill, his social-mindedness and human qualities were constantly extolled in the communist and liberal press. Then Dos Passos, too, went to Spain. He was horrified by the operations of the Stalinist camarilla in and behind the Loyalist lines, and he said so. The much-reiterated verdict on him was thereupon reversed. Comrade Gold was the trigger man in a column denouncing not merely Dos Passos' politics but his art:

Like the Frenchman Celine, Dos Passos hates communists because organically he seems to hate the human race. It is strange to see how little real humaneness there is in his book. He takes a dull, sadistic joy in showing human beings in their filthiest, meanest, most degenerate moments.

Comrade Gold pretended to find the clue to Dos Passos' character in his occasional use of four-letter words. Curiously, however, the communist press at the same time began acclaiming Ernest Hemingway, whose use of such words is more extensive and notorious. (Hemingway, after a honeymoon of Stalinist favor, would receive his share of comradely vituperation a few years later—when he, in his turn, would tell too much about the communists in Spain in his novel *For Whom the Bell Tolls*.)

Reviewers who watched their Stalinist p's and q's discovered that Dos Passos had never really known how to write. By the time his novel *Adventures of a Young Man* appeared, in the summer of 1939, he was among the top layer of "renegades." The critical ganging-up was no surprise to those familiar with the intellectual red terror. A few of the emancipated reviewers dealt with the book as a literary work, pro and con: Harry Hansen and John Chamberlain, for instance. Many of the other big-time reviewers simply excommunicated it on thinly disguised political grounds.

The novel traces the disillusionment of an idealistic young American with the communists at home and later on the Spanish battlefields. Although for years they had touted the novel of social consciousness, certain critics—Louis Kronenberger, Malcolm Cowley, Elliot Paul, Alfred Kazin, etc.—now realized belatedly that the introduction of politics spoils a novel. Several of them improvised the thesis that "disillusionment," being negative, cannot be the basis of a good novel. Since many of the world's greatest novels rest on disillusionment, it was apparently the author's specific disillusionment with Stalinism that evoked this theory.* As James T. Farrell summed it up:

The reception given *The Adventures of a Young Man* reads like a warning to writers not to stray off the reservations of the Stalinist-controlled League of American Writers, to which more than one of the critics belong. What renders these critics suspect is their striking tone of unanimity.†

Another revealing item: Boris Souvarine's *Stalin: A Critical Survey of Bolshevism* appeared in an American edition in the autumn of 1939. It is a scholarly volume that had long been known to students of Russian history. The daily reviewer of the New York *Times*, Ralph Thompson, dismissed the book in one casual and contemptuous paragraph, branding those who praised it as "local followers of Leon Trotsky." They were nothing of the sort—indeed, the book is as vigorously anti-Trotsky as it is anti-Stalin—and Mr. Thompson later apologized publicly for mislabeling, but he never got around to an intelligent appraisal of the book.

---

* A typical discussion, quoting many of the reviewers, appeared in the *New Masses*, July 4, 1939.

† The *American Mercury*, August, 1939.

It was no easy thing for a book unpalatable to the comrades to obtain an objective review in the leading metropolitan papers during the "best" years of the Red Decade. Men like Rascoe, Hansen, Brickell and Chamberlain risked it; many others either panned anti-Soviet books or ignored them. The silliest tourist account of Soviet glories rated their attention, but not books like those of Andrew Smith or George Kitchin. The Sunday book sections, under different editorial control, were far more fair, though *Books*, the New York *Herald Tribune* supplement, was honeycombed with Stalinists who did their stuff boldly under the innocent Irita Van Doren's nose.

When I published *Moscow Carrousel*, someone in Miss Van Doren's department gave it for review, of all people, to Louis Fischer! One might as well give an atheist tract to the bishop for calm appraisal. The resultant "review" was of such a nature that Miss Van Doren kept it out—and the volume was never reviewed at all. The daily *Herald Tribune* reviewer followed the current party strategy by stating that my "difficulties with the censors" were largely responsible for my acid pictures of Soviet life. I wrote him, pointing out that 90 per cent of the book had been written before the alleged difficulties, which were a communist post-factum invention anyhow. To which he replied with this curious and revealing explanation:

I think that any newspaperman who lived for years in Moscow seems to acquire a certain morbidity of mind, which expresses itself in various ways. Your book seemed to me to suggest that you had suffered less from it than might have been anticipated.

In other words, the "unfriendly" reports of the U.S.S.R. by men who lived there for long periods were the result of a sort of mental ailment! He did not inquire *why* Moscow gave resident reporters "a certain morbidity of mind"—the causes, for him, were in difficulties with the censors and not in the horrors of the Soviet reality.

By this time, of course, nearly all the literary fellow-travelers have presumably renounced their Stalinist associations. But curiously they do not yet find it possible to approach an anti-Stalinist book calmly. Either they puff aloud in the attempt to find reasons for discrediting it—see their reviews of Jan Valtin's *Out of the Night*—or they evade the issue by pretending not to notice the offending volume. One example must suffice:

In 1940 a remarkable book on her Soviet experiences was published by Freda Utley, an English economist. It was called *The Dream
We Lost*. It was at once a deeply touching personal narrative and a
detailed, documented analysis. Her books on foreign affairs had in
the past been reviewed and always favorably. This one was her most
ambitious and intensive work. It was put out by a reputable publisher.
Bertrand Russell, in *The Saturday Review of Literature*, described it
as the most important book as yet written on Russia. *Not a single one
of the regular daily reviewers of the major newspapers, however, even
mentioned it!* They shied away from it, perhaps because it was too annoying a reminder of their own gullibility and literary power-politics
of the years which Miss Utley described so well.

In the years of the Popular Front far-reaching sabotage of books
frowned upon by the comrades was almost automatic. A few—the
Tchernavins', Chamberlin's, my own—prospered despite this. Yet
every writer who indited a novel or biography or play likely to offend
the Browder boys knew as a certainty that he could expect to be hit
over the head by many of the leading critics. They would question the
motives of the author in "attacking Socialist Russia," though it never
occurred to them to question the motives of the Fischers and Hindus'
and Durantys in kowtowing to Russia. They would work in, as
though by accident, the special set of libels being circulated about the
author by the Stalinist character assassins.

Not infrequently the ganging-up began before an "undesirable"
book was published. I mentioned how a West Coast Writers Congress assailed *We Cover the World* in its prenatal stage, merely because they did not approve the editor. The campaign to discredit Stolberg's *Story of the C.I.O.* began months before it appeared. Dozens of
progressive union leaders inside the C.I.O. helped Mr. Stolberg with
the research; few books in the labor field had been so carefully checked
and supported by documentary citations. But no sooner was the
book announced than the publisher began receiving letters and telephone calls attacking the author's accuracy. One of the most virulent
attacks arrived on the letterhead of the League of American Writers,
signed by its secretary, Franklin Folsom. Mr. Folsom followed point
by point the arguments current in the communist press. Similar
letters reached the publisher from Ralph Roeder, Meyer Levin and
others closely associated at the time with fellow-traveler enterprises.

Longmans, Green & Co. publish the Living Thoughts Library. A volume in the series is devoted to Karl Marx, and the editor invited Trotsky to write a foreword. Before public announcement of this fact had been made, the tidings reached Stalinist headquarters. A representative of the Communist Party called on the publishers, another on the editor of the series. They urged that the use of Trotsky's foreword was a "mistake" and warned that if not corrected a boycott might be invoked against the whole series.

These publishers ignored the threats, which reached them in increasing volume. But the same cannot be said for all publishers. From experience they knew that anti-communist books started off with a heavy handicap not only in liberal and quasi-liberal publications but in the hands of many reviewers for major newspapers and magazines. The Book and Magazine Guild, strongly communist in its leadership, was also able to put in some good licks for the cause by undermining "undesirable" manuscripts and authors.

Books slanted to conform to the party line, by the same token, started with a critical advantage. All along the line there were hands eager to push them. There was the Book Union, devoted exclusively to promoting Stalinist books. There was a (Stalinoid) Wholesale Book Corporation, buying books in quantity for a series of Left Wing or workers' bookshops. These outlets do not add up to much, but they took the edge off the risk of publishing.

And all these pressures and threats and favors contributed to the cumulative cultural red terror. You either belonged or you didn't. And if you didn't the dice were loaded against you. What applied to literary callings applied no less to the theatre, the movies, painting, dancing. Preponderant Stalinist influence on the American Newspaper Guild extended the terror to a portion of the press. Secretly edited communist "shop papers" in the New York Times, on Time magazine and other publications made life miserable not only for the bosses (whose correspondence was regularly rifled for these papers and whose private lives were invaded) but for anti-Stalinist radicals on the staff. Virtual communist control on many Federal Writers', Theatre and Art Projects were also enormously useful to the comrades in holding the cultural front for Stalin. Many of the project and other W.P.A. offices resembled Communist Party headquarters, with communist literature for sale, party dues and assessments being collected, and party announcements on the bulletin boards.

From the loftiest penthouse to the lowliest W.P.A. ditchdigging, the intellectual red terror held sway. It all sounds like something out of Gilbert and Sullivan, but there was nothing in the least funny about it to the favorite victims. The imprint is still deep in the flesh of American culture. Philip Rhav, an editor of *Partisan Review* and thoroughly familiar with the politics of the intellectual Left, once summed it all up thus:

The result has been that a kind of unofficial censorship is now menacing the intellectual freedom of those Left-wing writers who are known to be opposed to the bureaucratic dictatorship in Moscow and to its representatives abroad. This G.P.U. of the mind is attempting—through intrigue, calumny and overt as well as covert pressure—to direct cultural opinion into totalitarian channels.*

If he erred, it was on the side of understatement.

---

* *New Leader,* December 10, 1938.

Chapter XXVIII

THE LAST LOONY SCENE

1

THE last days of the Red Decade were enlivened by a gesture more profligate in its absurdity, more tragic for the dignity of its dupes than anything that had gone before. As though with a premonition that the comedy was drawing to an abrupt end, the actors hurried to compound a document truly gargantuan in its grotesqueness. It is hard to believe that some satiric genius with a gift of prophecy did not have a hand in the manufacture of the situation. Two dates—with an interval of only nine days between them—compass the lunacy.

1. *August 14, 1939:* Some four hundred Americans, among them important figures in education, the arts, sciences and religion, issued a long Open Letter branding as "fascists" and "reactionaries" all those who dared suggest "the fantastic falsehood that the U.S.S.R. and the totalitarian states are basically alike." The letter in particular castigated the Committee for Cultural Freedom, formed some months earlier, for including Russia among the totalitarian nations that suppress cultural independence and deny civil freedoms.

2. *August 23, 1939:* Both Berlin and Moscow made it known that their respective dictatorships had entered into a pact of friendship, non-aggression and mutual economic aid—the pact which was the signal for the Second World War.

Some four hundred reputable Americans, including the most active fellow-travelers of the moment, had thus climbed way out on a limb to denounce those who saw totalitarian features on the face of the Soviet despotism. The echoes of their denunciation had not yet died down when Stalin, with all the dramatic skill of which he is capable, joined Herr von Ribbentrop, his guest at the Kremlin, in calling these four hundred—and millions the world over whose self-delusions and mendacity the fatuous four hundred typified—dupes. . . . Humiliated dupes of a four-year-old hoax. There were those among the betrayed

342

four hundred who would have given their right arms to have avoided this public exhibition of their naïveté. It took the shock of the Nazi-Soviet nuptials to make them aware that they had long been used to play a sinister game for an unprincipled foreign dictator.

A more clownish finale for the Red Decade, I submit, could hardly have been figured out by a Shakespeare with the assistance of George S. Kaufman. All the absurdity of the communist show, of the excited periphery, of the fertile Popular Front frauds, were summed up in this last gesture of political chicanery wedded to starry-eyed innocence.

2

But before we look more closely at the amazing document of self-revelation, we must touch on the Committee for Cultural Freedom. It was primarily as an "answer" to this Committee that the extra-ordinary Open Letter was conceived and carried through, although most of its signers were left in ignorance of that fact.

In the spring of 1939 a group of men and women opposed to all forms of suppression in the domain of culture—whether at home or abroad, whether under Nazi or Fascist or Bolshevik slogans—banded together to ward off the encroachments of totalitarian thinking in our own country. Among the prime movers of the undertaking were John Dewey, Sidney Hook, Victor Riesel, Benjamin Stolberg, Ferdinand Lundberg, Horace M. Kallen, Suzanne La Follette, Frank H. Trager, Henry Hazlitt, and the writer. Since all Stalinists would have been ready to defend, or pretend to defend, the arts, sciences and education against Nazi and Italian brands of totalitarian suppression, what really distinguished this group—and the hundreds who soon joined them—was that they refused to exempt Stalin and his cohorts from the general indictment. And that was the key to the bitterness against them not only in the frankly communist press but in the crypto-communist circles of which the Nation and the New Republic editors were both typical and in the leadership.

My own task was to compose a statement for this Committee for Cultural Freedom as the least common denominator of principle on which the intellectually honest could join together. The statement was adopted as I wrote it, except for some technical editing. It de-clared, among other things, that:

Under varying labels and colors, but with an unvarying hatred for the free mind, the totalitarian idea is already enthroned in Germany, Italy, Russia, Japan and Spain. There intellectual and creative independence is suppressed and punished as a form of treason. Art, science and education—all have been forcibly turned into lackeys for a supreme state, a deified leader and an official pseudo-philosophy. . . . Literally thousands of German, Italian, Russian and other victims of cultural dictatorship have been silenced, imprisoned, tortured or hounded into exile.

We then went on to warn that the totalitarian idea "threatens to overwhelm nations where the democratic way of life, with its cultural liberty, is still dominant," among them the United States. Then we hit out at the kind of "liberals" and "democrats" who hurrahed for the Soviet brand of suppression while excoriating other sorts:

Through subsidized propaganda, through energetic agents, through political pressure, the totalitarian states succeeded in infecting other countries with their false doctrines, in intimidating independent artists and scholars, and in spreading panic among the intellectuals. Already many of those who would be crippled or destroyed by totalitarianism are themselves yielding to panic. In fear or despair they hasten to exalt one brand of intellectual servitude over another; to make fine distinctions between various methods of humiliating the human spirit and outlawing intellectual integrity. Many of them have already declared a moratorium on reason and creative freedom. Instead of resisting and denouncing all attempts to straight-jacket the human mind, they glorify, under deceptive slogans and names, the color or the cut of one straight-jacket rather than another.

More than 140 men and women in intellectual pursuits had signed this manifesto by the time it was made public in May. Scores of additional adhesions to this basic formulation of free men's faith came in from all over the country, despite the fact that the Committee, having neither funds nor an organized party behind it, could give its work little or no publicity. A few perspicacious editors here and there realized that this was the first concerted move against Stalinist domination in the field of American thought, but altogether too few of them.

Among the signers, in addition to the few I have already mentioned, were the following—and in that period they constituted a true Roll of Honor:

Louis Adamic
Herbert Agar
Sherwood Anderson
Cyrus LeRoy Baldridge
Ernest Sutherland Bates
Carl Becker
Thomas H. Benton
Prof. P. J. Bridgman
Dr. Paul F. Brissenden
Dorothy Dunbar Bromley
Struthers Burt
Witter Bynner
V. F. Calverton
Henry Seidel Canby
Oliver Carlson
John Chamberlain
Albert Sprague Coolidge
Dr. George S. Counts
G. Watts Cunningham
Wendell P. Dabney
Walter Damrosch
Elmer Davis
Babette Deutsch
Max Eastman
Dr. Irwin Edman
Abraham Epstein
Morris L. Ernst
Edna Ferber
Dorothy Canfield Fisher
Ira Gershwin
Harry D. Gideonse
Abram Harris
George W. Hartman
Philip M. Hicks
Rev. John Haynes Holmes
Sidney Howard
Inez Haynes Irwin
Jerome Kern
William H. Kilpatrick
Irene Corbally Kuhn
Suzanne La Follette

Sinclair Lewis
Thomas Mann
Benjamin C. Marsh
Milton S. Mayer
Claude McKay
Ernest L. Meyer
Wesley C. Mitchell
Marston Morse
Gorham Munson
David S. Muzzey
Stephen Naft
Henry Neumann
James Oneal
H. A. Overstreet
Walter Pach
Saul K. Padover
John Dos Passos
Ralph Barton Perry
Lorine Pruette
Winifred Raushenbush
James Rorty
Leonard Q. Ross
Charles Edward Russell
Morrie Ryskind
George H. Sabine
J. Salwyn Schapiro
George S. Schuyler
Evelyn Scott
George N. Shuster
John Sloan
Louis Stark
Clara G. Stillman
Benjamin Stolberg
Norman Thomas
Dorothy Thompson
Frederic F. Van de Water
Oswald Garrison Villard
M. R. Werner
Frances Winwar
Helen Woodward

Branding these people as "fascists" and "friends of fascists," as "Trotskyites" and "reactionaries" took some daring. But the communists had what it took. An all-out attack on the Committee for Cultural Freedom was launched by the *Daily Worker* and followed obediently—though with face-saving reservations—by the *Nation* and the *New Republic*. Corliss Lamont yelled that it was just a pack of Trotskyites. Most communists yelled with him. Of course the official Trotskyist organs also attacked it, for their own sectarian reasons. Heywood Broun joined the assault—one of his last jobs for Stalin. The *New Republic* refused to print the Committee's statement, but gave lots of space to attacking what it didn't publish. It subtly conveyed the impression that it was a "Trotskyist" committee, and in effect agreed with the communist Open Letter smearing the committee as "fascists" and "reactionaries." The *Nation* did publish the manifesto but with it a long, obscure, panicky attack by editor Freda Kirchwey. In more roundabout style the liberals followed the *Daily Worker* line of ignoring the contents of the Committee's clear, concise statement and creating the misimpression of a Trotskyist in the woodpile.

Nothing that had happened on the Left in the whole course of the Red Decade, not even the Moscow trials had so upset the Thirteenth Street junta. Here was a rallying point for the intellectuals, who heretofore had to choose between Stalinist leadership and none at all. The whole structure of Innocents' Clubs seemed to them at stake. Something had to be done to counteract it, to discredit this cultural front for liberty. The task was entrusted to Corliss Lamont, the little general of the Friends of the Soviet Union, Stalin's equivalent of the German-American Bund.

3

The scheme was to produce a longer document with even more distinguished names to testify that the members of the Committee for Cultural Freedom, from John Dewey down, were just fascist agents of Trotsky. An Initiating Committee of ten members was formed to act as sponsors for this noble undertaking. The hardy ten were Professor Dorothy Brewster, Dashiell Hammett, Corliss Lamont, George Marshall, Professor Walter Rautenstrauch, Vincent Sheean, Donald Ogden Stewart, Maxwell S. Stewart, Rebecca Janney Timbres, Mary Van Kleeck—all hard-worked Popular Front names.

Over the signatures of these ten, Lamont sent out a form letter to thousands of potential signers. It was a masterpiece of political jugglery. For instance, the letter never mentioned the Committee of Cultural Freedom by name, although an attack on it, embedded in the draft of the Open Letter, was the clear purpose of the whole maneuver. "We count on you," it said, "as one of those who will appreciate the importance of answering those who are attempting to destroy the unity of the progressive forces by spreading the false idea that the Soviet Union and the totalitarian states are fundamentally alike." The purpose, it said, was "simply to help clarify the confusion that has been created in some minds by the attempts to bracket the Soviet Union with the Fascist States."

Moreover, they sent along a voluminous "summary" of "supporting material" to prove that Soviet Russia enjoys civil and cultural freedom. But "the names of those who sign the letter," it assured them, "will not be attached to the summary as well." Just an extra bit of the oil of chicanery to make it easier for victims to swallow the concoction.

The Open Letter proper was a gem, especially in the light of the bargain at that very moment being worked out by Molotov and von Ribbentrop. It denied "the fantastic falsehood" that Russia could have anything in common with Germany and called the purveyors of such lies "fascists and their allies" out "to prevent a united anti-aggression front." In particular it pointed the accusing finger at the Committee for Cultural Freedom which was "sowing suspicion between the Soviet Union and other nations interested in maintaining peace." It listed ten—count 'em, folks, exactly ten!—proofs that the Soviet Union differed from other dictatorships.

Among the ten were all the familiar delusions fostered about Russia by its cultists and professional press agents. Number 1, ironically, was that "The Soviet Union continues as always to be a consistent bulwark against war and aggression, and to support the goal of a peaceful international order." This less than a month before Russia marched into Poland! Number 5—that Russia "has built the trade unions," without indicating, of course, that these unions were tied hand and foot, and at bottom nothing more than the state's company unions. Number 7, dealing with the cultural aspect, is delicious. For instance, it indicates that "Those writers and thinkers whose books have been burned by the Nazis are published in the Soviet Union"; never mind the obverse—that books outlawed in

Russia were being published in Germany and Italy. . . . Not a word, of course, of the thousands of writers and scientists in the concentration camps and places of exile.

Point 8 in the line-up is worth special notice. It hails the suppression of "the myths and superstitions of old Russia"—in plain English, the suppression of religion. Any doubt on that score is dispelled by the "supporting material," wherein Point 8 specifies "the superstitions of old-time religion." Now there is no reason why four hundred Americans, even if most of them do go to church occasionally, should not exult over the elimination of religion if they so wish. But when we find among them the Rev. Harry F. Ward of the Union Theological Seminary, the Rev. Otis Jackson, the Rev. Thomas L. Harris and other clergymen, the logic does get a bit thick.

The ultimate news release on the Open Letter was mailed from the office of an American Council for Soviet Affairs, whatever it may be. It claimed that four hundred had signed the amazing document assailing those who dared assert that Russia was a totalitarian regime which interfered with creative freedom. Those who formed the Initiating Committee presumably knew what they were doing; although the violent attacks on Russia by Vincent Sheean only a couple of months later—on the grounds that it was a totalitarian setup!—open even that assumption to doubt. Let us say, therefore, that those who put them up to it knew what they were doing. But the majority were men and women who let themselves be blindfolded and led into a dirty job of character assassination. Most of them would probably be astonished to learn that they had been used to smear "Fascist" in big yellow letters on Professor Dewey, Edna Ferber, Sinclair Lewis, Walter Damrosch and a few hundred others guilty of mentioning Russia along with Germany and Italy among countries denying cultural freedom.

Among the signatories of the 400-signature letter were at least 29 who had also graced the famous 150-signature letter whitewashing the Moscow trials and purges. To have given support to two such documents rates them a special listing as stooges-cum-laude, so here they are:

Marc Blitzstein	Edwin Berry Burgum
Millen Brand	Vera Caspary
Dorothy Brewster	Haakon M. Chevalier

Kyle Crichton
Robert Coates
Muriel Draper
Hugo Gellert
Robert Gessner
Dashiell Hammett
Granville Hicks
Langston Hughes
John Howard Lawson
Corliss Lamont
Jay Leyda
Prof. V. J. McGill

John Hyde Preston
Lynn Riggs
Harold J. Rome
George Seldes
E. Tredwell Smith
Hester Sondergaard
Bernhard J. Stern
Maxwell S. Stewart
Paul Strand
Max Weber
Richard Wright

These dauntless 29 deserve to lead all the rest when diplomas are handed out to the prime window dressers of the Red Decade. Not only had they condoned the blood purges in Stalin's domain, but they had attested that the quality of his oppression was unique and not to be lightly confused with the lines offered by Hitler and Mussolini. Those who joined in the latter public testimony, released to an indifferent world just nine days before Moscow announced its new-found love for Hitler, are listed herewith—precisely as published by the dependable *Daily Worker* on August 14, 1939:

Prof. Newton Arvin of Smith College, Prof. Robert A. Brady of the University of California, Prof. Dorothy Brewster of Columbia University, Prof. Edwin Berry Burgum of New York University, Prof. Haakon Chevalier of the University of California, Prof. Stanley D. Dodge of the University of Michigan, Prof. Dorothy Douglas of Smith College, Prof. L. C. Dunn of Columbia University, Prof. Henry Pratt Fairchild of New York University, Prof. Mildred Fairchild of Bryn Mawr, Prof. Robert Gessner of New York University, Dr. Wyllistine Goodsell of Teachers' College (retired), Prof. Samuel N. Harper of the University of Chicago, Prof. Norman E. Himes of Colgate University, Prof. Alexander Kaun of the University of California, Dr. Max Lerner of Williams College, Prof. Charles E. Lightbody of St. Lawrence College, Prof. Herbert A. Miller of Bryn Mawr College, Prof. F. O. Matthiessen of Harvard University, Anita Marburg of Sarah Lawrence College, Clifford T. McAvoy of C.C.N.Y., Prof. V. J. McGill of Hunter College, Prof. Robert McGregor of Reed College, Prof. Allan Porter of Vassar College, Prof. Paul Radin of the University of California, Prof. Frederick L. Schuman of Williams College,

Prof. Bernhard J. Stern of Columbia University, Prof. Vida D. Scudder of Wellesley College, Prof. Ernest J. Simmons of Harvard University, J. Raymond Walsh, Prof. Robert Morss Lovett of Chicago University, now Governor of the Virgin Islands, F. Tredwell Smith, Charles J. Hendley, President of the New York Teachers' Union.

AMONG THE SOCIAL SCIENTISTS AND SOCIAL WORKERS ARE:

T. A. Bisson of the Foreign Policy Association, Dr. John H. Gray, Leo Huberman, George Marshall, Mary van Kleeck, Mortimer Graves, Helen Alfred, Alice Stone Blackwell, Margaret I. Lamont, Dr. John A. Kingsbury, Mary White Ovington, Bertha Reynolds, Rebecca Janney Timbres, Katherine Deveraux Blake, Harriet G. Eddy.

AMONG THE SCIENTISTS AND ENGINEERS ARE:

Prof. Walter Rautenstrauch, Dean of the Columbia School of Industrial Engineering, Prof. George B. Cressey of Syracuse University, Prof. Robert Chambers of New York University, Earl P. Hanson, explorer, Dr. John P. Peters of Yale Medical School, Dr. Thomas Addis of Leland Stanford University, Prof. Dirk J. Struik of the Massachusetts Institute of Technology, Walter N. Polakov, Dr. Gerald Wendt, Director of Science and Education at the New York World's Fair.

AMONG THE WRITERS, JOURNALISTS AND EDITORS ARE:

Vincent Sheean, George Seldes, Robert Briffault, Louis P. Birk, Millen Brand, Fielding Burke, Robert M. Coates, Maria Cristina Chambers, Lester Cohen, Kyle Crichton, Pietro di Donato, Muriel Draper, Sara Bard Field, Irving Fineman, Marjorie Fischer, Waldo Frank, Angel Flores, Granville Hicks, Agatha Illes, Matthew Josephson, Fred C. Kelly, Beatrice A. Kinkead, Ruth McKenney, Katharine Dupre Lumpkin, Meridel LeSueur, Meyer Levin, Klaus Mann, Carey McWilliams, Harvey O'Connor, Shaemas O'Sheel, S. J. Perelman, John Hyde Preston, William Rollins, Jr., Ralph Roeder, Isobel Walker Soule, Irina Skariatina, Christina Stead, Clara Weatherwax, William Carlos Williams, Ella Winter, Richard Wright, Leane Zugsmith, Albert Rhys Williams, Dashiell Hammett, Corliss Lamont, Bessie Beatty, Maurice Halperin, Associate Editor *Books Abroad*, Frank C. Bancroft, Editor "*Social Work Today*," I. F. Stone, Associate Editor the *Nation*, Jean Starr Untermeyer, Louis Untermeyer, Alfred Kreymborg, Orrick Johns, Langston Hughes, Kenneth Fearing, Stirling Bowen, Vera Caspary, Arthur Kober, George Kauffman, John Howard Lawson, Clifford Odets, Lynn Riggs, Viola Brothers Shore, Donald Ogden Stewart.

AMONG THE ARTISTS, ARCHITECTS AND THEATRICAL PEOPLE ARE:

Hugo Gellert, Wanda Gag, William Gropper, A. E. Steig, James

Thurber, Max Weber, Lynd Ward, Rockwell Kent, Stuyvesant van Veen, Art Young, Maurice Becker, Simon Breines, Eugene Schoen, Anita Block, Lincoln Kirstein, Sam Jaffe, Jay Leyda, Aline MacMahon, Hester Sondergaard, Herman Shumlin, Paul Strand, Marc Blitzstein, Harold J. Rome.

OTHER WELL-KNOWN PEOPLE AMONG THE SIGNERS ARE:

Rev. Otis G. Jackson, Rev. Thomas L. Harris, Prof. Harold E. Luccock, Dr. Harry F. Ward, Dr. Charles S. Bacon, Dr. Williams Henry Walsh, Col. Raymond Robins, former head of the American Red Cross Mission in Russia, S. Stephenson Smith, president of the Oregon Commonwealth Federation, Dr. Joseph A. Rosen, Edward Lamb, Meta Berger, Darwin J. Meserole, George D. Pratt, Jr., Alfred K. Stern, William Osgood Field, Jr., Alice Withrow Field, Dr. Emily M. Pierson, Bernard J. Reis, C. Fayette Taylor, Robert Whitaker, William Dodd, Jr., and many other prominent people from all sections of the country.*

Then came the deluge: the announcement of the Soviet-Nazi alliance, the hasty abandonment of the anti-fascist and pro-democratic pretensions by the communists, the flop-over from "collective security" to unmitigated isolationism, the return to the attack on the New Deal and the "economic royalist" at its head. The most pathetically drenched were these 400 who had charged so bravely under the generalship of Corliss Lamont. Most of them ran to cover. All of them looked silly in their waterlogged condition. A few dozen of them have tried to make amends by outdoing all others in denunciation of the Stalinist betrayers. The *Nation* published the Open Letter of the 400 and the news of the Soviet-Nazi Pact in the same issue! A goofy epoch had exploded in farce. And in the tragedy of war.

4

In the first weeks after Joachim von Ribbentrop and Viacheslav Molotov, in the smug and beaming presence of Joseph Stalin, signed their Moscow-Berlin pact, the most uncomfortable human beings outside a German or Russian concentration camp were the communists and their assorted associates. Most of them in time would memorize the healing rigamarole of ready-made rationalizations of the event.

---

* There are less than the claimed 400 in this list; the absentees must be taken on the *Worker's* say-so.

In those fearful days before the new catechism came through, however, every last comrade felt himself cast tragically in the role of "he who gets slapped."

Stalin's treatment of his foreign employees and friends was peculiarly brutal. With characteristic relish for trickery expertly compounded, he rubbed in his scorn for pensioners in other lands. This time the branch-office managers were not even vouchsafed a preview of the new line. They were not even allowed a period of grace in which to prepare the regular clientele, at least, for the new political goods. The Browders of America, the Harry Pollitts of England, the Thorez' of France were in the middle of their serenades to democracy and anti-fascist collective security when the slop pails of Muscovite contempt were emptied on their heads.

The first report of the pact was flashed on the radio on a Monday evening. That night the early editions of the Tuesday papers carried the story. But the official organ of the Communist Party of the United States of America, the *Daily Worker*, was without information on the matter for over twenty-four hours. Party leaders could not be reached for comment—they were all in hiding. Not until Wednesday did their mouthpiece confirm that the capitalist press for once had told the truth. Russia had indeed made a great contribution to peace by getting together with Germany.

Browder recovered from a brief diplomatic illness and conceded an interview to the press. He analyzed Stalin's "master stroke" for the preservation of peace. The Axis was smashed. The pact, he asserted with an air of inside knowledge, would have an "escape clause" under which the Soviets could repudiate the agreement if this fellow Hitler tried any aggression against Poland or Rumania. The reporters had scarcely filed out of his chromium-fitted office when the text of the Soviet-Nazi agreement was made public. Alas, there was no such escape clause.

Nevertheless, Israel Amter, one of Stalin's yes men, climbed out on a limb to inform his customers that if Poland were invaded the Soviet fatherland would rush to its aid. The confusion and panicky alibis were not limited to American comrades. In all countries they were equally at sea. The British communist leader, Harry Pollitt, made the blunder of writing a pamphlet for his party brethren urging support of Poland against Nazi aggression. Almost immediately, on word from Moscow, he was removed from the leadership and his pamphlet was destroyed. Later Pollitt publicly confessed his sins in this outrageous assumption that communists should protest Hitler's war and was reinstated in Stalin's good graces. Sir Stafford Cripps— who might be described unkindly as the Corliss Lamont of England—recorded his panic in these searching phrases: "A pact of non-aggression between Russia and Germany will be a great reinforcement for peace in Eastern Europe. At the same time it is a lie to suggest it leaves Germany a free hand against Poland or anyone else." Such sagacity clearly qualified him as British Ambassador to Moscow soon thereafter.

Amter and Cripps notwithstanding, it was precisely in Eastern Europe that peace was first shattered. Stalin did rush into Poland— to knife it in the back as it fought Hitler face to face. Day after day the world watched the discomfiture and humiliation of the Stalinist agents. No sooner had they adjusted their story, than Moscow proceeded to kick it into a shapeless and ludicrous heap. If Stalin had decided, sadistically, to humble his foreign henchmen and underscore their moral and intellectual servitude to the Kremlin, he could not have done it more effectively. After that any pretense of independence or political initiative on the part of the American, or any other, national Communist Party became impossible.

The Soviet-Nazi rapprochement did not come unexpectedly to neutral observers, as I have indicated elsewhere. A dozen or more prominent journalists had long foretold its advent. Many of us had been aware of the intensive negotiations between Nazis and Bolsheviks all through the years of the "democratic" party line. Significant hints of the get-together maneuvers could be detected even in the fantasies developed around the Moscow trials and the shootings of the Red Army commanders. In a series of articles in the Saturday Evening Post the late General Krivitsky, for years in charge of Soviet military intelligence in Western Europe, had disclosed the details of Stalin's unrelenting efforts to win over Hitler.

But clearly it had come as a surprise to Stalin's own faithful. Six weeks before the pact Comrade Browder had been asked at a session of the Institute of Public Affairs in Charlottesville, Virginia, whether there was a possibility "of the Soviet Union entering into an agreement with Germany." The Thirteenth Street Führer sneered at such an absurdity. "The most active source of such rumors," he explained, "is Berlin, which has hopes of confusing the democracies with such

stories. There is about as much chance of such an agreement as of
Earl Browder being elected president of the American Chamber of
Commerce." The *Daily Worker* had indignantly dismissed similar
suggestions as "the filthy falsehood that the Soviet Union was considering an agreement . . . with the bestial Nazi regime." Back in
November, 1938, the blundering Browder had declared in a public
address:

The reactionaries openly speculate that the Soviet Union may try
to beat Chamberlain at his own game by joining hands with Hitler.
But even those who hate the land of socialism cannot believe it, when
they see that the Soviet Union alone rounds up the traitorous agents
of Hitler within its own land and puts them beyond the possibility
of doing any more of their wrecking, spying and diversions for fascism.

Less than three months before the "filthy falsehood" came true,
the *Daily Worker* wrote:

The whispered lies to the effect that the Soviet Union will enter
into a treaty of understanding with Nazi Germany are nothing but
poison spread by the enemies of peace and democracy, the appease-
ment-mongers, the Munich-men of fascism.

Of course the Nazis had been left no less in the dark about the
business. Fritz Kuhn, the Brown Browder, had warned his followers:
"Rumors that Germany will enter into a pact with communist Russia
are part of a campaign to smear Hitler with the communist brush."
Marshal Goering's own paper had declared: "As long as we remain
National Socialists, true to our ideals, there can never be any commerce between Nordic Germany and Asiatic Russia."

But their respective masters knew better.

CHAPTER **XXIX**

THE MELANCHOLY RETREAT OF
THE LIBERALS

1

THE most pitiful victims of the pact were not the Browders and
Amters. The contemptuous blows of their master's whip were,
after all, the occupational hazards of stooging for a headstrong dictator. The real victims were the fellow-travelers in Stalin's entourage,
self-deluded and self-righteous. They were not only struck but made
ludicrous. They found themselves stripped in the market place, their
most intimate intellectual parts exposed. They had not even a decent
alibi for gullibility to cover their nakedness. Their acceptance of the
Kremlin's "democracy" had been a feat of faith, since the oppression
and totalitarian horrors inside Russia were spread for all to see who
cared to open their eyes. The inner core of moral identity between
Hitlerism and Stalinism had been attested year after year by experts
on both dispensations. Our fellow-travelers could not claim that they
had been fooled—they had so conspicuously fooled themselves.

For years they had preferred pretty fables to grim realities. They
had drugged themselves with ideological cocktail parties, make-believe
united fronts, puerile rationalizations of the horrors. Having swallowed
a man-made famine, the purge trials and mass executions of the preceding years, they could not even squawk about the natural climax
of the process in the temporary merging of the Red and Brown streams
of fascism. To American fellow-travelers the Kremlin's alignment with
Hitler must have seemed the Russian dictator's greatest atrocity, with
themselves as the victims.

The more self-respecting among them faced the truth of their
own nakedness. Dr. John Haynes Holmes, for instance, courageously
admitted that he and other liberals had been taken for a ride. "I
am sick over this business," he said in a Sunday sermon, "as though
I saw my father drunk and my daughter on the street. And all the
more, since I feel that I have deceived myself as well as been deceived."

355

He might have added to the indictment, in justice to his admirers, that he had helped to deceive others on this subject. He went on:

If we liberals were right on certain single aspects of the Russian Revolution, we were wrong, disgracefully wrong, on the question as a whole. We were wrong because, in our enthusiasm over Russia's liberation from the Czar, our hope for the further liberation of the Russian people from economic as well as political serfdom and our vision of a new world springing from the womb of this Russian experiment, we permitted ourselves to condone wrongs that we knew must be wrongs. We consented to violations of principle that we knew to be fatal to the moral integrity of mankind.

We defended, or at least apologized for, evils in the case of Russia which horrified us wherever else they appeared, and by whomsoever else they were done. We accepted covertly, if not openly, the most dangerous and ultimately disastrous idea that can lodge within the human mind, namely, that the end justifies the means.

But not many had Dr. Holmes' moral gumption. The liberal magazines and the vast majority of the fellow-travelers, including those who broke publicly with the communists, preferred to transfer the deception to another level. Everything had been lovely in their red Utopia, they now pretended, until August 23, 1939, when things went haywire. They preferred to see themselves as the victims of an accident rather than as dupes of a deliberate hoax. Steadfastly, therefore, they refused to see the Russian alliance with Nazi Germany as a product of the Stalinist counter-revolution, as a natural consequence and historical confirmation of the long steady drift of the Russian Revolution from its original moorings.

It was more comforting to regard the whole thing as a sudden aberration or even as a masterpiece of Machiavellism to trip up Hitler. Always the cultists of Russia-worship managed to dispose of unpleasant truths piecemeal—now explaining away a famine, now wishing away a blood purge, now finding alibis for oil shipments to Mussolini. As long as they could evade drawing a line under all these things, they could keep themselves in a state of ideological hypnosis. Even thus they now "approved" or "attacked" the line-up with the Nazis as though it were in a historical void, rather than an act conditioned by the amoralism of Bolshevik thinking, the totalitarian trends of Stalin's epoch, the whole Soviet tragedy of these years.

Despite all the rationalizations, however, the incredible revolution was over. It had been snuffed out by Stalin, as arbitrarily as it had been ignited. Long official explanations of the Soviet betrayal of the millions in its periphery finally came from headquarters. The anti-fascist and anti-Nazi slogans were dropped. Criticism of Hitler disappeared from the party press and Innocents' Clubs. The boycott of Nazi goods was called off. The illicit Popular Front in Washington collapsed—what remained of it functioned as an internal opposition to the New Deal and as a secret partnership on specific issues.

Moscow's Fourth Period, with its high hopes and low chicaneries, its grotesque pretensions and bizarre social amalgams, died a sudden and humiliating death.

2

Those who observed the intellectual scene in America with open eyes during the Red Decade often remarked that nothing could surpass, for moral confusion, the co-operation of men of letters and of learning with every Stalinist crime at home and abroad. They were wrong. In the last months of 1939 and the first months of 1940 it was surpassed, with considerable margin to spare, by some of these same intellectuals in the panicky retreat from Moscow after the pact.

Few of them broke clean. Having admitted so late the villainies of the Kremlin, they stopped short of admitting also their own share in those villainies. Not one of them apologized manfully to colleagues whom they had so long plastered with sticky epithets for the crime of seeing sooner through the Kremlin's crimes. Few of them worked up the intellectual fortitude to express decent regret over former vehemence in approving man-made famines, bloody purges, routine ganging-up on heretics, or over former cowardice in approving these things by silence.

Worse. Most of these post-pact renegades adopted sanctimonious attitudes of hurt innocence. Stalin, Browder and Mike Gold had misled the poor dears, promising them Utopia and delivering the Mannerheim Line. . . . A dozen years of counter-revolution, millions of corpses, the Soviet fueling of Mussolini's war on Abyssinia and other such trifles might have suggested to these gentry that their virtue was in danger. But no, nothing short of the rape of Poland and Finland could suffice to disabuse their trustful simplicity! For some of them even the marriage with Hitler was not enough—they waited for the bloody honeymoon in Poland. The novelist Ralph Bates waited for the invasion of Finland before giving up the Stalinist ghost, and the Kremlin *golom* possessed Malcolm Cowley even beyond that.

In viewing these post-pact penitents, we have only the alternative of deciding whether the fault is with their understanding or with their integrity. Here we do not confront men who wrestled with their consciences and emerged into the light after a long, slow, soul-searing climb from the pit. There was no interval of searching and study such as others went through; no slow, painful cycle from illusion through doubt to disillusionment. They simply kicked over the traces as suddenly as they had once adopted their totalitarian faiths. It is possible to agree with the communist charge that such "conversions" smelled of opportunism.

A few of them—fantastic though it sounds—even made a virtue out of their long silence or their long defense of what they now admitted were horrible crimes and injustices and betrayals. They actually patted themselves on the back for their heroism in keeping quiet— or in shouting hurrah, as the case may be—while the horrors were transpiring under their intellectual noses. They did not blame themselves for stupidity or moral callousness in supporting a criminal regime—they blamed Stalin for shaming them with a Soviet-Nazi pact and the robbing of helpless neighbors. Which is a good deal like being indignant with a weasel for behaving—like a weasel.

Sidney Hook wrote a brilliant essay about these strange intellectuals who remained superior and self-righteous in the midst of a conspicuous demonstration of their tragic blundering.* He questioned the sincerity of men who were offended with Stalin's most recent crimes but failed to disavow the whole inseparably linked chain of crimes. Professor Hook wrote in part:

It does not betoken a change of heart to appeal from Stalin drunk to Stalin not-so-drunk! It betokens fear—a fear that Stalin has carried his crimes too far, a fear that may be allayed if Stalin proves that he can get away with it.

What shall we say of the political philosophy of a group whose proclamation of emancipation from Stalin reduces itself to the charge

---

* The *Socialist Call*, January 13, 1940.

that he has murdered one man too many, committed one crime too many; which deplores merely the extra stroke that betrays the butcher in one who had been applauded as a master of a fine art? Why should we trust those who are outraged by the broken bodies of Finnish workers, women and children but who still see nothing amiss in the Stalinist massacre and mutilation of their working class opponents in Spain, and who openly admit that they would still glorify Stalin if he confined his tortures to the cellars of the Lubianka and the wastes of the Russian Arctic. Is Finnish blood more precious than Spanish or Russian blood?

And yet we can, with an effort of the will, find a little compassion for the men in their panic of fear and despair. The fact is that Stalin *had* gone too far. It was as though you had connived with a criminal in a matter of simple forgery or theft and he had made you a party to multiple murder. The *New Yorker* found words of sympathy for the betrayed liberals and literati on which I cannot improve. It pointed out editorially that the Moscow-Berlin alliance had made a laughing stock out of these people. Then it added:

The attack on Finland, however, as calculated and bloody as anything that happened in Spain or Poland or Czecho-Slovakia, will probably temper the general amusement. It is easy to laugh at a man whose religion merely turns out to be disreputable politics; it is something else when it comes down to cold-hearted murder.

3

Vincent Sheean was one of those who prided himself, in the midst of his confessional, that he had never before attacked Stalin's Russia. Not, mind you, through ignorance of Stalin's crimes. The confessional—a series of articles in the *New Republic* in November, 1939—bears overwhelming witness to the fact that he knew the unpleasant truth all along. The Soviet regime, he affirmed, had resulted in "the most horrifying and bloodthirsty terrorism of modern times," in which "every vital principle of socialism from Marx to Lenin had been . . . vitiated, perverted or ignored." What is more, he backed up these views with the kind of detailed facts and theoretical discussion which no human being could have stored up or thought out in a month or a year. Clearly he knew all along—and now congratulated himself

on his noble forbearance in saying nothing about it to the men and
women who had hung on his every word and looked to him for
guidance.

Strange logic! With all the "horrifying" facts in his possession,
he said he had yet reserved "a special patience and understanding for
the Soviet Union," no matter how "deeply disturbed and apprehen-
sive" he had been all the time. A few weeks later he explained in
a letter "how difficult it had been for me to surrender an obstinate
hope."* This is not the language of reason but the language of un-
reasoning faith. Not until the solemn hour of this confessional had
he "been willing to discuss Stalin (or even, in fact, to mention him)
in print."

To begin with, this assertion must be put down as a curious understatement. It happens that his reports on Spain had been accurately
on the party line, at a time when other observers were trying to tell
some disturbing truths about the Stalinist invasion of Loyalist Spain.
If that isn't "discussing Stalin," his "out" is pretty technical. When
Sheean contributed his name to resolutions and manifestoes condoning
the "horrifying and bloodthirsty terrorism," perhaps he was likewise
detouring "discussion of Stalin."

But then we come to the notorious "letter of the 400," in
which the octogenarian John Dewey and several hundred others were
assailed as "fascists and allies of fascists" for pronouncing Stalin's ineffable name in the same breath with Hitler's. Sheean was not simply
one of the herd of four hundred, but one of the select ten of the
Initiating Committee which corralled the herd. What is more, his
letter soliciting signatures was attached to a lengthy document out-
lining ten specific points wherein Russia's purity contrasted with
Germany's and Italy's sinfulness.

At this juncture I rise to protest that we can no longer exempt
him from the sin of discussing Stalin. I have the document at hand.
It's a comprehensive document in support of Stalin and Stalinism.
When Sheean took part in the concoction he not only knew the
truth but three months later specifically demonstrated that in all ten
of the enumerated points Stalin's guilt was at least equal to Hitler's
and Mussolini's!

To have evaded that truth year after year, at the same time assailing

---

* The *Nation*, December 13, 1939.

those who tried to reveal it, is hardly a record deserving the laurels which Sheean awards himself. Professor Hook can scarcely be blamed for characterizing the thing as a "voluntary petition in intellectual bankruptcy." Sheean's claim that he had not actually approved Stalin's major crimes hardly saves him from that bankruptcy. He was writing and lecturing continually on the state of the world in those years, and failure to tell what he knew about one-sixth part of that world— a part, moreover, which profoundly affected life in the other five-sixths—was, to put it mildly, scarcely playing fair with his audiences.

He carried rationalization so far that after the announcement of the Moscow-Berlin Axis he went on the air to "explain" and defend it; that he did a creditable job of it is attested by the fact that the *New Masses* proudly published his explanation. With the cocksureness of blind faith he predicted that Russia would not invade Poland, whatever wicked anti-Soviet commentators might say on the subject. The chronology of his "conversion" reads more like the record of a breathless race: *August 14*—publication of his attack on the low "fascists" who compared Russia with Germany. *August 23*—his open-minded exoneration of Stalin in the matter of the pact which touched off a world war. *November 1*—his flaming denunciation of Russia as the Thermidor, the counter-revolution and fascism rolled into one.

I have enlarged on Vincent Sheean only because, being among the most confused of the lot, he offers such a tempting clinical case of the neuropathology of Stalinism. Because Sheean is a brilliant and sensitive writer, as well as a peerless reporter, his strange career among Stalinists is the more remarkable. I present him only as a type. If a man of his talents could have blundered so pathetically, it is easier to understand the hundreds of lesser men who blundered.

Cases like those of Hindus and Fischer are too complicated by professionalism. Hindus, for example, continued to speak thickly, his mouth full of "buts," "ifs" and "maybes." True, he now attacked Stalin's foreign policies and sometimes went so far as to imply that a dictator's foreign behavior is not unrelated to the character of his behavior at home. But through his labored formulas one could still hear the hopeful refrain: "And yet like the tide of the ocean in the midst of wind and storm the revolution continues to roll on and on." He was still suffering and not a little upset that the revolution was rolling on and on into Finland, the Baltic states and Rumania.

Fischer's assault on Russia was sudden, clumsy and rather hyster-

ical. Small wonder, considering how long and how loudly he had
defended the Soviet counter-revolution and attacked Stalin's critics.
A somersault of such dimensions cannot be expected to be as neat
and clean-edged as an ordinary flip-flop. He had held his tongue as
long as he could, he told his *Nation* customers in effect, but he could
hold it no longer. Enough is enough. He, too, demanded applause
for his heroic restraint! Like the Scotchman whose wife tumbled out
of the airplane, he said not a word until he was safely on the ground,
his family out of Russia, the Spanish party line on which he collaborated nicely washed out in blood, and the bankruptcy of Stalinism
so clear that even the *Nation* began to suspect the fact. One
of Fischer's manuscripts indicting the horrors of Stalin's rule came
to my desk at the *American Mercury.* Having read it, I returned it
with the notation, "Nothing new in this except the signature." In
1941 he published his astonishing book *Men and Politics.* In it he
attacked the Soviet regime as vigorously as anyone had ever done
but avoided mention of Soviet episodes which he had been especially
industrious in blurring, such as the man-made famine. Moreover,
he awarded a series of medals to Louis Fischer for valor in not disturbing the delusions of *Nation* readers for some seventeen years.

The late Heywood Broun had started the parade of deserters with
a trenchant column on the day after the pact was consummated. "The
masquerade is over. The dominoes are dropped," he wrote, "and it
now becomes possible to look at the faces of the various ones who
pretend to be devoted to the maintenance of democracy." But there
was nothing in that column to suggest that Broun himself for many
years had not only taken part in the masquerade but served as literary
trigger man for the Browders and Jeromes. Others followed suit in
slurring over their own role in the incredible revolution.

Take Granville Hicks. In resigning from the Communist Party
he did not indicate disapproval of the bloodletting or the bargain with
Nazism. He resigned only because party leaders, to quote his words,
"made it clear that, if I eventually found it impossible to defend
the pact, and defend it in their terms, there was nothing for me to
do but resign." He left the impression that this dictatorship of the
party was something new—until then, the public was left to surmise,
Hicks had been allowed to defend his views and in his own words.

Not for another year did he come around to attesting: "In practice today supporting the Communist Party means giving *carte blanche*

not merely to the leaders in this country but also to a little group
of men five thousand miles away."* Today, let us note, as if things
were any different in the years when Hicks was more amenable. "I
think," he wrote in another article, "a great deal, though by no means
all, of Left criticism has been invalidated by the events of last year."
Again the self-consoling pretense that "the last year" changed everything, and that the horrors which went before the Hitler pact were
somehow haloed by the Hicks imprimatur. But a page farther Dr.
Hicks does make a reluctant admission of error in that flawless past:

> By joining the Communist Party I had committed my future to
> a group of politicians, and I ought to have kept a much sharper eye
> on them than I did. Politics is no game for a person whose attention
> is mostly directed elsewhere.

It was perhaps the nudge of conscience revealed in these words
that prompted Hicks, in the first months of his escape from Browder's
cultural concentration camp, to put out a mimeographed bulletin
for other refugees like himself. Therein Max Lerner, Hicks and others
discussed "What now, little fellow-traveler?" without finding an answer. Jim Farrell in his inimitable fashion dubbed the bulletin a
"Stalinist Lonely Hearts Club." One wonders whether the Hickses
even recalled that not long ago they had given a blanket endorsement
of Stalinism, executions of Old Bolsheviks and all, and hissed "Fascist!" at those who demurred.

Once I found myself, for my sins, on the same radio program with
Ralph Bates, then in the throes of his Stalinist fever. Waiting our
turn at the microphone, we reluctantly made conversation. In some
connection or other I mentioned the French Revolution. Whereupon
Comrade Bates flared up in righteous anger. "We communists understand that revolution," he all but snarled. The incident stuck in my
mind. These people had taken over not only the Russian Revolution
and its terror but the French Revolution and its terror, and all revolutions since the day Cain turned on Abel. In a kind of political
megalomania they had identified themselves with History.

Whether Bates is now ready to share the French Revolution with
heretics or still regards it as his private property, I cannot say. In any
case, he jumped off Stalin's band wagon suddenly at the Finland

* The *Nation*, September 28, 1940.

station. "A specter is haunting the world, a specter of a revolution that is dead," he exclaimed. It died, he contended, in Finland. Why not in Poland, or before that in the G.P.U. slaughterhouses where the revolutionists were done in? Why not in the Arctic wastelands crowded with exiles and prisoners, or in the vast regions piled high with the victims of preventable famine? Because it is the only way to salvage his delusions of revolutionary grandeur, he placed the demise arbitrarily at the point where *he* jumped off. But not before he made a speech—

I am getting off the train. It will be a flying jump, and no doubt the passengers in the compartments behind will shoot at me as they clatter by. I had thought the train was bound for a fertile place in the sun; but I have found out that it is rushing toward the Arctic north, where it will be buried beneath vast drifts of snow and be forever more silent.

No one would guess, from this peroration that Bates himself had spent years shooting from compartment windows at people who sought to warn him that the train was not headed for sun and fertility. He even refers to certain accusations against anti-Stalinist groups in Loyalist Spain as an "utterly unscrupulous charge." But he fails to note that he was among those loudest in making just such charges.

Those few penitents must do as examples of the retreat from Moscow. Dozens, perhaps hundreds, jumped off without speechifying and slunk away with hunched shoulders. The abusive Mr. Crichton liquidated his Robert Forsythe personality by quietly removing him from the *New Masses* masthead. (That masthead, once fat with juicy names, grew thinner and thinner until the bosses removed it altogether to avoid further embarrassment. . . .) A few of the pro-Soviet book reviewers began to take sideswipes at Stalin by way of protective coloration, without actually breaking the psychological umbilical cord that connected them with Mother Volga.

It was, when all is said and done, a most melancholy and unheroic retreat.

CHAPTER XXX

NEW FRONTS FOR OLD

1

THERE is nothing either remarkable or reprehensible in people changing their minds. Consistency is an overrated virtue—too often merely a euphemism for congealed and outlived attitudes. It takes a lot more courage to renounce a cherished faith that has soured than to pretend it still smells sweetly. Loyalty to one's conscience and intellectual integrity may transcend loyalty to a set of beliefs.

But when millions of people in all parts of the world change their minds on the same subject *simultaneously*, as if on a signal, there is cause for suspicion. When the simultaneous somersaults are executed everywhere with the same gestures, accompanied by the same shouting, the suspicion is deepened to a certainty. Only a miracle or a conspiracy can explain such extraordinary coincidence. The complete about-turn in communist policy and principle with the consummation of the red-and-brown merger was no miracle.

The ideological summer of communism-as-twentieth-century-Americanism ended with the abruptness of a shot in the back of the neck, which is said to be the favorite G.P.U. method of execution. Winter came without the sere prelude of autumn. Portraits of Lincoln and Washington simply disappeared from communist walls and communist hearts; democratic verbiage evaporated from party and fellow-traveler literature and conversation; tolerance for the sinful bourgeoisie dried up in the comradely bosoms.

By merely holding on to anti-fascist and collective-security views learned by rote from Browder's textbooks, people found themselves damned in Browder's press as war mongers, imperialists and enemies of the people. The order of the day was no longer "stop Hitler" but "stop the imperialists." The distinctions which the Comintern had developed in endless speeches and theses and manifestoes—between good wars and bad wars, between democratic nations and fascist nations—were not even abolished. They were treated as if they had never existed.

365

Only yesterday, one recalled with amazement, Browder had declared in his book *Fighting for Peace*, "It is my conviction that the fascist dictatorships can be halted only by superior force." "It is the height of futility, and that means, in the last analysis, of stupidity," he had warned, "in foreign affairs to be 'neutral' as between fascist and democratic, between war-making and peace-seeking governments, to retreat before and surrender to the bandit governments."

Only yesterday, the full energies of the American League for Peace and Democracy were focused on the "fight for collective security." The American Youth Congress was piling up resolutions demanding action against Hitler and Mussolini. TAC was parading under banners inscribed "STOP HITLER!" The Workers Alliance, the American Writers Congress, the American Student Union, the League of Women Shoppers, the Friends of the Soviet Union, the Lawyers Guild—all, all were agreed that the aggressors must be halted by the joint force of the democracies with Uncle Sam in the lead.

In August, 1939, those war cries were forgotten; nay, reversed. The same organizations now affirmed with no less heat that the fighting democracies were no better than Nazi Germany, so that it did not matter who won the war. They clamored for an immediate "negotiated" peace every time Berlin launched one of its "peace offensives." Because it was making no secret of its support of the anti-Hitler forces, the Roosevelt Administration now shared standing room in the Stalinist purgatory with Trotskyists and renegades. The Good Neighbor policy toward the Latin American nations, until then applauded and abetted by the comrades, had been transformed overnight into "dollar diplomacy" for "Yankee imperialism." Investment in national security, demanded so passionately by every Stalinist newspaper and Innocents' Club, was now exposed by the same papers and clubs as a trick to rob the sharecroppers and enslave India.

It was as though the four years of mass courtship of existing institutions had never taken place. Both the marriages of convenience—with liberals, labor, churches, literati—and the illicit love affairs (with the New Deal, for instance)—were canceled out. Only the offspring of these unions, legitimate and otherwise, remained around as a reminder of the liquidated Fourth Period. Some of them were too embarrassing a reminder and therefore had to be expeditiously choked. This was especially true of front organizations whose primary excuse for existence was to fight fascism, like the League for Peace and Democracy. Others were spared on condition that they change their reminiscent names. The Hollywood Anti-Nazi League, for example, shamelessly dropped the "Anti-Nazi" label, converting itself into the Hollywood League for Democratic Action. And all those organizations which remained alive immediately readjusted their principles by the simple procedure of turning them inside out.

The whole phenomenon added up to a public and indubitable demonstration of communist control. In every one of the red planets in the Kuusinen system, those who refused to follow the new catechism had to depart, silently or in a burst of angry eloquence. What better testimony could be offered that the party-liners were the bosses? David Lasser of the Workers Alliance and Joe Lash of the American Youth Congress had been vehement in denying the "lies" about communist domination. When these organizations, like every other about which similar "lies" were circulated, turned violently isolationist and anti-New Deal, Lasser and Lash refused to go along. Were the communists thereupon expelled? Not at all—Lasser and Lash had to depart. It is not overstraining logic to assume that those who remain in control of a disputed fort have the control in it. Both these young men acknowledged that logic by denouncing their respective organizations belatedly as communist-controlled. Membership in most of the Stalinist booby clubs fell sharply, but the party grip on the machinery of every such organization was only tightened in the crisis.

2

For a few weeks the officials of the League for Peace and Democracy talked incoherently in a panic of uncertainty; the new line was still a bit vague. Then the league came through. On October 29, 1939, hand-picked delegations from "safe" branches met in Philadelphia and duly renounced everything that they had preached in the past. Roger Baldwin, James Waterman Wise and other prominent leaguers had resigned. But stalwarts like the pious Dr. Harry F. Ward, Max Yergan, Alice Barrows, as well as a whole battalion of job holders were on hand to reaffirm faith in "Stalin's peace policy," as on display in Poland, Estonia, Latvia, Lithuania and soon thereafter Finland.

But defections were too general, the fraud too transparent. The most successful of the front organizations, precisely because of its magnitude and influence, became a red elephant. Dr. Ward and six of his comrades met in a cafeteria on February 2, 1940, and decided that the animal must be removed. Neither the 20,000 claimed as dues-paying members nor the 7,500,000 claimed as affiliates through co-operating units were consulted. The noisiest false front of them all was simply killed off by its hierarchs. Comrade Urevich, if he had not been purged in the meantime, must have shaken his head sadly.

The American Friends of the Soviet Union could not face the storm. Moscow had offered a test of friendship beyond their collective strength. The organization was strangled so quietly, however, and expired so meekly that the American public did not hear the sad news for months after the corpse had been burned in Corliss Lamont's luxurious cellar. By accident the newspapers learned, and Dr. Lamont confirmed, that the organization had been dead for some time. Dr. Lamont himself never faltered. As proudly as ever he rejected the communist label while continuing to do the most onerous jobs for the communists.

The American Youth Congress survived. All but a handful of the church and liberal affiliates pulled out, some of them in a churlish and vituperative mood. In effect the American Student Union and the Communist Youth League remained in control of an army without soldiers. But the congress did manage to stage one last and raucous show. The Roosevelt family, which had so long pampered and protected the communist leadership, was treated to a sample of class-angled gratitude. The President, because he dared to describe Russia as a dictatorship, was booed on his own front lawn by delegates to the February, 1940, convention in Washington. Mrs. Roosevelt was a pathetic figure when she tried to chide her obstreperous "children" the following day. They gave her the cold treatment. Only John L. Lewis—who contributed to the coincidence by becoming isolationist and anti-New Deal along with the communists—now touched the dialectical heart of the congress in its post-pact incarnation.

TAC, the Theatre Arts Committee, hastily purged its repertory of anti-Hitler and collective-security skits and songs. Russia's attack on Finland stirred the sentimental heart of Broadway as few things had done in recent years. For a few "Broadway figures," in fact, the tragedy provided the chance to do public penance for past association with Stalin's movements. The great mass of actors, producers and playwrights had been deeply touched by Finland's heroic resistance—there was a David-and-Goliath quality to the struggle that appealed to their dramatic natures. A great theatrical relief effort got under way.

The counter-effort was undertaken by the same TAC which had once yelled "Stop Hitler!" and by a handful of theatre folk whom even the Nazi-Kremlin alliance had not cured of their Soviet illusions—people like Lillian Hellman, Herman Shumlin, Paul Robeson, Will Geer. Louis Schaffer, manager of Labor Stage, until then an occasional collaborator of TAC, was singled out for special contumely by this organization now that he took an active part in the Finnish relief enterprise. The same people who had helped raise money year after year for Spain and China and other causes beyond our own shores now decided and brayed to the world that "charity begins at home," not in Europe.

The pattern held true everywhere. A. Philip Randolph, president of the National Negro Congress, retreated, leaving Max Yergan, John P. Davis and the other party-liners in full command. A group of prominent members of the American Artists Congress—George Biddle, William Zorach, Lewis Mumford, Ralph M. Pearson, Stuart Davis—refusing to join in a whitewash of the Soviet aggression in Finland, had to resign publicly, surrendering the field to Lynd Ward, Rockwell Kent and other fellow-travelers.

Resignations from the League of American Writers, beginning with Thomas Mann, Van Wyck Brooks, Louis Bromfield and other innocents, reached a climax with the lugubrious departure of many not-so-innocents even unto Malcolm Cowley. The first post-pact Writers Congress, held in New York early in June, 1941, was a dismal and emaciated affair, even though the gathering was merged with conventions of the Artists Congress and the United American Artists of the C.I.O. to fill out the shrunken contours a bit. The signatures under the regulation summons to the faithful included a few of the bigger figures out of the league's glorious Stalinoid past. But these only underlined the mediocrity of the new recruits: a long list of unknown writers and artists—thickly strewn with pulp magazine *litterateurs* and comic-strip colleagues of Rembrandt—evidently seeking collective notoriety as a consolation for individual obscurity.

Said the *New Masses* consolingly on the eve of the congress: "All of the *New Masses* editorial staff belong to the League of American Writers and we intend to be on hand for as many sessions as possible. It's a beautiful program. . . ." They were on hand all right, together with practically all their current contributors: the proceedings, indeed, looked and sounded like an enlarged plenum of the *New Masses* editors. But, alas, it was not a beautiful program. It was a drab and dispirited program compared with the recent past. True, stalwarts like Donald Ogden Stewart, Dashiell Hammett, John Howard Lawson and Dudley Nichols were still among the front names, as well as Orson Welles, who discovered the revolution in his advanced youth. But the fabulous and supercolossal Hollywood delegation of yore was not in attendance; even Dorothy Parker was mysteriously unaccounted for.

A "critics' panel" session which once upon a time could have counted on command performances by dozens of glamorous critical names, now contented itself with such obscure celebrities in the domain of literary criticism as Samuel Sillen, Herbert Aptheker, Michael Gold, Dorothy Brewster and Edwin Burgum. The main bouts, which a few short years ago presented champions like Hemingway and Thomas Mann, Waldo Frank and Archibald MacLeish, now announced the ever serviceable Congressman Marcantonio, Edgar Snow, Lawson, Samuel Putnam, Rockwell Kent, Genevieve Taggard, Robert K. Speer, etc.

At past congresses the literary-political discussions had moved in the exalted spheres of the higher culture, but now the emphasis was on cheap fiction for the "pulps," the concoction of standardized detective yarns and even the art of inventing "true story" tales; that, in fact, is the nearest the congress came to truth in literature. The detective category had a narrow escape from ideological catastrophe. It seems that a certain Ken Crossen had been prevailed upon to discuss "New Heroes in the Pulp Field." Now it happens that one of Mr. Crossen's own heroes, familiar to dime-detective addicts, is none other than the Green Lama who, unfortunately, invests a lot of his heroism on fighting communists! So it was lucky for the Lama and the league alike that the speaker withdrew. All in all, the Fourth Congress of the writing fellow-travelers demonstrated that the typewriter front had not only grown thin and haggard but had lost its former elevated tone and caviar atmosphere. The Donald Ogden Stewartship of the organization passed to Dashiell Hammett, the new president, which was scarcely a literary triumph for the congress.

Not until two weeks later did the few writers and the mass of pseudo-writers who took part in this ill-fated congress realize that history was playing a nasty practical joke on them. Ignoring the "capitalistic lies" about Comrade Hitler's aggressive intentions against Führer Stalin, the muddled literati went all-out in support of Moscow's "peace" policy for the U.S.A. They passed resolutions condemning our "war mongering" aid to Hitler's victims, supporting outlaw strikers in our defense plants and glorifying Stalin's genius in keeping out of the unsavory imperialist squabble. They indicated their adherence to the "peace vigil" picket line maintained by the American Peace Mobilization around the White House. An entire session was given over to the memory of Randolph Bourne, who opposed American participation in the first World War and Theodore Dreiser was honored with a Randolph Bourne citation as the current embodiment of Left isolationism.

But a fortnight later Hitler invaded Russia; Stalin's "peace" diplomacy appeared in its true light as a ghastly and futile super-appeasement; and the party line on war was switched again!

The deepening breach between the communists and the government—by no means complete even at this writing—was manifest in a changing climate in the N.L.R.B. and in legal proceedings against Browder and other party chieftains for self-confessed passport frauds. It was reflected in the belated and rather shamefaced withdrawal of Berle, Jackson and other New Dealers from the Lawyers Guild. The communist social lobby became somewhat more circumspect, and a few of the innocent ladies became less eager to lend their names and their homes to the party camouflage experts.

Let no one imagine, however, that the elaborate false front collapsed or that the periphery behind it turned into a ghost town. True, it was temporarily bewildered and demoralized, but it remained—and remains—populous. The thousandfold communist bureaucracy held tight, with only a few defections. Those with an economic stake in the literary markets, the lecture audiences, the trade-union posts and even Federal patronage at the disposal of the party held on grimly. Thousands for whom the allegiance had lost all rational content, for whom it was plainly a religious experience, accepted the new party line without a murmur of protest or a glimmer of understanding.

The communist and fellow-traveler leadership in a long series of C.I.O. unions, of course, was unaffected by the Soviet-Nazi pact; like the party officials, such leaders were at bottom simply inert agents of a foreign power, obeying automatically. Indeed, as long as the Moscow-Berlin Axis lasted, they were now able to express their political bias in the language of action on the labor front. The series of airplane, aluminum, die-casting and other defense strikes fomented and led by communists is fresh in memory—the New Deal fellow-traveler contingents were reaping the whirlwind where they had sowed the wind.

And the Fifth Period, like every other, quickly found expression in its own planets, operating on the steam power of the revised ideology. New fronts for old, with suckers enough and to spare! Indeed, some of those duped and humiliated in the preceding period limped back eagerly for more punishment—and the inevitable new disillusionment. Barnum was an amateur compared to the Union Square entrepreneurs.

3

The building of a new array of Innocents' Clubs after the outbreak of the Second World War revolved around two main sets of slogans. First, the comrades sought to capture and control anti-war and isolationist sentiment. Second, they discovered a new and almost hysterical solicitude for civil liberties and the Bill of Rights. The motivations in both respects are clear enough. The anti-war propaganda was calculated to head off American defense effort and aid to Hitler's enemies; it was a Stalinist job synchronized with the Nazi-inspired propaganda and paid off by Hitler, after twenty-two months, with invasion of the U.S.S.R. The to-do about constitutional rights derived from a healthy suspicion—now that the "democratic" Popular Front honeymoon had been wrecked—that government agencies might act to curb the agents of foreign dictatorships. As always, the frank proponents of state terror were organizing to exercise all civil rights in their war to destroy civil rights.

An additional impetus to the second of these new communist enterprises was provided by the action of the American Civil Liberties Union, at long last, in expelling a few communist leaders from their midst, although a bevy of active fellow-travelers remained. The presence of Stalin's henchmen on an American organization of this type had long been a piece of irony which no amount of sophistry could erase. If Browder's boys sat on the board of the A.C.L.U., why not Fritz Kuhn's boys? The irony was turned to farce by the circumstance that the Rev. Dr. Harry Ward headed the Union at the same time that he generaled the League of Peace and Democracy and other Muscovite planets. Certainly an extraordinary alignment for a person presumably dedicating his life to civil freedoms!

In any case, in the months after the Stalin-Hitler pact the Civil Liberties Union found it increasingly awkward to maintain its united front with the Communist Party and finally voted' to oust the more notorious Moscow comrades. (Well-known Stalinist figures remained on the face-saving theory that they were not *officially* members of Browder's conspiracy.) Dr. Ward eased the tension by resigning. The Union was thereupon subjected to a standardized mud barrage in communist circles and the party's campaign for "civil liberty" fronts under its own control was intensified.

The party-line "democracy" of the preceding years had been a mischievous nuisance to genuine democrats. The sudden communist passion for "peace" and "isolation" became a no less mischievous nuisance to honest peace advocates and honest isolationists, who were much relieved when the end of this fake-pacifism came in June, 1941. Some of them in their anxiety for allies failed to distinguish between non-intervention sentiment rooted in patriotic American self-interests and the temporary isolationism of people selling a bill of goods for their Moscow or Berlin bosses.

The Muscovite junta in our midst used its old bait in new waters and a number of genuine peace organizations took the hook. Others were more wary. *Uncensored*, an isolationist publication issued by American liberals and socialists, warned their friends against the Stalinist fishing expeditions. The Brooklyn Church and Mission Federation felt it necessary to caution Protestant ministers against camouflaged communists active in enticing religious groups into their newly formed "peace" fronts. Comrade Harry Bridges' crowd on the West Coast started a Keep-America-Out-of-War movement apparently intended to lure an existing organization of the same name into suicide by merger. John T. Flynn and others of the original organization sounded the tocsin of alarm in time, forcing the Bridges outfit to change its name and tactics.

But thousands did bite. A new chapter in the grotesque history of the American Gullible's Travels was written, as obscene as any that had come before. By April, 1940, only seven months after the launching of the new party line, the Committee for Cultural Freedom headed by Professor Dewey was able to list for the guidance of its

members the following "New Organizations under Outright Communist Party Control," all of them started after January 1, 1939:

American Committee for Friendship with the Soviet Union (suc-
cessor to the discontinued Friends of the Soviet Union)
Baltimore Statewide Conference on Civil Liberties
Boston Citizens Union
Committee for Civil Rights for Communists
Coordinating Committee Against Profiteering
Defense Committee for Civil Rights
Detroit Bill of Rights Defense Committee
Emergency Conference to Save Spanish Refugees
Greater New York Emergency Conference on Inalienable Rights
Hollywood League for Democratic Action
Los Angeles Conference on Civil Liberties
Miami League for Peace and Human Welfare
Michigan Civil Rights Federation
Minneapolis Civil Rights Committee
National Emergency Conference
Needle Workers' Council for Peace and Civil Rights
New Bedford Conference on American Democracy
New York Citizens Peace Council
North American Spanish Aid
Pan-American Conference on Democratic Rights
Progressive Committee to Rebuild the American Labor Party
San Francisco Academic and Civil Rights Council
Sharecroppers' Aid Committee
Washington Council for Democratic Rights
Yanks-Are-Not-Coming Committee*

Most of the local groups listed were in due time absorbed by
national groupings. They were stop-gap formations to keep the now
homeless members of the liquidated united-front organizations in
line until new organizational garrisons could be constructed for them.
The most important of these was the self-styled American Peace
Mobilization, which became, in a sense, the central reservoir into
which the most effective personnel and energies of other communist
fronts were channeled. Association with this front became tanta-
mount to public acceptance of the Hitler-Stalin line for America—

---

* *Stalinist Outposts in the United States,* Report No. 2, by the Committee for
Cultural Freedom.

except where it was merely proof of bottomless political naïveté. Because of its key position, we shall consider the history and activities of the Mobilization in some detail in the following chapter.

There are still enough totalitarian liberals and Stalinoid writers available to embellish divers manifestoes and to serve as a source of camouflage-names for new false-front organizations as they are hatched. There are still stalwarts by the score who seem ready to sign anything Stalin shoves under their noses, even if they have to pinch their nostrils to avoid asphyxiation.

4

The Committee for Cultural Freedom analysis of April, 1940, also listed old organizations under "outright communist control." With the caution that a few of them may have died of Soviet-Nazi pneumonia since then, here is the list as vouchsafed by the committee:

American Council on Soviet Relations
American Society for Race Tolerance
American Student Union
Association of American Law Students
Artkino, Distributor of Soviet Films in the United States
Book Union
Book-and-Play-of-the-Month Club
Finnish Workers Federation
Friends of the Abraham Lincoln Brigade
International Juridical Association
International Labor Defense
International Publishers
International Workers Order
Intourist (Soviet travel agency)
Jewish People's Committee
Jimmy Collins Flying Club
Labor Research Association
League of American Writers
League of Struggle for Negro Rights
National Committee for People's Rights
National Negro Congress
New Theatre League
New York Committee to Aid Agricultural Workers
Southern Negro Youth Congress

Veterans of the Abraham Lincoln Brigade
Wholesale Book Corporation
Workers Alliance
Workers Bookshops (a national chain, some branches called
   "Progressive Bookshops")
Workers Cultural Federation
Workers International Relief
Workers Library Publishers
World Tourists
Young Pioneers

The report, further, listed two other categories of organization, in a spirit of utmost caution:

1. "Groups under communist influence, with non-communists present:"
American Artists Congress
American Friends of the Chinese People
China Aid Council
Council for Pan-American Democracy
League of Women Shoppers
Medical Bureau for Spain
National Committee for People's Rights
United Student Peace Committee

2. "Organizations in close collaboration with the Communist Party:"
American Committee for the Protection of the Foreign Born
American Investors Union
American Youth Congress
Consumers Union
Descendants of the American Revolution ("Committee of 1776")
Film Audiences for Democracy
Frontier Films
National Council for the Protection of the Foreign Born
Spanish Intellectual Aid
Theatre Arts Committee (TAC)
West Side Council for Race Tolerance

For the sake of completeness, let us also list a batch of the pro-Soviet or communist-influenced publications: New York *Daily Worker*, *Equality*, *Bulletin of the League of American Writers*, *The Com-*

munist, Communist International, Dialectics, Die Freiheit, Labor Defender, Labor Fact Book, Chicago Mid-West Record, New Masses, People's Press, San Francisco People's World, Soviet Russia Today, World News and Views, Science and Society, TAC, In Fact, Friday.

The incredible revolution in its lush and lunatic luxuriance was no more. But Comrade Kuusinen's universe of communist frauds remained with us. The forms change, the spirit of abject subservience to Moscow remains. Under all the seeming contradictions of policies and battle cries there is that one significant element of consistency.

5

Within the gigantic tragedy of Moscow's betrayal of millions of its trustful foreign enthusiasts in kicking over their cherished Popular Front illusions, we may isolate one minor tragedy. It is a tale edged with irony and splotched with absurdity, but it remains tragic none the less. Elsewhere I called it *The Strange Case of PM*, and the title still seems appropriate at this writing, more than a year after June 18, 1940, when the fellow-traveling *New York PM*, an afternoon tabloid, was launched.

The tragedy lies in the timing. "What we would have, of course," Ralph Ingersoll, editor of the *PM* a-borning, explained in a memorandum early in 1939 when the staff was being mobilized, "would be an organ of the United Front." He went on to qualify this statement, but he had hit on the central fact about the whole business. But by the time the scheme jelled, alas, the Popular Front was dead. Mr. Ingersoll and his wealthy backers, who put up more than $1,500,000, had on their hands "an organ of the United Front" without a United Front. They had a staff strongly fellow-traveler in affiliation and temper and in spots openly communist at a time when this breed was losing its grip on life in New York. Had the editor been a communist, matters would have been simpler; he would have made the hairpin turn like the rest of them. But he wasn't. He had carried over his United-Front principles into a frontless epoch but was saddled with lieutenants devoted fanatically to the new party line. New York thereafter watched the paradox of a relentlessly pro-British and anti-Hitler paper which, outside of this one vital matter, was undisguised in its pro-communist bias. In the same issues it read brilliant editorials urging American action against the Axis—and stories giving aid and comfort to Russia, Left Wing C.I.O. leaders and others openly seeking to prevent such action. Not until Germany considerately attacked Russia was the paradox in part resolved.

The mystery of the case was provided at the outset by the startling contrast between the financial angels of the paper and its political character. It began, appropriately, with a writer of mystery stories: Dashiell Hammett, a ranking fellow-traveler. In November, 1938, he started interviewing applicants for jobs on the nebulous paper that eventually crystallized as *PM*. Eleven thousand applicants were canvassed in the next eighteen months, and 151 were chosen. With so many trained newspapermen to choose from, the final list was startlingly loaded with the kind of names familiar to communist readers, a few of them with little if any experience except on Stalin's kept press.

Far from being grateful, Ingersoll seemed furious when tipped off that dozens of his employees had been intimately connected with divers communist activities—one of them having served as *Daily Worker* managing editor, another as editor of *The Communist*, a third as leader of the Young Communist League, a fourth as a Soviet government official, a fifth as staff cartoonist of the *Daily Worker*, a score or more as contributors to divers Muscovite publications here. Naturally there were many non-Stalinists on the staff and an in-between group of professional newspapermen. But the pervasive color was the sickly red of latter-day revolutionism.

Now for the financial backing of the Popular Front paper without a Popular Front. The two largest stockholders were Marshall Field III and John Hay Whitney. Among the others were Mrs. Louis Gimbel, Philip A. Wrigley, Mrs. Marion Rosenwald, Lessing Rosenwald, George Huntington Hartford II, Dwight Deere Wiman and other representatives of the class and the interests to the liquidation of which the great majority of the *PM*'ers were dedicated. Obviously such people did not begin to understand what they were stepping into. And there was not much any of them could do about it when they did begin to find out, having signed over full editorial authority to Ingersoll. Someone along the line deserves special citation for exceptional salesmanship.

The communist permeation of the paper was analyzed by *Har-*

per's, the *American Mercury*, the *New Leader* and others. Under this pressure—and, we must assume, because of horrified protests from the richer backers—the paper began to tone down its Stalinist bias. But at critical moments that bias reasserted itself blatantly. There was the *PM* coverage of the murder of Leon Trotsky, for instance. Only the *Daily Worker*, by a slight margin, exceeded *PM* in cynical misrepresentation of the affair. Of all the writers in Mexico, Ingersoll chose the Federated Press man, Frank Jellinek, a contributor to the *Daily Worker*, to report the affair for him!

The paper soon ran through its million and a half dollars. It was saved from collapse by Marshall Field, who bought out the others and poured some more gold into the project. Many of the more notorious fellow-travelers were dropped, though plenty of them held on. It was generally understood that the communist phase was ended. But at the beginning of February, 1941, the readers learned differently. More blatantly than ever *PM* went all-out to aid the Moscow cause, in defiance of ordinary good sense and decent journalism. The occasion was the death under mysterious circumstances of General Walter Krivitsky, the former Soviet military intelligence officer who had broken with the Kremlin, revealed Moscow's terror secrets and worked with the British intelligence in fighting Fifth Columnists.

Despite superficial appearances of suicide, there were—and there remain—serious doubts. It may well be that the death, if not outright murder, was a "forced suicide" on the pattern familiar to students of G.P.U. and Gestapo techniques. The press almost unanimously voiced doubts of the suicide, and many urged an intensive investigation to smoke out Moscow agents. Only *PM* blazoned its certainty that this *was* simple suicide and worked itself into hysterics in attacking those who wanted to expose the network of foreign terrorists by initiating an investigation. If its purpose had been to protect Stalin's espionage here, it could scarcely have gone any stronger. The paper surpassed the *Daily Worker* in ridiculing the dead man and those who wanted his death looked into. *PM's* "reporting" of the event took the form of a gleefully jocular column captioned, "OK, Coroner, Skip the OGPU." In the same ghoulish playfulness it then stuck pins into the corpse, into Krivitsky's friends and into the editors who dared demand an investigation. The performance was macabre.

Let us assume for a moment that the G.P.U. had staged or forced

Krivitsky's "suicide." Nothing would then suit its killers better than that the case should be closed as soon as possible and written off as simple self-destruction. Even if they had not been directly responsible in this instance, Moscow agents would hardly relish an intensive Federal inquiry. Whatever its motives, *PM* in effect did a job for these agents. The reaction of *PM* to the Krivitsky episode was violently Stalinist. The suspicions aroused by this reaction were bolstered soon thereafter by a campaign of persecution against Jan Valtin, author of *Out of the Night*. Again, only friends of the G.P.U. could be so heatedly eager to "expose" Valtin and so industrious in promoting his deportation.

The news that the paper had been cleaned of its totalitarian influences was evidently premature. Small wonder that in certain New York circles the saying went that "the communists are having a Marshall Field day."

And while we are on the subject, a few lines must be accorded to another post-pact fellow-traveling publication. *Friday*, edited and reportedly financed by a young Stalinist sympathizer named Dan Gilmor, has faithfully toed the party line. Its writers are in large part from the same drawer as those of the *New Masses*. Though covered with a froth of popular features, the basic stuff in it parallels the official party press. In its very first issue, dated March 15, 1940, *Friday* led off with an attack on "foreign agents"—not, God forbid, the agents of Hitler, Stalin or Mussolini, but the agents of Great Britain! Another leading article in that number ridiculed the charge that Hollywood was touched by communist propaganda. A third glorified the West Coast comrade, Mike Quin, who had written a pamphlet called *The Yanks Are Not Coming*.

The post-pact fellow-travelers also have at their disposal a new publishing firm: Modern Age Books, subsidized by Richard Storrs Childs, an enormously wealthy young man. "Its list," Benjamin Stolberg remarked in the *Saturday Evening Post*, "reads like an American Bolshevik Five Foot Shelf." Its authors include Bruce Minton and John Stuart of the *New Masses*, Granville Hicks, John Strachey, Dr. Harry F. Ward, Leon Goodelman and a raft of others of this caliber. Its subject matter includes hallucinatory literature on the Soviet myth in its various manifestations, the latest sample being the Dean of Canterbury's imaginative work on his Never-Never Land in Russia.

Some of those who in the less hospitable climate of the post-pact days might hesitate to write for out-and-out communist publications thus have other, safer outlets for their talents. If the money holds out—from the "muddled millions" on this side and the bloody millions in Stalin's hands—there will be more such outlets.

Chapter XXXI

AND THEY CALLED IT "PEACE"

IN ANNOUNCING the demise of the League for Peace and Democracy, the *Daily Worker* had called for the formation of a "new and greater peace movement." For a time it looked as if The-Yanks-Are-Not-Coming groups, started by the West Coast maritime comrades and widely imitated, might be that greater movement. The slogan became a hallmark of Stalinist undertakings, although a few outsiders picked it up by accident; even the canny William Allen White was indiscreet enough to borrow it once without realizing its ancestry. But ultimately the experimental and regional outfits devoted to selling Uncle Sam the spurious Moscow-Berlin brand of "peace" were gathered into the fold of the American Peace Mobilization, which flourished as the central repository of the Stalinist sabotage-potential in America.

The technique of its formation, its leadership and ramifications are so quintessentially Kremlinesque that it became the best available test of Stalinoid infection. What obtrudes as the story unfolds is the extent to which this front was integrated into practically all other communist-dominated enterprises. Holding companies of the pre-S.E.C. era could have taken lessons in the arts of interlocking directorates from the communist maestros.

What needs to be noted especially is the dominant role played in it by the leaders of C.I.O. trade unions most closely connected with defense industries, transportation and communications—the unions, that is to say, which were in the best position to translate anti-defense, anti-convoy, pro-Soviet slogans into obstructive action. In California where half the airplanes made in the U.S.A. are turned out, the American Peace Mobilization was largely another name for the C.I.O., and the C.I.O. is in effect another headquarters for the Communist Party. Throughout the nation the triumvirate—Communist Party, American Peace Mobilization, Congress of Industrial Organizations— were inextricably interwoven. If our Washington monitors were tough-liberal instead of mushy-liberal, they would have been less astonished to find sabotage of defense production under a union label.

The collective-security league had been dissolved, but the framework of paid functionaries, volunteer enthusiasts and sucker lists remained. Many of the league leaders simply waited for the shock of the pact to wear off, then faced their constituencies with a new inside-out story. By the end of 1939 all Communist Party institutions were feeding the press with publicity on a brand-new Emergency Peace Mobilization Committee of Greater New York. The old local headquarters of the League for Peace throughout the country emerged from the confusion under shiny new titles.

The Brooklyn section of the American League became the Brooklyn Community Peace Council; other sections turned into the Hollywood Peace Forum, the Massachusetts Peace Council, the Northern California Peace Mobilization Committee, the Peace Committee of the Medical Profession, even the Mothers' Day Peace Council and the Milwaukee Indians' Peace Group. In our national capital the transformation was carried out with beautiful candor: the announcement of the new peace organization reached members in the same envelope that transmitted news of the liquidation of the old one. The scores of local bodies were then formed into district "mobilizations," among which the New York City outfit held first place. Its first active leaders included Morris Watson, vice-president of the American Newspaper Guild; Jean Horie, executive secretary of the New York Youth Congress; Congressman Vito Marcantonio, head of the International Labor Defense; John P. Davis and Max Yergan, chiefs of the National Negro Congress; Bella Dodd, a leader of Local 5 of the Teachers Union; Dan Gilmor, editor of *Friday*; Walter Scott Neff, one of the teachers subsequently suspended by the College of the City of New York along with Yergan and others for alleged communist activity; and others whose multiple Stalinist affiliations underscore the integration of which I have spoken.

The first Peace Mobilization demonstration in New York was called for April 5, 1940, in Washington Square Park. A batch of unsuspecting innocents were corralled by Miss Dagmar Norgord, whose spouse, Douglas Jacobs, was at the moment directing the picketing of the French Consulate as part of Hitler's drive against France. Among those who later resigned from the growing roster, charging that they had been gathered in by misrepresentation or that their names had been used without authorization, were Mary Simkhovitch, the famous social worker; Dr. Emanuel Chapman of Fordham University; Professor George Shuster, then acting president and now president of Hunter College—which shows how easy it is to trap people with a fine speech about "peace." The committee on arrangements met at the home of Mrs. Bertha Foss, executive secretary of the National Emergency Conference for Civil Liberties, another of the post-pact Muscovite fronts, and in its number were such trusted friends as Austin Hogan of Mike Quill's Transport Workers Union, and Robert K. Speer, head of the Teachers Union Local 537.

The demonstration took place under the resounding title "It Must Not Happen Again Peace Rally," with the familiar New York Stalinist crowd out in full force and decorative figures like Dean Ned Dearborn of New York University shoved into the forefront for effect. Joe Curran, generalissimo of the Maritime Workers Union, was among the speakers. Comrades the nation over took up the work, and demonstrations were reported from everywhere. Earl Robinson and Paul Robeson and TAC toured the country to provide entertainment relief for the Mobilization revival meetings.

Some three hundred "emergency" committees came into being and in the East alone some four thousand religious, political and fraternal organizations were approached with the emergency "peace" message. In Chicago and Detroit and Cleveland, wherever the Left Wing of the C.I.O. had large strength, it served as the main support of the campaign. A drive was launched to obtain 500,000 signatures to a "peace petition." At the meetings the orators were usually drawn from the same frayed hat: people like Bella Dodd, Harry Van Arsdale, John P. Davis, Yergan, Jean Horie, Mike Quill, Marcantonio. The way the lines cross and recross in an intricate and close-meshed pattern is truly wonderful to behold!

Then came the first big blast. The Mobilization announced through Mrs. Aline Davis Hays that a "People's Rally for Peace" would be held at Randall's Stadium, New York, on August 4, with Marcantonio as chief speaker. The gathering was played up as a curtain raiser for a big national show in Chicago over the Labor Day week end. Other mass meetings by way of prelude to Chicago were held in other large cities. The Boston act was endorsed by Harvard Professors Kirtley Mather, Marcell Francon and Russell Nixon, by Edgar Brightman of Boston University and the Rev. Alfred Pool of the Presbyterian University. In San Francisco, proud of its Yanks-Are-

Not-Coming slogan, the Peace Mobilization Committee was run by the State Industrial Council and its director, Harry Bridges, with the Maritime Federation doing a lot of the work. In Jamestown, New York, Mayor Leon F. Roberts endorsed the holy work. Harold Christoffel, C.I.O. organizer who later won nationwide notoriety as leader of the Allis-Chalmers strike which tied up a third of the nation's defense production, played a lead role in the Wisconsin branch of the newly minted "peace" movement. In Cleveland the job was done by the central body of the C.I.O. in that city, including the unions which later pulled some notorious strikes in defense plants. Almost everywhere John L. Lewis' Labor's Non-Partisan League joined the Mobilization as a matter of course.

I go into these details only because they provide a glimpse of the conduits between the Moscow-dictated fake-pacifist movement and the subsequent strikes and other obstruction to American defense work. It is safe to guess that not one in a thousand striking aluminum or aviation or other defense factory workers realized that his leaders were, like as not, publicly on record as violently condemning the whole national defense effort. Had they realized it they might have suspected that the strikes had purposes not specified in the formal list of demands.

The Chicago show instantly received the endorsement of the California, Wisconsin, Connecticut and Washington C.I.O. State Councils. These are states in which defense strikes were particularly numerous and embittered in the following year. Endorsement also came quickly from the National Maritime Union, the International Woodworkers Union, the Farm Equipment Workers Organizing Committee, the Maritime Federation of the Pacific, the Federation of Architects, Chemists, Engineers and Technicians, the Fur and Leather Workers Union, the American Newspaper Guild and the Greater New York Industrial Council—all C.I.O. affiliates. Joe Curran's Maritime Union prepared to send seven hundred delegates, the American Youth Congress undertook to provide a delegation of four hundred or more and several hundred were announced by the National Negro Congress. Locals of the United Automobile Workers Union— locals which would soon figure in defense production blockades— sent a thousand delegates. The great purveyor of panaceas for the aged, Dr. Francis Townsend, gave his pontifical approval to the convention.

This was big-time stuff, Stalin's newest and biggest and most important American venture. The faithful were apprised that Senators Arthur Capper of Kansas and Edwin C. Johnson of Colorado had sent in their blessings to the gathering and that the speakers would include Senator Nye, Senator Clark and Oswald Garrison Villard. But before the convention got started, the press caught on to what was happening. There were disclosures of the paternity of the Chicago baby. Thereupon Nye, Clark and Villard, having been inveigled by the cooing peace talk, withdrew as speakers. Mr. Villard's statement is worth quoting, because it speaks for tens of thousands who have at various times been lured into the communist corrals.

"I went in under a mistaken impression," he explained. "When they came to me they showed me a list of half a dozen sponsors, friends of mine and known non-fellow-travelers. I gave my name on the strength of theirs. I learned that it was actually being run by the communists and got out just as fast as I could. The trouble is that liberals are always being roped in by seeing names of their friends."

The press exposure, however, did not cut down the attendance. The stooges had known it anyhow and the incurable innocents shrugged it off as more red-baiting. The New York delegation chartered special trains. The impressarios ate crow and announced Vito Marcantonio, Dr. Townsend and Paul Robeson instead of the resigned Senators. The three-day session at the Chicago Stadium echoed with damnation of President Roosevelt and other "war mongers." Mike Quill exclaimed, "We will not be drawn into any war in Europe or South America to make profits for Wall Street." Joe Curran expounded the theory that "peace time conscription is directed solely against the wage earners as part of an effort to destroy the social and economic gains of the last three years." Robeson sang. The comrades cheered.

On September 2, 1940, the delegates dropped the emergency title and set up the American Peace Mobilization. It named officers and adjourned to carry the good work through the nation.

2

The comrades managed to round up an unknown clergyman, a Rev. John B. Thompson of Oklahoma, and made him president. They have a natural preference for clerical figureheads everywhere, even in anti-God movements, and there are always a few eager to serve. The rest of the officers were with few exceptions people already familiar to us from our journey through the Kremlin's planetary system. A Vanderbilt scion, Frederic Vanderbilt Field, long associated with obscure radical publications, was chosen as national secretary. Those haloed with the title of vice-president were Reid Robinson, Paul Robeson, Vito Marcantonio, Jack McMichael, Theodore Dreiser and Katherine Terrell, executive secretary of the Institute for Pacific Relations.

The following were elected to the National Council of the American Peace Mobilization; how many of them thereafter resigned I do not know, since the communists broadcast adhesions but soft-pedal defections:

Prof. Walter Rautenstrauch; Howard Bay; Marc Blitzstein; Donald Ogden Stewart; Harry Van Arsdale; James Carey; Hugh DeLacy president of the Washington Commonwealth Federation; Herbert Biberman; Joseph Cadden, executive secretary of the American Youth Congress; Walter Neff; George Marshall, editor of *Soviet Russia Today*; Elmer Fehlhaber, secretary of the Ohio Labor's Non-Partisan League; John P. Davis; Harvey O'Conner; Morris Watson, vice-president of the American Newspaper Guild; Rev. Owen Knox; Leonard Goldsmith; Gerald Harris, Sr., of the Alabama Farmers Union; Carl Swanson, executive member of the United Automobile Workers Union; Grace Makepeace, president of the Ohio Townsend Movement; Herbert Long and Howard Lee of the Southern Conference on Human Welfare; Donald Henderson; Rev. Chad Wilson; Virgil Mason, of the National Association of Die-Casters; Harry Donaghue; Mervyn Rathborne; Charles Doraine; Pearl Hart; Abram Flaxer, president of the State, County and Municipal Workers Union; Rabbi Moses Miller of the Jewish People's Committee; Revels Cayton of the Maritime Federation of the Pacific; Joseph Curran; John DeBoer; Max Yergan; Millen Brand; Carl Sandburg; Richard Wright; Langston Hughes; Carey McWilliams; Earl Robinson; Rev. Frank Smith; Michael Quill; Dr. Abraham Crombach; George S. Murphy; State Senator Charles Fine of North Dakota; Clinton Clark of the Louisiana Farmers Union; Bella Dodd of the New York Teachers Union; Rev. Owen Whitfield, of the United Cannery Workers (C.I.O.); Manuel Lucas of the Florida Cigar Workers Union; Virgil O'Conner; Father Smith of the Society of Catholic Commonwealth; Grant Oakes, chairman of the Farm Equipment Workers Organizing Committee;

William Hixon; Norman McKibben, president of the Workers Alliance; Enoch Price; Prof. Franz Boas; Mrs. Margaret Gayle of the Georgia Conference of Social Workers; Oscar Ameringer, editor of the *American Guardian*; William Ross of the United Mine Workers; William Harrison, editor of the Boston *Chronicle*; Clifford O'Brien; Philip Connolly, head of the California C.I.O. Council; Meyer Adelman; Louis Berne, president of the Federation of Architects, Chemists, Engineers and Technicians; George Seldes, editor of the party-line propaganda sheet *In Fact*; State Senator Charles Bigg of Michigan; Saul Brunin; Mrs. Aline Davis Hays, chairman of the New York League of Women Shoppers.

These were the chosen. Many of them, no doubt, did not suspect that they were fulfilling a promise made to Nazi Germany by Stalinist Russia—a promise, moreover, for which Germany paid with a ghastly betrayal. For the most part they represented a reshuffling of the same old crowd under a new name. "Peace" being a seductive word, any number of unsuspecting long-established anti-war organizations had sent delegates to Chicago. Notwithstanding a growing public sophistication in such matters, there were still plenty of suckers to serve as respectable window dressing for every picket line, every mass meeting, every publication of the Mobilization.

3

The "isolationism" of the Mobilization was a rather bizarre hybrid, since it was made in the image of the current Soviet foreign policy. Thus in its first year hysterical demands for absentation from the European war were coupled, illogically but emphatically, with demands for full aid to China, total embargo against Japan, and entangling alliances with Soviet Russia. After Moscow and Tokyo built their own axis, the anti-Japanese and pro-Chinese notes were not entirely squelched—apparently Stalin was still bargaining at that end—but carefully muted.*

---

* In his first draft of this chapter, written just before the Nazi assault on Russia, Mr. Lyons had at this point the following passage, which seems to us worth preserving:

The chance of Stalin turning against Germany seems, at this writing, extremely remote; the chance of Hitler turning against Russia seems exceedingly real. In either contingency, the American Peace Mobilization would either fold up or reverse its

After its launching at the Chicago Stadium the A.P.M. was indefatigable in damning Roosevelt, Britain, the lend-lease bill, conscription and official measures against sabotage of defense industries. Nearly every strike in a bottleneck industry of the defense effort could be readily traced through its leaders and supporters to the A.P.M. On December 9, 1940, a meeting was called to plan a "march on Washington." Freddy (Blackie) Myers, organizer for Curran's maritime union, told the A.P.M. leaders there that "the time for action has arrived, our telegrams and resolutions are being disregarded, the time may come when nothing less than a nationwide strike against war will be effective. But we've got to hurry." The threat of a general strike to paralyze America's potential action to stop Hitler was advanced with growing emphasis in the propaganda.

Demonstrations in Washington under Mobilization banners became a routine event. Delegations tried unsuccessfully to see the President, Mr. Morgenthau, Jesse Jones and Senator George. They were cordially received, however, by Senator Burton Wheeler, and by the Coughlinite Congressman Martin L. Sweeney; the latter even inserted some of the propaganda into the Congressional Record. Rallies to protest aid to Britain became epidemic, always cut to the master pattern. In the New York area, Congressman Marcantonio, Bella Dodd, Jean Horie, Eugene Connolly, Morris Watson and Walter Neff yelled themselves hoarse in the service of Stalin's American Peace Mobilization. Poor Robeson sang and sang and sang.

Another Randall's Stadium demonstration, on April 5, 1941, anniversary of the fledgling rally on Washington Square, was called in a flamboyant message signed by "220 delegates from 53 cities in 25 states and 77 unions, meeting in Washington, D. C., on January 27, 1941." The "Working Conference for Peace," a strongly ecclesiastic pacifist body, seems to have been drawn into joint sponsorship of the event, which styled itself an "American People's Meeting."

The Rev. Mr. Thompson, the scowling Dreiser, the pushing Marcantonio and Jack McMichael, chairman of the American Youth Congress, led all the rest of the signatories. The curious political confection included such ingredients as Hollywood's Biberman; Rev.

---

line. So we may still have the thrill of hearing Paul Robeson sing and Vito Marcantonio shout and Mike Quill bluster for America's entry into the war. The *Daily Worker*, the Hollywood brethren of the faith, Theodore Dreiser, the American Youth Congress and John L. Lewis may still discover miraculously that this "imperialist" war is a holy crusade for justice and freedom after all.—*The Publishers.*

Albert W. Buck of the Evangelical and Reformed Church, Chicago; Russell N. Chase of the Civil Liberties Union of Ohio; Morris Carnovsky, Broadway actor; Henry Wadsworth Longfellow Dana, a much-worn Stalinist stage prop; a Y.M.C.A. Secretary from Hartford named Leonard Detweiler; Robert W. Geiger, president of the Pennsylvania Workers Alliance; Dashiell Hammett, the current president of the redoubtable League of American Writers; Mrs. Aline Davis Hays; Rev. Lee A. Howe, Jr., of the Oneida, N. Y., Baptist Church; Julius Klyman and Morris Watson, vice-presidents of the American Newspaper Guild; Canada Lee, actor; William Levner, president of the W.P.A. Teachers Local 453, A.F. of L.; Father Thomas Logan of Philadelphia; Norman McKibben, president of the Workers Alliance; Lewis Merrill, president of the United Office and Professional Workers of America; the Right Rev. Walter Mitchell, Bishop of Arizona; O. M. Orton, president of the International Woodworkers of America, C.I.O.; Dean Elbert Russell of Duke University; Joseph Selly, president of the American Communications Association, C.I.O.; Artie Shaw, the swing maestro; Eda Lou Walton, literary critic; Richard Wright, the novelist; and Art Young, the cartoonist.

Among the organizations listed as behind this "call" were the American Youth Congress, the usual array of C.I.O. unions and regional Councils, the Farmer-Labor Party of Minnesota, the International Workers Order, the League of Young Southerners, the Southern Negro Youth Congress, the Washington (State) Commonwealth Federation. The "call" told how "democracy had been blacked out" in Germany, France, England and now the United States—but remained discreetly silent on the state of democracy in beloved Russia. "This is not a war to wipe out the evils of Hitlerism and tyranny," it proclaimed. ". . . It is a war to line the pockets of corporate interests at the expense of the peoples of the world." Hasty words destined to boomerang when Hitler broke faith with the Peace Mobilization!

Despite the imposing list of signatories and the shrill call to action, the meeting fizzled. The *Daily Worker* expected an attendance of 30,000 and claimed that 4,225 delegates and 748 "observers" had been "elected" to participate. But less romantic reporters said that only 200 delegates were in the stand, along with a thinnish sprinkling of guests. However, indoor sessions took place at Mecca Temple at which, for the sake of variety, Paul Robeson sang, Vito Marcantonio damned Roosevelt and Britannia, and Corliss Lamont praised Stalin's noble foreign policies.

The main open activities of the A.P.M. were picketing the White House and giving testimonial dinners to Marcantonio. The perpetual picket line around the Roosevelts at one point was joined by a contingent of Curran's sailor boys carrying "No Convoy" signs—a rather broad hint, everything considered. At another time a delegation from the American Communications Association joined the White House parade. The "vigil" had the blessings of the League of American Writers and every other party-line setup. The Dies Committee presented testimony that at least 150 Federal employees were among the 500 persons who went from Washington to New York for the April "People's Meeting" of the A.P.M., among them a number holding tactically important posts in the government. It has also been disclosed that when the Mobilization got stuck for cash to finance the White House parade, its organizers wired to nine of the muddled-millions coterie, among them Lionel Stander, the movie comedian; Broadway producer Herman Shumlin; George Marshall, one of the editors of *Soviet Russia Today*; Mrs. Ellen Brandsteader of Chicago; and Alfred K. Stern.

From an intimate source it is learned that decisions for dramatic anti-defense action on American docks, harbors and ships were taken at a secret meeting in a Greenwich Village apartment. The Communist Party commissar for shipping, Roy Hudson, told about twenty-five leading communists to prepare for an all-out test of "our party's strength in the maritime industry." The meeting was attended by the leaders of communist "fractions" in such shipyards and ports as Mobile, San Francisco, San Diego, Philadelphia, Boston, New Orleans and New York.

The real significance of the Mobilization, of course, was not in its open activities. It was in the wires connecting it with hundreds of big and little groups under Muscovite influence and especially with trade-union fractions owned and controlled by communist agents in munitions, shipping, radio and telegraphy and other industries basic to national security.

The organization was fated to a short if busy life. The Nazi attack on Stalin's country, of course, turned all the A.P.M. slogans and activities to ashes. As these words are set down, it is not yet clear what disposition will be made of the humiliated organization whose very existence must remain a reminder of the Kremlin's stupidity. Should Soviet Russia find itself once more in the Hitlerite camp—through capitulation or compromise—then the Mobilization or another outfit of the same kind could take up the noble task of a Hitler-styled "peace" where it was interrupted by Herr Adolf Schicklgruber's ingratitude.

Meanwhile, American communism and its manifold extensions have made a complete swing around the circle in less than two years: from the superpatriotic interventionism of the League for Peace and Democracy, through the perfervid isolationism of the American Peace Mobilization and back to the starting point. And the merry-go-round is still turning.

CHAPTER **XXXII**

THE MENACE OF TODAY

1

NOW that the panic has abated, it is possible to take stock, in a general way, of what remained after the collapse of the incredible revolution which climaxed the Red Decade.

The Communist Party of the United States lost a few leaders and a great many members but was not seriously shaken organizationally. From its Fourth Period peak of some 75,000, it probably slid down to 35,000 or 40,000; one guess is nearly as good as another. Its income from American sources dropped off sharply, now that the cocktail front had been all but abolished. But its major publications continued to appear, indicating that the foreign subsidy had been increased by headquarters to help a branch office in its time of depression.

The party let the crease out of its pants and became more negligent about shaving. Browder's boys lost their appetite for lecturing in universities and keeping other such low bourgeois company. Agreeing with Broun that the masquerade was over, the party leaders ordered a general retreat underground. The aboveground skeleton of an organization was retained, but the essential business of the party was transferred to reorganized small groupings, meeting conspiratively. The secret members became even more secretive, and extreme precautions were ordered to conceal membership lists. As a transparent legalistic stratagem, the "severance" of relations with the Communist International was formally announced to the press—at the very moment when those relations were more intimate, the Moscow control more jealous, than ever in the past. Even the ostensible ownership of the *Daily Worker* was transferred to three very old ladies of D.A.R. vintage by way of legal camouflage. Margaret Marshall suggested that if the ladies intended to write for "their" paper, they might adopt Estonia, Latvia and Lithuania as pen names.

Outside the party itself there remained, as we have seen, a vast array of old and new Innocents' Clubs, though none of them, old or new, even approached the size and the political weight of the former League for Peace and Democracy or the American Youth Congress at the zenith of its glory. There remained—and that is the most vital fact, practically—the whole complex of those C.I.O. unions wholly or in part under communist leadership.

There is no real difficulty in identifying these unions. In nearly all of them there is an anti-Muscovite opposition which has the detailed facts—should our government or the press ever work up the courage to expose this alien strangle hold on a portion of American labor. They have identified themselves repeatedly at regional and national conventions, voting always as a bloc under the command of good Left-Wingers like Harry Bridges, Joe Curran, Mike Quill and Morris Watson. At the C.I.O. convention soon after the 1940 Presidential election, the division between the Stalinist minority and the American majority was clear-cut. Stalinist union leaders have been on all the new and old front organizations. As we have seen, they constituted the most conspicuous façade embellishments for all the "peace" and "civil liberties" outfits under Moscow's inspiration. They revealed themselves on any test vote on resolutions implying criticism of Russia.

In a survey of the situation published in the *American Mercury* in February, 1941, Victor Riesel, an exceptionally well-informed labor journalist, wrote:

Comrade Browder ... had ample reason for self-satisfaction. The communists had succeeded in developing significant strength in the fields of machine tools, steel, aircraft production, munitions, communications, transportation—in the fields, that is, of most critical importance in connection with defense preparations. This was no accident. In the United States, as in all other countries, the Communist International from the very beginning of its career had focussed its energies and its cash investments on precisely those industries which were of most strategic value in relation to war and defense efforts. . . . The result is that a foreign dictator, operating through subsidized American agents or unsubsidized enthusiasts for his cause, is in a position to throw a monkey-wrench into the machinery of American defense.

The epidemic of defense strikes was no surprise to those who had been watching the communist penetration of American life. There was for them no mystery in the circumstance that those strikes always developed particular virulence in plants whose products were essential for the operation of a large number of other industries. Of course, there were usually genuine grievances which the comrades skillfully exploited to stir up trouble. The rank and file of strikers are as patriotic as any other group of working men and women in America—like the rest of the country, they were victimized by the communist conspiracy in our midst.

It would be silly to deny that the series of defense tie-ups was communist in origin. The very newspapers and commentators who had been cautious or silent on the subject said in chorus, when the Russo-German war started, "Now the defense strikes will decline or stop altogether!" thus acknowledging Soviet string-pulling. It's an old communist trick to make people "prove" the obvious. The pattern of these defense industry "insurrections," to use Robert Jackson's word for one of the strikes, was always the same. Wage and other legitimate demands would be made; the official mediation machinery would show itself quite capable of effecting a settlement; but always the pro-Soviet leadership would select and concentrate on some far-fetched issue not easily adjustable, and the strike was protracted.

In the first six months of 1941 some 2,500,000 man-hours were lost in vital defense industries. The subsequent reversal of the party line must not expunge the memory of that deliberate piece of sabotage in a moment of national crisis. *The same machinery for new attacks on America is still extant and still under orders from a foreign totalitarian dictatorship.* Here are a few of the more publicized anti-defense strikes:

The Vultee Aircraft plant at Downey, California, was tied up in mid-November. Its real leader was the notorious Wyndham Mortimer whose Communist Party name is—or was—Baker. The negotiations were broken off on minor technicalities of the kind straightened out without difficulty as soon as the leaders, under War Department pressure, decided to co-operate.

Vastly more serious was the strike at the Allis-Chalmers plant which lasted seventy-six days, from January to April, 1941, affected $45,000,-000 of military contracts and delayed our destroyer program by three months. At the head of the union, Local 248 of the United Automobile Workers, stands Harold Christoffel whose Stalinism is undisguised. In eight months he called seventeen stoppages, practically all on ludicrous pretexts. The seventy-six day strike involved nothing more momentous than the charge that a tiny number of A.F. of L. workers were engaged in their own union propaganda.

Among the most loyal henchmen of Bridges is O. M. Orton, who on May 9 pulled out 12,000 workers from logging camps and sawmills in the Puget Sound region. Negotiations for settlement were going normally when Orton suddenly withdrew, charging that the Defense Mediation Board was "an all-out labor-busting and strike-breaking device." This of a board whose membership included President Murray of the C.I.O. and Thomas Kennedy, secretary-treasurer of the United Mine Workers!

The aluminum industry, basic to aviation production, naturally was compassed by the obstruction strike movement. The Die-Casters Union brought about a strike at the Cleveland plant of the Aluminum Company, shutting down work on $60,000,000 of aluminum castings vital for airplane output. The leaders of the union included Edward T. Cheyfitz, a former member of the Young Communist League. Another aluminum strike, involving 5,000 workers at the Bohn plants in Detroit, was led by John Anderson, once communist candidate for governor in Michigan.

The most dramatic of the strikes was at the Inglewood, California, plant of the North American Aircraft Company, closed on June 6 by the local C.I.O. crowd and reopened several weeks later by the U. S. Army. Mortimer was again among the leaders, seconded by Elmer Freitag, who had registered as a communist in 1938, and by Lew Michener, an old hand in Muscovite movements. Some $200,000,000 worth of aviation work was menaced and the pro-Soviet leadership could not be budged by the chiding and the threats of their central organization.

At the time the President ordered the Army to take over the Inglewood plants, it looked as if the C.I.O. might finally crack down on its totalitarian sector. From Washington came news dispatches under reputable by-lines, evidently inspired by C.I.O. tip-offs, forecasting an earnest house-cleaning effort. But optimism on this matter soon petered out. Murray, allegedly after conferences with Lewis and Pressman, changed his tune sharply, disowned those dispatches and left small doubt that the fantastic *status quo* of communist control would for the time being remain undisturbed.

The strike climate changed .overnight—specifically over the night of June 22—when the Nazi-Soviet entente was smashed by Hitler's armies. What neither the government nor the anti-Stalin leaders of the C.I.O. could achieve by pleading or menacing, Hitler did for them. One must pause to savor this fact. An allegedly American labor movement, engaged in the life-and-death task of building a national defense structure, decided to work or to desist from work in accordance with the shifting preference of a foreign dictator!

2

Among liberals, writers, artists, professors—on the so-called intellectual front—Stalinist influence is still effective, notwithstanding the retreat and the attention it attracted. The myth of a "socialist Russia" and its "happy life" persists. A topsy-turvy book like the Dean of Canterbury's *Soviet Power*—an Alice-in-Wonderland volume that can only be catalogued as literature of hallucination—not only finds publication but is seriously discussed by alleged intellectuals.

Discomfited by the "strange" conduct of that country in the war crisis, the Russian-worshippers yet consoled themselves desperately. Surely, they told themselves, there must be something deeply Machiavellian in the business which ordinary mortals cannot see or understand. They must take Moscow on faith. In the make-believe world of their political religion, the chivalrous Stalin was "saving" the Poles and Finns when he invaded their lands, "protecting" the ungrateful Baltic countries and sections of Rumania. The ineffable one in the Kremlin was secretly "undermining Hitler," they whispered, even though he was openly acting as a shameless stooge for Hitler in every country and colony of the earth. In every rumor or troop movement in Eastern Europe they detected Stalin's readiness to "join the democracies."

Stalin, alas, did not join the democracies. *He was violently shoved in among them against his will.* On the basis of such facts as are now available it seems likely that Hitler did not even give him an opportunity to capitulate without fighting. When Molotov said pitiably, on the morning after the Hitler double cross, that Russia had been honestly abiding by its promises to Germany and had not even had any complaints on the subject, he was probably telling the truth.

The aggression was, indeed, undeserved: the Kremlin had worked overtime to please Berlin and to impress the Führer with the Comintern's usefulness in its new role as Dr. Goebbels' handmaiden. The fact that the Nazis betrayed their Soviet partner does not in the slightest detract from Stalin's crime in entering that partnership. It merely demonstrated that the most extreme appeasement was futile.

The outbreak of the Russo-German war stripped the Soviet dictatorship of its last shred of self-respect. It had not merely betrayed its millions of Fourth Period united-fronters but was being deprived of the fruit of its crime. Few parallels for sheer blundering in foreign policy can be found in modern history. During four years the Kremlin labored to construct a Popular collective-security Front, whatever its motives. In the spring of 1939 the effort finally succeeded. The very statesmen who had most bitterly opposed it were begging, hat in hand, for just what Moscow had been offering all along. They showed their earnestness by guaranteeing the frontiers of Poland and Rumania, thereby in effect guaranteeing the safety of Russia.

But Stalin decided to destroy his four years' effort. He decided to touch off a European war, remain in the side lines, and serve his fascist partner as a benevolent non-belligerent. At one blow he sacrificed the goodwill of millions the world over, wrecked hundreds of his communist organizations, evoked hurricanes of hatred everywhere. Then he hastened to grab territories belonging to weak neighbors in a mood of cynical disdain for civilized opinion. As the military might of the Nazis became more apparent, a desperate eagerness to serve entered into Russia's behavior as a Hitlerite agent. It called "people's conventions" in England to preach compromise. It strove to set every Latin American country against the United States. It fomented strikes and subsidized "peace" movements in America.

When the news that Hitler was turning his strength against Russia spread through the world, Moscow officially denied it all as "capitalist rumors." It was, Tass charged, "quite clumsily concocted propaganda" by forces "interested in further extension of the war." Communist publications featuring such denials were still on the newsstands when the brown hordes began to overrun the Soviet land. Scores of "anti-war" and "anti-imperialist" organizations built up by Stalin throughout the world remained as living monuments to a totalitarian despot's stupidity, even while he cried out for the help of England and America.

Suddenly he was the despised and pitied ward of the democracies he had baited only yesterday, surrounded by neighbors who hated Stalin even more than they feared Hitler, facing a continent for once united on one project of destruction. This when it had been within his power to head off the Second World War, or at worst to force a real two-front war on Germany as a respected member of a world-wide anti-Nazi coalition. He may have received the formal help of Britain and the United States, but not an iota of their trust. For his betrayal of the anti-fascist cause Stalin collected only war and contempt.

Among the intellectuals who recanted and retreated and were duly chastised in communist editorials, Stalin's party still retains a significant hold. Psychologically these latest "renegades" remain tied to the Stalinist movement *by their sense of guilt*. Having been deeply involved in communist skulduggery for so many years, some of them find it difficult to speak out or to deal tolerantly with those who do speak out. They are under pressure always to blur or conceal the ugly story. Perhaps some of them harbor a hope that their investment of emotion has not been entirely lost.

Avidly they grab at any scrap of information or rumor, however tenuous or withered, that might sustain this hope. Consciously or in a fog of self-justification, they still find ways of attacking or ignoring anti-Soviet books, of aiding (or at least tolerating) new Soviet rackets. Stalin may have betrayed and shamed them, but he is still their Little Father and the family scandals had best be kept out of the papers. Such ex-fellow-travelers, their spirits yearning toward Moscow despite everything, are entrenched in the government, in the schools, in literature, everywhere. All that many of them need is a halfway decent pretext to return to their old ideological loves. For many of these "unreconstructed fellow-travelers," to use Professor Hook's phrase, the German attack on Russia came like a blessed release. Once again they were able to exhibit their suppressed affection for the Kremlin and its works.

3

The communist planetary system is with us despite the ending of the Red Decade. What the current task of the communists will be when these pages are published cannot now be guessed. The only certainty is that it will be a task conditioned by Russia's and not by America's national interests. By definition the communist and his fellow-travelers, though not all of them are aware of it, in fact serve

a foreign nation before their own. The most self-respecting and conscientious among them can merely rationalize their allegiance to the
Soviet dictatorship in terms of higher duty. However they may rationalize their conduct as pro-American, their readiness to support an outside power against the United States has been a demonstrated fact.

I submit, on the basis of what has been summarized in these pages,
that the Communist Party and its manifold affiliates and stooge outfits
have no more claim on the tolerance of democratic-minded Americans
than the German Bund or any other subservient agency of a foreign
totalitarian regime. They have as little title to the protection of the
Bill of Rights as any other espionage and propaganda agencies of
foreign dictatorships. The circumstance that they deck themselves
in pseudo-idealistic verbiage and Left slogans should not exempt them
from moral and legal responsibility for their Trojan Horsemanship,
any more than its exempts a Nazi spy posing as a superpatriot. It
merely adds the count of charlatanism to the indictment against them.
We are not concerned, after all, with the skill of their disguise but
with the practical functions under the camouflage.

The spectacle of a foreign-owned and foreign-controlled agency
putting up candidates for the highest and lowest offices in the land,
enjoying the privileges reserved for American political parties and
cynically exploiting the magnanimity of the Bill of Rights and the
mores of a democratic tradition, is amusing in normal times. It is a
type of self-indulgence which a democratic nation can permit itself at
certain times, if only as a disdainful gesture of self-confidence.

But there is a point at which self-confidence becomes foolish and
even suicidal. Such indulgence in a period of crisis when democracy
is admittedly on the defensive is worse than frivolous. It is close to
social insanity. It means risking the liberties of the present and endless
coming generations through squeamishness in diagnosing and treating
social dangers. Not one of the European democracies prostrate under
the heel of Hitler or Stalin would again permit itself the luxury of
indulging avowed enemies of democracy and agents of totalitarian aggressors if it could turn back the clock and live its last decade over
again.

We cannot and must not deny to any American the right to believe
anything he wishes—and that includes socialism and communism and
anarchism in all their endless variations. But by no stretch of common
sense can this principle be distorted to provide shelter for the agents

of any totalitarian nation and to facilitate the success of Hitler's or Stalin's assignments in America. It is not tolerance but stupidity to risk our democracy out of fear of sullying it. We must make a clear and indubitable distinction between an American's personal beliefs, however unorthodox or cockeyed, and automatic submission to dictation from outside. It is, in the final checkup, the difference between an honest opinion and an order from headquarters.

The Kremlin's right to carry on conspiracies for the expunging of your liberties and mine—for subordinating American independence to Stalin's whims or needs—is in no way guaranteed by the Bill of Rights. Despite the outcries of muddled liberals under shrewd Muscovite cheerleaders, Stalin's prerogative of placing a candidate for President of the United States on our ballot is not exactly an "inalienable right."

I submit that the right to survival is the first law for democracies as for any other society. We must face the fact that the Communist Party and the organizations under its control do not constitute an American political unit but merely the American segment of a world-wide Soviet conspiracy. The objection is not to an international organization within which the American member has an equal status with other nations. The objection is to a bogus "international" in which the American member is a willing tool in the hands of a foreign nation.

The "liberalism" which defends the right of Stalin to wipe out all our rights places the forms and the formulas of democracy above the substance of democratic self-defense and democratic survival. It is, of course, unfortunate that there is no rule-of-thumb by which democratic freedoms may be applied or denied. Admittedly there is a central zone between the obvious extremes where the good sense of the community must assert itself as best it can. The right of free speech, press and assemblage cannot be exercised indiscriminately to the point of producing violence and panic through deliberate inflaming of crowd passions, racial hatreds and group phobias. By the same token the right to political organization cannot be extended indiscriminately to conspiracies against American democratic modes of existence.

I am not unmindful of the risks involved. Unfortunately nothing that we do, from crossing the street to developing a policy of national security, is without an element of hazard. Both principle and expediency dictate circumspection and calmness in dealing with the problems of foreign agencies which function through American personnel. Wherever feasible, the techniques of exposure are self-evidently preferable to the techniques of legal restraint. But wounds must not be allowed to fester and spread their poison because of squeamishness in applying antiseptic.

In taking action against the communist penetration of American life there are clearly dangers involved. The chief of these is that innocent bystanders may get hurt. But the danger of letting Nazi or Stalinist agents function freely in this time of world-wide crisis is infinitely greater. Soviet Russia stands convicted of crimes against the laws of God and man. No far-fetched sophistries can remove it from the category of totalitarian, brutal and horrifying dictatorships. Its agents have no more claim to special "democratic" prerogatives than the agents of any other regime in that category.

THE END

INDEX

INDEX

Abbott, George, 290
Abbott, Grace, 272
Abolitionists, 29
Abraham Lincoln Brigade, 283, 326
Ackley, John C., 254
A.C.L.U. *See* American Civil Liberties Union
Adamic, Louis, 345
Addams, Jane, 154
Addis, Thomas, 350
Adelante, 278
Adelman, Meyer, 224, 388
Adler, Stella, 293
Adventures of a Young Man, 337
A. F. of L. *See* American Federation of Labor
"Against an American Third Party," 80
Agar, Herbert, 345
Aircraft and Machinists Division of the U.A.W., 229
Alabama Farmers Union, 230, 387
Alexander, Henry, 136
Alfred, Helen, 350
Algren, Nelson, 147, 248
Allen, Jay, 270
Allis-Chalmers, strike, 227, 385, 395
Aluminum Company, 396
Aluminum Workers, 230
Amalgamated Clothing Workers of America, 40, 43, 221
Amalgamated Food Workers, 85
American Artists Congress, 369, 376
American Civil Liberties Union, 148, 372
American Committee for the Defense of Leon Trotsky, 251
American Committee for Friendship with the Soviet Union, 374
American Committee for the Protection of the Foreign Born, 376
American Committee for Struggle Against War, 150
American Committee for the World Congress Against War, 149
American Communications Association, 212, 226, 229, 390
American Council for Soviet Affairs, 348
American Council on Soviet Relations, 375
American Federation of Labor, 35, 39, 42, 70, 72, 82, 170, 175, 219, 220, 221, 222, 223, 226, 230, 396
American Federation of Teachers, 212

American Friends of the Chinese People, 157, 376
American Friends of Spanish Democracy, The, 280n.
American Guardian, 388
American Investors Union, 376
American Labor Party, 175, 264, 301
American Labor Pictures, Inc., 290
American Legion, 33-34, 172, 196
American Magazine, 63
American Mercury, 225, 272, 284, 337n., 362, 379, 394
American Negro Labor Congress. *See* League for Struggle for Negro Rights, 78
American Newspaper Guild, 185, 212, 222, 229, 230, 340, 383, 385, 387, 390
American Peace Mobilization, 9, 50, 307, 371, 374, 382-392
American Rescue Ship Mission, 212
American Revolutionary Dancers, 138
American Socialist Monthly, 217
American Socialist Party, 53
American Society for Race Tolerance, 375
American Student Union, 154, 156, 212-215, 216, 218, 305, 366, 375
American Writers Congress, 177, 202, 256, 366
American Youth Congress, 9, 154-156, 202, 206, 209-212, 299, 309, 366, 368, 376, 387, 390
Ameringer, Oscar, 388
Amsterdam, Congress, 149, 195
Anderson, John, 396
Anderson, Sherwood, 129, 144, 349
Anglo-Russian Committee in England, 23
Anschluss, 14
Anti-Imperialist League, 50, 75, 141, 148
Anvil, The, 137, 143
Appel, Benjamin, 320
Aptheker, Herbert, 370
Araquistan, Luis, 270, 271, 273, 280
Arent, Arthur, 248
Arlen, Richard, 293
Armstrong, Arnold B., 147
Arnold, Benedict, 173
Arnold, Edward, 293
Arnold, Mrs. Thurman, 308
Artef, 75, 139
Artists in Uniform, 130
Artists Union, 230

405

Artkino, Distributor of Soviet Films in the United States, 375
Arvin, Newton, 254, 318, 320, 349
Asch, Nathan, 147
Assignment in Utopia, 14, 96, 100, 116
Association of American Law Students, 375
Atkinson, Brooks, 297
Attasheva, Pearl, 139
Attempts by Communists to Seize the American Labor Movement, 219
Auerbach, Leopold, 130
Authors' League of America, 288
Azaña, 279

Bainter, Fay, 294
Baker, George. *See* Mortimer, Wyndham
Baldridge, Cyrus LeRoy, 345
Baldwin, Roger, 148, 367
Baltimore, 230
Baltimore *Evening Sun,* 187
Baltimore Statewide Conference on Civil Liberties, 374
Balzac, 135
Bancroft, Frank C., 350
Barbusse, Henri, 80, 133, 149, 151, 154
Barnes, Harry Elmer, 198
Baron, Sam, 19, 271, 273, 334
Barrows, Alice, 367
Basic industries, 42
Bates, Ernest Sutherland, 345
Bates, Ralph, 270, 321, 358, 363
Bay, Howard, 387
Beal, Fred E., 265, 331-332
Beard, Professor Charles A., 202
Beatty, Bessie, 350
Beausobre, Julia de, 94
Becker, Beril, 248
Becker, Carl, 345
Becker, Mrs. William A., 187
Bedacht, Max, 53, 197, 265
Bein, Albert, 290, 320
Benchley, Robert, 291, 296
Benjamin, Herbert, 89
Bennett, Joan, 294
Bennett, Thomas B., 248
Benson, Governor, 196
Benton, Thos. H., 345
Berkman, Alexander, 51
Berle, Adolph A., 304, 371
Berlin Anti-Comitern Pact, 165
Berne, Lewis Allen, 224, 388
Bernhard, Bern, 295
Bernstein, Aline, 320
Bethlehem Steel, 223
Biberman, Herbert, 286, 287, 288, 290, 291, 292, 293, 294, 295, 387, 389
Biddle, George, 369

Biedenkapp, Fred H., 189
Bigg, State Senator Charles, of Michigan, 388
Billings, 14, 331
Bioff, Willie, 289
Birk, Louis P., 350
Bishop, Dr. Hillman, 196
Bisson, L. A., 350
Bittelman, Alex, 36, 53, 189
Black, Justice, 301
Blackwell, Alice Stone, 350
Blake, Bishop Edgar F., 196
Blake, Katherine Deveraux, 350
Blanch, Arnold, 248
Blankfort, Michael, 148
Blast, 138, 143
Bledsoe, William, 284-285, 287, 288, 289, 295
Blitzstein, Marc, 248, 249, 348, 387
Bliven, Bruce, 103, 107, 242
Block, Anita, 139
Block, Dr. Louis, 303, 308
Bloor, Ella Reeves, 40, 189, 190, 265
Blum, Leon, 24, 27, 298, 318
Boas, Franz, 388
Bodenheim, Maxwell, 147
Bohn plants, 396
Bohnen, Roman, 248
Bonham, R. P., 231, 232
Book and Magazine Guild, 230, 340
Book-and-Play-of-the-Month Club, 375
Books, 338
Books Abroad, 350
Book Union, 340, 375
Boston *Chronicle,* 388
Boston Citizens Union, 374
Boston Tea Party, 29
Boston University, 384
Bouck, William, 45
Bowen, Stirling, 350
Boyd, Thomas, 147
Brady, Robert A., 349
Brand, Millen, 248, 320, 348, 350, 387
Brand, Phoebe, 248
Brandsteader, Mrs. Ellen, 391
Breakdown, 136
Brenner, Anita, 271, 279
Brent, George, 294
Breuer, Bessie, 320
Brewster, Dorothy, 248, 320, 346, 348, 349, 370
Brickell, 338
Brickner, Rabbi Barnett R., 196
Bridgeman, Michigan, Convention, 35
Bridgeport, 230
Bridges, Harry, 12, 85, 151, 223, 224, 225, 226, 227, 231, 289, 302, 303, 304, 385, 394

Bridgman, P. J., 345
Briffault, Robert, 136-137, 350
Briggs, Marian, 216
Brightman, Edgar, 384
Brissenden, Paul F., 345
British Labor Party, 216
Bromberg, J. Edward, 290, 295
Bromfield, 369
Bromley, Dorothy Dunbar, 345
Brook Farm, 29
Brooklyn Church and Mission Federation, 373
Brooklyn College, 213, 214
Brooks, Van Wyck, 148, 314, 315-316, 317, 318, 320, 369
Brophy, John, 41, 219
Brotherhood of Railway Trainmen, 198
Broun, Heywood, 193, 194, 222, 254, 290, 322, 327, 335, 346, 362
Browder, Earl, 12, 21, 22, 35, 36, 40, 53, 54, 62, 63-69, 78, 83, 142, 144, 146, 147, 150-152, 153, 154, 156, 170, 171, 173, 175, 179, 180, 182, 189, 190, 193, 195, 196, 197, 198, 202, 207, 215, 222, 233, 265, 266, 301, 311, 317, 318, 319, 321, 323, 329, 352-354, 355, 357, 362, 365
Browder, Irene, 189
Brown, Bob, 147
Brown, John, 16, 29
Brown, J. R., 248
Brunin, Saul, 388
Brussels, 215
Bryant, Louise, 111
Bryn Mawr College, 349
Buchman, Mrs. Beatrice, 295
Buchman, Sidney, 291, 292, 320
Buck, Rev. Albert W., 390
Bufano, Remo, 296
Bukharin, Nikolai, 59, 126, 240, 241, 314
Bulkley, Robert, 305
Bulletin of the League of American Writers, 376
Bund, German-American, 181, 346
Burgum, Edwin Berry, 136, 248, 254, 348, 349, 370
Burke, Fielding, 147, 350
Burke, Kenneth, 147, 320
Burr, Aaron, 173
Burt, Struthers, 345
Burton, Harold L., 196
Butler, Major General Smedley D., 196
Bynner, Witter, 345
Byrne, Professor, 295

Caballero, Largo, 268, 269, 271, 273, 277-278
Cabot, Bruce, 294
Cadden, Joseph, 206, 216, 387

Cagney, James, 288, 290, 294
Caldwell, Erskine, 129, 134, 147, 318, 320
California, 230. See also Hollywood; San Francisco
California C.I.O. Council, 388
Calmer, Alan, 147
Calverton, V. F., 133, 326, 345
Campbell, Alan, 248, 254, 291
Canby, Henry Seidel, 345
Cannon, James, 32, 50, 53, 57, 259
Cannon, Dr. Walter, B., 272
Can These Things Be!, 90, 313
Cantwell, Robert, 147
Capper, Arthur, 386
Carey, James B., 228-229, 387
Carlisle, Harry, 148
Carlson, Oliver, 345
Carmody, John, 308
Carnovsky, Morris, 248, 390
Caspary, Vera, 248, 348, 350
Catechism of the Revolutionist, 309
Catholic Church, 176, 193, 220
Cauldron, 143
Cayton, Revels, 387
C. C. N. Y., See College of the City of New York
Chabrun, Mme. César, 255
Chamberlain, John, 131, 133, 255, 338, 345
Chamberlin, William Henry, 107, 116, 326, 332, 339
Chambers, Maria Cristena, 350
Chambers, Robert, 350
Chambless, Edgar, 108
Champion of Youth, 216
Ch'ao-ting Chi, 248
Chapin, Katherine Gibson, 320
Chapman, Dr. Emanuel, 384
Chappell, Winifred, 157
Charlottesville, Virginia, 353
Chase, Russell N., 390
Chase, Stuart, 102
Chevalier, Haakon M., 248, 254, 349
Cheyfitz, Edward T., 396
Chiang Kai-shek, 23, 68
Chicago, 175, 230, 296
Chicago Federation of Labor, 41
Chicago Group Theatre, 139
Chicago Tribune, 313
Chicago, University of, 314, 349, 350
Chicherin, 117
Childs, Richard Storrs, 380
China, 191, 201, 369
China Aid Council of the American League for Peace and Democracy, 212, 376
China Today, 282
Chinese Anti-Imperialist Alliance, 75

Chodoroff, Edward, 295
Christian Science Monitor, 332
Christoffel, Harold, 224, 227, 385, 395
Churchill, Winston, 296
Church League for Industrial Democracy, 198
Ciliga, 94
C.I.O. *See* Committee for Industrial Organization
C.I.O. News, 225
City Council of Associated Workers Clubs, 75
Civil Liberties Union, 390
Clark, Clinton, 387
Clark, Joe. *See* Cohen, Joseph
Clark, Senator, 386
Clay, Eugene, 148
Cleveland, Ohio, 44-46, 196, 228, 230
Close, Upton, 154
Clurman, Harold, 248
Clyde, Ethel, 254
C. N. T., 275
Coates, Robert, 147, 248, 249, 349, 350
Cobb, Humphrey, 254, 289, 292, 320
Cochran, Gifford, 254
Cohen, Joseph, 149, 154
Cohen, Lester, 147, 320
Colby, Merle, 148, 248
Cole, Lester, 248, 289, 350
Colgate University, 349
College News, 154
College of the City of New York, 196, 213, 349, 383
College Teachers Union, Local 537, 230
Collier's, 328
Columbia School of Industrial Engineering, 350
Columbia University, 349, 350
"Comintern Reps," 34
Commissariat for Internal Affairs, 168
Committee for Civil Rights for Communists, 374
Committee for Cultural Freedom, 280n., 342, 373, 375
Committee for Industrial Organization, 17, 175, 184, 213, 220, 289, 302, 309, 330, 339, 378, 382, 394, 396-397
Common Sense, 75
Commonwealth Federation (Washington State), 198, 390
Communism in the United States, 208
"Communism Is the Americanism of the Twentieth Century," 180
Communist, The, 90, 282, 378
Communist International, First Period, 22-23, 37, 39; Second Period, 23, 38, 47, 50, 56; Third Period, 23, 56, 70-76, 84-86, 99, 138, 146, 150, 153, 170, 171,

Communist International, Third Period— *Continued*
173-174, 193, 199, 258; Fourth Period, 26-27, 137, 140, 161, 165, 166, 169, 173, 174, 178, 199, 216, 283, 284, 300, 357, 366, 398; Fifth Period, 28, 372
Communist International, 87
Communist Labor Party, 33
Communist League of America (Opposition), 58
Communist Party, 12, 19, 20, 30, 31-34, 37, 61, 71, 75, 137, 160, 191, 196, 199, 220-223, 258, 265, 267, 272, 281, 286, 302, 331, 340, 352, 353
"Communists the Heirs of the Revolution of '76," 180
Communist Workers' School, 297
Communist Youth, 146
Community Church of New York, 194
Conference for Progressive Political Action, 35, 43
Congress of American Revolutionary Writers, 145
Connecticut, 230
Connelly, Marc, 319
Connolly, Philip M., 224, 388
Conroy, Jack, 135, 147, 248
Consumers National Federation, 305
Conway, Curt, 248
Coolidge, Albert Sprague, 345
Coordinating Committee Against Profiteering, 374
Corcoran, 304
Costigan, Howard G., 198
Couday, Ted, 248
Coughlin, Father, 181
Council for Pan-American Democracy, 376
Counts, Dr. George S., 94, 107, 124, 133, 154, 345
Cowan, Emmett, 248
Cowley, Malcolm, 103, 134, 146, 147, 148, 242, 248, 249, 250, 254, 259, 317, 318, 319, 320, 321, 327, 337, 358, 369
Craft, Hy, 295
Crawford, Bruce, 248
Crawford, Joan, 293-294
Cressey, George B., 350
Crichton, Kyle, 139, 248, 327, 349, 350, 364
Cripps, Sir Stafford, 353
Crombach, Dr. Abraham, 387
Cromwell, John, 294
Cronbach, Robert M., 248
Crossen, 370
Cummings, Constance, 296
Cunningham, G. Watts, 345

Curran, Joseph, 85, 223-225, 226, 303, 304, 384, 387, 394
Current History, 63, 133, 168
Cutler, Addison T., 254
Czecho-Slovakia, 359

Dabney, Walter P., 345
Dahlberg, Edward, 147
Dailes, Ida, 152
Daily Worker, 13, 44, 88, 89, 116, 119, 124, 135, 142, 154, 155, 171, 179, 180, 183, 189, 200, 201, 203, 216, 245, 246, 247, 264, 282, 286, 287, 290, 291n., 292, 293, 294, 295n., 297, 307, 312, 330, 332, 335, 346, 349, 352, 354, 376, 378, 379, 382, 390, 393
Damrosch, Walter, 345
Dana, H. W. L., 139, 140, 149, 154, 248, 259, 390
D. A. R., 172
Darcy, Sam, 286
Daughters of the American Depression, 212, 308
Davis, Bette, 294
Davis, Elmer, 345
Davis, Jerome, 111, 247, 248, 254, 259, 291
Davis, John P., 369, 383, 387
Davis, Stuart, 248, 249, 369
Dearborn, Ned H., 291, 384
De Boer, John, 387
Debs, Eugene V., 16, 53
De Caux, Len, 221, 225
Defense Committee for Civil Rights, 374
Defense Mediation Board, 396
De Kruif, Paul, 247, 248, 315, 318
DeLacy, Hugh, 387
De La Mora, Constancia, 268
Del Bagno, Paolo, 264
De Leon, Daniel, 12, 53
Delépine, Maurice, 255
Democratic Party, 175, 178, 289. *See also* New Deal
Dennen, Leon, 144, 326
Dennis, Gene, 189
Depression, 19, 72, 84, 86, 100, 153, 181, 190
Descendants of the American Revolution, 376
Detroit, 155
Detroit Bill of Rights Defense Committee, 374
Detweiler, Leon, 390
Deutsch, Babette, 345
Dewey, Dr. John, 94, 107, 244, 251-258, 314, 326-329, 343, 373
Diament, Heinrich, 139
Di Donato, Pietro, 350

Die-Casters Union, 396
Dies Committee, 147n., 224, 228, 271, 305-307, 311, 391
Dieterle, William, 287
Die Weltbühne, 163
Dillon, 320
Dimitrov, Georgi, 165-166, 171, 264
Dinamov, Sergei, 145
Divine, Father, 176, 200
Dodd, Bella, 383, 387
Dodd, William E., 291
Dodge, Stanley D., 349
Dolfuss, 79
Donaghue, Harry, 387
Doraine, Charles, 387
Doriot, Jacques, 12, 21, 68
Dorothy Parker's Spanish Children's Relief Fund, 280n.
Dos Passos, John, 129, 134, 147, 271, 314, 326, 336-337, 345
Dostoievski, 135
Douglas, Dorothy, 254, 349
Douglas, Melvyn, 294, 295
Douglas, William O., 300, 307
Downey, California, 395
Dozenberg, Nicholas, 67, 267, 302-303
Draper, Muriel, 247, 248, 315, 320, 349, 350
Dream We Lost, The, 339
Dreiser, Theodore, 80, 128, 129, 144, 147, 254, 389n.
Dublin, Mary, 254
Dudley, Jane, 296
Dunn, L. C., 349
Dunn, Robert W., 248, 259
Dunne, Philip, 320
Duranty, Walter, 111, 122-124, 127, 243, 319
Dynamo, 138

Eastman, Max, 130, 182, 257, 262, 326, 329-330, 345
Eddy, Harriet G., 350
Eddy, Sherwood, 109, 111, 244
Eden, Anthony, 238
Edman, Irwin, 345
Ehrlich, Leonard, 148
Einstein, Albert, 149, 272
Eisenstein, Sergei, 139
Eldridge, Florence, 293
Elistratova, 144
Emergency Conference to Save Spanish Refugees, 280n., 374
Emerson, Thomas I., 303, 304n.
Emstach, Jules, 220, 228
Endore, Guy, 147, 248, 254, 292, 320
Engdahl, 53
Engels, 180

England, 200, 238, 274, 276, 280, 298, 389, 398, 399
Enters, Angna, 296
EPIC, 170-171, 289
Epstein, Abraham, 345
Equality, 376
Ernst, Morris, 345
Estonia, 367
Ethel, Dr. Garland, 248
Ethical Culture School, 194
Ethiopian War, 200
Evergood, Phil, 248
Ezekiel, Mrs., 307

Fadiman, Clifton, 131, 133, 136
Fairchild, H. P., 320, 349
Fairchild, Mildred, 254, 349
Famine, in Russia, 49, 71, 97, 106, 115, 117-119
Faragoh, Francis, 295, 320
Farm Equipment Workers Organizing Committee, 230, 284, 387
Farmer, Frances, 294, 296
Farmer-Labor Party, 43, 390
Farmers Union, 38
Farrell, James T., 129, 147, 326, 335-336, 363
Fascization of Russia, 239
F. B. I. *See* Federal Bureau of Investigation, 89
Fearing, Kenneth, 147, 320, 350
Federal Art Project, 340
Federal Bureau of Investigation, 304
Federal Theatre Project, 139, 340
Federal Workers School, 212
Federal Writers' Project, 334, 340
Federated Farmer-Labor Party, 44
Federation of Architects, Chemists, Engineers and Technicians, 230, 384, 388
Federation of Motion Picture Crafts, 289
Fehlhaber, Elmer, 387
"Fellow-Travelers," 136
Ferber, Edna, 345
Ferstadt, Louis, 248
Feuchtwanger, Lion, 331
Ficke, Arthur Davison, 320
Field, Ben, 147
Field, Frederik V., 248
Field, Marshall, III, 378, 379
Field, Sara Bard, 350
Fight, 216, 333
Fighting for Peace, 366
Film and Photo League, 75
Film Audiences for Democracy, 376
Film Daily, 286
Films for Democracy, 300

Fine, State Senator Charles, of North Dakota, 387
Fineman, Irving, 350
Finerty, John F., 255
Finland, 357, 358, 361, 363, 364, 367, 368, 369
Finnish Workers Federation, 375
First All-Union Congress of Soviet Writers, 146
Fischer, Louis, 24, 103, 111, 116-120, 122, 123, 124, 125, 127, 131-132, 168-169, 254, 259, 278, 317, 338, 361-362
Fischer, Marjorie, 320, 350
Fisher, Dorothy Canfield, 345
Fishermen's Union, 230
Fitzpatrick, John, 41
Five Year Plan, 24, 72, 88, 89, 92, 104, 332
Flanagan, Hallie, 139
Flaxer, Abram, 224, 387
Flores, Angel, 148, 350
Florida Cigar Workers Union, 387
Flynn, Elizabeth G., 248, 303
Flynn, John T., 373
Folsom, Franklin, 339
Fonda, Henry, 294
"forced labor," 108
Ford, James W., 78, 145, 151, 189, 190, 265
Ford, John, 53, 294
Ford Motors, 223, 227
Foreign Policy Association, 350
Forsythe, Robert. *See* Crichton, Kyle
For Whom the Bell Tolls, 336
Foss, Mrs. Bertha, 384
Foster, William Z., 32, 35, 40, 53, 56, 57, 60, 62, 66, 72, 78, 145, 176, 189, 202, 228, 265
Foster Parents Plan for Spanish Children, 212
France, 17, 165, 200, 238, 270, 274, 276, 280, 298
Franco, 269, 272, 273, 274, 275, 276, 277
Francon, Marcel, 384
Franco-Soviet Treaty, 162
Frank, Nelson, 19
Frank, Waldo, 112, 129, 131, 144, 146, 147, 255, 292, 318, 334-335, 350, 370
Franklin, 29
Freeman, Joseph, 113, 131, 133, 135, 147, 148, 154, 318, 319, 320
Free Tom Mooney Congress, 156
Freitag, Elmer, 396
French Revolution, 363
Friday, 380, 383
Friedman, Dr. Elisha M., 110

Friends of the Abraham Lincoln Brigade, 375
Friends of Soviet Russia. *See* Friends of the Soviet Union
Friends of the Soviet Union, 49, 75, 141, 146, 148, 177, 202, 208, 258, 263, 346, 366, 368
Friends of Spanish Democracy, 308
Frontier Films, 376
F.S.U. *See* Friends of the Soviet Union
Fuchs, 320
Furniture Workers Union, 230
Fur Workers Union, 41, 230
Fusionists, 175

Gabriel, Gilbert, 291
Gag, Wanda, 350
Gahagan, Helen, 291
Gallagher, Leo, 154
Galtier-Boissière, Jean, 255
Gamarnik, 237
Gannes, Harry, 189
Gannett, Lewis, 133
Gardner, Joseph, 149
Garfield, John, 294, 296
Garfield, Jules, 248
Garrett, Oliver H. P., 289
Gas and Chemical Workers Union, 230
Gastonia, North Carolina, 82, 265, 331
Gayle, Mrs. Margaret, 388
Geddes, Virgil, 139
Geer, Will, 369
Geiger, Robert W., 390
Gelbert, Hugo, 248, 349, 350
General Motors, 227
General Strike (Seattle), 29
George, Harrison, 180, 332, 335
"George Washington—American Revolutionist," 181
Georgia Conference of Social Workers, 388
Germany, 165, 174, 200, 202, 205, 239, 273, 274, 276, 298, 344, 353, 356, 361, 366, 398-399
Gershwin, Ira, 345
Gessner, Robert, 136, 248, 254, 349
Gide, André, 274, 326, 330-331
Gideonse, Dr. Harry D., 214, 326, 345
Gilmore, Dan, 383
Gimbel, Mrs. Louis, 378
Gitlow, Benjamin, 19, 32, 36, 45, 50, 51, 57-61, 69, 233, 265, 267, 326
Glebov, Anatoli, 139
Glinka, 135
Goering, Marshal, 354
Goethe, 135

Gold, Michael, 131, 133, 134, 142, 146, 147, 148, 179, 180, 222, 224, 265, 316, 318, 327, 357, 370
Goldberg, B. Z., 254
Golden Book of American Friendship with the Soviet Union, 259, 260
Goldman, Emma, 16, 51, 53
Goldschmidt, Alphonse, 254
Goldsmith, Leonard, 387
Gollon, John, 216
Gompers, Samuel, 35, 53
Goodelman, Leon, 380
Good Neighbor policy, 366
Goodsell, Wyllistine, 254, 349
Gordon, Eugene, 147
Gorney, Jay, 290, 295
Gottlieb, Harry, 248
G. P. U., 91, 97, 99, 100, 103, 105, 108, 111, 119, 124, 168, 181, 189, 236, 240, 243, 249, 250, 251, 255, 277, 279, 282, 299, 319, 326, 333, 341, 364, 365, 379-380
Grady, Mrs. Henry F., 308
Graham, Martha, 140
Grand Rapids, Michigan, 143
Grapes of Wrath, The, 285
Graves, Mortimer, 350
Gray, Dr. John H., 350
Greater New York Emergency Conference on Inalienable Rights, 374
Great Offensive, The, 115
Grebanier, Dr. B. D. N., 214, 248, 324
Grecht, Rebecca, 189
Green, Gil, 78, 189, 207, 209, 215
Green, William, 71, 171, 220
Greenleaf, Richard, 248
Gregory, Horace, 133, 147
Gropper, William, 350
Group Theatre, 146
Guidice, Ernesto, 216
Guyot, Raymond, 216

Hackett, Frances, 289
Hague, Mayor, 184
Hall, Helen, 291
Hallgren, Mauritz, 259, 320
Halperin, Maurice, 350
Hamilton, 173
Hammett, Dashiell, 247, 248, 294, 314, 346, 349, 350, 370, 390
Hanson, Earl P., 338, 350
Hapgood, Powers, 219
Harcourt, Brace & Co., 292
Harding, 43
Hardman, J. B. S., 85
Harlem Prolets, 138
Harper, Samuel N., 349

Harper's, 378-379
Harris, Abram, 345
Harris, Gerald, Sr., 387
Harris, Marvin, 295
Harris, Rev. Thomas L., 348
Harrison, Charles Yale, 326
Harrison, William, 388
Harriton, Abraham, 248
Hart, Henry, 147, 248, 320
Hart, Pearl, 387
Hartford, George Huntington, II, 378
Hartman, Geo. W., 345
Harvard University, 349, 350, 384
Haskell, General William N., 108-109
Hathaway, Clarence, 44, 53, 78, 141, 147, 155, 157, 189, 215, 259, 265, 316
Hayes, Helen, 297
Hays, Mrs. Aline Davis, 307, 384, 388, 390
Haywood, Big Bill, 29, 53
Haywood, Harry, 78
Hazlitt, Henry, 343
Health and Hygiene, 282
Hearst, William Randolph, 13, 116, 181, 184, 324
Hecht, Ben, 294
Heller, A. A., 148, 259
Hellman, Lillian, 248, 254, 289, 291, 296, 320, 369
Hemingway, Ernest, 269, 270, 319, 336, 370
Henderson, Donald, 148, 151, 152, 154, 224, 228, 259, 387
Henderson, Leon, 174, 300, 302, 307, 308
Hendley, Chas. J., 350
Herbst, Josephine, 107, 147
Herrick, Robert, 147
Heyward, DuBose, 320
Hicks, Granville, 131, 133, 134, 135, 142, 146, 248, 254, 317, 319, 349, 350, 362-363, 380
Hicks, Philip M., 345
High, Stanley, 179
Hillman, Sidney, 40, 43, 221, 225
Hillquit, Morris, 31, 53
Himes, Norman E., 349
Hinckley, William, 206, 216
Hindus, Maurice, 97, 111, 114-116, 122, 123, 125, 127, 317, 361
Hitler, 9, 11, 13, 15, 24, 25, 26, 77, 83, 84, 88, 109, 149, 150, 161-166, 181, 190, 203, 261, 267, 269, 274, 275, 286, 288, 294, 295-297, 314, 324, 332, 349, 352, 354, 356, 357, 358, 360, 365, 366, 372, 380, 397, 398
Hixon, William, 388
Hogan, Austin, 227, 228, 384
Hollywood, 143, 184, 185, 191, 284, 324

Hollywood Anti-Nazi League, 202, 289, 290, 294
Hollywood Citizens Committee for the Federal Theatre, 291
Hollywood League for Democratic Action, 374
Hollywood Peace Forum, 383
Holman, Libby, 291
Holmes, Eugene, 320
Holmes, John Haynes, 326, 345, 355-356
Hook, Sidney, 145, 193, 257, 260, 326, 343, 358, 361
Hoover, 70, 73, 87
Hopkins, Miriam, 294
Horie, Jean, 383
Howard, Roy W., 172
Howard, Sidney, 148, 345
Howat, Alexander, 41
Howe, Rev. Lee A., Jr., 390
Howells, William Dean, 129
Huberman, John, 350
Huberman, Leo, 244
Hudson, Roy B., 85, 189
Hughes, Langston, 78-79, 139, 147, 248, 318, 349, 350, 387
Humphries, Rolph, 248
Hunter College, 349, 384
Hurwitz, Leo, 248
Hypocrisy, in Red Decade, 15

Ickes, Harold, 174, 181, 207, 300, 305
Ickes, Mrs. Harold, 308
I Confess, 19
Icor, 75
I. L. D. *See* International Labor Defense
Illes, Agatha, 350
Ilma, Viola, 154
Independent Shoe Workers Union, 85
Industrial Councils, 230
In Fact, 313, 388
Ingersoll, Ralph, 377
Inglewood, California, 396
Ingram, Rex, 290, 296
Ingster, Boris, 289
Inland Boatmen's Union, 230
Innocents' Clubs, 16, 18, 48-49, 50, 55, 141, 155, 157, 174, 177, 185, 188, 191, 221, 228, 265, 272, 305, 308, 346, 357, 366, 372
In Place of Profit, Social Incentives in the Soviet Union, 95n.
Institute of Public Affairs, 353
International Association of Writers for the Defense of Culture, 321
International Class War Prisoners Aid Society. *See* MOPR
International Juridical Association, 375

International Labor Defense, 49, 50, 75, 141, 195, 259, 263, 264-265, 299-300, 305, 375, 383
International Ladies Garment Workers Union, 41
International Literature, 142, 144
International Longshoremen and Warehouse Workers Union, 225, 230
International Publishers, 75, 375
International Red Aid, 50
International Union of Revolutionary Theatres, 139
International Union of Revolutionary Writers, 130, 142, 148
International Union of Seamen and Harborworkers, 85
International Union of Workers Theatres, 139
International Woodworkers Union, 230, 385, 390
International Workers Order, 75, 197, 213, 375, 390
Intourist, 375
"Iron Age," 81
Irwin, Inez Haynes, 345
"Is Human Nature Changing in Russia?", 105
Italy, 165, 174, 200, 205, 239, 273, 276, 344
Ivan the Terrible, 159, 240, 241
Ivens, Joris, 291
Iwan, Chen, 140
I Was a Soviet Worker, 331
I Write as I Please, 111, 122
I. W. W., 29, 35, 53, 184
Izvestia, 95, 116

Jackson, Andrew, 29
Jackson, Gardner, 291, 307
Jackson, Rev. Otis, 348
Jackson, Robert H., 174, 207, 210, 300, 302, 304, 309, 371, 395
Jackson, Mrs. Robert H., 308
Jacobs, Douglas, 383
James, Burton C., 248
James, Florence B., 248
Jamestown, New York, 385
Japan, 165, 174, 197, 200, 201, 324, 344
Jefferson, 29, 172
Jerome, V. J., 189, 190, 286, 290, 316, 317
Jewish People's Committee, 375, 387
Jimmy Collins Flying Club, 375
John Reed Clubs, 75, 130, 137, 138, 142, 144, 145, 148
Johns, Orrick, 147, 350
Johnson, Edwin C., 386
Johnson, Hewlett, 127

Johnson, James Weldon, 318
Johnson, Nunnally, 294
Johnson, Oakley, 148
Jones, Jesse, 389
Jones, Joe, 248
Josephson, Matthew, 133, 146, 350
Jungle, The, 335

Kaganovich, 126
Kallen, Horace M., 343
Kallet, Arthur, 147, 254
Kamenev, 240, 243
Karakhan, 237
Kashton, Dave, 216
Katterfeld, 36
Katz, Charles, 295
Kauffman, George, 350
Kaufman, Milton, 224
Kaun, Alexander, 349
Kay, Helen, 307
Kazakevich, V. D., 248, 254
Kazin, 337
Keating, Fred, 288, 296
Kelley, Hubert, 63
Kellogg Pact, 26
Kelly, Fred C., 350
Kelly, Mayor, 175, 220
Kennedy, Thomas, 396
Kent, Rockwell, 254, 315, 369, 370
Kern, Edward, 296
Kern, Jerome, 345
Kern, Paul, 254
Keymborg, Alfred, 320
Kilpatrick, Wm. H., 345
Kimbrough, Jess, 320
King, Earl, 232
Kingsbury, John A., 254, 259, 350
Kinkead, Beatrice A., 350
Kirchwey, Freda, 103, 242, 346
Kirov, Sergei, 167
Kirstein, Lincoln, 147
Kitchin, George, 94, 338
Kleeck, Mary Van. See Van Kleeck
Klein, Adelaide, 248
Kline, Herbert, 147
Klyman, Julius, 390
Knights of Labor, 29
Knox, Rev. Owen, 387
Kober, Arthur, 320, 350
Kolarov, 46
Kraft, H. S., 248
Krestinsky, 240
Krestintern, 38
Kreymborg, Alfred, 350
Krivitsky, Walter, 12, 162, 281, 326, 353, 379-380
Kronenberger, Louis, 337
Krumbein, Charles, 53, 189

Kruse, Bill, 57
Kuhn, Fritz, 354
Kuhn, Irene, 345
kulaks, 71, 96
Kunitz, Joshua, 147, 148, 259, 320
Kuomintang revolution, 23
Kuusinen, Otto, 47, 48, 207, 322, 377

Labor Defender, 263
Labor Herald, 40
Labor Party, 171
Labor Research Association, 75, 375
Labor's Non-Partisan League, 175, 301, 385
Labor Sports Union, 75, 138
Laemmle, Carl, 294
La Follette, Robert M., 43
La Follette, Suzanne, 19, 255, 326, 343, 345
La Follette Civil Liberties Committee, 222
La Guardia, 79, 175, 215
Lamont, Corliss, 49, 80, 146, 154, 248, 254, 257, 314, 315, 346, 349, 350, 351, 353, 368, 391
Lamont, Margaret I., 350
Lamont, Thomas W., 257
Lamson, David, 320
Landis, Dr. James McCauley, 231-234
Landy, Avram, 189
Lane, Priscilla, 294
Lane, Rosemary, 294
Lansbury, George, 24
Lapin, Adam, 154
Lardner, Ring, Jr., 254
Larkin, Jim, 36
Lash, Joseph P., 155-156, 206, 216
Laski, Harold, 133, 317
Lasky, Jesse, Jr., 321
Lasser, David, 86-87
Latimer, Murray, W., 308
Latvia, 367
Lawrence, Catherine, 248
"Lawrence, David," 140
Lawson, John Howard, 147, 248, 289, 318, 321, 349, 370
Lawyers Guild, 366, 371
League Against War and Fascism, 50, 75, 152, 176. See also League for Peace and Democracy
League for Peace and Democracy, 50, 153, 192, 195-199, 201, 202, 203, 208, 213, 216, 296, 299, 305, 333-334, 366, 367, 373, 382
League of American Writers, 142, 146, 185, 255, 284, 292, 315, 316, 318, 335, 337, 339, 369, 375, 390, 391
League of Nations, 26, 161, 200

League of Professional Groups, 142, 145
League of Professional Groups for Foster and Ford, 313
League of Struggle for Negro Rights, 75, 375
League of Women Shoppers, 212, 300, 307, 366, 376
League of Workers Theatres, 138, 139
League of Young Southerners, 390
Lee, Canada, 390
Lee, Gypsy Rose, 287, 293, 313
Lee, Howard, 387
Left, 137
Left Front, 137, 142
Left Review, 137, 143
Leftward, 138, 142
Left-Wing Communism, 37
Leghorn Congress (Socialist Party), 21
Leiserson, Dr. William, 304
Leland Stanford University, 350
Lenin, 22, 26, 37, 124, 135, 141, 159, 180, 181, 240, 242, 315
Leonardo da Vinci Art School, 264
Lerner, James, 206, 216
Lerner, Max, 133, 254, 314, 349, 363
Lerner, Tillie, 147
Le Sueur, Meridel, 147, 350
Levin, Meyer, 321, 339, 350
Levine, Isaac Don, 326
Levner, William, 390
Levy, Melvin, 147, 248
Lewis, John L., 17, 41, 71, 170, 175, 219, 302, 368
Lewis, Sinclair, 134, 326, 345
Lewisohn, Irene, 291
Leyda, Jay, 139, 248, 349
L'Humanite, 140
Lightbody, Chas. E., 349
Lincoln, 172, 173, 180
Lindeman, Eduard C., 105-106
Littlepage, 261, 262
Litvinov, 117, 126
Lodge, Henry Cabot, 219
Loeb, Philip, 247, 248, 296
Logan, Father Thomas, 390
London, Jack, 129
Long, Herbert, 387
Longmans, Green & Co., 339
Lore, Ludwig, 36, 56, 326
Los Angeles, 29, 230
Los Angeles Conference on Civil Liberties, 374
Louisiana Farmers Union, 387
Lovestone, Jay, 32, 53, 57, 151, 152, 171, 179, 265
Lovett, Robert Morss, 43, 147, 154, 198, 254, 318, 350
Loy, Myrna, 294

Loyalists, Spanish, 268-283
Lozovsky, Comrade, 82
Lozowick, Louis, 147, 248
Lucas, Manuel, 387
Lumpkin, Grace, 147
Lumpkin, Katherine, 254, 350
Lundberg, Ferdinand, 314, 326, 343
Lundeen, Ernest, 259
Lynd, Helen Merrell, 321
Lynd, Robert S., 254
Lyons, Eugene, 326

MacArthur, Charles, 294
McAvoy, Clifford, T., 254, 349
McCarten, John, 63
McConnell, Francis J., 280n.
McCracken, Dr. Henry N., 217
McDonald, Duncan, 45
MacDonald, Dwight, 318
McGill, V. J., 248, 254, 329, 349
Macgowan, Kenneth, 294
McGregor, Robert, 349
McHenry, Beth, 286
McKay, Claude, 318, 326, 345
McKenney, Ruth, 321, 350
McKibben, Norman, 388, 390
MacLeish, Archibald, 317, 318, 319, 370
McMichael, Jack, 206, 389
McNutt, Waldo, 206
McWilliam, Carey, 254, 321, 350, 387
Machinists Union, 43
Macleod, William C., 248
Madaule, Professor Jacques, 255
Madden, J. Warren, 300, 303
Magazine, The, 137
Magil, A. B., 131, 133
Makepeace, Grace, 387
Malisoff, William, 254
Malraux, André, 270, 317
Maltz, Albert, 248, 290, 321
Mandel, Ben, 19
Mangabas, Frederico, 321
Mangold, Nathan, 384
Mangold, William P., 254
Mann, Erika, 291
Mann, Klaus, 350
Mann, Thomas, 322, 345, 369, 370
Manufacturers Association, 231
Manuilsky, D. Z., 199
Marburg, Anita, 254, 349
Marcantonio, Vito, 12, 49, 259, 264, 305, 331, 383, 386, 390
Marching! Marching!, 133
Marine Cooks and Stewards Union, 230
Marine Workers Industrial Union, 85, 225
Maritime Federation of the Pacific, 230, 384, 387

Maritime Labor Board, 222, 302, 303
Maritime Workers Union, 85, 223, 225
Marsh, Benjamin C., 345
Marshall, Elizabeth Dublin, 254
Marshall, George, 254, 346, 350, 387, 391
Marshall, Margaret, 393
Marshall, Robert, 308
Martin, Homer, 226
Marx, Groucho, 294
Marx, Karl, 30, 159, 180, 185, 315, 340
Mason, Virgil, 387
Massachusetts Institute of Technology, 350
Massachusetts Peace Council, 383
Mathe, M., 255
Mathew, Kirtley, 384
Matles, James, 220, 228
Matthew, Dr. J. B., 150-157, 196
Matthews, Herbert L., 270
Matthiessen, F. O., 349
May, Dr. Ernst, 108
Mayer, Milton S., 345
Mdivani, 237
Medical Bureau and North American Committee to Aid Spanish Democracy, 280n.
Medical Bureau for Spain, 376
Medical Bureau to Aid Spanish Democracy, 271, 272, 280
Meierhold, 139
Men and Politics, 362
Mencken, H. L., 134
Menefee, Selden C., 248
Menzhinsky, Comrade, 100
Merlin, Milton, 294
Merrill, Lewis, 224
Message from Hollywood, A, 290
Meyer, Ernest L., 345
Miaja, General Jose, 279
Miami League for Peace and Human Welfare, 374
Michener, Lew, 224, 227
Michigan Civil Rights Federation, 374
Milestone, Lewis, 254, 292
Millen, John McAlpin, 254
Miller, Herbert A., 254, 349
Miller, Loren, 254
Miller, Rabbi Moses, 387
Millis, Harry, 304
Milwaukee, 230
Milwaukee Indians Peace Group, 383
Milwaukee Industrial Union Council, 227
Mine, Mill and Smelter Workers Union, 230
Mingulen, Comrade, 82
Mink, George, 85

Minneapolis Civil Rights Committee, 374
Minor, Robert, 36, 53, 57, 170, 189, 259, 265, 272
Minton, Bruce, 321, 380
Mitchell, Martha E., 271
Mitchell, Right Rev. Walter, 390
Mitchell, Wesley C., 345
Moberly, Missouri, 143
Modern Age Books, 232, 380
Modern Monthly, 260
Modern Quarterly, 133, 136, 193, 244, 279
Modigliani, G. E., 255
Molotov, Viacheslav, 9, 60, 126, 351, 397
Mooney, 14, 242, 331
MOPR, 49, 50, 305
Morang, Alfred, 248
More, Thomas, 125
Morgenthau, Mrs., 307
Morgenthau, Secretary, 389
Morris, Newbold, 272
Morrow, Donald, 134
Morrow, Felix, 145
Morse, Marston, 345
Mortimer, Wyndham, 220, 223, 224, 227, 395, 396
Moscow, 11, 16, 21, 29, 39, 42, 44, 54, 64, 72, 77, 83, 85, 87, 89, 90, 100, 104, 117, 130, 139, 143, 144, 156, 160, 161, 164, 165, 173, 176, 177, 182, 183, 193, 195, 200, 201, 202, 203, 206, 207, 265, 266, 305, 329, 352, 357
Moscow-Berlin Pact, 77, 301. *See also* Nazi-Soviet Pact
Moscow Carrousel, 338
Moscow *Daily News*, 125, 140, 282, 332
Moscow *Literary Gazette*, 145
"Moscow trials," 162, 236-246, 330, 353
Mothers' Day Peace Council, 383
Motion Picture Artists Committee, 212, 284
Motion Picture Democratic Committee, 289
Motion Picture Guild, 289, 291
Moussinac, Leon, 140
Muezenberg, Willi, 47-48, 50, 149, 259
Mumford, Lewis, 147, 317, 318, 369
Muni, Paul, 272, 294
Munson, Gorham, 345
Munson, M. Y., 254
Murphy, George S., 387
Murray, Philip, 221-222, 226, 396
Music Vanguard, The, 137
Mussolini, 11, 13, 21, 24, 109, 160, 200, 269, 275, 349, 356, 360, 366
Muste, 156
Muster, Morris, 224

Muzzey, David S., 345
Myers, Frederick N., 224, 389

Nadir, Moishe, 148
Naft, Stephen, 345
Nation, 103, 116, 118, 120, 157, 194, 206, 278, 318n., 326, 343, 350, 351, 362
National Association for the Advancement of Colored Peoples, 152
National Association of Die-Casters, 229, 387
National Committee for the Defense of Political Prisoners, 75
National Committee for People's Rights, 375, 376
National Committee to Aid Victims of German Fascism, 75, 156
National Congress for Social and Unemployment Insurance, 171
National Council for the Protection of the Foreign Born, 376
National Emergency Conference for Civil Liberties, 374, 384
National Farmer-Labor Party, 45
National Film and Photo League, 139
National Labor Relations Board, 222, 229, 302, 304, 371
National Lawyer's Guild, 300, 304
National Maritime Union, 9, 229, 303, 385
National Mine Workers Union, 85
National Negro Congress, 202, 212, 213, 369, 375
National Scottsboro Committee of Action, 156
National Student League, 75, 148, 153, 154. *See also* American Student Union
National Textile Workers Union, 84
National Tom Mooney Council of Action, 156
Nazis, 13, 25, 160, 191, 223, 241, 298, 347, 397-398
Nazi-Soviet Pact, 14, 22, 27, 183, 208, 294, 359, 361, 371, 373
Nearing, Scott, 154
Nechayev, 309-310
Needle Workers' Council for Peace and Civil Rights, 374
Needle Workers Industrial Union, 84
Neff, Walter Scott, 383, 387
Negrin, Dr. Juan, 268, 277, 278, 279
Negro People's Theatre of the South, 139
Nelson, Steve, 189
"Nepmen," 23
Neumann, Henry, 345
New Bedford Conference on American Democracy, 374

New Dance, 138
New Dance Group, 138, 140
New Deal, 87, 153, 158, 170, 173, 185, 191, 207, 220, 221, 289, 298
New Deal, A, 102
New Duncan Dance Group, 138
New Force, 142
Newhouse, Edward, 147
New Leader, 13, 280n., 295, 334, 379
New Masses, 66, 88, 131, 132, 133, 138, 142, 143, 154, 156, 180, 183, 186, 201, 216, 247, 262, 282, 297, 328, 329, 330, 337n., 361, 364, 369, 370, 380
New Republic, 103, 104-105, 107, 110, 116, 134, 181, 182, 193, 194, 200, 208, 231, 241, 256, 314, 326, 328, 335, 336, 343, 346, 359
New School for Social Research, 146
News Letter, 307
New Theatre, 137, 139, 186, 296
New Theatre League, 139, 140, 295, 375
New Theatre of Hollywood, 139
New Theatre School, 140
New York, 15, 19, 40, 72, 126, 142, 143, 146, 155, 171, 184, 208, 228, 230, 266, 296, 324
New York *American,* 109
New York Citizens Peace Council, 374
New York Committee to Aid Agricultural Workers, 375
New Yorker, 63, 133, 359
New York *Herald Tribune,* 124, 131, 133, 312, 338
New York Teachers' Union, 350, 387
New York *Times,* 122, 124, 243, 333, 337, 340
New York University, 349, 350, 384
New York *World-Telegram,* 228
Nichols, Dudley, 254, 289, 291, 293, 295, 370
Nixon, Russell, 384
Nockles, Edward, 41
Norgord, Dagmar, 383
North, Joseph, 147, 318
North American Aircraft Company, 396
North American Committee to Aid Spanish Democracy, 280n.
North American Spanish Aid Committee, 280
Northern California Peace Mobilization Committee, 383
Nugent, Elliot, 294
Nye, Gerald P., 386

Oak, Liston, 271, 326, 333-334
Oakes, Grant, 387
O'Brien, Clifford, 388
O'Conner, Virgil, 387

O'Connor, Harvey, 321, 350, 387
Odets, Clifford, 140, 148, 287, 350
Odyssey of a Fellow-Traveler, 150
Ohio Labor's Non-Partisan League, 387
Ohio Townsend Movement, 387
Old Bolsheviks, 238, 246
Olds, Elizabeth, 248
Olgin, Moissaye, 53, 65, 146, 147, 265, 318
O'Malley, John, 248
Oneal, James, 345
O'Neil, George, 294
Opatoshu, Joseph, 148
Open Letter of the 400, 342-351
Ordeal of Mark Twain, The, 315
Ornitz, Samuel, 147, 247, 254, 288, 289
Orton, O. M., 224, 390, 396
O'Shea, Thomas, 228
O'Sheel, Shaemas, 350
Otis, Raymond, 248
Ottenheimer, A. L., 248
Out of the Night, 85, 267, 380
Overstreet, H. A., 345
Ovington, Mary White, 350
Oxford Pledge, 155, 209

Pach, Walter, 345
Packing House Workers Organizing Committee, 230
Padover, Saul K., 345
Page, Mrs. Charles, 295
Page, Myra, 147
Paine, Thomas, 16, 29, 172
Painters District Council No. 9, 230
Palmer, Attorney General Mitchell, 33-34, 51
Pan-American Conference on Democratic Rights, 374
Pan-Pacific Trade Union Secretariat, 68
Parker, Dorothy, 247, 248, 254, 294, 308, 313, 314, 315, 317, 321, 370
Partisan, The, 138
Partisan Magazine, 143
Partisan Review, The, 137, 143, 341
Party Organizer, 74, 195, 199, 228
Passaic, New Jersey, 42
Patel, 149
Patterson, 289
Paul, Elliot, 337
Peace Committee of the Medical Profession, 383
Pearson, Ralph M., 369
Pen and Hammer, 75, 137
People's Front. *See* Popular Front
Perelman, S. J., 321, 350
Perkins, Frances, 174, 231, 300, 302
Perry, Ralph Barton, 345
Peter the Great, 159, 172, 240, 241

Peters, John P., 350
Peters, Paul, 147, 248
Petersen, Arnold, 179
Pflaum, Irving, 272, 274
Phelan, Arthur J., 232
Philadelphia, 143
Philippine Writers League, 321
Piatikov, 237, 261
Pickens, William, 152
Pierre Degeyter Club, 137
Pilnyak, Boris, 110
Pinchot, Mrs. Gifford, 307
Piscator, Erwin, 140
Pitts, Rebecca, 148, 248
Platten, Fritz, 22
Plavner, Murray, 218
PM, 12
Polakov, Walter N., 254, 350
Poland, 352, 353, 357, 358, 359, 361, 364, 367
Pollitt, Harry, 21, 352-353
Pollock, Hugo, 19
Pool, Rev. Alfred, 384
Popular Front, 15, 17, 26, 27, 79, 161, 163, 165, 206, 207, 216, 266, 272, 274, 286, 288, 298, 317, 326, 335, 339, 343, 346, 357, 372, 377, 398
Porter, Allen, 147, 349
Portland, 230
Posner, Dr. John Jacob, 271, 272
P. O. U. M., 268
Powell, Dick, 294
Prall, D. W., 254
Pravda, 158, 276
Preece, Harold, 147
Presbyterian University, 384
Pressman, Lee, 221, 225, 232, 291, 304
Pressman, Mrs., 307
Preston, John Hyde, 248, 349, 350
Price, Enoch, 388
Profintern, 38, 40, 67, 68, 71, 82, 85, 130
Progressive Committee to Rebuild the American Labor Party, 374
Progressive Miners Committee, 41
Prokosch, Frederick, 321
Proletarian Culture. *See* Proletcult
Proletarian Journey, A, 332
Proletarian Literature in the United States, 133
Proletarian Party, 33
Proletcult, 128-140, 142, 177
Proust, 136
Pro-War Communism, 201
Pruette, Lorine, 321, 345
Pullman strike, 29
Putnam, Samuel, 248, 370

Quarry Workers Union, 230

Queens, 230
Quill, Michael, 223, 224, 227, 228, 384, 387, 394
Quin, Mike, 380

Radek, Karl, 47, 117, 243, 261, 314
Radicalism in America, 29
Radin, Paul, 349
Railroad Workers Amalgamation Committee, 41
Rainey, Henry T., 109
Rains, Claude, 294
Rakovsky, Christian, 22, 241, 314
Randolph, A. Philip, 369
Rapallo Treaty, 162
Raphaelson, Samson, 254
RAPP, 131
Rascoe, Burton, 328, 338
Rathborne, Mervyn, 224, 226, 387
Ratner, Ira, 295
Raushenbush, Winifred, 345
Rautenstrauch, Walter, 346, 350, 387
Ray, Tom, 85
Rebel Dancers, 138
Recht, Charles, 249
Red Dancers, 130, 137
Redfield, A., 282
Red Peasant International. *See* Krestintern
Red Trade Union International. *See* Profintern, 38
Reed, John, 32, 53, 111
Reed, Robert, 296
Reed College, 349
Reid, Ogden, 312
Reis, Bernard, 297
Reiss, Irving, 291
Reissig, Herman F., 280n.
"Reps," 69
Republican Party, 175, 178, 264
"Rescue Ship Mission," 309
Retail and Wholesale Workers, 230
Review, 154
Reynolds, Bertha, 350
Rhav, Philip, 341
Riegger, Wallingford, 249
Riesel, Victor, 19, 343, 394
Riggs, Lynn, 249, 349, 350
River, W. L., 321
Roberts, Holland D., 249
Roberts, Leon F., 384
Robeson, Paul, 369, 384, 386, 389n., 390
Robins, Col. Raymond, 254
Robinson, Earl, 384, 387
Robinson, Edward G., 294
Robinson, Reid, 224
Robinson-Rubens case, 266
Roche, Mrs. Josephine, 308

Rochester, Anna, 249
Rockefeller, Nelson, 323
Rodman, Sam, 29
Roeder, Ralph, 321, 339, 350
Rolland, R., 149
Rollins, William, Jr., 147, 350
Romaine, Paul, 147, 249
Rome, Harold J., 247, 249, 321, 349
Roosevelt, Mrs. Eleanor, 156n., 174, 183, 206, 207, 209-215, 217, 300, 305, 307, 308, 309, 332, 368
Roosevelt, Franklin D., 87, 171, 174, 181, 183, 192, 215, 295, 296, 301, 305, 368
Rorty, James, 145, 326, 345
Rose, Donald, 295
Rosenwald, Lessing, 378
Rosenwald, Mrs. Marion, 378
Rosmer, Alfred, 255
Ross, Professor Edward Alsworth, 255
Ross, Leonard Q., 345
Ross, William, 388
Roth, Henry, 249, 254
Royce, Edward, 148
Ruble, 127n.
Ruehle, Otto, 255
Rukeyser, Muriel, 139, 321
Rukeyser, Walter A., 111
Rumania, 352, 361, 397
Russell, Bertrand, 339
Russell, Charles Edward, 345
Russell, Elbert, 390
Russell, Rosalind, 294
Russia in Transition, 111n.
Russian-American Institute, 49
Russian Embassy, 187
Russia's Iron Age, 332
Russia-worship, 92-100, 181
Ruthenberg, Charles E., 32, 33, 36, 53, 56, 57
Ruthven, Madeline, 289
Ryan, William G., 19, 333
Rykov, Premier, 59, 240, 241, 261, 314
Ryskind, Morrie, 285, 291, 326, 345

Sabine, George H., 345
Sacco, 14, 181, 242
Sacher, Harry, 297
Sackheim, Mrs. Jerome, 295
St. Lawrence College, 349
St. Louis, 78
St. Paul, 44, 46
Salvemini, Professor, 264
Sandburg, Carl, 387
San Francisco, 230, 384-385
San Francisco Academic and Civil Rights Council, 374
San Francisco C.I.O. Industrial Council, 226

Santley, Joseph, 291
Santo, John, 220, 227, 228
Saposs, Dr. David, 303, 304
Sarah Lawrence College, 349
Saturday Evening Post, 179, 223, 225, 261, 353, 380
Saturday Review of Literature, 292, 339
Sayre, Joel, 289
Schaffer, Louis, 369
Schapiro, J. Salwyn, 345
Schappes, Morris U., 249, 291
Schlamm, Willi, 163-164
Schlauch, Margaret, 149, 154, 249, 254
Schlochower, Harry, 249
Schneider, Isidor, 131, 133, 147, 316
School for Barbarians, 291
Schulberg, Budd Wilson, 321
Schuman, Frederick L., 154, 200, 259, 313-314, 349
Schuyler, George S., 345
Science and Society Quarterly, 282
Scott, Evelyn, 326, 345
Scott, Profintern overseer, 40
Scottsboro case, 156, 291
Screen Actors Guild, 289
Screen Guild Magazine, 284
Screen Writers' Guild, 288
Scudder, Vida D., 321, 350
Scully, Frank, 288, 289, 295
Seagle, William, 254
Seattle, 230; general strike, 29
Seaver, Edwin, 147, 249, 321
Seldes, George, 90, 249, 313, 349, 350, 388
Selly, Joseph, 224, 226
Selsam, Howard, 249, 254
Serebriakov, 240, 314
"Serfs of the Soviet, The," 261
Serge, Victor, 94, 102-103
Shachtman, Max, 58
Shakespeare, 134
Shane, Maxwell, 295
Sharecroppers' Aid Committee, 374
Shaughnessy, Edward J., 231
Shaw, Artie, 390
Shaw, Bernard, 127
Shaw, Irwin, 249, 289, 321
Sheean, Vincent, 270, 314, 317, 318, 321, 346, 348, 350, 359, 360-361
Sherer, Marcel, 224
Sheridan, Ann, 294
Shields-Collins, Betty, 217
Shoemaker, Mr., 232
Shore, Viola Brothers, 254, 291, 321, 350
Shukutoff, Arnold, 254
Shumlin, Herman, 290, 291, 296, 369, 391
Shuster, George, 345, 384

Sidney, Sylvia, 291, 294
Sifton, Claire, 139, 147
Sifton, Paul, 139, 147
Sigerist, Dr. Henry E., 247, 249, 254, 259
Si-lan Chen, 248
Sillen, Samuel, 370
Silone, Ignazio, 113
Silver Shirts, 13
Simkhovitch, Mary, 384
Simmons, Ernest J., 350
Simons, William, 149
Simonson, Lee, 297
Simpson, Mr., 110
Sinclair, Upton, 129, 170-171, 289, 318, 321, 335
Single Tax, 29
sit-down strikes, 227
Skariatina, Countess Irina, 254, 350
Sklar, George, 147, 249
Slesinger, Tess, 254, 289, 291, 321
Sloan, John, 345
Smedley, Agnes, 148
Smilga, 240, 314
Smirnov, 240
Smith, Andrew, 331, 338
Smith, Bernard, 249, 254
Smith, Edwin S., 303
Smith, Mrs. Edwin S., 308
Smith, E. Tredwell, 249, 254, 349, 350
Smith, Rev. Frank, 387
Smith, Jessica, 249
Smith College, 349
Smolny, 33
Snow, Edgar, 370
Social-Democrats, German, 24, 161
"social facist," 71, 133
Socialist Call, 13
Socialist Labor Party, 53, 179
Socialist Party, 31, 86-87
"socialized medicine," 94
"Social Work Today," 350
Society of Catholic Commonwealth, 387
Sokolnikov, 241
Solon, S. L., 19
Solonevich, 94
Solow, Herbert, 198, 266
Sondergaard, Gale, 293, 294
Sondergaard, Hester, 249, 349
Soule, George, 103, 318
Soule, Isobel Walker, 259, 350
Southern Conference on Human Welfare, 212, 305, 387
Southern Negro Youth Congress, 212, 375
Southern Review, 314
Souvarine, Boris, 326, 337

Soviet Communism, A New Civilization, 124, 127
Soviet Journey, 117
Soviet Power, 127, 397
Soviet Russia Today, 253, 259, 263, 387, 391
Soviet Worker, The, 113
Soyer, Raphael, 249
Spain, 17, 201, 326, 344, 359, 369
Spanish Civil War, 201, 269-283
Spanish Intellectual Aid, 376
Spartacus, 16
Speer, Robert K., 254, 370, 384
Spender, Stephen, 136
Spitzer, Marion, 295
Spivak, John L., 147
Spofford, Rev. William B., 198, 254
Stachel, Jack, 53, 69, 144, 189
Stadt, Dr. Z. M., 271
Stalin, 9, 10, 11, 12, 14, 15, 21, 23, 24, 25, 30, 47, 54, 57-61, 64-69, 70, 81, 85, 93, 97, 99, 103, 105, 112, 113, 116, 120, 123, 125, 126, 134, 137, 138, 141, 144, 149, 159, 160, 162, 166, 167, 168, 172, 175, 176, 179, 181, 186, 190, 197, 200, 203, 206, 236, 238, 239, 242, 245, 246, 247, 249, 250, 252, 253, 255, 257, 261, 266, 269, 271, 273, 274, 276, 278, 282, 283, 294, 295, 311, 314, 322, 346, 355, 358, 359, 360, 363, 364, 397
Stalin: A Critical Survey of Bolshevism, 337
Stalin Constitution, 26, 168, 240
"Stalin's Great American Hoax," 198
Stampfer, Dr. Friedrich, 160
Stander, Lionel, 247, 249, 288, 314
Stark, Louis, 345
Starobin, Joseph, 154
State, County and Municipal Workers Union, 230, 387
State Industrial Councils, 230
State of Affairs, 282
Stead, Christina, 350
Steffens, Lincoln, 110, 111, 147, 193
Steig, A. E., 350
Stern, Alfred K., 391
Stern, Bernhard J., 148, 249, 254, 349, 350
Stevens, Housely, Jr., 249
Stevens, Virginia, 296
Stevenson, Philip, 147, 249, 321
Stewart, Donald O., 232, 254, 256, 289, 290, 292, 293, 294, 295, 318, 319, 321, 346, 350, 387
Stewart, Mrs. D. O. See Ella Winter
Stewart, Maxwell S., 103, 157, 245, 249, 254, 259, 346, 349
Stillman, Clara G., 345

Stolberg, Benjamin, 19, 223, 255, 326, 330, 339, 343, 345
Stone, Irving, 321
Stone, I. F., 350
Story of the C.I.O., 339
Stowe, Leland, 321
Strachey, John, 80, 111, 133, 193, 317, 380
Strack, Celeste, 154, 216
Strand, Paul, 249, 296, 349
Straus, Leon, 216
Strebel, Gustav, 225
Strong, Anna Louise, 111, 120-123, 127, 168, 169, 254
Strong, Edward E., 206, 216
Struik, Dirk J., 350
Stuart, Gloria, 294
Stuart, John, 249, 380
Student, The, 154
Student Congress Against War and Fascism, 215
Student League for Industrial Democracy, 153, 155. *See also* American Student League
Studs Lonnigan, 335
Sugar, Maurice, 227
Suicide, 106
Swanson, Carl, 387
Sweezy, Paul M., 254
Symes, Lillian, 318, 326
Syndicalist League of North America, 66
Syracuse University, 350
System of Accounts for a Small Cooperative, A, 67

Taboo, against criticism, 11
TAC. *See* Theatre Arts Committee
Taggard, Genevieve, 147, 249, 318, 321, 370
Tairov, 139
Taub, Belle, 148
Teachers' College, 349
Teachers Union, 194, 214; Local 5, 230, 383
Tead, Dr. Ordway, 215, 291
Teapot Dome scandal, 43
Technocracy, 13, 29
Texas, 230
Thaelmann, 21
Theatre Arts Committee, 296, 368, 369, 376
Theatre Collective, 137, 139
Theatre Committee for the Defense of the Spanish Republic, 290
Theatre of Action, 130, 137, 139
Theatre Union, 137, 146
Theatre Union Dance Group, 138
This Soviet World, 121
Thomas, Norman, 13, 24, 71, 171, 345

Thomas, R. J., 225, 226
Thomas, Wendelin, 255
Thompson, Dorothy, 345
Thompson, Rev. John B., 386, 389
Thompson, Ralph, 337
Thorez, 352
Timbres, Rebecca Janney, 346, 350
Time, 340
Tomsky, Mikhail, 59, 237, 240, 314
Tone, Franchot, 292
Townsend, Dr., 171, 385
Trachtenberg, Alexander, 53, 146, 147, 259, 316, 318
Trade Union Educational League, 39, 57, 67, 72, 82. *See also* Trade Union Unity League
Trade Union Unity League, 72, 84, 130, 141, 148, 175, 228
Trager, Frank H., 343
Transmission belts, 141
Transport Workers Bulletin, 228
Transport Workers Union, 223, 228, 229, 297
Travels in Two Democracies, 112
Tresca, Carlo, 255
Tretyakov, Sergei, 140
Trotsky, Leon, 22, 56-57, 58, 59, 117, 124, 159, 237, 240, 244, 250-251, 315, 318, 337, 340, 346, 379
Trotsky, Sedov, 250
Trotsky Commission, 257
Trumbo, Dalton, 289
Tschabasov, Nahum, 249
Tsik, 125
TUEL. *See* Trade Union Educational League
Tukhachevsky, General, 237, 241
Turner, Ethel, 249
Tuttle, 290, 294, 295
TUUL. *See* Trade Union Unity League
Twentieth-Century Fox, 294
Tzik Committee, 240

U.G.T., 275
Uj Elore, 228
Uncensored, 373
Unemployment Councils, 86, 141. *See also* Workers Alliance
United American Artists, 369
United Automobile Workers Union, 385, 387
United Cannery, Agricultural, Packing and Allied Workers of America, 228, 230, 387
United Council of Working Class Women, 75
United Electrical, Radio and Machinists Union, 228, 230

United Federal Workers, 230, 309
United Front, 17. *See also* Popular Front
United Mine Workers, 41, 175, 388, 396
United Office and Professional Workers Union, 230
United Press, 272
United Shoe Workers, 230
United Student Peace Committee, 376
United Tannery Workers Union, 230
University of California, 349
University of Michigan, 349
University of Wisconsin, 213
Untermeyer, Jean Starr, 318, 321, 350
Untermeyer, Louis, 321, 350
Upsurge, 136
Urevich, 149, 183, 198, 368
U. S. Daily, 109
Utley, Freda, 339

Valtin, Jan, 12, 85, 267, 338, 380
Valuta episode, 98
VanArsdale, Harry, 387
Van de Water, Frederic F., 345
Van Doren, Carl, 318, 321
Van Doren, Irita, 338
Vanguard, 140
Vanguard Dance Group, 138
Van Kleeck, Mary, 254, 259, 346, 350
Vanzetti, 14, 181, 242
Variety, 286
Vassar College, 215, 217, 349
Veiller, Anthony, 291
Versailles, 160
Veterans of the Abraham Lincoln Brigade, 376
Vidor, King, 287
Villard, Oswald G., 345, 386
Vincent, Merle D., 303, 305
Vinton, Betty, 307
Virgin Islands, 198, 350
Vishinsky, 245
Vladimir, Prince, 172
Von Ribbentrop, 342, 351
Von Sternberg, Joseph, 294
Voorhis, Jerry, 306
Vorvärts, 160
Vultee Aircraft, strike, 395

Wagenknecht, 36
Wagner Act, 222, 229
Wald, Lillian D., 253, 254, 272
Waldman, Mark, 254
Walker, Charles Rumford, 326
Wallace, Henry A., 305
Walling, Metcalfe, 307
Wallis, Keene, 249
Walsh, Frank P., 291
Walsh, J. Raymond, 350

Walton, Eda Lou, 254, 390
Wanger, Walter, 291, 294
War Crisis, The, 203
Ward, E. E., 232, 233
Ward, Dr. Harry F., 111, 195, 196, 197, 348, 367, 372, 380
Ward, Lynd, 254, 369
Warner, H. M., 294
Warner, Jack, 294
Warner, S. T., 321
Washington, George, 172-173, 180
Washington, 171, 183, 184, 187, 192, 207, 211, 296, 300, 302, 309, 310, 324, 357
Washington Commonwealth Federation, 387
Washington Council for Democratic Rights, 374
Watson, Morris, 224, 383, 387, 390, 394
Weatherwax, Clara, 133, 254, 350
Webb, Sidney and Beatrice, 111, 124-127, 169
Weber, Max, 249, 254, 349
We Cover the World, 292, 339
Weimar Republic, 160
Weinstone, 57
Weisner, Louis, 254
Wellesley College, 350
Wendt, Dr. Gerald, 350
Werner, M. R., 345
West, Nathaniel, 147, 254
West Coast Writers, 292
West Side Council for Race Tolerance, 376
Wexley, John, 321
White, David McElvy, 254
White, William C., 107
White Sea Canal, 108
Whitfield, Rev. Owen, 387
Whitney, A. F., 198
Whitney, John Hay, 323, 378
Wholesale Book Corporation, 340, 376
Wilde, Percival, 291
Wilder, Thornton, 134, 319
Williams, Albert Rhys, 111, 319, 350
Williams, Aubrey, 207, 305
Williams, Mrs. Aubrey, 308
Williams, William Carlos, 321, 350
Williams College, 313, 349
Willison, George T., 249
Wilson, Rev. Chad, 387
Wilson, Edmund, 111, 128, 129, 131, 134, 326
Wiman, Dwight Deere, 378
Winter, Ella, 111, 147, 232, 296, 318, 321, 350
Winwar, Frances, 249, 345
W.I.R. *See* Workers International Relief
Wisconsin, 230

Wise, James Waterman, 148, 255, 259, 367
Witt, Bert, 154, 304n.
Witt, Mrs., 307
Wolfe, Bertram, 32
Wolfson, Martin, 249, 296
Woodward, Helen, 345
Workers Alliance, 17, 86, 87, 89, 141, 212, 213, 230, 300, 305, 309, 334, 366, 376, 388
Workers Bookshop, 75, 376
Workers Cultural Federation, 376
Workers Dance League, 137, 139. See also New Dance League
Workers Ex-Servicemen's League, 75
Workers Film and Photo League, The, 137
Workers International Relief, 48, 75, 156, 376
Workers Laboratory Theatre, 138
Workers Library Publishers, 75, 376
Workers Music League, 75, 137
Workers Party, 34, 37, 39, 43
Workers School, 75
Workers' Theatre. See New Theatre
Working for the Soviets, 111n.
World Congress Against War, 149
World Tourists, 75, 376
World War, first, 29, 30, 35, 66, 160
World War, second, 15, 77, 182, 399
World Youth Congress, 212, 215, 216
Wortis, Rose, 189, 228
W.P.A., 319, 340; Teachers Local 453, 390

Wright, Richard, 147, 249, 349, 350, 387, 390
Wrigley, Philip A., 378

Yagoda, Henry, 100, 105, 119, 120, 130, 245
Yakhontoff, Victor A., 249, 259
Yale Medical School, 350
Yanks Are Not Coming, The, 374, 380
Yard, Molly, 206
Yegorov, General, 237
Yenukidze, Abel, 237, 240
Yergan, Max, 367, 369, 383, 387
Yezhov, 245
Yipsels, 206
Young, Art, 255, 390
Young, Roland, 294
Young, Stanley, 321
Young Communist League, 75, 153, 154, 155, 206, 212-216, 396
Young Democrats, 207
Young Methodists, 206
Young Pioneers, 146, 153, 376
Young Republicans, 207
"Youth Peace Strike," 155

Zack, Joseph, 233
Zamora, Francisco, 255
Zetkin, Klara, 50
Zinoviev, Gregory, 22, 49, 59, 240, 241, 242, 243, 261
Zionists, 117
Zorach, William, 255, 369
Zugsmith, Leane, 255, 282, 321, 351

CPSIA information can be obtained
at www.ICGtesting.com
Printed in the USA
LVHW091305280619
622656LV00001B/93/P